Mustangs & Unicorns

A History of the 359th Fighter Group

MUSTANGS & UNICORNS

A HISTORY OF THE 359TH FIGHTER GROUP

by JACK H. SMITH

Pictorial Histories Publishing Company
Missoula, Montana

Library of Congress Catalog Card No. 97-68918

ISBN 1-57510-029-0

TYPOGRAPHY & COMPOSITION Arrow Graphics
COVER DESIGN Bill Vaughn
COVER PAINTING Jack H. Smith

Pictorial Histories Publishing Company
713 South Third Street West, Missoula, Montana 59801

HARD TACK

This book is dedicated to Colonel Avelin P. Tacon Jr., commander of the 359th Fighter Group from Jan. 1943 to Nov. of 1944. Tacon was a West Pointer and ran a tight ship. Aggressive pilots like John Oliphint all to often found themselves standing in front of Hard Tack's desk receiving a lecture on combat discipline. It must have been difficult for commanders to hold youthful tigers in check and not destroy the edge that made them fighter pilots with very few equals in the world. The pilots felt like Tacon was preventing them from winning the war single handedly but in truth the mental discipline he instilled in the Group kept many of them alive, while those who broke ranks to do combat with the Hun often failed to return. Oliphint and Tacon joined forces during 1994 to have a plaque displayed at West Point commemorating the 359th Fighter Group's eight West Point men (the most in any fighter group during World War II).

Contents

Introduction

IT WAS MY ASSUMPTION that as I grew older life would gradually slow down along with my workload. Don't count on it! Having spent the better part of six years of my spare time writing three books on the West Virginia Air National Guard, I was just getting back into my groove, during Oct. of 1991, when M/Sgt. Bill Wolfinger called me from Martinsburg, West Virginia with the following announcement; "Jack! Do I have a project for you!" Knowing Wolfie has a persuasive line my reply was "Oh no, what?" The result of the conversation that followed is this book.

One contemporary aviation historian has described the 359th FG as a "colorless unit". I think that after reading this book you will find that statement is not true.

Certainly other fighter groups scored more air kills but it must be remembered that the 359th was one of the last groups to enter service. Also they would undoubtedly have scored more kills had not more than two-thirds of their missions been close escort for bombers, a job closely supervised by Col. Tacon who didn't tolerate a mass exodus from the bomber stream to chase small numbers of enemy fighters. On the other hand close escort earned them the undying gratitude of the airmen in those bombers. This affection the bomber crews felt for their *little friends* is amply exemplified in the following story.

Lt. David B. Archibald spotted a crippled B-24 Liberator being attacked by a Me 109 and dived on it, chasing it away. Archibald then moved in close to the bomber and motioned for the pilot to follow him. With two engines out and a third on fire, the bomber's crew began jettisoning equipment to lighten their aircraft. Flying through an overcast sky at treetop level Archibald led the B-24 towards an advanced Allied airfield in France. After gaining enough altitude to safely bail out and assured by Archy they were over friendly territory, the crew jumped. Archibald then landed at the airfield and minutes later met the bomber-pilot, who gave him a grateful hug. And that's what escorting is all about, saving lives.

The 359th ranked high as train killers, a very hazardous job. Likewise the unit excelled at destroying aircraft on the ground, another deadly undertaking. Any ground target is extremely dangerous for the fighter pilot. Unlike a dogfight ground attack exposes the fighter and its pilot to weapons of various calibers, sometimes from several directions, thereby increasing the odds of being nailed. It's like riding a motorcycle, it's not a matter of *if* you're going down it's a matter of *when*. The targets can also be lethal and a prime example is an exploding steam locomotive hurling tons of debris into the path of an attacker.

The 359th can lay claim to several firsts. On May 23, 1944 the Group used their P-51B Mustangs to dive bomb a bridge. It was the first recorded instance of a Merlin powered Mustang performing that type of mission. Col. Avelin P. Tacon became the first 8th Air Force pilot to sight and give chase to the Me163, rocket fighter, on July 28, 1944. The first Me163 lost in combat, fell to the guns of Lt. Col. John B. Murphy on Aug. 16, 1944. It was on Dec. 18, 1944 that Lts. Paul E. Olson and David B. Archibald,

These events are definitely colorful!

War is a dirty business and the side that presses the advantage quickly and relentlessly will usually win, bringing the conflict to a mercifully swift conclusion. To that end the 359th carried out its assignments with aggressiveness and some-times pure abandon. That spirit was exemplified by Capt. Ralph E. Kibler, of the 370th FS, when he chased a Fw190 down the streets of Hamm, Germany, until it crashed head-on into a three story building, becoming one of two victories he scored on April 22, 1944.

Never again will the world witness vast fleets of bombers and fighters, like those that blackened the heavens over Germany. All that is left of that bygone era are combat films and memories. This book is a collective memory of the 359th FG.

Lt. Ralph E. Kibler Jr. poses with the 370th's ubiquitous mascot Flak. Kibler was an aggressive pilot as witnessed by his pursuit of a Fw 190 down the streets of Hamm, Germany below the rooftops. He like so many other talented dogfighters was the victim of groundfire while strafing.

both of the 368th FS, became aces during the same mission, downing five Fw190s each, a feat duplicated only once in the history of the 8th Air Force. On Aug. 27, 1944 Lt. Lawrence A. Zizka shot down a twin engine German aircraft which was the only kill scored by the VIII Fighter Command on that day. In a repeat performance Capt. Ray S. Wetmore bagged a Me163 on March 15, 1945. What are the odds of the same fighter group scoring the only kill of the day twice? Astronomical, no doubt, especially with hundreds of Allied fighters prowling the sky.

Acknowledgments

ONCE MORE I MUST THANK M/Sgt. Bill Wolfinger for his assistance in gathering data that made this project possible. Helping Wolfie was S/Sgt. Tim Shipway, another history buff.

Aviation historian Jeff Ethell made available his photo collection, a selection of which appear in this work. William Hess and Danny Morris also furnished photos.

With Tom Ivie and Charles W. Arrington's permission, their articles on the Kentucky ANG, which appeared in the March and April issues of *Air Classics* during 1987, served as a guide in the writing of that units activities. Tom and Charlie also furnished most of the photos of the Kentucky aircraft and Charlie furnished a starter list of Kentucky P-51 and F-86 serial numbers.

Lt.Col. Benny A. Huffman of the W. Va. ANG was most helpful in looking up the combat records of the 167th pilots who served in Korea. Col. Huffman is a fine gentleman, with whom I have spent many instructive hours on the firing range with the 1911, .45 ACP.

The strike photos came from the collection of Andrew J. Treat, who was a photo interpreter in the 7th PG and were sent to me by Char Baldridge. Char's husband's brother, Arlen Baldridge, was a pilot in the 368th FS and was murdered after being taken prisoner on May 21, 1944. Char is also the 359th Historian.

My brother Tom N. Smith, who flew with the 398th Bomb Group, loaned me his silk bail out map of Germany which was very helpful in following missions and finding towns not on today's maps.

Of all the former members of the 359th that contributed to this book, one name stands out, if for no other reason than the huge volume of data and photos he donated. Anthony Chardella deserves everyone's thanks. For a deep look into a warriors soul I thank John H. Oliphint, a man I respectfully call *The Predator*. Other former members that deserve recognition are; Glen C. Bach, Jack Bateman, Ira J. Bisher, Lawrence Bouchard, Dr. Paul Bruns, Rene Burtner, Ernest De Graves, Charles Doersam, George A. Doersch, Phillip Dupont, Howard Fogg, Charlie Foster, Robert Guggemos, Benjamin Hagen, Robert Hatter, Robert Hawkinson, Ralph Klaver, Andrew Lemmens, Larry Lovell, T. P. Smith who furnished color slides of the 370th, Paul E. Sundheim and Sid Wheeler. Charles H. Staley, a former pilot with the 369th FS, and his wife Martha are co-editors of *The Outer Circle*, the 359th's newsletter. Elsie Palicka contributed photos from her late husband Ed's collection.

Richard Ward the noted aviation artist and historian, from England, furnished several photos of German aircraft, which came from the Bundesarchiv and I would be remiss in failing to mention Richard; we have shared data on several occasions.

Contributors to the West Virginia ANG section are; J. O. Bail, John Bailey, Martin Bambrick, H. Kemp Copenhaver, James H. Guthrie, John Boone Harris, John R. Hoylman, Kenneth C. Hoylman, Jack Koch, Jim Miller, Sheldon Miller, James K. McLaughlin, Edward R. Morton, Max Richardson, William O. Starks and Douglas Wilburn. Duncan Curtis and Dave McLaren helped research aircraft serial numbers.

It is with great sadness I recognize the assistance of the late James M. Burns, a brother Irishman who eagerly proofread this book. Jim was a very close friend and a veteran of Vietnam and the Gulf War. Stricken by a rare, terminal disease that destroys the kidneys and having watched his mother die from the same illness Jim resolved to cheat The Reaper of his sometimes sadistic pleasure. On the morning of April 19, 1994 my friend decided it was a good day to die. He walked from his home to an adjacent wooded park, put a .357 magnum to his heart and pulled the trigger. *"We are all headed for the same destination, some of us just take an earlier train,"* was one of Jim's favorite quotes.

These beautiful ladies once adorned the walls of Wretham Hall. The paintings are signed by the artist Capt. James L. Way Jr. a pilot from the 368th Squadron. The painting on the right was in Ray Wetmore's room. Note the five pointed star with five kill crosses that no doubt signified his ace status. In the center of the star is an ace of hearts playing card. The artwork shown here is typical of that found in combat units of the 8th AF and shows the strong influence of the Vargas and Petty centerfolds of Esquire Magazine during this era.

The Home Team

THE 359TH FLEW TWO TYPES of fighters, the P-47 Thunderbolt and the P-51 Mustang. Assuming that not everyone who reads this book will be familiar with these two great aircraft I have included a brief outline covering the design and performance of each.

P-51 MUSTANG

The Mustang was designed by Edgar Schmued of North American Aviation. Following the mandate of James H. 'Dutch' Kindelberger, the president of NAA, to "keep all of the bumps on the inside", Schmued came through with a sleek aircraft that was destined to defeat the mighty Luftwaffe. Ironic is it not that German-American engineers were responsible for the winning American fighter design? I will now touch briefly on the features that contributed the most to the Mustang's outstanding military record and performance.

At the head of my list is the unique engine cooling system, which was designed in a manner that created little drag and at speed developed 300 lbs. of thrust. In turning what was, on other aircraft powered by liquid cooled engines, a speed robbing handicap into a propulsion system the P-51 is without equal. Much as the P-51's coolant system is highly efficient, it is also the fighter's *Achilles heel*. One well placed hit means the ride is over and the pilot can count on just a few minutes of power before his Merlin grinds to an abrupt halt.

The Mustang's high speed and relatively small size made it a difficult target for all but the most experienced anti-aircraft gunners. And that brings us to the laminar flow wing which also added to the Mustang's speed. Here again the P-51 led the world, by being the first mass produced aircraft to incorporate this feature. Laminar flow is achieved by moving the thickest point of the wing's cross section (airfoil) back toward the middle. This delays the formation of shock waves that cause drag. The superior design of the P-51 was first shown when the A model, powered by an Allison engine, proved to be thirty m.p.h. faster than the P-40 Warhawk powered by the same engine.

The crowning jewel of the Mustang's design is the Packard built, Rolls-Royce Merlin V-12 engine. While Allison engineers stuck their heads soundly in the sand and refused to take advantage of such items as intake manifold backfire screens or multiple stage superchargers, the Merlin marched on to become a legend in its own right. The Merlin's ability to churn out maximum power, for extended periods without failing, saved many a pilot's life when being chased home out of ammo.

When Lt. Olin C. Everhart was assigned as a pilot to the 368th FS, in February of 1945, he had previously been associated with tests on the Merlin engine. He informed his fellow pilots if their engines ever lost oil pressure to hit the oil dilute switch until the crankcase filled with fuel. The gasoline would pick up residual oil and serve as a lubricant for possibly up to an hour. Lt. Arthur B. Morris of the 369th FS applied that knowledge over Germany on March 9, 1945 and flew back to England.

During the final months of the war, two items became standard equipment that improved the Mustang and its pilot's ability to survive in combat. The K-14 gunsight improved the chances of the less tal-

Top: never before published shot of Ray Wetmore's P-51B, serial number 42-106894, fuselage code letters CS-P. Wetmore scored four kills with this Mustang. The invasion stripes date this photo. Of particular note is the fact this Mustang has had its exhaust shrouds removed, not an uncommon practice. Although rearward vision was not as good as in the later D model Mustang a number of pilots preferred the extra margin of speed the early models were capable of. Below, Capt. James L. Way Jr. of the 368th runs up the Merlin in P-51D, serial number 44-15371, CV-Z. Note the once glossy white star and bar of the national insignia has been subdued with the application of flat grey paint. Not much help in being inconspicuous when the majority of the aircraft's skin is bright aluminum.

ented gunnery graduates to acquire and destroy a target. The other hot item was the Berger G-Suit, an inflatable device that covered the pilot's abdomen and thighs. The suit kept blood in the upper half of the body and thereby preventing blackouts.

The ultimate production Mustang, the P-51H, barely missed the chance to prove itself in combat. The war ended in early May and the first H models were scheduled to arrive later that month.

When the final tally was made, the P-51 had established a kill ratio of four to one, twice that of the P-47. During diverse engagements, the Mustangs often went up against numerically superior enemy forces, inflicting losses as high as thirty-seven to nothing! That just about says it all.

P-47 THUNDERBOLT

The P-47 Thunderbolt was designed and built by Republic Aviation. The 'Jug' was a huge fighter tipping the scales some 4,000 lbs. heavier than the P-51. And therein lies the P-47's main handicap. As anyone who is familiar with high performance automobiles will tell you, weight is the nemesis of speed and handling.

To its credit the Thunderbolt was very sturdy and its initial acceleration in a dive outstanding. These two features helped the Jug survive combat, but the ability to sustain major damage or dive away from a combat disadvantage doesn't put victory markers on the side of ones fighter. According to Pop Doersch, the Jug did instill confidence in its pilots that they could survive. But after flying the

P-51 he felt they could actually win the air war.

The P-47 was powered by a Pratt and Whitney eighteen cylinder, double row, radial engine, also known as a *round motor*. The strong points of this design were lots of power and the ability to take a licking and keep on ticking.

While the Mustang's powerplant was a proven unit, having already been used in the British Spitfire, Hurricane and Lancaster, the Thunderbolt's engine had several bugs that required sorting out before the aircraft could be called a dependable weapon. The most notable problem with the P&W engine was a faulty ignition harness that grounded, no pun intended, a lot of P-47s until replacement units could be produced and shipped to England. There was also a spate of replacement engine failures. This was traced to improper pickling of the engine prior to shipment.

The P-47 could carry a heavier bomb load than the P-51 and was an excellent ground attack platform, while the P-51 was *The* air superiority fighter. The Jug's eight .50 calibre machine guns have been pointed to as an advantage over the six carried by the P-51D but this is only true as far as strafing is concerned. In a dogfight accuracy counts more. In fact, many P-51D and Thunderbolt pilots had the two outboard guns removed to lighten the plane and make room for additional ammo. Their theory was, "if you can't hit a target with four guns, two more won't help."

The argument will always exist as to which was the better fighter, the P-51 or the P-47, but the kill statistics speak for themselves.

One of the few natural metal finish P-47D-22-REs received by the 359th. It is believed none of these birds saw combat before being passed on to the 9th AF. LARRY LOVELL

Belly landing sequence taken at Dover, Delaware. Although this P-47 wasn't one of those used for training by the 359th it shows a scene too often repeated to go unnoticed. The 359th's monthly combat reports mentioned a number of cases where landing gear on P-47s failed to extend , also noting this happened frequently during training. SHELDON MILLER PHOTOS.

For the adventuresome modeler a nice clear photo of the P-47's R-2800 engine. While initially plagued with bugs the big Pratt & Whitney proved reliable and capable of running with entire cylinders shot away. From top left to lower right are: T/Sgt. Jack Linder, S/Sgt. Earl Sneddon, Sgt. Carrol Erickson and Sgt. Chester Sawyer.

Miscellaneous British Aircraft

THE 359TH FG WORKED in concert with the RAF on several occasions. Below are three types of RAF aircraft mentioned in the Mission Diary. There are two other types shown elsewhere and they are; the Westland Lysander and Supermarine Walrus.

AVRO LANCASTER

The Avro Lancaster was the pride of Bomber Command and most of its missions were flown under cover of night. The British believed bombers stood a better chance of surviving cloaked in darkness. They also pursued a policy of area bombing in contrast to the American strategy of precision bombing. German ground radar which not only located targets but controlled search lights and laid the anti-aircraft guns made the night a poor cover. Meanwhile the German night fighter force was directed to the bomber stream where their airborne radar aided in selection of individual targets. This combined with upward firing cannon called *Schräge Musik* (Jazz Music) proved a devastating combination. Indeed the RAF lost nearly 100 aircraft a night on several missions. American bomber losses pale by comparison and since they were flying by day gunners were able to exact a heavy, although sometimes exaggerated, toll on their tormentors.

VICKERS-ARMSTRONG WELLINGTON

The Wellington was a medium bomber and its heyday in the night skies over Europe were long past when the 359th began operations. It had an aluminum geodetic structure which proved amazingly strong and was covered mostly by linen. The lack of self sealing fuel tanks and adequate armor protection for the crew were serious flaws in its design. Like most RAF bombers the Wellington was armed with light caliber .303 machine guns and if a gunner was lucky enough to hit an enemy fighter his chances of disabling it were slim.

A RAF Coastal Command Wellington Mk XIII equipped with A. S. V. Mk II Radar. On July 6, 1944 an ASR Wellington arrived too late to help a B-24 crew down at sea and being covered by Col. Tacon and his section. MILITARY AIRCRAFT PHOTO

One of nineteen Lancasters modified to carry the drum shaped bombs used against the Ruhr dams in Germany. Note the top turret was removed from these special purpose aircraft. The Lancasters escorted by the 359th on Mar. 20, 1945 were supposed to drop 22,000 lb. *Grand Slam* bombs and would have looked much like one shown above; unfortunately the RAF sent conventional Lancs on that mission. MILITARY AIRCRAFT PHOTO

VICKERS-ARMSTRONG WARWICK

The Warwick was essentially a stretched and improved Wellington and by the time it arrived was far outclassed and Bomber Command had no need for it, their attention being rightfully focused on the Lancaster heavy bomber. Consequently the Warwick and the Wellington were relegated to other duties, notably coastal patrols and ASR work. Between Feb. 1, 1941 and May 8, 1945 Coastal Command accounted for saving 5,721 Allied and 277 enemy airmen.

The Opposition

A Me109G-2 Gustav the prettiest of the series. The engine cowling of succeeding versions would be covered with bumps, some quite large, to enclose a bigger supercharger and other items that no longer fit within the narrow confines of the aging design's fuselage. The factory applied code letters were supplanted by operational markings after delivery to a combat unit. MILITARY AIRCRAFT PHOTO

THIS SECTION BRIEFLY DESCRIBES the enemy aircraft encountered by the 359th. It gives their performance and notes each ones vices and virtues, hopefully without bias. Let no one doubt that the Luftwaffe was a mighty foe. Laying aside political beliefs, the German Air Force was staffed with a lot of intelligent, brave men. Their ultimate defeat was in a large degree fostered by inept leadership at the highest level with Adolf Hitler at the head of the list.

Had the Me262 been allotted to combat units a year earlier the war might have ended in a negotiated peace instead of an unconditional surrender, this was a very real prospect that weighed heavily on the minds of 8th Air Force command. But it wasn't to be, due mainly to a shortage of engines, and the Americans managed to cope with the *jet menace*, to the extent that it did materialize. To be sure there were missions on which the gunners aboard Flying Fortresses and Liberators had the almost impossible task of combating these *Buck Rogers* aircraft and it is of little consolation to those who died during these encounters that they were minor in scope.

The lion's share of aerial combat involved the famous Me109 and Fw190, so let's explore this pair first.

MESSERSCHMITT 109

The Me109 was designed by Willy Messerschmitt in 1934 and was the main fighter of the Luftwaffe far longer than it should have been, but Willy had the right political connections. The 109, like most of its contemporaries, was a low wing design powered by a liquid cooled, V-12 engine which was inverted, as were most of these engines used by the Germans. This fighter reached its peak, in my opinion, with the early G model. The later G models grew increasingly ugly, being covered with bumps and bulges to enclose equipment that no longer fit within

The Fw190D-9 or *Langnasen Dora*. This particular aircraft survived the war and is marked for U.S. Foreign Evaluation (FE-121 in this case). MILITARY AIRCRAFT PHOTOGRAPHS

The fastest fighter aircraft of WW II were the Me262 and the Me163. ABOVE, a Me262A-1B as it appeared during April of 1945. This aircraft was capable of 540 m.p.h. in level flight. BELOW, the Me163B-1A, or Devil's Sled, was rocket powered and could burn along at 596 m.p.h. Both were impossible to catch in level flight but in a dogfight the edge went to the piston engine aircraft which were usually more maneuverable. MILITARY AIRCRAFT PHOTOGRAPHS

its small and aging airframe. At this point a complete redesign was in order, but fighters were in demand so cobbled-up versions of the 109 pervaded the ranks of the Luftwaffe's flight lines.

Mediocre performance became a millstone around the pilot's neck. Power increases were followed by a proportionate increase in weight and drag resulting in no significant gains. It is also worth mentioning that the narrow track landing gear caused a lot of grief during landings, especially in a crosswind. More disturbing is the fact that some 1,200 fledgling pilots died trying to master this beast. In spite of these handicaps experts like Erich Hartmann, with 352 victories, scored an mazing number of victories flying the 109, but they are the exceptions and not the rule.

FOCKE-WULF 190

Although the company name Focke-Wulf appears at the head of the 190's designation, it was designed by Prof. Kurt Tank. It was a much better aircraft than the Me109 and managed to keep apace, or one jump ahead, of its foes. The 190 started out being powered by a BMW fourteen cylinder, double row, radial engine. Later versions were powered by a liquid cooled V-12, which created a more streamlined nose and gave a boost in speed. This model was the Fw190D and it was quickly dubbed the *Langnasen-Dora* (Longnose-Dora).

The superior speed enjoyed by pilots of the 190D during the early part of 1944 was experienced by Maj. Albert R. Tyrrell of the 368th FS on Feb. 22, 1944. Tyrrell, who was leading the 368th, bounced a 190D that was attacking a B-17 near Hamm, Germany. Cruising at 20,000' he nosed his P-47 over and chased the enemy from 18,000' down to 10,000'. Going full-bore and with an indicated speed of 525 m.p.h., Tyrrell was surprised that the 190 maintained a 300 yard lead. The German pilot then made a diving turn into the cover of clouds and the chase ended.

MESSERSCHMITT 262

The Me262 was the ultimate German fighter of WWII and for some time it was the bench mark against which the first Allied jet fighters were judged. It was also a product of German national pride as its builders realized the war was going badly and their revolutionary fighter was the last hope for their country to regain air supremacy.

The 262's airframe was a mixture of steel and aluminum parts. This blend was the result of a hurried construction schedule and had time allowed for replacing the steel parts, with those made from lighter material, then the airframe would have been considerably lighter, resulting in even greater performance.

In those pioneering days materials technology lagged far behind the ability of man's mind to conceive new designs. The first production jet engines were marvels of engineering, hamstrung by an inability to build them with anything approaching a reasonable working life span. The Messerschmitt team set a fifty hour goal for time between major servicing of the jet engines, but only achieved half that time span.

The Me262 Swallow was a case of too little, too late. Those that crossed swords with the 8th AF caused a real sensation, blasting through formations of bombers with near total immunity. The Mustangs were usually fast enough in a dive to overtake the jets when they broke for home and 118.5 Me262s fell to the P-51's guns, while the P-47 claimed an additional 20.5. The limiting factor in the operation of this aircraft was its high rate of fuel consumption a problem shared by all early jets. The 262's average time aloft was about fifty minutes, after which came the deadly proposition of trying to land with Mustangs circling over the jet's airfields.

MESSERSCHMITT 163

"The Devil's Sled" was one nickname given the Me163 Komet by its pilots. This was an aircraft that proved to be more dangerous to the Germans than to those against which it was pitted. Although the pilots of the 8th AF called it a 'jettie', the same as they did the 262, the 163 was actually powered by a rocket motor which used extremely volatile and corrosive fuels. There was a constant danger that the smallest leak in a fuel line fitting , even while parked, would result in a catastrophic explosion. Likewise the pilot, who sat between two fuel tanks filled with hydrogen-peroxide, knew that if these tanks ruptured during a crash his chances of survival were slim, despite the fact he wore a protective suit made of PVC fabric impregnated with neoprene.

On the positive side, this tiny fighter was even faster than the 262 and its flying wing design, engineered by Dr. Alexander Lippish, enabled it to stretch the use of its twelve minute fuel supply by making high speed gliding attacks through the seemingly endless streams of American bombers. When momentum tapered off the pilot would re-ignite the motor and quickly build his speed back past the 500 m.p.h. mark.

Also aiding in the use of this extremely limited range interceptor was the German ground radar vectoring system and the positioning of Komet airfields along paths known to be taken by 8th AF bombers.

While the Me163 was a beautiful, futuristic design, from an operational standpoint it was a failure. For the monetary expenditure required to field this little brute the returns were very small. The Komet claimed sixteen victories, a rather pathetic showing.

MESSERSCHMITT 110 / 210 / 410

Messerschmitt's model 110 was a twin engine aircraft with twin rudders that gave the gunner, who sat behind the pilot, a better field of fire. The Me 110 used two of the same V-12 engines that powered the Me109. It was used as a long range escort fighter during the Battle of Britain and took a terrible beating at the hands of the RAF Spitfires and Hurricanes.

While fast, for a twin engine fighter, it couldn't hold its own in a dogfight and as a result the 110 was then assigned as a bomber destroyer. In this role it was successful, until American long range escort fighters intruded on its hunting grounds, then it became almost suicidal to attack the bombers. The Me110 was also equipped with radar and used as a night fighter against the RAF bombers. And contrary to popular belief the losses sustained by the RAF on their night missions were even higher than those taken by the 8th AF bombers during daylight raids.

Progressive development of the Me110 led to the Me210 and 410, both marginally faster and better armed, but still easy prey for the ever present Mustangs and Thunderbolts.

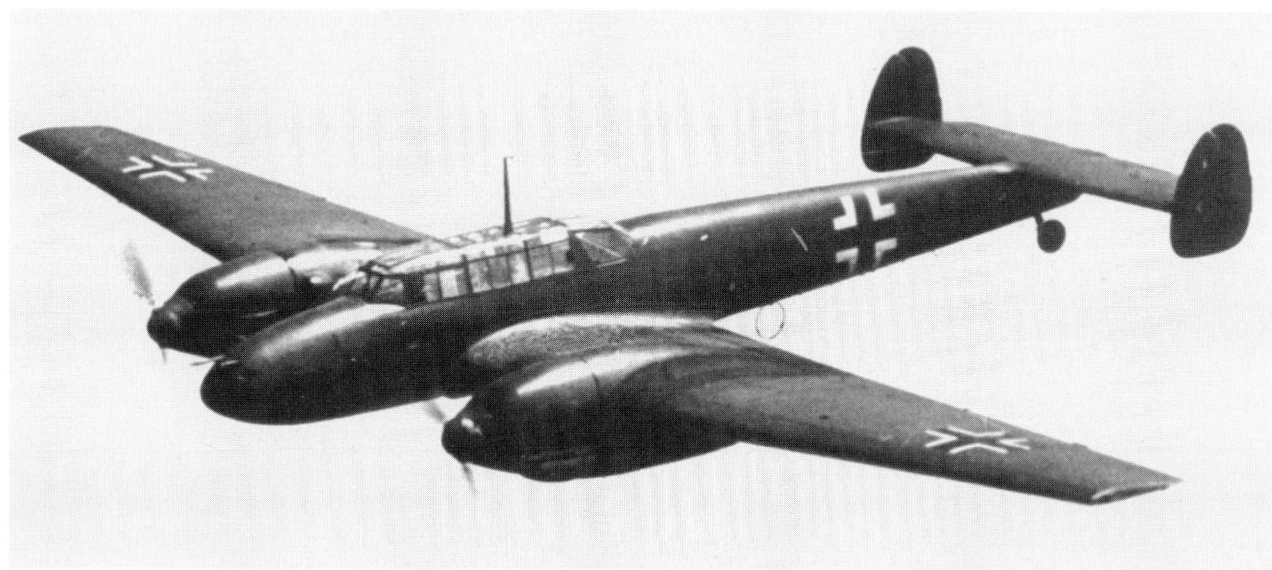

The top photo depicts a Me110C-4 which was equipped with 1,100 h.p. engines giving it a top speed of 336 m.p.h. at 19,685'. It was armed with two 20mm cannon and four 7.9 mm machine guns in the nose and a single 7.9 in the aft green-house for defence. Wingspan was 53'-3 3/4. MAP photos. Below Me210A-2s. Note nose and the single vertical stabilizer. Despite a boost in power, from two engines of 1,350 h.p. each, the speed raised to only 350 m.p.h. This was partly due to the drag caused by the two remote controlled gun barbettes, containing a single 13mm machine gun each, that were added to the waist of the fuselage. ETHELL PHOTOS

Battle Overview

TO GIVE THE READER who is not familiar with the air war over Europe during WWII a basic understanding of the 359th's operations against Festung Europa, it is necessary to give a brief sketch of how the campaign progressed.

When the 8th AF began its assault on Germany the art of modern air combat was still in a state of flux. Thanks to the Luftwaffe's fighters it quickly became evident that unescorted bombers were going to sustain an unacceptable percentage of losses.

The chances of a bomber crew surviving a twenty-five mission tour were very slim. With the arrival of the P-51 and its ability to penetrate anywhere in Germany, bomber losses diminished to the point that a tour was extended to thirty five missions and by late 1944 to fifty missions.

The invasion of France, or D-Day, forced the 8th AF to fly support for the Allied ground forces, but once these units were firmly established on the continent, attention shifted back on Germany.

Meanwhile, despite the heavy bombing of their factories, the Germans managed to increase fighter production. The two major handicaps that could not be remedied were fuel and pilot shortages. Time and safe areas were required to adequately train new pilots, but with 8th AF fighters roaming at will over Germany, these requirements could not be met.

Early on the Allies realized that the Reich depended heavily on imported oil and great emphasis was placed on the destruction of petroleum facilities. The oil fields of Ploesti, Rumania, which supplied 27% of Germany's oil, were bombed constantly, either by the 9th or 15th AF, although they were vigorously defended by Axis fighters and flak. As the tap shut tighter Germany was forced to depend on domestic supplies of synthetic oil and fuel. The city of Merseburg, in east-central Germany, produced these synthetics and the 359th FG escorted bombers to that target seven times.

Despite the heavy attrition of men and machines the Luftwaffe still managed to put up a creditable defence. With the rapid advance of Allied ground forces, especially those led by Gen. George S. Patton, the territory left to defend shrank, but the job didn't become easier, for by now raids consisting of over 1,000 8th AF bombers were commonplace.

The jets, which were the last hope of a crumbling German military-industrial complex, were obliged to stand down until enough fuel could be collected to mount sporadic attacks on the fleets of American bombers. To compensate for their loss of air power the Germans increased production of flak guns and the power of the legendary 88mm gun to bring down Allied aircraft reached mythic proportions.

And so it was, in the final days of the war in Europe, that without the fuel to put forth a significant effort, many of the idled Luftwaffe units were pressed into the ground defence of a rapidly collapsing Germany. The mighty Luftwaffe had fallen and with it went the last hope of the Reich that was to have lasted a thousand years.

What Is A Fighter Group?

THE 359TH FG WAS ASSIGNED to the VIII Fighter Command, as a part of the 66th Fighter Wing until Oct. of 1943. In Nov. of 1943 they were moved to the 67th FW and thus it would remain, except for a brief return to the 66th during the invasion of Normandy.

Ground support was furnished by the 448th Air Service Group (headquarters section and Base Services Squadron), 824th Air Engineering Squadron, 648th Air Material Squadron and the 3rd Gunnery and Tow-Target Flight.

The 359th (combat group) consisted of three squadrons: the 368th, 369th and 370th. Ideally each squadron contained sixteen fighters, not including spares, and a squadron was then divided into four flights, of four fighters. These four flights were identified as: Red, White, Blue and Yellow. Extra flights were designated as Black and, or Green. These colors were strictly for radio identification and visual

identification was not treated until near the end of the war, when the dorsal strakes on the P-51Ds flown by flight leaders were striped in the appropriate color.

Flights were further broken down into a pair of elements. So using Red Flight as an example we have: Red 1, the flight leader and his wingman Red 2 making up the first element. The second element is led by Red 3, with his wingman being Red 4.

To visually identify the three squadrons the rudders were painted: yellow for the 368th, red the 369th and dark blue the 370th. The noses of all 359th FG aircraft were painted a glossy deep green. The squadrons were also identified by code letters stenciled on the sides of the fuselage. These letters were: CV for the 368th, IV the 369th and CS the 370th. These double letter codes were applied forward of the national insignia (star and bars) and the individual aircraft code letter was located aft. When the number of fighters allotted to a squadron exceeded the

Lt. John D. Cooley's P-51K. This photo was taken after the war and the code letters CV-V are painted under the wing to deter buzzing the British countryside, a practice that could cause needless fatalities and destruction of property.
DOERSHAM

AT LEFT, a good comparison of the green noses as applied to the Thunderbolt which is on its way out and the P-51B which will fly its first combat mission, with the 359th FG, on May 4, 1944 two days after this picture was snapped. Left to right are S/Sgt. Marshall L. Binder, Lt. Harold L. Hollis and Cpl. Robert E. Erikson. Hollis was KIA on June 22, 1944. ABOVE, Capt. Rene L. Burtner's P-51D *HUBERT*. Canopy frame and rudder are painted red. Also note the three horizontal stripes on the dorsal strake, which denote a flight leader. Other P-51s flown by flight leaders had four vertical stripes on the strake. This photo was probably taken after the cessation of hostilities since the black identification bands on the wings and vertical stabilizer have been removed. Fred S. McGehee shot down two Me109s on Mar. 24, 1945 while flying *HUBERT*. RENE BURTNER

usable number of letters in the alphabet, then a duplication occurred. To distinguish between two fighters with the code letter A for instance, the A on one of the fighters would either be underlined thus <u>A</u>, or similarly capped. This reads BAR-A.

For radio identification of the group and its squadrons, the following call signs were used;

Date of Change	359th FG	368th	369th	370th
	Wallpaint	Beesnest	Tiretread	Weelass
Jan. 3, 1944	Wallpaint	Jackson	Tiretread	Wheeler
Apr. 17, 1944	Wallpaint	Sonnet	Tinplate	Tailer
Apr. 23, 1944	Chairman	Jigger	Tinplate	Redcross
B group call signs	Cavetop	Handy	Earnest	Rollo
C group call sign,	Ragtime			

The preceding call signs, codes and color schemes, represent the final system used by the 359th FG. As with any organization the symbols, codes, etc., go through an evolutionary process and often the reasons for those changes are lost in the mists of time. Since this may well be the last work written on the 359th while a considerable number of former members are still living, this is the time to record those previously mentioned changes.

When the Group went into combat, flying the P-47, all of their fighters were painted with the standard camouflage scheme of olive drab (green) on the topside and neutral grey below. Following another standard practice, to prevent gunners on bombers from mistaking the P-47 for a Fw190, an 18" white band was painted on the leading circumference of the engine cowling and 12" wide bands chordwise across the vertical and horizontal tail surfaces. This treatment was also applied to the P-51 when it arrived, to keep it from being mistaken for the Me109, which it did resemble head-on.

Hours before the invasion of France all Allied aircraft were painted with 'zebra stripes'. These were removed from the top surfaces of the wings and fuselage or sprayed over with coat of aluminum lacquer about a month later.

The green nose first appeared on the Group's P-47s, during March of 1944, in the form of a 24" band painted around the forward section of the engine cowling. The first green to grace the noses of 359th Mustangs, covered the spinner and the cowling back to the first exhaust stack. This was later extended back past the exhaust stacks in a downward curve to the front of the wingroot and wheel wells.

The letter codes only changed once and that was unique to the 359th FG. That change was made to the 370th Squadron's code letters some time after the middle of March 1944. The original letters CR were changed to CS.

Group and squadron insignia all featured the fabled unicorn, symbol of strength and virtue. The single horn denoted the Group flew single engine fighters. For the 368th FS the motif was a unicorn head with a lightning bolt clenched in its mouth (referred to as a thunderbolt during the P-47 period). The 369th had a unicorn in full stride, superimposed

on a lightning bolt. The 370th's unicorn was similarly displayed in a bucking posture. The colors for these badges were: yellow for the 368th's background disc, red for the 369th, dark blue 370th and white for the unicorn. The lightning bolt was red outlined in white (later the 167th FS would change the bolt to yellow). The Group emblem was a left profile of a unicorn head on an escutcheon. Above the head were three stars, having three, five and nine points. Below the escutcheon, in Latin, were the words "CUM LEONE" (with lions), denoting that the Americans of the 359th were fighting alongside the RAF. The unicorn was a profound choice for the Group's symbol and reference to it can be found in the Bible as well as Buddhist and Confucian text. This stanza of an old German ballad is a sufficient look into the nature of the creature at this time.

The unicorn is noble
He keeps him safe and high
Upon a narrow path and steep
Climbing to the sky;
And there no man can take him.
He scorns the hunters dart
And only a virgin's magic power
Shall tame his haughty heart.

That covers the machines of war and leaves us with the men who made it all happen. It took about 2,000 men to staff the Group's combat and support units. Starting at the top we have the command structure and then the officers in charge of the various sub-units: Weather, Supplies, Engineering, etc. Next come the pilots, crew chiefs, armorers, fuelers, maintenance men, radio technicians, cooks, doctors, clerks and guards. It took all of these men, working as a team, to keep the Group's fighters in the air and ready to fight the Hun.

The 359th was based at East Wretham (Army Station 133), on what was formerly a country estate in Norfolk County, England. Wretham Hall was an imposing three-story, masonry structure consisting of some seventy-five rooms and it was used as living quarters by the officers. The base had been previously occupied by bomber units of the RAF. Wretham Hall was destroyed by a fire in 1949.

Naturally it was the fighter pilots that captured the public's attention. Fighter pilots have been and still are described by many adjectives: bold, dashing, flamboyant and sometimes irreverent, but the word that perhaps best describes them is proud!

The Second World War has been called "the last good war". If any war can be called good, then WWII fills the bill nicely. The enemy was well defined, his purpose and his atrocities documented. This gave the Americans a bond that was not emulated until our recent war with Iraq. The Axis powers: Germany, Italy and Japan, were a threat to the freedom of the entire world, the magnitude of which, many people today don't realize. Nazi Germany was working on an atomic bomb as were the Japanese, and some proof has recently surfaced indicating Japan detonated an atomic device just before the war ended. Food for thought, for those who say that we Americans were wrong in using atomic bombs on Japan. Clearly Germany and Japan would have not hesitated to use these weapons on us.

So it was with a sense of pride, knowing that they were fighting for a truly just cause, that the men of the 359th and their brothers-in-arms went to war. For their actions on Sept. 11,1944, they would receive a Distinguished Unit Citation and for their participation in other major operations six Battle Ribbons to adorn their Guidon. The six ribbons are; *Air Offensive Europe* (preparation for invasion of Normandy), *Normandy* (invasion support), *Northern France* (support for the drive across France), *Rhineland* (support for the airborne invasion of the Netherlands and the drive into the Rhine), *Ardennes-Alsace* (support during the Battle of the Bulge) and *Central Europe* (support for the final drive across Germany).

◄ On the facing page are some of the men who kept the Group functioning. Starting in the top left corner we have the Weathermen, left to right, S/Sgt. Melvin E. Kazek, Lt. ?-Stauco, Lt. Ralph Platt (Stormy) and M/Sgt. Gerald P. Baker. Top right, Radio Repair (today this section is called Avionics). Second row on the left, the men in who worked in supply. On the right the Infirmary Staff. Third row on the left the Motor Pool. On the right, some of the 368th's Armorers. Fourth row on the left, the 368th's Communications Staff with Lt. Irvin Segal in the center. On the right the 370th's Cooks.

Mission Diary

THE FOLLOWING IS an explanation of terms and abbreviations used in this work.

ANG—Air National Guard

API—Armor Piercing Incendiary, the ammunition preferred by fighter pilots. In calibre .50 it was capable of penetrating nearly any armor plate to be found on aircraft and light tanks.

ASR—Air-Sea-Rescue, aircraft and boats devoted to the task of finding and retrieving airmen that were lost, or forced down over water.

Category E—Denotes an aircraft that is damaged beyond the point of economical repair.

F/O— Flight Officer, noncommissioned officer, one grade below 2nd Lieutenant.

Fort— B-17 Flying Fortress

KIA—Killed in action.

Lib —B-24 Liberator

MEW and Type 16 control— Micro-Wave Early Warning and Type 16 are ground based radar systems, used to direct fighters to suspected enemy aircraft. MEW was the more advanced system.

MIA—Missing in action.

Noball target— V-1 missile launch site. These pilotless flying bombs were called Buzz-Bombs or Doodle-bugs.

POW—Prisoner of war.

RAF—Royal Air Force

R/T—Radio transmission

R/V—Rendezvous, the time and place escorting fighters join with the bombers.

Most of the cities are shown using wartime spellings. Contemporary spelling is used only when the reader might not recognize the old name. The notable changes are: Braunschweig / Brunswick, Germany, Koln / Cologne, Germany, Dunkerque / Dunkirk, France and München / Munich, Germany.

Air to ground scores are shown thus: 25-38 trucks, as an example. The first number, denotes 25 trucks destroyed and 38 the number of trucks damaged.

Air victories are shown thus: 14-3-5, fourteen being the number of kills, three denoting probable kills and five the number of aircraft damaged.

Time is shown using the standard military system. At the head of each mission the reader will find the takeoff and landing times shown thus: **(0944-1458)** in this instance the group took off at 9:44 in the morning and landed at 2:58 in the afternoon.

The Air Force credits the 359th FG with 346 combat missions and that will never change. During my research I found three additional missions, which the Group was not given credit for. This book embraces all 349 missions.

Those not familiar with the air war over Europe will note that the Group didn't fly every mission they were scheduled for. The infamous British fog or rain, or a combination of both, would often keep a base closed, while one just a few miles away managed to get its aircraft airborne. But these occasions were rare as the 359th gained a reputation for completing missions in the worst weather, continuing on to the target while entire groups of bombers turned back for England.

It took ten months to digest and record this diary and I have attempted to keep it from being dry reading. But before embarking on the 359th's first mis-

All of the photos on this page show the 359th FG during training. Starting at the top and working left to right: Anthony Chardella squats in front of the 369th FS's enlisted men's quarters at Grenier Field, New Hampshire, note the 369th's unicorn laid out in painted stones; unidentified trio of mechanics and a training command P-47 (these were built by Republic but those built by Curtiss didn't meet spec. for combat duty due to shoddy workmanship and ended up trainers); Chardella, on wing, arming guns; unidentified armorer kneeling at a P-47's gun bay; 368th's armament workshop at Farmingdale, New York (note the crude lighting consisting of incandescent bulbs strung along the ceiling); Larry Lovell; last photo, an unidentified radio technician doing a systems check. PHILLIP DUPONT PHOTOS

Front of Wretham Hall. The kitchen wing is obscured by the greenery on the left. This imposing masonry structure comprised of some seventy-five rooms was home for the 359th's officers. Wretham Hall was destroyed by a fire in 1949.

sion let's cover the Group's background leading up to that point.

On Dec. 20, 1942, the 359th FG came in to being by the issuance of War Department Order AG 320.2. The 1st Air Force then issued an order on Jan. 15, 1943 activating the Group at Westover Field, Massachusetts. Lt.Col. Avelin P. Tacon Jr. was placed in command.

Throughout March the 359th received enlisted men from various units already stationed at Westover, the bulk however came from training schools. During that month the first squadron leaders were assigned: Captain Albert R. Tyrrell to the 368th FS, Major Rockford V. Gray the 369th FS and Major John B. Murphy the 370th FS. Murphy was the only one with combat experience, having flown with the 11th FS of the 343rd FG, in the Aleutians and sharing in the destruction of a Japanese 'Dave' floatplane on June 3, 1942.

Training began in earnest during April of 1943, with the squadrons moving to other bases. The 368th and 369th flew to Grenier Field, New Hampshire, while the 370th went to Bedford Army Air Base, New Hampshire. Flying time was limited, since each squadron had only two or three P-47s for training. Through May and into July the squadrons rotated to Republic Field, Long Island to obtain new Thunderbolts. With an adequate supply of fighters on hand the pilots quickly improved their skills.

The squadrons gravitated back to Westover Field during August and on the dawn of October 2, 1943 the majority of the Group departed by train for Camp Kilmer, New Jersey, arriving there in the afternoon. On October 7 the Group boarded ships in New York Harbor. Headquarters and the 368th boarded the USAT *Argentina*, formerly a Good Neighbor Liner; the 369th was assigned to the *Thurston*, a converted freighter and the 370th took the former Dutch motor vessel, *Sloterdyjk*. These three ships were part of a large convoy that sailed just before dawn on Oct. 8, 1943.

The *Argentina* docked at Liverpool, England on Oct. 19 and Headquarters, along with the 368th, immediately boarded trains for East Wretham. The trains arrived at Thetford, about five miles south of East Wretham, with the troops being obliged to march to their new home. The citizens of Thetford held their noses, while they cheered the passing Yanks. As Phillip Dupont, a radio technician, explained "we were quite ripe, after all those days on ship, without a shower". Meanwhile the 369th and 370th debarked at Glasgow and Gourock, Scotland respectively.

Lt. Col. Tacon went to work instantly, organizing the unit. The serious business of preparing for war went straight forward, with little emphasis placed on close order drill or spit and polish. The result was, in less than eight weeks the base was ready to begin flying combat missions.

The VIII Fighter Command required every new fighter group to be led into combat by experienced pilots. To achieve this, the 359th's senior flying officers: Lt. Col. Avelin P. Tacon Jr., Majors William H. Swanson, John B. Murphy, Albert R. Tyrrell and Rockford V. Gray, plus twelve captains and lieutenants, were put on detached service with the 84th FS of the 78th FG, based at Duxford. In their absence, Major Luther H. Richmond of the 352nd FG moved from Bodney to East Wretham, to act as the 359th's flying group commander.

December 11, 1943 (1102-1304)

The 78th FG flies withdrawal support for B-24s returning from Emden, Germany. The 78th scores one kill for no losses. During the action Capt. Chauncey S. Irvine, the group leader, and his wingman Lt.Col. Avelin P. Tacon, unsuccessfully bounce a Me109, while Lt. James R. Pino, who is leading a top cover flight, is bounced by German fighters that also come up empty handed. During the night the 359th's detachment returns to East Wretham.

1 December 13, 1943 (1352-1539)

During the morning forty-two P-47s fly a practice mission over England, returning to base just before noon. At 1155, while the fighters are still landing, the 359th receives a field order assigning them a high altitude sweep over France. Not all of the Thunderbolts are refueled in time to participate, due to inadequate facilities. Maj. Luther H. Richmond of the 352nd FG, 'The Blue Nose Bastards of Bodney', leads the 359th FG on its operational debut. The force consists of thirty-six P-47s, eleven each from the 368th and 369th FSs and fourteen from the

Top, an aerial view of Station 133 looking west and taken just prior to the 359th FGs arrival. The field had received the Luftwaffe's attention as evidenced by the bomb craters. The wingtip of the photo platform aircraft which is visible in the upper right obscures the control tower. The hangar which is right of center became the 370th FS's hangar. The runway running parallel to the trailing edge of the wing and cutting diagonally across the upper right of the field was the main runway and was eventually covered with perforated steel planking during the winter of 1944-45. The control tower didn't look like most of the others found on 8th AF bases. The typical control tower was a smaller glazed enclosure on top of a rectangular masonry building. Emergency vehicles are in an advantageous position parked near the tower.

370th. They cross in over Gravelines, France at 1437 and 28,000', make a sweep in the area of St. Omer and come out near Le Treport. The flight is routine despite the fact Abbeville, home of Germany's elite fighter unit JG 26, is in the vicinity. All of the Group returns safely.

* **December 16, 1943**

The Group is scheduled to fly a withdrawal support mission but at 1200, fifteen minutes before engine warm-up time, the mission is scrubbed due to the poor weather.

2 December 20, 1943 (1000-1240)

Maj. Richmond leads again and the 359th flies penetration escort for B-17s headed for Bremen, Germany. Of the fifty-nine P-47s taking off twenty-two return early. Seventeen are aborts and five are assigned as escorts. Eight of the aborts are due to engine trouble and seven from failure of drop tanks to release. R/V is made off Texel Island at 1101 and 29,000'. During escort a flight of Jugs, providing top cover at 32,000', spots six enemy aircraft at 35,000' shadowing the bombers. They are not pursued. Escort is dropped at Zuidlaarder Lake and the 359th returns on a reciprocal course. During the return flight an unidentified P-47 follows the leader of the 368th FS for five minutes. The Group returns safely to base and an investigation is begun concerning the possible sabotage of Lt. Herman E. King's Thunderbolt.

As a result of reporting the enemy aircraft flying reconnaissance over the bombers, a "smack the Hun" order is issued instructing fighter groups to "pursue and destroy."

3 December 21, 1943 (1052-1255)

Maj. Richmond leads the 359th for the last time. The mission is area support for 9th AF B-26 Marauders bombing Noball targets in the Calais area of France. Fifty-seven P-47s take-off and a malfunctioning prop causes the only abort. The Group crosses in at Gravelines, France at 1130 and patrols until 1200. During the patrol a Spitfire is seen exploding as the result of an attack by an unidentified Thunderbolt. The 359th then crosses out at Gravelines and all of the pilots, except Lt. Herman E. King of the 370th FS, return safely to base. King makes a crash landing on the emergency airfield at Manston, England and while he escapes injury the P-47 is declared Category E. A second investigation is opened in connection with the possible sabotage of King's fighter.

4 December 22, 1943 (1218-1436)

Lt.Col. Avelin P. Tacon Jr. CO of the 359th FG leads for the first time. The assignment is penetration support for B-17s and B-24s attacking Osnabruck, Germany. R/V is made near Zwolle, Netherlands at 1315 and 27,500'. Escort is provided until 1330, when the limited range of the P-47 demands returning to base. After the mission pilots complain that the radio call signs for the 368th and 370th, Beesnest and Weelass respectively, sounded too much alike on the radio. A change to Jackson for the 368th and Wheeler for the 370th will take place on January 3, 1944.

* **December 22, 1943**

A practice escort mission with B-24s is flown over East Anglia. Fourteen Jugs from the 370th FS participate.

5 December 23, 1943 (1233-1537)

Lt.Col. Tacon leads an area support mission for B-17s, over northern France. Noball targets are the objective again. R/V is made at Berck-Sur-Mer, France at 1320 and 14,000'. The flight is routine until returning to England, where Lt. Charles V. Cunningham, of the 370th, makes a belly landing at Reigate. Once more the pilot is all right, while the aircraft is Category E.

* **December 27, 1943**

A saboteur is spotted on the aircraft dispersal area and is fired on as he makes good his escape. Damage to a belly tank's connections are found.

* **December 29, 1943 (1334-1504)**

Today the 359th and the 352nd FGs practice escorting B-24s. Maj. William H. Swanson, of the 369th FS, leads the Group and Lt.Col. Tacon flies as an independent observer.

6 December 30, 1943 (1059-1407)

Lt.Col. Tacon leads the Group on a penetration support mission for heavy bombers hitting Ludwigshafen, Germany. R/V is not made at a point east of Roye, France as scheduled, so the Group orbits until 1219, then returns to base crossing out near Cayeux-Sur-Mer, France at 1303.

7 December 31, 1943 (1035-1336)

Lt.Col. Tacon leads again, as the 359th provides escort for sixty-four B-17s bombing a ball bearing fac-

Top, two men from the 369th FS have just finished hanging a 500 lb General Purpose Bomb on the belly of a Jug. This photo was most likely taken on Jan. 28, 1944, the only bombing mission flown before Valentine's Day (see message on bomb).

tory at Paris, France. R/V is made over Cayeux-Sur-Mer, France at 1120 and 24,000'. The bombing results are observed to be good and no bombers are lost. Six Fw190s are chased, although not caught, by twelve P-47s led by Lt.Col. Tacon and Maj. Rockford V. Gray.

8   January 4, 1944 (0858-1133)

Lt.Col. Tacon flies lead as the Group provides penetration support for B-17s raiding Münster, Germany. The 359th crosses in at 0959, north of Terschelling Island, Netherlands and R/V is made east of Dokkum at1002 and 27,000'. Escort is given until 1014, when the Group turns homeward from the Westerbork area of the Netherlands. The 359th returns without incident.

9   January 5, 1944 (1010-1305)

Lt.Col. Tacon is in the lead as the Group flies penetration escort for B-17s scheduled to bomb the ball bearing plants at Elberfeld, Germany. R/V is made

near Dinteloord at 1106 and 27,000'. The escort continues until 1129, in the area of Elsdorf, where a B-17 gunner fires on the P-47 flown by Lt. William N. Tucker of the 370th and misses. The 359th crosses out at 1151 over Schouwen Island, Netherlands.

10   January 7, 1944 (1135-1423)

Fifty-nine Thunderbolts led by Lt.Col. Tacon provide withdrawal support for B-17s and B-24s blasting the industrial areas of Ludwigshafen, Germany. The 359th crosses the coast of Belgium at 1219 near Ostende and makes R/V north of Sedan, France at 1241 and 25,000'. The bombers are then escorted as far as Bapaume, where they are left at 1318. The 359th then returns safely to England, crossing out near Gravelines, France at 1357. Thirty of the P-47s land at other bases due to low fuel.

11   January 11, 1944 (1115-1420)

Sixty-one P-47s of the 359th provide withdrawal support for B-17s and B-24s bombing aviation industry

Left, Lt. John Houston Oliphint and on the right, Maj. Rockford Vance Gray. Olie and Rocky scored the Group's first kill on Jan. 29, 1944 when they shared in the destruction of a Me110. Grey would transfer to the 9th AF during the next month and score five additional kills. He died in a crash in Sept. of 1944.

targets at Halberstadt and Oschersleben, Germany. This is the first mission the Group will use the new 108 gallon belly tanks, which are replacing the previous 75 gallon units. Lt.Col. Tacon aborts over the English Channel when his instruments fail and Maj. William H. Swanson takes the lead. The Group crosses the coast near Bergen, Belgium at 1205 and the lead section makes R/V with the bombers close to Amelo, Belgium at 1215 and 19,000'. Nine Me109s are spotted in the vicinity and promptly chased off. The 359th then takes the lead section of bombers out to Amsterdam and returns to pick up the rest of the force. At 1232, twenty miles south of Diepholz, the 368th FS breaks up an attack on the rear box of B-17s being made by three Me210s. The 368th is then bounced by three Me109s, one painted blue and the other two light green, with red bands around the fuselage. During a brief engagement Lt. Edward J. Hyland is shot down, becoming the Group's first pilot to be KIA. A few minutes later Captain James E. Buckley, who is leading Yellow Flight of the 370th, enters a steep dive and disappears, the probable victim of oxygen equipment failure. Buckley was a West

Point graduate. On returning to England two pilots from the 370th are killed during crash landings. Lt. William N. Tucker dies at Radnal, Shrops and Lt. Lynn W. Hair perishes at Chipping Warden as his P-47 hits a tree and explodes. Lt. Glenn C. Bach, of the 370th FS, becomes lost in the overcast while returning from flying radio relay, along the northern French coast, and is forced to make a wheels up landing in a pasture in northern England. A member of the Home Guard watches over his fighter while Bach goes to Bardon Mill to contact East Wretham.

12   January 14, 1944 (1402-1715)

Lt.Col. Tacon leads the Group on an area support mission for B-17s hitting Noball targets, in the Pas de Calais sector of France. The Group crosses in at 1449 and 15,000', near Pointe-Haut-Banc, France and patrols until 1626. On returning to England two pilots from the 369th make crash landings, Lt. Glenn C. Bach at East Wretham and Lt. Homer L. Rodeheaver at Wormingford. Neither pilot is injured.

A lineup of 368th FS Thunderbolts all named for characters in Al Capp's comic strip Li'l Abner. Names are; Marryin' Sam, Pappy Yokum, Daisy Mae, Mammy Yokum, Li'l Abner and Lonesom' Polecat. Tony Chardella donated the ID plate from Pappy Yokum to the 167th's Heritage Museum in 1992.

13   January 21, 1944 (1307-1640)

Another area support mission for 8th AF heavies blasting Noball targets in the Pas de Calais sector. R/V is at Pointe-Haut-Banc. The 359th returns safely.

14   January 24, 1944 (1121-1440)

This mission is penetration area support, with Lt. Col. Tacon in the lead. The bombers are recalled when their bases begin closing due to the weather. The 359th is not notified of the recall and proceeds on, crossing in near Blankenberghe, Belgium at 1204. The bombers are not found but the 359th flies its assigned mission, receiving several vectors that prove to be false alarms. The Group then crosses out at 1330, south of Knocke, Belgium.

*   January 26, 27, 1944

A dive bombing mission is scheduled and scrubbed, both days.

15   January 28, 1944 (1305-1647)

Four P-47s led by Lt. Lester G. Taylor, of the 369th, fly a weather reconnaissance flight in the vicinity of Leeuwarden, Netherlands. On the way out Taylor's Jug is hit by flak, near Mardyck, France. The Thun-derbolts land at Manston, England before returning to East Wretham.

16   January 28, 1944 (1505-1727)

After receiving a favorable weather report from the previously dispatched flight, the remainder of the Group heads off to Leeuwarden to dive bomb an airfield. The 368th and 370th carry 500 lb. General Purpose bombs, while the 369th provides top cover. A heavy overcast blankets the target area and R/V with the 352nd FG, which is to provide area support, fails. The Group returns home with their bombs.

17   January 29, 1944 (1050-1405)

Definitely a red-letter day for the 359th as they score their first kill. Tacon, now a full Colonel, leads a withdrawal support mission for B-17s and B-24s returning from Frankfurt, Germany. The coast is crossed at 1113 near Walcheren, Belgium and R/V is made at 1203. At 1215 near Malmedy, Belgium, Red Flight of the 368th is flying at 27,000' when Lt. Emer H. Cater sights a glossy, light green Me110 5,000' below. Cater and Capt. Clifton Shaw give chase and Shaw scores hits on the 110's port engine, which begins trailing smoke. Several other pilots get snap shots at the 110 before it goes into a dive, pursued by Maj. Rockford V. Gray and Lt. John H. Oliphint of the 369th, who ultimately share in its destruction. The pilot is observed bailing out.

18   January 30, 1944 (1139-1450)

Col. Tacon leads a withdrawal support mission for B-17s and B-24s returning from the Brunswick and Hannover areas of Germany, where they have bombed targets of opportunity, since the primaries were obscured by clouds. The P-47s cross in at Ijmuiden, Netherlands at 1225 and make R/V close to Herzlake at 1251 and 19,000'. The 369th attacks eight Ju88s, flying line abreast, preparing to attack the bombers near Haselunne. During this combat Lt. Robert L. Thacker downs one and claims a probable, while Lts. Robert L. Pherson and Luster H. Prewitt damage two others. In a following action six Me109s are engaged, with Maj. Rockford V. Gray and Lt. Robert J. Booth scoring one kill each, while Capt. Niven K. Cranfill damages a 109 near Lingen. The Group then crosses out at 1345. On landing at East Wretham Maj. Gray's P-47 is found to have bits of the pilot he killed stuck to it. A gruesome reminder that when a fighter explodes a human life usually ends.

*   January 31, 1944

Another dive bombing mission is scrubbed, this one shortly after the briefing.

*   February 1944

During this period the 359th manages to put up more fighters than any other fighter group in the 8th AF, and the pilots show a remarkable ability to fly on instruments in extremely poor weather. Also begining on the 23rd of this month water injection is installed on the Group's P-47s, under the supervision of Lt. George M. Hesser, the Station Engineering Officer.

19   February 2, 1944 (1310-1555)

The assignment for today is escort for 9th AF B-26 Marauders bombing an airfield at Tricqueville, France. Take-off is delayed twenty five minutes because of bad weather and as a result the 359th fails to make R/V, arriving just in time to see the Marauders leaving the target area. All fourty-four P-47s return safely to England where Lt. John H. Oliphint, of the 369th FS, hits a barrage balloon near Southend, due to limited visibility. The Jug's prop is

scratched and the wing dented in several places as a result.

20   February 3, 1944 (0954-1328)

Col. Tacon leads the 359th on a penetration support mission for B-17s bombing Emden and Wilhelmshaven, Germany. R/V is made at 1042 and 27,000' over Meppel, Netherlands. Lt. Lester G. Taylor, of the 369th, aborts and heads home with Lt. Robert C. Thomson as escort. Thirty miles from the Netherlands coast they encounter two Fw190s and Thomson executes a head-on attack against one, scoring a kill. The remaining 190 exits and the Jugs resume their flight back unhindered. Over Emden, Germany three P-47s of the 369th's White Flight are damaged by flak. Lt. Cecil W. Crawford, White 2, leaves his flight and heads for another flight up ahead, which is led by Capt. Nevin K. Cranfill. Crawford is last seen going west, near Texel Island. Escort is then broken at1120. On returning to England Lt. Charles W. Hipsher, of the 370th FS, runs low on fuel and makes a wheels up landing at Oulton, Norfolk RAF base, striking several objects on the runway, which is under construction. Lt. Robert C. Thomson of the 369th lands on the emergency airfield at Woodbridge with his battle damaged P-47.

21   February 4, 1944 (1011-1248)

The first mission today is penetration support for B-17s and B-24s headed for the marshalling yards at Frankfurt, Germany. Fifty-two Jugs leave the sod at East Wretham in a lapsed time of 5 minutes and 47 seconds. With Col. Tacon in the lead the 359th crosses in over Schowen, Netherlands at 1057 and R/V is made at 1110 near Woensdrecht at 24,000'. Escort is dropped at 1119 and the Group makes a sweep through the Netherlands before crossing out at 1150.

22   February 4, 1944 (1328-1555)

Col. Tacon also leads the second mission today, which is withdrawal support for the bombers returning from Germany. Forty-six P-47s take part in this mission. Once more the primary targets have been obscured by clouds and targets of opportunity have been hit. The 359th crosses in near Dunkirk, France at 1405 and makes a sweep of the withdrawal area, while Capt. Benjamin H. Albertson takes a flight from the 370th FS to patrol the Calais area of France.

This flight crosses out at 1445 near Berck-Ser-Mer, France and the remainder of the Group crosses out in the vicinity of Dunkirk at 1440.

23 February 5, 1944 (0958-1335)

Col. Tacon leads a penetration support mission for B-24s raiding six airfields in northern and central France. The Group takes off with a light snow falling and crosses in at 20,000' over St. Aubin, France at 1059, where R/V is also made. The Liberators are taken to La Ferte-Bernard, where the escort is dropped at 1123. The 359th then makes a sweep north and turns west at 1132, leaving the continent over Dieppe at 1159.

24 February 6, 1944 (0925-1230)

Col. Tacon is in the lead of a penetration escort for bombers going to Epernay, France. The fighters cross in over Le Treport at 1020 and make R/V northeast of Beauvais, France at 1027 and 25,000'. The bombers are then taken to the target. At 1040 Col. Tacon leads Blue and White Flights of the 368th, (eight P-47s), in a diving attack from 25,000' on four Fw190s at 12,000'. As they close in for the kill, sixteen more 190s appear from the clouds. The P-47s scatter the enemy fighters into protective cloud cover and they do not reappear. Meanwhile Lt. Howard E. Grimes, of the 370th, is forced to make three successive high speed dives, to shake three Fw190s off his tail. The dives take Grimes from 29,000' to the deck and he leaves the enemy fighters at the French coast. His post mission report is filed with the Group, to record enemy tactics. Escort is broken near Epernay and the 359th exits France at 1145, near Gravelines.

25 February 8, 1944 (0909-1136)

Col. Tacon leads again as the 359th provides the sole penetration support for 110 B-24s blasting Noball targets at Siracourt, France. R/V is made at Pointe-Haut-Banc at 18,000' and the escort is routine. No bombers are lost and no enemy aircraft are encountered.

26 February 10, 1944 (0942-1236)

Fifty-one Thunderbolts, under the command of Col. Tacon, fly penetration support for B-17s raiding industrial targets at Brunswick, Germany. Nine P-47s return early, including five that fail to find the Group because of cloud formations reaching to 20,000'. R/V is made at 25,000' near Egmond, Netherlands and the force crosses in at 1039. At 1110 near Gramsbergen, Netherlands the 369th and 370th FSs are bounced by fifteen to twenty Me109Es. During the ensuing fight the Group downs seven 109s and damages an eighth. Claims for the 369th are; Capt. Charles E. Ettlesen, one destroyed and Lt. Clifford E. Carter, one damaged. 370th kills; Lt. William R. Hodges, two destroyed, Capt. Carey H. Brown and Lts. Ralph E. Kibler, Ross O. Major and Ray S. Wetmore one each destroyed. The 368th maintains escort until reaching Bawinkel, Germany and turns for home. This mission is deemed such a success that the 359th FG receives a letter of commendation from Lt.Gen. Carl Spaatz, commanding general of U.S. Strategic Air Forces in Europe.

The day ends on a tragic note for the 370th FS when Lts. Alexander M. Cosmos and Elmer N. Dunlap take off from East Wretham at 1645, on a test flight and run into a blinding snowstorm. At 1714 Cosmos' P-47 spins in from 800' and explodes in a field near Somersham, England.

27 February 11, 1944 (1157-1505)

Col. Tacon is in the lead as the Group provides withdrawal support for B-17s returning from Frankfurt, Germany. During takeoff Lt. Clifford E. Carter, of the 369th, hits a tree and makes a safe belly landing just as the last of the Group becomes airborne. Carter escapes injury but his fighter sustains major damage to the wing. The P-47s cross the Belgium coast south of Nieuport at 1237 and R/V occurs near Ciney, Belgium at 1310 and 23,000'. An estimated ten to fifteen Me109s and Fw190s dart upward from a cloud layer at 10,000' to attack the bombers and duck back before they can be intercepted. One B-17 is seen going down west of Abbeville, France at 1344 with eight chutes being counted. A second Fort is downed east of Abbeville at 1345 with only four chutes observed. The remaining B-17s are then taken to Le Treport, France and left at 1400.

* February 12-19, 1944 (bad weather)

28 February 20, 1944 (1034-1352)

This is the first day of *Big Week*, the assault on German aircraft production and airfields. Today B-

There aren't names to go with all the faces on this page but they deserve recognition for their contribution to the Group. Top left, base Military Police. Top right, the Group's intelligence officers from left to right: Capt. Maurice F. X. Donahue, Major John R. Fitzpatrick and Lt. Philip R. McTiernan. Middle left, the base fire fighters. Middle right, the Parachute Shop. Front row left to right: Sgt. Joseph T. Mitchell and S/Sgt. Joseph P. Nash. Back row left to right: Cpl. Elmo L. Garrett, T/Sgt. Edward F. Goldhesky, Pfc. Joseph J. Mancusco and S/Sgt. Franklin P. Daves. Their job was to inspect chutes periodically and repack them. This crew was evidently a good one for there is no recorded instance of a 359th FG parachute failing to open. Bottom, the men responsible for periodic inspection of the pilot's personal equipment seen here checking a dinghy. Other items included life jackets and oxygen masks.

17s are to bomb an airfield at Leipzig, Germany and the 359th provides penetration escort, with Col. Tacon leading. The Group crosses in near Egmond, Netherlands at 1133, passes the bomber formations and makes a sweep west of the Zuider Zee. Turning east they R/V with the Forts near Meppen, Germany at 1215 and 23,000'. The escort continues until 1233, when the 359th turns back and is replaced by P-47s of the 56th FG.

An anti-jamming device built into the Group's radios by Capt. Alfred M. Swiren, the Group Communications Officer, proves successful on this its first outing.

29   February 21, 1944 (1232-1541)

Maj. William H. Swanson leads the group on a penetration escort for B-17s raiding the city of Brunswick, Germany. The 359th crosses in at 1332 near Egmond and makes R/V near Hardenberg, Netherlands at 1349 and 20,000'. Escort is dropped east of Osnabruck, Germany and the Group crosses out at Egmond.

30   February 22, 1944 (1116-1425)

Col. Tacon is back in the lead as the 359th furnishes penetration escort for B-17s bombing several cities across Germany. The force enters Germany from the vicinity of Valkenberg, Belgium at 1215. At 1300 near Hamm, Germany Lt. George A. Doersch, of the 370th, observes a B-17 exploding, off to his left. Doersch and Tacon move in to investigate and encounter a Fw190D, long nose. Doersch gets the kill and Tacon is awarded a damaged. At 1305 the 370th is jumped by ten plus Me109s. Maj. John B. Murphy bags one and Lt. Albert T. Niccolai damages another. The 368th enters the action at 1312 when three Me109s are seen attacking an aborting B-17. All three enemy fighters are destroyed, with kills going to Capt. Charles E. Mosse and Lts. Andrew T. Lemmens and Emer H. Cater. Cater's kill is observed crashing into the center of a small town, after the pilot bails out. Five 370th Thunderbolts are damaged by flak during the mission.

31   February 24, 1944 (1034-1330)

Two missions are on tap today, the first is penetration escort for B-17s hitting Schweinfurt, Germany. Col. Tacon leads the first mission and R/V is made one minute off Egmond, Netherlands at 1133 and 24,000'. At 1157 near Hardenbergh, Netherlands Maj. John B. Murphy, of the 370th, leads White Flight in an attack on two Me109s approaching the lead box of B-17s from the rear. Murphy nails one and it goes into a vertical dive trailing black smoke, as the pilot bails out. Lt. Albert T. Niccolai is last seen diving after the lead Me109 and is listed as MIA. At 1215 near Neunhaus, Germany the 368th's Red and Green Flights engage seven Fw190s headed for the bombers. Lt. Thomas J. McGeever destroys one of the 190s during a turning dog fight that takes them from 26,000' to 10,000', where the German pilot bails out. Maj. Albert R. Tyrrell bags two 190s before the Group heads back to England at staggered intervals.

32   February 24, 1944 (1336-1626)

Col. Tacon also leads the second mission today, which is withdrawal support for the B-17s returning from Schweinfurt. R/V occurs over Ninove, Belgium at 1450 and 22,000'. No enemy aircraft are encountered and the 359th returns without loss.

33   February 25th, 1944 (1112-1432)

Col. Tacon institutes a policy of giving squadron commanders experience at briefing and leading the Group. Maj. William H. Swanson, of the 369th FS flies the lead as the Group provides penetration escort for B-17s raiding Regensburg, Germany. The bombers notify the 359th by R/T that they (the bombers) are ten minutes early and the fighters alter their course to intercept. R/V is made near Sedan, France at 1227 and 25,000'. Escort is then dropped at Lebach, Germany and the Group turns for home. Four twin engine enemy aircraft are chased near Chatillon at 1242 and they escape by diving into cloud cover. The 359th then exits the continent near Knockne, Belgium at 1351.

34   February 29, 1944 (1040-1350)

Maj. John B. Murphy of the 370th FS leads the Group on a withdrawal support mission for B-17s bombing aircraft factories in the vicinity of Brunswick, Germany. R/V is made near Wetrup, Germany at 1158 and 25,000'. No action occurs and the Group returns safely to England. After landing a 7.5mm bullet hole is found in the cowling of Col. Tacon's P-47, a minor mystery since no enemy aircraft were seen.

The photos on this page give proof positive the Jug could take a licking and keep on ticking. Top left, crew chief Sgt. George M. Rinaldi poses beside the flak damaged vertical stabilizer of a P-47 from the 368th FS. Top right, exit hole from what appears to be a hit by a 20mm round. Ethell. Center right, looks like a 20mm round pierced a prop blade. This would cause an imbalance resulting in a potentially destructive vibration throughout the aircraft.

The pilots are informed that the Group will be re-equipped with the P-51.

* March 1, 1944 (1100-1245)

Three pilots from the 368th FS fly a weather reconnaissance flight to Brussels, Belgium.

35 March 2, 1944 (1037-1351)

Maj. Albert R. Tyrrell, of the 368th FS, leads as the Group furnishes penetration escort for B-17s and B-24s blasting Frankfurt, Germany. Snow is falling as forty-nine of the Group's P-47s lift off. R/V is made near St. Hubert, Belgium at 1135 and 26,000'. At 1140 near Neufchateau, Belgium, Red Flight of the 370th FS spots and engages five Fw190s, with Capt. Daniel D. McKee bagging one before the enemy pilot is aware of his presence.

Escort is dropped by the 368th at 1150 and 1153 by the 369th. The 370th proceeds on until 1200 waiting for the replacement escort of P-51s, that fails to appear. The Group leaves Fortress Europe close to The Hague, Netherlands from 1242-1245.

36 March 3, 1944 (1322-1634)

Maj. William H. Swanson, of the 369th, is in command as the Group flies an area patrol in support of B-17s heading for targets in the vicinity of Berlin, Germany. The 359th establishes a patrol in the area of Louvain, France at 20,000'. No enemy aircraft are seen during the patrol. On the way home Capt. Charles E. Mosse of the 368th and Lt. John L. Downing, of the 370th, spot five dinghies in the

Left, Capt. Charles Edward Mosse and his Scottish wife the former Nina Wilson. They met while Mosse (Carlos) was visiting friends of his family in Scotland. The wedding took place on Mar. 1, 1944. Right, Lt. John L. Downing of the 370th FS and his crew chief S/Sgt. Charles Boskin. Downing. On Mar. 3, 1944 Mosse and Downing flew cover over three occupied dinghies in the English Channel until help arrived. Mosse shot down three Me109s on May 19, 1944. One kill was confirmed by his wingman and the other two occurred minutes later after he exited the cloud cover directly behind the two 109s he was chasing. Both German pilots bailed out of their 109s after being hammered by Mosse. Now about 50 miles north of Berlin, low on fuel and alone he set a course for home. About this time a 109 attacked Mosse low and from the rear. The throttle quadrant was blown out of his hand by a 20mm round and flames burst from the instrument panel. Mosse jettisoned the canopy, released his shoulder and lap belts, nosed the P-51 over and was left sitting in mid-air. While floating down in his chute the German pilot buzzed him and waved. Mosse landed safely and after walking north, about ten minutes, he was taken prisoner by a German paratrooper who escorted him to a nearby airfield where he was treated for burns around the wrists and eyes. A few days later Mosse was in a POW camp with 2,000 other Allied airmen. As for the two Me109s he shot down without a witness he never filed a claim, he said, "I was just getting the job done."

English Channel, close to the French coast. Three of the dinghies are occupied and two are empty. The position is relayed to ASR and the P-47s remain on station until help arrives.

37   March 4, 1944 (1045-1354)

A snowfall stops and ground crews thaw the P-47s control surfaces, allowing Maj. John B. Murphy, of the 370th, to lead the Group off to provide penetration escort for B-17s raiding Berlin, Germany. During the previous mission to Berlin the bombers ran into progressively bad weather and were forced to hit targets of opportunity. The 359th crosses the Netherlands coast near Flushing at 1129. R/V occurs at 1205 and ten minutes later, near Bonn, Germany, Lt. Ray S. Wetmore of the 370th observes about seventy-five enemy fighters high and to the left of the bombers. Blue and White Flights turn into the approaching bandits, breaking up their attack. During the ensuing clash the following claims are made by the 370th: Lt. Wetmore one Me109 destroyed and one damaged, Lt. William R. Hodges, one Me 109 probable, Lt. Harold D. Hollis and Capt. Charles E. Mosse, one Me109 each damaged, Maj. John B. Murphy, one Me109 destroyed/shared with Lts. Alan C. Porter and Paul Bateman, Murphy also damages a Fw190D and shares in the destruction of a second with Bateman. The Group then penetrates to Neuenkirchen, forty miles past Bonn, before withdrawing to Malmedy, Belgium and setting up an area patrol. Meanwhile Blue and Yellow Flights of the 369th have run into forty to fifty Me109s near Cologne, Germany at 1225. In the running defensive battle that follows Lt. Robert L. Pherson takes a 20mm hit in the right wing of his Jug and Lt. Richard H. Broach claims a Me109F as a probable. A crippled B-17 is then escorted out to Ostende, Belgium by Lt. Ralph E. Kibler's flight from the 370th. The Group returns safely to East Wretham.

Boeing B-29A from the 15th AF landing at Kanawha Airport circa 1950. The B-29 was the only US heavy bomber not obsolete at the end of WW II, its performance being a quantum leap over the B-17 and B-24. As of this writing it is the only aircraft to have dropped atomic weapons operationally. After WW II the RAF aquired 87 of the 3,960 B-29s built and named them Washingtons. The B-29 served well in Korea, but the Mig-15 signaled the end of its combat effectiveness. Although the Central Fire Control System enabled the B-29 to defend itself daylight losses became intolerable and missions were switched to night (shades of the RAF during WW II). The B-29s greatest problem was chronic engine failures and fires, a problem that was never entirely solved. ROSS TAYLOR

38   March 6, 1944 (0952-1220)

There are two missions today, with the first being penetration escort for B-17s headed for Berlin, Germany again. The Group is led by Maj. John B. Murphy, after Col. Tacon aborts with radio trouble. The 359th crosses in near Egmond, Netherlands at 1050 and 24,000'. R/V is made one minute later. The Forts are then taken to Hardenburgh, Netherlands where escort is dropped at 1117. The 359th exits the coast near Egmond at 1132.

39   March 6, 1944 (1306-1613)

The second mission today is withdrawal escort for the B-17s returning from Berlin. Maj. Clifton Shaw, of the 368th, leads as Col. Tacon aborts, again due to radio transmitter trouble. The 359th crosses in north of Egmond and R/V is made near Vechta, Germany at 1443 and 23,000'. Immediately the 368th and 369th engage enemy fighters attacking B-17s and B-24s in the area. Claims for the 368th FS are: Capt. Wayne N. Bolefahr, one Me109 destroyed, Lt. Emer H. Cater, one Fw 190 damaged and Lt. Raymond B. Janney III, one Me109 probable. The

369th claims: Lt. Robert L. Pherson, one Me109F destroyed, left with the engine smoking and a fire in the cockpit. Lt. Robert J. Booth destroys a Fw190 from which the pilot bails out. The chute opens but the canopy splits. On the way out Lt. Clifford E. Carter, of the 369th, spots a 350' steamship, damaged and smoking, heading for Den Helder, Netherlands. Carter strafes the ship twice. Back at East Wretham Lt. Harry L. Matthew, of the 369th, is injured in a crash landing.

On this mission two significant events take place. First the 8th AF Bomber Command suffers its highest losses of the war in Europe as a total of seventy-two B-17s and B-24s are destroyed. Also, flying as an observer, in a B-17 of the 100th Bomb Group, is Col. Alva Harvey Commanding Officer of a B-29 group (444th) being formed in the United States. The vicious battle he witnesses today convinces him that the B-29 could not survive in the hostile skies over Germany. As a result the decision is made to use the B-29 exclusively in the Pacific. It is also decided to lead the Germans into believing the Superfortress will be flown against them, thereby giving them another worry.

Top, the station's Westland Lysander. This was probably the aircraft reporting a ceiling of less than 700' on March 9, 1944. The *Lizzie*, as the British called it, was a superb design that was used for close ground support, dropping supplies, target tug and for dropping agents behind enemy lines at night. This was the type of aircraft used to extract John Oliphint from occupied France. PALICKA

*   March 7, 1944

A weather reconnaissance mission is cancelled and at 1645 news is received that a Boeing B-29 Superfortress is in England and available for inspection.

40   March 8, 1944 (1107-1402)

Another double mission day and Col. Tacon leads the first one which is penetration escort for B-17s and B-24s bombing Berlin, Germany. The Group crosses in and makes R/V over Egmond, Netherlands at 1207 and 25,000'. Ten miles north of Minden, Germany at 1255 Blue Flight of the 368th bounces five Me109Gs and Lt. Raymond B. Janney III claims a probable. The Group returns without loss but Lt. Howard E. Grimes, of the 370th, crash lands at Bungay Airdrome, England. Grimes is not injured but his P-47 is Category E.

41   March 8, 1944 (1449-1745)

Col. Tacon leads the second mission as the 359th provides withdrawal escort for the Berlin raiders. The Group crosses in south of Egmond and at 1540. Blue Flight of the 369th, which has become separated from the Squadron, engages twenty to twenty-five Fw190s over the Zuider Zee, near Muiden. During the ensuing melee Lt. Charles W. Staley damages one of the enemy fighters. The remainder of the Group makes R/V with the returning bombers at 1600, near Urk, Netherlands. The 359th then returns safely to England.

42   March 9, 1944 (1016-1251)

Two missions are flown again today, with Col. Tacon leading the first one as the 359th furnishes penetration support for B-17s pounding Berlin, Germany for the fourth mission in a row. When the pilot of a Lysander, flying at 700', reports he can not see the ground, Col. Tacon recommends that the mission be scrubbed. The order is to go regardless of the lack of visibility and the 359th manages to get off safely but fifteen minutes behind schedule. The bombers are also late and R/V is made at 1118 and 26,000' over the Zuider Zee. There is no combat and the Group returns safely.

43   March 9, 1944 (1332-1646)

Maj. John B. Murphy, of the 370th FS, leads the second mission of the day, which is withdrawal support for the Forts returning from Berlin. R/V is

Top left, Lt. Robert W. Hawkinson and his P-47 *Lonesom' Polecat*. Top right, Sgt. Anthony C. Chardella an armorer with the 369th FS poses for the camera with Lt. Charles H. Kruger's Jug *Nancy June* in the background. That's a fleece-lined leather suit Tony is wearing and it could make you break a sweat even when the temperature dipped far below zero. Bottom, *Oily Boid* the Jug flown by Lt. Robert J. Booth. The serial number of this P-47 was 42-8695 and Booth was flying this aircraft when he destroyed a Me109 on April 25, 1944.

made at 1437 and 26,000' over Enkhuizen, on the west coast of the Zuider Zee. The mission is uneventful and the Group returns without incident.

44   March 11, 1944 (0954-1156)

Three assignments are scrubbed today before fifty-one P-47s from the 359th FG provide withdrawal support for B-17s that have raided the marshalling yards at Münster, Germany. Maj. Clifton Shaw leads and R/V is made at 1040 and 23,000' over Geertruidenberg, Netherlands. The Group then makes a sweep through an area southeast of Nijmegen, before returning safely to base.

45   March 13, 1944 (0947-1245)

Today the 359th draws an assignment closer to home as they furnish area support for B-17s and B-24s blasting Noball targets in the Pas de Calais area of France. Lt.Col. William H. Swanson leads the Group and R/V is made over Cayeux, France at 1035 and 18,000'. Due to the poor weather, only seven of the 271 bombers participating in the mission manage to bomb a target of opportunity, Poix Airdrome. No enemy aircraft are encountered.

*   March 14, 1944

A practice mission to escort and make mock attacks on eighteen new bombers is flown by four P-47s from the 368th FS and twelve from the 369th FS.

46   March 15, 1944 (1017-1338)

Col. Tacon leads as the 359th provides withdrawal support for B-24s bombing Brunswick, Germany. R/V is made at 1150 and 20,000' over Hannover, Germany. At 1210, near Steinhuder Lake, about a dozen Me109s approach the 368th FS in close formation and at their altitude of 24,000'. Two flights of P-47s break into the bandits and Lt. Thomas J. McGeever destroys one and damages two more. At 1215 Yellow and Green Flights of the 369th engage six to ten Me109Fs and Lt. Charles H. Kruger claims one kill and a probable. Low on fuel, Kruger and Lts. Frank S. Fong and Robert L. Thacker hit the deck and head for home. Minutes later, thirty miles west of Hannover, Kruger strafes a train and damages the locomotive. Thacker then follows suit by damaging another locomotive, a mile down the

tracks. As the trio crosses the Netherlands they observe twenty-five to thirty Me109s flying a parallel course, over the Zuider Zee. Kruger, Fong and Thacker hug the terrain and escape detection, snagging trees and powerlines in the process. The Group returns intact.

47   March 16, 1944 (0904-1216)

Maj. Albert R. Tyrrell, of the 368th FS leads the Group on a penetration escort mission for B-17s bombing Augsburg, Germany. The Group crosses in over Gravelines, France at 0944 and makes R/V near Compiegne, France at 1000 and 22,000'. At 1025 near St. Dizier, France the bombers are attacked by four Me109s diving from 30,000'. The 368th and 369th break up the attack and Lt. Howard A. Linderer, of the 369th, flames one of the bandits. Escort is dropped during the engagement and on the way out, thirty-five miles west of St. Dizier at Sommesous, Lt. Ray S. Wetmore who is leading Blue Flight of the 370th sees twenty-five bandits diving on a formation of B-17s. As the Germans pass through the Forts, Wetmore leads a diving attack on two Fw190s. Firing a long burst into one as he enters compressibility, Wetmore is surprised to see it explode. As the P-47s climb back to the bombers two more Fw190s appear and in a repeat performance Wetmore explodes his second kill. Climbing back again the flight has to dodge two parachutes from a damaged B-17, which is still under attack by a 190. As Blue Flight turns toward the bandit it breaks off the attack and heads for the deck. Low on fuel and ammo the Jugs head for home.

48   March 16, 1944 (1250-1546)

Col. Tacon leads the second mission today which is withdrawal support for the B-17s returning from Augsburg. The Group crosses in north of Dunkirk, France at 1333 and makes R/V over Esternay, France at 1400 and 15,000'. The Forts are escorted out near Le Treport, France and left over the English Channel.

49   March 17, 1944 (1412-1708)

The Group is briefed to strafe airfields in the Beauvais-Tille area of France. On the way in they are vectored to search for enemy aircraft but none are found. Due to poor visibility the 359th is forced to drop down to 150' to find their target. Beauvais

Left, Capt. Benjamin Henry Albertson as he appeared during training with the 369th FS. Benjy transferred to the 370th in Oct. of 1943. On March 18, 1944 the right wing of his Thunderbolt was shattered by flak and he bailed out in the Pas de Calais area of France, where he was taken prisoner. Right, Lt. Joseph Ashenmacher, of the 368th FS, poses while standing on the right main wheel of a natural metal P-47. On Mar. 19, 1944 Ashenmacher was wounded by flak requiring the amputation of his left index finger. He received the first Purple Heart in the Group.

is seen twice through the haze but an attempt to line up on the field for a strafing run is also foiled by the haze. With the element of surprise gone and with instructions not to make a second pass, the mission is aborted. All the pilots can report is French peasants waved vigorously at them as they thundered over the countryside.

50   March 18, 1944 (1118-1428)

Col. Tacon leads the 359th on a penetration escort for B-17s raiding Oberpfaffenhofen, twenty miles northeast of Augsburg, Germany. The Group crosses into France near Calais at 1150 and R/V occurs at 1221 and 25,000' over Moreuil, France. No contact is made with enemy aircraft and the escort is broken near St. Dizier, France. The P-47s then cross out over Calais.

51   March 18, 1944 (1445-1802)

The second mission today is withdrawal support for B-24s returning from Friedrichshafen, Germany and Col. Tacon leads again. The B-24s are forty-four minutes late so the 359th escorts the B-17s returning from Oberpfaffenhofen. The 368th FS makes R/V at Epernay, France while the 369th and 370th FSs join up at 1603 near Soissons at 22,000'. No contact is made with the Luftwaffe and the bombers are left in the vicinity of Oisemont, France at 1656. Capt. Benjamin H. Albertson, of the 370th, is lost when the right wing of his P-47 is shattered

by flak. Albertson bails out at 1705 in the Pas de Calais area and becomes a POW.

52   March 19, 1944 (1657-1930)

After Maj. Albert R. Tyrrell aborts with engine trouble Maj. William H. Swanson, of the 369th, leads as the Group furnishes area support for B-17s bombing Noball targets in the vicinity of Lens, France. One Fort is lost to flak over St. Omer and eighty-eight are damaged. No enemy aircraft are encountered. Lt. Joseph M. Ashenmacher, of the 368th, is hit in the left hand by a piece of flak but makes it back to England for a safe landing. His left index finger requires amputation, which earns him the Group's first Purple Heart.

53   March 20, 1944 (0959-1255)

Today's mission is penetration support for B-17s raiding Frankfurt, Germany and Maj. Niven K. Cranfill, of the 369th FS, leads the Group for the first time. R/V is made at 1110 and 29,000' over St. Hubert, Belgium. Due to poor visibility most of the bombers abort but a few manage to hit targets of opportunity. No contact is made with the Luftwaffe. Lt. Paul H. Bateman's P-47 is damaged by flak but returns safely.

54   March 22, 1944 (1312-1628)

Today the 359th provides withdrawal support for

B-17s returning from the area of Berlin, Germany, where targets of opportunity have been hit, due to cloud cover over the primaries. Lt.Col. Willam H. Swanson leads and R/V is made near Oldenburg, Germany at 1440 and 20,000'. Escort is provided to Terschelling Island, Netherlands. Twelve German fighters are observed during the escort but no attacks are made. At 1512 near Meppel, Netherlands Lt. John E. Kerns' P-47 is struck on the bottom of the left wing by the prop on Capt. Edwin F. Pezda's P-47. Both pilots, who are from the 370th FS, return safely but the wing on Kerns' Thunderbolt is replaced.

55   March 23, 1944 (0844-1203)

With Col. Tacon leading, the 359th furnishes penetration support for B-17s and B-24s that are forced to bomb targets of opportunity in the vicinity of Münster, Germany. The Group crosses the Netherlands coast at 0947 near Egmond and R/V occurs at 1013 close to Meppen, Germany at 24,000'. The bombers are then escorted to Bramsche, which is in the target area. The 359th does some patrolling before turning for home.

56   March 26, 1944 (1330-1649)

The 359th flies area support for B-17s and B-24s pounding Noball targets in the Pas de Calais sector of France. Maj. Chauncey S. Irvine leads the Group and R/V is made over Pointe-Haute-Banc, France at 20,000'. While enemy fighters seldom appear in the Calais area it is noteworthy that the Germans have increased the number of flak guns in this location, forcing the 8th AF to fly higher to reduce the odds of getting hit. Missions that were previously flown at 14,000' are now increased by 6,000'. Four bombers are seen going down in the target area today due to flak.

Also on this day six P-51Bs are delivered, two for each squadron. The Group begins preparation for transition to the type.

A B-17 named *Sunrise Serenade* buzzes the base and drops a message in a bottle, which is attached to a parachute made from a handkerchief. The message reads;

"To The P47 Boys"

"To you who fly and keep them flying the P47s. Many thanks for the wonderful work you are doing for us who

Above, one of the first six P-51Bs to arrive at East Wretham on March 26, 1944. This picture was taken the day after arrival. Notice the white identification bands on the wings and vertical stabilizer. These bands were to prevent gunners on allied bombers from mistaking the P-51 for a Me109, though it didn't always work.

are up here in the big ones. You are to all of us a million dollar sight when you help us on every mission. Again we the boys of this Fort "Sunrise Serenade" want to thank you each and every one of you for your protection to us as we make each mission. Thanks a million.

Signed: The crew of the
SUNRISE SERENADE

(The Sunrise Serenade was a B-17G from the 452nd Bomb Group.)

BILL'S BUZZ BOYS

The special group of P-47 pilots known as Bill's Buzz Boys was formed by Col. Glenn E. Duncan, commander of the 353rd FG, with the approval of Maj.Gen. William E. Kepner Commanding General VIII Fighter Command. Their purpose was to formulate and test methods for attacking ground targets, especially airfields. They were literally "writing the book."

Sixteen volunteers, four each from the 353rd, 359th, 361st and 355th FGs reported to Col. Duncan on March 15, 1944. The four pilots from the 359th FG were members of the 369th FS and their leader was Capt. Charles C. Ettlesen, a man considered one the 359th's best pilots. His fellow volunteers were Lts. John H. Oliphint, Clifford E. Carter and Robert L. Thacker. The unit called themselves *Bill's Buzz Boys* in respect of Gen. Bill Kepner. *Most* of the P-47s flown by the Boys were equipped with paddle blade props that improved performance.

Left, the man for whom the *Buzz Boys* named themselves, Maj.Gen. William E. Kepner. Lt.Col. Grady L. Smith group exec. in the background. Above, the three survivors of the 369th FS contingent. Left to right, Lt. John H. Oliphint, Lt. Robert Leroy Thacker and Capt. Charles Campbell Ettlesen. The cardinal rules for attacking ground targets formulated by the *Boys* were: come in fast, come in low **and only make one pass**. Violation of the last rule cost a lot of good pilots, for after the first pass anti-aircraft guns were usually manned and already warmed up on the last fighters to pass over the target.

MISSIONS

(Only the claims of 359th pilots listed.)

1   March 26, 1944 (1407-1658)

Col. Duncan leads twelve Thunderbolts, of the so called 353rd 'C' Fighter Group on their first mission. Attacks are slated to be made on French airfields at Chartes, Chateaudun, St. Andre de L'Eure and Beauvais/Tille. Blue Flight, comprised of the 359th pilots, attacks the field at Chateaudun. Capt. Ettlesen leads as they approach the target at 425 m.p.h. Ettlesen strafes a hangar and in the process hits a high tension power pole that cuts halfway through his P-47's wing, before snapping. The P-47 is thrown 200' upward and he regains control just in time to blast a water tower before exiting the target. On landing in England 30 ft. of cable is found hanging from the wing. Oliphint destroys a twin engine aircraft, damages two blister hangars and one large hangar. During the pass his P-47 is hit by a 20mm shell in the main fuel tank, which miraculously fails to explode. Carter damages a He111 and one blister hangar.

2   March 27, 1944 (1238-1610)

Col. Duncan leads again as eleven P-47s provide penetration support for B-17s, until reaching La Rochelle, France. There are no claims or losses.

3   March 29, 1944 (1150-1454)

Twelve Thunderbolts, led by Col. Duncan, take off to attack the following airfields in northwest Germany: Quackenbruck, Vechta, Bohmte, Hesepe, Rhine, Twente/Enshede and Bramsche. Ettlesen again leads Blue Flight, as they attack the airfield at Quackenbruck, setting a hangar housing an unidentifiable aircraft, on fire and damaging a barracks. Moving on Ettlesen destroys a locomotive and shares in the destruction of four others. Oliphint strafes two passenger trains damaging the locomotives and nineteen coaches, one freight train destroying the

Scenes from Thetford, unless noted otherwise, starting in the upper left and moving from left to right; plaque commemorating the birth place of the American patriot Thomas Paine; railway station; Courthouse; downtown scene showing the Bell Hotel on the right and St. James Congregational Church straight ahead; line of shops, Odeon Theatre; Dog and Partridge in East Wretham was the 359th's favorite watering hole and known to them as the Pig and Whistle; The Green Dragon, another pub frequented by the group.

locomotive and damaging several boxcars, two coal trains destroying the locomotives and derailing several cars, damaging a barge and killing five German soldiers. Thacker damages a barracks and a railroad station plus sharing damage to the locomotives. Carter destroys two Me410s on the airfield and as he pulls up from the pass throws a hail of fire into an administration building. Later Carter also shares in strafing five locomotives.

4   April 1, 1944 (0750-1123)

Capt. Charles C. Ettlesen leads eleven P-47s on another raid against airfields in northwest Germany. Ettlesen's White Flight fails to find its assigned target due to poor visibility and proceeds to Bohmte, where they find eight locomotives parked close together and as Ettlesen states in his report, "shot the hell out of them." Other shared claims are: one tugboat left on fire and a second damaged along with a barge. On the way out, over the eastern edge of the Zuider Zee at 16,000', Ettlesen is bounced out of the sun by two Me109s. Carter answers his call for help and scores hits in the right wing root of one of the attackers. The 109 begins trailing black smoke but is lost in cloud cover and is counted as a probable.

5   April 3, 1944 (1357-1601)

Mission number five is led by Capt. Albert B. Starr, of the 355th FG and the *Boys* again head for northwest Germany. Bad weather forces them to turn back.

6   April 8, 1944 (1123-1438)

Ettlesen leads twelve P-47s off and one aborts, as they head back to the same area of Germany. This time the unit makes a sweep thirty miles ahead of a force of B-17s. On reaching Havern the *Boys* double back but forego attacking the airfields they had previously passed over when heavy flak is encountered. Ettlesen then leads White Flight as they strafe targets of opportunity in the vicinity of Dummer Lake with the following claims being made, all shared: one locomotive destroyed and two probables, one tugboat left on fire and sinking, plus one power launch left burning. Thacker shares in strafing the three locomotives and the tugboat. Oliphint shares in blasting both tugboats and the power launch; he also riddles the control tower of a drawbridge and shares in strafing three barges. After the attack on

the power launch Oliphint notes that Carter is missing and circles the area of Bohmte. During his scouting he notices the side of a two-story house has been damaged but no aircraft debris are present. It us assumed that Carter was hit by flak, struck the house with the wing of his P-47 and continued on before sending a R/T that he was bailing out. Carter is listed as MIA. On the way out the remainder of White Flight escorts a B-24 straggler to the coast.

7   April 10, 1944 (0803-1113)

Capt. Starr leads eight Thunderbolts off today and one aborts. The *Boys* first provide target support for the 55th FG and then attack targets in the area of Paris, France. No claims are filed by the 359th's pilots.

8   April 12, 1944 (1434-1739)

Capt. Starr leads twelve of the *Boys* off, on this their last mission, and one aborts. They return to northwest Germany, where Blue Flight which is comprised of the pilots from the 359th, fails to find any German aircraft in the air or on the ground. Oliphint, *The Predator*, makes Blue Flight's only claim when he finds a small train parked in the center of a German hamlet, makes three passes down the street destroying the locomotive and setting two boxcars on fire.

On returning to their base at Metfield, England the unit is disbanded and the 359th's pilots return to East Wretham the next day.

As a result of the successful experiments carried out by the *Buzz Boys* Col. Duncan is assigned the command of a special strafing school, located in Scotland, there to pass on the tactics developed during the units brief existence.

57   March 27, 1944 (1257-1610)

Col. Avelin P. Tacon Jr. leads the 359th FG as they provide penetration, target and withdrawal support for B-17s bombing airfields at Chartes, Tours and La Rochelle, France. The Group crosses the French coast near Veules at 1344. At 1410 near Chateaudun the 368th FS has a brief and scoreless skirmish with some Me109s. At 1410 near Chartes the 370th FS has just made R/V at 15,000', when fifteen plus bandits are spotted at 10,000' heading for the bombers. As Capt. Daniel D. McKee leads Red Flight in a diving attack Lt. Howard E. Grimes aborts due to a malfunctioning prop, caused by an electrical short.

Left, Lt. Frank S. Fong in the cockpit of a stateside P-47. During the combat of Mar. 27, 1944 Fong, the only Chinese-American pilot in the theatre at that time, destroyed a Fw190 in the air. Lt. Robert Laughry Pherson, right, destroyed a Me109E on Mar. 27.

During the encounter McKee claims a Fw190 as a probable and is hammering a Me109 when another Me109 latches onto his tail and scores some minor damage. McKee shakes his attacker and as the three remaining P-47s form up to return to base they are jumped by five Me109s. Lt. John E. Kerns is last seen being pursued by three of the 109s. McKee and the other survivor from Red Flight shake their adversaries and head for England. Lt. Charles V. Cunningham's Jug sustains major damage from a German fighter that bounces him from out of the sun. The wing spar is severed, a cylinder is shot off of the engine and a tire is blown. Despite this ravaging Cunningham flies the P-47 190 miles back and makes a safe landing at Shoreham Airdrome, England. Meanwhile at 1430 the 369th FS engages enemy fighters near Gallardon, France and Lt. Frank S. Fong, the only Chinese-American pilot in the E.T.O. at this time, bags a Fw190 while Lt. Robert L. Pherson downs a Me109E.

58   March 28, 1944 (1509-1826)

Col. Tacon leads again as the Group furnishes area support for B-17s bombing four airfields at Chateaudun and Chartes, France. R/V occurs at 1605 and 23,000' over Beauvais. The fighters are under Type 16 control but the vectors received by the 359th turn up nothing. Lt. William R. Hodges, of the 370th, does spot a Ju52 transport but cannot relay his find because of radio failure and decides not to engage alone. The force crosses out over Cayeux, France at 1718.

59   March 29, 1944 (1134-1519)

Maj. John B. Murphy, of the 370th FS, leads fifty-three P-47s off today on a penetration escort mission for B-17s raiding Brunswick, Germany. There are five aborts and R/V is made near Egmond, Netherlands at 1226 and 24,000'. The Forts are left at 1310 in the vicinity of Steinhurder Lake. No enemy aircraft are encountered and the 359th returns without incident.

60   March 30, 1944 (1000- ?)

The first of two missions flown today is weather reconnaissance in the area of Brussels, Belgium.

Mary, the P-47 flown by Lt. Lawrence W. Bouchard, alias Frenchy. There are 55 mission markers on the nose of his Jug. Note the star painted on the wheel.

Lt.Col. William H. Swanson, of the 369th FS, leads eight P-47s from his squadron off and they all return safely.

61 March 30 (1406-1626)

The second mission today is to dive bomb an airfield at Soesterberg, Netherlands. Col. Tacon leads twelve P-47s, of the 369th FS, armed with two 500 lb. General Purpose bombs each and a dozen P-47s from the 368th and 370th each, as escort. Time over the target is 1502 at 22,000'. Seven hits are scored on the base buildings and runways; flak is intense but no enemy fighters are encountered. The 8th AF summary describes the mission as a success. A submarine is spotted three miles off the coast from Ijmuiden. On returning to England, from this the Group's first completed bombing mission, Col. Tacon leads his formation in a low level review over East Wretham and then takes them to Bodney, the 352nd FG's base, for a buzz job.

At the morning briefing Col. Tacon reports that he has flown the P-51 Mustang and that it is the finest fighter he has ever flown.

* March 31, 1944

The scheduled mission is scrubbed at 0855 and the

Group does some non-operational flying. At 1100 Lt. John B. Hunter is approaching East Wretham when his engine quits. Hunter bellies his P-47 in a mile north of the base and emerges from the crash shaken and with scratches on his forehead. The P-47 is destroyed by the resulting fire.

62 April 5, 1994 (1341-1623)

Col. Tacon leads the Group on a mission to strafe airfields in the vicinity of Oldenburg, Germany. The P-47s cross in south of De Kooi, Netherlands at 1431 and find heavy clouds obscure most of the continent. The 359th returns without incident.

* April 7, 1944 (bad weather)

63 April 8, 1944 (1229-1555)

Today's mission is withdrawal support for B-17s raiding airfields at Quackenbruck, Rheine, Hesepe and other locations in northern Germany. Col. Tacon leads and of the forty-eight P-47s taking off three return early. R/V is made over Dummer Lake at 1452 and 22,000'. Good bombing results are observed and no enemy aircraft are encountered. One of four B-17s lost today is seen crashing east of the

On March 31, 1944, Lt. John B. Hunter of the 368th FS was approaching East Wretham when the engine in his Thunderbolt quit. Hunter bellied his fighter in a mile north of base and except for a few scratches was not the worse for wear. The photo shows the remains of Hunter's Jug after it caught fire.

Zuider Zee and eleven chutes are noted in the vicinity. The 359th exits the Netherlands over Egmond from 1452-1459.

64   April 9, 1944 (1324-1640)

The Station's Miles Master is sent up on a mid-morning local weather recon and is caught in hard rain that forces the pilot to land in a cow pasture. After several delays Col. Tacon leads the 359th on a withdrawal support mission for B-24s bombing Tutow, Germany. Forty-eight Thunderbolts take off and four return early. Crossing in south of De Kooi, Netherlands at 1422 the Group proceeds to Hannover, Germany where the flak is heavy but no hits are taken by the 359th. The weather is poor and no bombers are found. The Group returns without loss and six pilots from the 370th FS bring back drop tanks that failed to release. Coincidentally this is the last mission for the 108 gal. drop tanks, henceforth 150 gal. tanks are to be utilized.

65   April 10, 1944 (0817-1124)

Col. Tacon leads as the 359th flies a withdrawal support mission for B-17s raiding airfields near Paris, France. For the third consecutive day the Group puts up forty-eight aircraft and there is only one abort. R/V is made at 0925 and 20,000' over Reims, France. Good bombing results are noted on two airfields and no contact is made with the Luftwaffe. The trip out is without incident.

66   April 10, 1944 (1425-1739)

The second mission today is target support for twenty-seven Droop Snoot P-38s, of the 20th FG, bombing an airfield at Gutersloh, Germany. Maj. Albert R. Tyrrell, of the 368th FS, leads forty-eight P-47s off, with two aborts. The P-38s arrive at the R/V point, which is just off the enemy coast, early and proceed on without the 359th FG as escort. R/V is made over the target and excellent bombing results are observed, with the airfield's buildings getting a good concentration of hits. On the way out, near Osnabruck, Germany, one P-47 from the 370th FS is hit in the right wing by flak but the entire Group returns safely.

Today was the combat debut of the P-38 Droop Snoot bomber.

67   April 11, 1944 (0913-1315)

Maj. Chauncey S. Irvine leads the 359th on a penetration support mission for B-17s blasting avia-

During the second mission of April 10, 1944, the 359th FG provided target and withdrawal cover for 20th FG Droop Snoot P-38s. Above photo shows the modifications made to the P-38 enabling it to carry a bombardier. ETHELL Top right: Lt. Will D. Burgsteiner poses with 1/72 scale, black I.D. models. On April 11, 1944 Burgsteiner destroyed four Fw190s on the ground and damaged a fifth, the only victories he scored during his tour. On the same mission Lt. Thomas P. Smith, bottom right, holding Flak the 370th's mascot, ran out of fuel over the Netherlands and bailed out. Wigwam (T. P. Smith) evaded capture and returned on September 16, 1944.

tion industry targets at Sorau, Germany, with strafing to follow the escort job. Support for the bombers is provided from Holdorf to Fallersleben, Germany, where at 1107 Red Flight of the 370th bounces seven bandits attacking the bombers. Lt. George A. Doersch downs a Fw190 after a long chase at an altitude of 50' and Lt. Ralph E. Kibler damages a Me109. As Lt. Elmer N. Dunlap tries to climb back with Red Flight he experiences a problem with the throttle to his engine and while separated is bounced by five bandits. Dunlap bags one Fw190 and damages another before being hit in the engine by a 20mm shell fired from a Me109. As he heads for home the engine quits west of Lingen, Germany and the P-47 crashes into some trees. Dunlap is still unconscious when he is taken prisoner. After escort is dropped at Fallersleben the 370th searches for ground targets. At 1115 near Gutersloh, Yellow Flight is escorting two crippled bombers out when they spot an airfield and drop down to strafe with the following results: Lt. Will D. Burgsteiner, four Fw190s destroyed and one damaged, Capt. Samuel R. Smith, two Fw190s destroyed on the ground and a third shot down over the airfield, which does a cartwheel on impact to only be awarded as a probable and Lt. Robert M. Callahan damages five Fw190s. Yellow Flight then heads back to England.

Meanwhile Blue and White Flights strafe an airfield near Volkenrod, which is forty miles east of Steinhuder Lake, with the following claims being made: Lt. Ray S. Wetmore, one Ju88 destroyed and one damaged plus one single engine aircraft damaged, Lt. Robert M. Borg, one single engine aircraft and its hangar damaged plus one twin engine transport damaged, Lt. Joseph E. Shupe, one Ju88 destroyed and one damaged, Capt. Daniel D. McKee, one Ju88 destroyed and two damaged, Lt. Harold D. Hollis, one Ju88 destroyed, Lt. Alan C. Porter, one Ju88 damaged along with a control tower and barracks area and wrapping up Lt. Vincent W. Ambrose, one twin engine aircraft destroyed. As Blue and White Flights are returning Lt. Thomas P. "Wigwam" Smith runs out of fuel over the Netherlands, bails out and evades capture, returning on Sept. 16, 1944. Lt. James R. Pino, of the 368th, is also lost on the way out over the Netherlands when his engine loses oil pressure and seizes. Pino bellies his Jug in, hitting an outhouse and burrowing into a haystack. He is not as lucky as Smith and becomes a POW.

The Thunderbolt flown by Pino today was usually flown by Lt. Raymond B. Janney III and had completed fifty-five missions without an abort.

68   April 12, 1944 (1313-1703)

Maj. Clifton Shaw, of the 368th FS, leads the Group off on a scheduled withdrawal support mission for B-17s raiding Leipzig, Germany. Thirty-nine P-47s leave East Wretham but five return early. As the 359th is becoming airborne a message is received that the bombers have aborted but the Group is to continue on to Germany. The Group crosses in north of Ijmuiden, Netherlands at 1403 and is vectored to Hannover, Germany where they make a sweep through the Lingen-Steinhuder Lake-Walsrode sector. No enemy aircraft are encountered so several flights drop down to look for targets to strafe but soon give up due to limited visibility.

69   April 13, 1944 (1350-1702)

Col. Tacon is flying lead today as the Group heads off to provide withdrawal support for B-17s bombing Schweinfurt, Germany. Forty-four P-47s takeoff with four returning early. R/V occurs over Prum, Germany at 1511 and 23,000'. One Fort is observed to be hit by flak and explode over Ghent, Belgium. No enemy aircraft are encountered and

Top, Capt. Wilbur C. Zeigler, the Station Chaplain, gives a pre-mission prayer. At the beginning of the 359th's operations Wing issued an order forbidding pre-mission prayers in the briefing room. This action was prompted as the result of some doltish chaplain preparing a group of fliers to die whereupon they refused to fly the day's mission. Col. Tacon met with Zeigler and offered the solution of how to continue with the prayer by pointing out the order read "*in* the briefing room." Henceforth all pre-mission prayers were conducted outside before the pilots boarded the trucks taking them to their fighters. Below, Capt. Howard L. Fogg Jr. of the 368th FS poses with one of his oil paintings based on his combat experiences. Photo was taken on April 14, 1944. Today Fogg is renowned in railroading circles for his paintings of trains.

the escort is broken at 1612 over Niewport, Belgium. The Group also does some strafing with the following claims being made: 3-8 locomotives, 0-5 railcars, 1-4 barges and 1-0 tugboat. Lt. Cecil R. Brown, of the 368th, bails out over the North Sea twenty miles northwest of Knocke, Belgium and Maj. Albert R. Tyrrell radios the position to ASR. Red Flight of the 368th FS remains on station five minutes, before low fuel demands breaking the pa-

On April 15, 1944 Lt. George A. Doersch, left, riddled a Ju88 that refused to crash. On the same mission Lt. Jack H. Bateman, right, strafed a barracks area damaging several buildings.

trol. ASR arrives five minutes later but no trace is found of Brown and he is listed MIA.

*   April 14, 1944

Maj. Luther H. Richmond, of the 352nd FG, who led the 359th FG on its first three missions, is downed by flak while leading an attack on an airfield near Vechta, Germany and spends the remainder of the war in Stalag Luft 1.

70   April 15, 1944 (1236-1556)

Maj. Niven K. Cranfill, of the 369th FS, is in the lead as the Group flies a strafing mission to Oldenburg, Germany. Forty-two Jugs are launched and seven abort. Time over the target is 1352 and the 369th FS provides top cover while the 368th and 370th FSs deal out the destruction. The 368th is assigned one airfield for each of its four flights but the fields are empty of planes and targets of opportunity are hit. Near Aurich, Germany at 1400 Blue and White Flights make the following claims:

1-0 locomotive, 0-3 radar installations, 0-2 flak towers, 0-2 barracks and 0-1 powerline. During the same period the 370th is also engaged in a similar action. Red Flight strafes an airfield near Oldenburg where Lts. Robert M. Callahan and Harold D. Hollis each explode a Ju88, Capt. Daniel D. McKee damages an aircraft resembling a P-47 and a biplane plus one gun position, and Lt. Jack H. Bateman strafes a barracks area damaging several buildings. Meanwhile Blue Flight strafes an airfield at Kayhauserfeld, where no aircraft are found. Lt. Samuel J. Huskins damages a flak tower and Lt. George A. "Pop" Doersch almost collides with a Ju88 that is approaching the field. Separated from his flight while dodging flak from the airfield, Doersch spots the Ju88 again, near Varel. After being fired on, the Ju88 lowers its wheels and leads Doersch over an army camp. During numerous passes the rear gunner is evidently killed and severe damage dealt to the German bomber but it still remains airworthy. Flak becomes intense so Pop breaks for home. Back at East Wretham five P-47s from the 370th are found to have flak damage. The pilots are Lts. Vincent W.

Above, a Ju88 bomber. Note the close grouping of the crew under an extensively glazed nose. Also visible are the two small caliber machine-guns located at the rear of the crew compartment. Bundesarchiv.

Ambrose, Harold D. Hollis, Raymond B. Lancaster, Joseph E. Shupe and Capt. Samuel R. Smith.

71   April 18, 1944 (1216-1606)

Lt.Col. John B. Murphy, of the 370th FS, leads as the Group furnishes penetration escort for B-17s hitting targets in the area of Berlin, Germany. R/V occurs at 1345 and the escort is dropped at 1407 near Cuxhaven, Germany. No contact is made with the Luftwaffe but the 359th is fired on by P-38s and B-24s. The Group returns safely to base despite the "friendly" fire.

72   April 19, 1944 (0833-1212)

With Maj. Albert R. Tyrrell in the lead the 359th flies penetration escort for B-24s raiding airfields at Paderborn and Gutersloh, Germany. Only thirty-two P-47s fly this mission, ten less than normally expected. This is due to a spate of engine oil pressure failures, which requires an abnormally high num-ber of engine changes. R/V is made over Horn, Netherlands at 0926 and 22,000'. The escort is dropped at 1025 and the 369th strafes between Osnabruck and Minden, Germany. The Group then crosses out near Egmond, Netherlands from 1103-1114.

73   April 20, 1944 (1726-2050)

Lt.Col. John B. Murphy leads the Group on a practice strafing mission from 1340-1430. The Group then provides area support for B-17s and B-24s bombing Noball targets in the Pas de Calais sector of France. Maj. Chauncey S. Irvine leads forty-one Jugs off and there is only one abort. The 359th arrives on station at 1824, no bombers are seen in trouble and no enemy aircraft are encountered.

*   April 21, 1944 (1512-1540)

Capt. Daniel D. McKee, of the 370th FS, leads forty-two P-47s off but the mission is scrubbed while the Group is still over England.

Capt. Daniel D. McKee leads the Group for the first time on a complete mission. The 359th leads the entire 8th AF as it furnishes penetration and target support for B-17s raiding the marshalling yards at Hamm, Germany. Forty-seven Thunderbolts leave East Wretham and five return early. R/V occurs over the Zuider Zee at 1823 and 24,000'. At 1850 over the target, Yellow Flight of the 370th FS sights about twenty bandits at 9 o'clock to the bombers, preparing to attack. With Red Flight providing cover, Yellow Flight breaks into the enemy fighters. All but one of the German pilots turn to meet the P-47s and the now lone attacker is promptly shot down by a B-17 gunner. During the encounter the following claims are made by the 370th: Lt. Ralph E. Kibler, two Fw190s destroyed with one of the pilots bailing out, Lt. Harold D. Hollis, one Fw 190D destroyed and Lt. Raymond B. Lancaster, one Fw190 destroyed with the pilot bailing out and one damaged. On the debit side of the ledger, Lt. Earl W. Thomas Jr. is shot down over Hamm and dies in the resulting crash. It was his first mission. The bombing results are observed as excellent and one Fort is seen to go down as a result of enemy fighter attacks, with five chutes noted. The 369th also gets a piece of the action with Lts. Harry L. Matthew and Robert J. "Posty" Booth each bagging a Fw190. Matthew's kill is notable since he catches the Hun hugging the ground and dragging a section of wire fence on his tailwheel. On the way out, about forty miles north of Hamm, Blue Flight of the 370th strafes a marshalling yard and while looking for someone to join up with Lt. Ray S. Wetmore slides in next to a Fw190. The German pilot, Leutnant Herbert-Konrad Eh, realizes what has happened but fails to escape as Wetmore hammers the 190 and Eh pulls up to 1,500' and bails out. Ground claims are: 7-6 locomotives, 0-4 boxcars, 0-1 rail station, 0-1 switch house, 0-1 factory, 0-1 searchlight, 0-1 oil tanker and 0-1 barge. Lt. Harry F. Cuzner, of the 369th, nurses his P-47, which is leaking oil, back for a safe landing at Woodbridge, Suffolk, England.

75   April 23, 1944 (1406-1626)

Col. Tacon leads the Group on a dive bombing mission to Le Culot Airfield, Belgium. Seventeen P-47s from the 370th provide escort and top cover for a total of seventeen P-47s from the 368th and 369th, armed with two 500 lb. General Purpose Bombs each. Time over the target is 1505 at 17,000' and the results of the attack are regarded as good. No enemy aircraft are encountered and the Group returns safely. Lt. Luster H. Prewitt, of the 369th, brings an armed bomb with a broken vane back to East Wretham. The release gear is found to be jammed and the bomb is safely removed by a RAF bomb disposal squad.

Lt. Andrew T. Lemmens, of the 368th takes his P-47 up on a test flight and discovers the landing gear will not come back down. After trying every trick in the book, to no avail, Lemmens makes a safe belly landing at Wattisham. It is later discovered that a landing gear strut had broken, exactly as it had happened on a P-47 flown by Thomas J. McGeever, at Republic Field months before.

76   April 24, 1944 (1050-1443)

Maj. Chauncey S. Irvine leads the 359th on a penetration escort, under Type 16 control, for B-17s raiding Erding Airdrome, Germany. Forty-four P-47s take off and five abort. R/V is made at 1143 and 19,000' near Ault and escort is broken at 1250 near Luneville, France. On the way out Blue Flight, of the 370th FS, strafes an airfield at St. Dizier, France with the following claims: Lt. Ray S. Wetmore, one Me109 destroyed and one damaged, Lt. Paul H. Bateman, one Me109 destroyed, Lt. Alan C. Porter, one Me109 destroyed and Capt. Samuel R. Smith, one twin engine aircraft destroyed. These pilots also share in the destruction of a second twin engine aircraft. Red Flight, of the 368th FS, consisting of Capt. Charles E. Mosse (Red 1), Lts. Raymond E. Burton, Andrew T. Lemmens and Raymond B. Janney III strafe an airfield at Champenoise destroying two aircraft, damaging two hangars, an administration building and a barracks. The Group then returns without loss.

77   April 25, 1944 (0728-1050)

The first mission today is penetration escort for B-17s blasting airfields at Dijon, Laon, Metz and Nancy, France. Forty-three Thunderbolts take off with only one returning early. Lt.Col. John B. Murphy, of the 370th FS, leads the Group and R/V is made at 0895 over Hornu, Belgium. The escort continues until 0859 near Espagene, where fifteen plus Me109s make a diving attack on the Forts. Lt. Robert J. Booth, of the 369th FS, downs one Me109 and then destroys a radar station. Lt. Robert M.

During the months the Thunderbolt was flown by the 359th FG several pilots' names occur with regularity in the destruction diary. Top left, Lt. D. H. Laing who parachuted near Berlin on May 19, 1944 and became a POW. Top center, Lt. Howard Ado Linderer who was MIA near Paris, France on June 12 also became a POW. *Briney Marlin* was the name of his aircraft. Top right, Lt. Andrew T. Lemmens. Andy would return after completing his first tour and fly a total of 133 missions. Bottom left, Lt. Robert Michael Borg. Builder as he was called completed his tour. Bottom right, Lt. John B. Hunter, of the 368th FS poses with his brother Cpl. Robert C., an armorer in the same squadron. Hunter completed his tour with three enemy aircraft destroyed, one in the air and two on the ground.

Callahan, of the 370th FS, bags a Fw190 on an airfield at Suippes, France. Other claims are: one flak tower and one barracks damaged.

Back at base Lt. Will D. Burgsteiner, of the 370th FS, suffers a broken elbow when he is accidently hit by a weapons carrier vehicle.

78 April 25, 1944 (1335-1554)

Capt. Daniel D. McKee, of the 370th FS, leads the second mission today, which is withdrawal support

for B-24s bombing Noball targets at Wizernes, France. Forty P-47s are launched from East Wretham and there are no aborts. R/V is made near the target at 1416 and escort is broken at 1445, west of Gravelines, France. No enemy aircraft are encountered and the Group returns without incident.

79 April 26, 1944 (0734-1051)

Col. Tacon leads today as the 359th flies penetration support for B-17s raiding industrial targets at

Brunswick, Hannover and Hildesheim, Germany. Forty-one P-47s take off and four abort. R/V is made with B-24s (B-17s not seen) at 0847 and 23,000' over Balkburg. Escort is dropped near Quackenbruck, Germany. No enemy fighters are encountered and no bombers are lost.

80   April 27, 1944 (0839-1216)

On the first of two missions flown today the 359th furnishes area support for B-17s and B-24s bombing Noball targets in the Pas de Calais sector of France. Col. Tacon leads forty Jugs off and there are no aborts. Three Forts are seen going down as a result of flak, with only ten chutes noted. The boring job of providing support during Noball missions isn't made any easier today when one group of bombers is observed making seven runs over a wooded area, apparently without dropping their loads. No contact is made with the Luftwaffe and the patrol ends at 1110 near Amiens, France.

81   April 27, 1944 (1902-2146)

Capt. Daniel D. McKee leads as the Group provides withdrawal support for B-17s raiding an airfield at Nancy, France. Forty-seven P-47s leave East Wretham and four return early. R/V is made over Charleroi, Belgium at 1957 and 20,000'. No enemy aircraft are encountered and the escort is dropped at 2037 north of Brussels, Belgium. A section of P-47s led by McKee follows the Forts all the way back to England to prevent German night intruders from slipping into the bomber formations during the gathering darkness and turning a landing pattern into a shooting gallery. Such an incident had occurred on the night of April 22 and the Germans shot down, or caused collisions that destroyed thirteen B-24s and one B-17.

The 369th FS receives twelve P-51s, eleven more will arrive tomorrow.

82   April 29, 1944 (0849-1336)

Maj. Clifton Shaw, of the 368th FS, leads the Group on a penetration escort for B-17s bombing Berlin, Germany. R/V is made near Egmond, Netherlands at 0945 and 22,000'. The Forts are taken to the vicinity of Hannover, where at 1041 a large force of bandits approach them. The 370th breaks up the attack and Lt. Charles V. Cunningham chases and destroys a Fw190. Escort having been dropped, Red

Top: Capt. Carey H. Brown of the 370th FS, one of nine West Pointers who were members of the 359th FG. He was killed while performing aerobatics in a Mustang on May 1, 1944. C. BROWN PHOTO Bottom: A typical flight shack of the 369th FS. These buildings were constructed from shipping crates and located next to the aircraft hardstands where they afforded shelter from inclement weather for mechanics that were forced to work in the open.

and Yellow Flights of the 370th are orbiting an airfield near Hannover when they are bounced by about fifteen Me109s. After a brief encounter, in which there are no claims or losses, the flights strafe a marshalling yard in the same area, with Lt. Charles W. Hipsher claiming seven of the fourteen locomotives destroyed. See destruction diary at the back of the book for a complete list of claims. On returning to England Capt. Daniel D. McKee, whose windscreen is obscured by oil as a result of a cylinder that blew over Germany, finds his P-47 on fire and shoots an emergency landing at Framlingham. The Jug noses over and flips on its back. McKee crawls out of the twisted remains in good shape but the Jug is Category E.

Top left, Lt. Robert John Booth, of the 369th FS, on the left poses with Lt. George Albert Doersch, of the 370th FS. On May 8, 1944 Booth scored the Group's first triple kill and achieved acedom. Booth has been described as the smoothest of all the 359th's pilots, an accomplished aerobatic flier who traveled to other bases in England to give demonstrations. When asked his opinion of the P-51 he stated it was his favorite fighter and the only time he wished he wasn't in one was the day flak brought him down. On the day Booth became an ace Doersch got two kills and a damaged. Also scoring on May 8 was Lt. Joseph E. Shupe, top right, who bagged two Fw190s. The two 190s downed by Shupe that day would be his only aerial victories before he was listed MIA on May 21. Bottom right, Lt. Emer H. Cater's P-51B, *Wanna Honey*. Note the single kill marking representing the Me109 he shot down while flying a P-47. The dark streak down the fuselage appears to be the result of an oil leak. The serial number was 43-6491.

83   April 30, 1944 (0809-1208)

Maj. Chauncey S. Irvine is in the lead as the Group flies penetration support for B-17s pounding airfields at Aulnut, Clermont and Lyon, France. Forty-six P-47s start the mission and three abort. R/V occurs at 0923 close to Chandai, France and the escort is dropped near Nevers at 0952. The 368th FS then strafes Bricey Airfield, Orleans at 1000 with these results: Capt. Charles E. Mosse, one Me210 destroyed, Lt. Raymond B. Janney III, one Me210 destroyed and one damaged plus an ammo dump blown, Lts. Samuel A. White and Robert E. Burton strafe Nissen hangars and dispersal areas. All of the Group returns to base except Lt. Robert V. Beaupre, of the 368th, who crash-lands at Wyton and sustains a broken right ankle.

At the end of April the 359th FG has about 140 fighters on hand, seventy-six of which are Mustangs. Most of their P-47D-22 models will be passed on to the

9th AF, after the Group completes transition to P-51.

84 May 1, 1944 (0740-1057)

Lt.Col. William H. Swanson leads thirty of the Group's P-47s as they provide area support for B-17s and B-24s blasting twenty-three Noball targets in the vicinity of Amiens, France. The 369th FS is off of operations today as they are refitting their newly acquired Mustangs. No enemy aircraft are encountered and no bombers are lost.

The fighter pilots have developed an intense dislike for Noball missions, which are mostly routine flights with no chance to see any action.

85 May 1, 1944 (1315-1618)

Eight Thunderbolts from the 370th FS, led by Capt. Carey H. Brown, fly the second mission today which is weather reconnaissance over enemy territory. The weather is reported as mediocre and no contact is made with the Luftwaffe.

86 May 1, 1944 (1803– 2040)

Maj. Albert R. Tyrrell, of the 368th FS, leads the third and final mission today, which is escort for B-17s bombing the marshalling yards at Troyes and Reims, France. Twenty-nine P-47s take off in a bad ground haze. R/V is made at 1905 and 22,000' over Mezieres, France. The bombing is done visually and one Fort is lost to flak, with only one chute observed. No enemy aircraft are encountered and the Group returns without incident.

Capt. Carey H. Brown, who led the second mission today, dies in the crash of his P-51 at 1900 near Knettishall, England while on a familiarization flight and practicing aerobatics. Brown was from the West Point Class of 1941.

* May 2, 1944

Lt. Raymond L. Botsford, of the 368th FS, is killed in the crash of his P-51 during a flight to test its guns. His engine quit and while trying to belly-in on a field the P-51 struck some trees. The fighter then narrowly missed a house, stalled and crashed. The cause of the crash was determined to be failure of the pilot to firmly position the fuel tank selector handle, causing the engine to quit from fuel starvation. Botsford is remembered as a capable young man who neither smoked or drank.

Later in the day Lt. John H. Oliphint, of the 369th FS, damages the wing on his P-51 when a gust of wind catches the fighter during a landing at East Wretham.

* May 3, 1944

The pilots of the 359th FG attend a lecture on flying the Mustang, given by Lt.Col. John C. Meyer of the 352nd FG. A ninety minute question and answer period follows. The remainder of the day is devoted to transitional flying.

87 May 4, 1944 (0836-1148)

Lt.Col. William H. Swanson leads the Group, which is flying a mixed bag of Thunderbolts and Mustangs, on a penetration support mission for B-17s that will have to hit targets of opportunity around Brunswick, Germany. R/V is made over Egmond, Netherlands at 0936 and 22,000'. Southeast of Meppel, Netherlands Blue Flight from the 368th FS, which is flying P-47s, strafes an airfield damaging a hangar and five to six barracks. Lt. Emer H. Cater takes a 20mm hit in the wing of his fighter but returns safely to England.

* May 5, 1944

No mission today as the Group gains proficiency with the P-51.

88 May 6, 1944 (0832-1120)

Lt.Col. Swanson leads the first all-Mustang mission, which is an area patrol, under Type 16 control, in the vicinity of Siracourt, France. Thirty-three P-51s participate even though the 368th FS is non-operational today. R/V is made at 0925 over Lille, France and the Group provides cover for B-24s hitting Noball targets. No bombers are lost and no enemy fighters are encountered.

89 May 7, 1944 (0817-1140)

Lt.Col. Swanson leads again as the 359th FG provides penetration, target and withdrawal support for B-24s bombing Osnabruck, Germany. Swanson aborts when his radio expires and Maj. Albert R. Tyrrell, of the 368th FS, takes the lead. R/V occurs over the Zuider Zee at 0923 and 23,000'. The bombing is by radar and the 359th encounters no

Left, Pop Doersch's P-51B after an altercation with a runway at Reims, France on May 11, 1944. Needless to say this badly mangled prop caused a severe vibration and it's a miracle Doersch made it back. Below, Capt. William R. Hodges was forced to bail out on the same mission after his P-51 was hit by flak. Hodges evaded capture and returned in September. Modelers might note the prop on this P-51D is flat black with no yellow on the tips of the blades.

enemy aircraft. Flak is noted to follow the fighters' evasive moves closely. One bomber is lost, a Liberator from the 389th Bomb Group. Only two survivors are found by ASR.

90   May 8, 1944 (0742-1255)

Today's mission is another escort job for B-24s and the target is Brunswick, Germany. Col. Avelin P. Tacon leads forty-three Mustangs across the Netherlands coast near Ijmuiden at 0842 and R/V is made twenty-five minutes later over Hasselt at 24,000'. The Libs are attacked by 50-75 Me109s southeast of Bremen, Germany at 0935. One B-24 is observed going down as a possible result of rockets fired by the enemy fighters. The 359th drops its tanks and engages the Luftwaffe with claims of twelve destroyed, one probable and three damaged. Lt. Robert J. Booth, of the 369th FS, downs two Me109s and a Fw190, the Groups first triple kill and he becomes an ace to boot! Booth also strafes and destroys a locomotive. Other 369th claims are: Maj. Niven K. Cranfill, Capt. Charles C. Ettlesen and Lt. Herbert C. Burton one Me109 each. The 368th tally includes: Lt. Benjamin M. "Horrible" Hagen III, one Me109 destroyed, Lt. Andrew T. Lemmens, one Me109 damaged, Lt. Albert G. Homeyer Jr., one Me109 probable and Capt. Wayne N. Bolefahr, one Me109 destroyed and one damaged. The 370th claims are: Lt. George A. Doersch, one Me109 destroyed , one Fw190 destroyed and one damaged, while Lt. Joseph E. Shupe downs two Fw190s. The 109 claimed by Doersch is engaged with only one gun firing, which then runs out of ammo. The German jettisons his canopy and

Doersch presses the attack bluffing the enemy pilot into bailing out. On the debit side of the ledger two pilots are lost. Lt. Stanley E. Sackett, of the 369th, becomes separated from his flight during the engagement and is not seen again. Sackett's body is found in the wreckage of his P-51B by the Germans, northeast of Neustadt, Germany, his skull crushed as a result of the crash. Lt. Alan C. Porter, of the 370th, is listed MIA. The Germans find his body near the crashed remains of his P-51B, in a forest near Celle, Germany.

After the mission Maj. Chauncey S. Irvine files a complaint that the 369th FS was jumped by P-38s from the 20th FG.

91   May 9, 1944 (0723-1056)

Col. Tacon leads once more as the Group furnishes target and withdrawal support for B-17s raiding Laon-Couvren Airfield in France. After the bombing a section from the 368th FS is to strafe the field and destroy any remaining aircraft. R/V is made over Laon at 0910 and 22,000'. The sequence of events becomes altered and Capt. Charles C. Mosse leads part of the 368th down between the bombing groups' attacks. As a result the fighters are hampered by poor visibility due to the dust and smoke from the just exploded bombs and they are followed closely by the next groups' bombs. Despite the con-

To counter the threat of German parachutists attacking Allied airfields, during the build-up for the Normandy invasion, all fighter groups were required to keep four fighters on ready alert, during daylight hours, with pilots sitting shifts in the cockpits. Top, to further enhance the defence of East Wretham three speedy, light-armored, vehicles were used. There must have been some *esprit de corp* among the crews of these vehicles for they named them all. Left to right, *The Flying Frenchman*, *The Green Hornet* and *The Stinger*. Bottom photo, also obviously posed, shows a crew with their water-cooled caliber 50 machine-gun.

fusion the 368th manages to strafe the buildings on the airfield. No enemy fighters are encountered. Two Forts are lost and no are chutes seen.

The afternoon is spent practicing dive-bombing on the Thetford range.

92 May 10, 1944 (0921-1026)

Maj. Albert R. Tyrrell, of the 368th FS, leads the Group off on a scheduled escort to Germany. The mission is scrubbed as the planes cross the English Channel.

93 May 11, 1944 (1325-1750)

Col. Tacon leads as the Group provides target and withdrawal escort for B-24s blasting the marshalling yards at Mulhouse, France. A preliminary sweep is followed by an early R/V over Besancon, France at 1507 and 23,000'. The results of the bombing are noted to be good, with one Liberator lost to flak. No enemy aircraft are encountered. Escort is dropped near Epinal at 1537 and the 370th FS drops down to strafe. At 1620 the squadron attacks an airfield at Reims, France with these results: Lt. Harold D. Hollis destroys one Me410; Lt. Ray S. Wetmore damages two flak towers and two gun emplacements; Capt. Daniel D. McKee strafes some hangars and the German gunners acquire the range. As Lt. William R. Hodges is making his pass the P-51 is hit in the hydraulic system and while trying to make it back to England the prop locks up forcing him to bail out near Peronne. Hodges evades capture and returns in September. Red Flight is last across the field and they are nailed badly. Lt. Ralph E. Kibler's P-51B is hit and he dies in the resulting crash. Lt. Edward J. Maslow is hit, bails out and is taken prisoner. Lt. George A. Doersch's P-51 is hit by a 20mm explosive round that drains his right wing fuel tank and ruptures the hydraulic system. Following the advice that "if you are hit by ground fire you're flying too high," Pop drops down and his prop hits a runway. With the blades bent back about 12" and the Mustang vibrating severely, Pop makes his way slowly back to England and lands at Manston. Lt. Daniel R. Tuchscherer also crash lands at Manston with battle damage and escapes injury.

94 May 12, 1944 (1100-1631)

Maj. Clifton Shaw, of the 368th FS, leads as the Group furnishes penetration, target and withdrawal support for 326 B-17s blasting the synthetic oil plant at Merseburg, Germany. R/V occurs over Fulda, Germany at 1304 and 24,000'. The bombing results are noted to be good, with several fires started in the target area. No enemy aircraft are encountered but the flak is heavy. One Fort is lost, three are Category E and 189 are damaged. At 1420 just prior to dropping the escort, Red Flight of the 369th FS led by Capt. Charles C. Ettlesen, with two P-51s from Yellow Flight acting as top cover, break off and make a 600 m.p.h. dive toward an airfield at Thamsbruck, about sixty miles west of Merseburg. Hitting the deck three miles out the four P-51s line up for the attack. Lt. D. H. Laing burns one twin engine aircraft and Capt. Ettlesen destroys another which is shared with Lt. Robert L. Thacker and damages a second. Thacker cuts across Ettlesen's line of fire and receives three holes in the tail of his Mustang. Lt. Herbert C. Burton hits a flagpole during the attack, wrenching the wing on his Mustang but returns safely to base. With the element of surprise gone Red Flight and their top cover rejoin the Group and head back, escort having ended at 1432 over Langensalza, near Thamsbruck.

95 May 13, 1944 (1312-1837)

Col. Tacon leads as the 359th FG heads out to give withdrawal support for B-17s bombing the Focke-Wulf factories at Krzensinki and Poznan, Poland. The Group arrives over Dramburg, the R/V point, at 1549 to find that the bombers were forty minutes early and already departed. The Mustangs flown by Capt. Charles E. Mosse and Lt. Robert H. Addleman, of the 368th, FS receive minor flak damage over Stettin. 8/10 cloud cover prevents any observations and no contact is made with the Luftwaffe. The Group lands safely in a bad haze.

* May 15, 1944

Four Mustangs are ordered to be kept on alert against possible German paratroop attacks on the base. Also a tour of duty is extended from 200 to 300 combat hours.

* May 17,18, 1944 (Bad weather over England.)

96 May 19, 1944 (1118-1700)

Col. Tacon is in the lead again as the 359th flies penetration, target and withdrawal escort for B-17s

May 19, 1944 was a busy day for the 359th and three pilots who scored are shown on this page. Top left, Lt. Herbert C. Burton, of the 369th FS, who destroyed two Me109s. Top right, Lt. Ray S. Wetmore, of the 370th FS, being carried by his ground crew, after downing two Me109s. Left, Lt. Raymond B. Janney III, of the 368th FS, bagged one Me109.

raiding Berlin, Germany. The takeoff is made, as the landing will also be, in a ground fog with hazy skies. R/V occurs over Neumunster, Germany at 1313 and 25,000'. At 1350 in the vicinity of Rathenow, sixty miles west of Berlin, the returning bombers are attacked by 100-150 Me109s and Fw190Ds. The 359th is so successful in breaking up the attack that no bombers are seen to go down as a result of enemy fighter action. The Group claims ten and one-half aerial kills and one damaged, with the action broken down as follows, by

squadron. For the 370th: Lt. Ray S. Wetmore destroys two Me109s, one of which was on the tail of a P-51. Lt. Paul H. Bateman bags one Fw190D from which the pilot bails out and Lt. Charles W. Hipsher damages a Me109. The 370th resumes escort after this combat. 369th action: Lt. Herbert C. Burton causes the mid-air collision and disintegration of two Me109s during a head-on attack, Lt. Charles H. Kruger destroys a Me109 on the tail of a P-51, Lt. Robert C. Thomson destroys a Me109 from which the pilot bails out and Lt. Charles C. Ettlesen

Three types of German aircraft destroyed by the 368th FS on May 21, 1944. Top, a Ju52 transport, the backbone of the Luftwaffe's supply system. It was similar in design to the Ford Trimotor with corrugated aluminum skin, but with a low mounted wing. Middle, the He111H medium bomber, another Luftwaffe workhorse. Bottom, Go242A-1 assault glider. Note its similarity to the C-119 Flying Boxcar. BUNDESARCHIVS PHOTOS

shares in the destruction of a Me 109 with a pilot from the 352nd FG. Ettlesen's shared victory is hard earned, with the combat starting at 23,000' and the German having the advantage. As the two fighters work down to tree top level the only gun on Ettlesen's P-51 that is firing runs out of ammo and he considers ramming the 109. The two fighters are so close the pilots exchange stares and the P-51 is caught in the 109's prop wash causing Ettlesen to hit a tree, damaging the wing and oil cooler. At this time a P-51 from the 352nd FG shows up and downs the enemy fighter. Ettlesen returns to England with only eight lbs. of oil pressure. Lt. John H. Oliphint chases a Me109 repeatedly scoring hits as the target sheds parts. Oliphint pulls in so close that his next burst of fire causes

the 109 to spray fuel and oil on his Mustang. As he pulls away the P-51's prop slices off the 109's left horizontal stabilizer. The 369th loses Lt. D. H. Laing near Berlin when his engine quits and he bails out to become a POW. The 368th's claims are: Lt. Raymond B. Janney III, one Me109 destroyed and Capt. Charles E. Mosse, one Me109 destroyed before he is shot down and taken prisoner. Lt. James B. Smith is also shot down and becomes a POW. Also in this area Lts. Emer H. Cater and Olin P. Drake strafe a railroad station, with each claiming one locomotive destroyed. Drake explodes an ammo car and Cater gets a large hole in a prop blade and a hole in the right aileron as a result. A few minutes later the pair crosses an airfield where they damage three gun emplacements, a control tower, headquarters building, oil derrick and a powerline. At 1500, just before exiting Germany through its northern border with the Netherlands, Lts. Homer L. Rodeheaver, John H. Oliphint, Robert C. Thomson and Myron C. Morrill Jr., the 369th's Blue Flight, strafe along the Wesser Ems Canal with these results: 1-2 barges, 1-1 oil storage tanks and 0-1 flak tower.

It has been stated concerning the P-51B's guns that the ammo feed chutes, coupled with the canted machine-gun installation, caused frequent jams. Some work in the field alleviated the problem but Larry Lovell, who was an armorer in the 368th FS, brought to light another factor concerning these jams. According to Lovell the machine-guns manufactured by Kelsey Hayes, under contract to Browning, the designer, were of inferior quality and even after much reworking would still jam after firing a few rounds. The problem was so acute shipments of replacement guns with the Kelsey Hayes name on the crates were not accepted by the 368th.

97 May 20, 1944 (0940-1306)

Col. Tacon leads again as the Group furnishes penetration, target and withdrawal support for B-24s bombing an airfield and the marshalling yards at Reims, France. The results of the bombing are observed to be excellent and no Libs are lost. No contact is made with the Luftwaffe and escort is dropped at 1205 as the force exits the French coast north of Cayeux. The 359th returns without incident.

98 May 21, 1944 (1018-1520)

Lt.Col. William H. Swanson leads the 359th on a *Chattanooga* mission to Ratzburg, Germany. The

On May 21, 1944, Lt. Thomas J. McGeever, top left, nailed a Ju52 making a landing approach and destroyed an unidentified aircraft on the ground. Top right, Lt. Homer Logan Rodeheaver. Rody died when his P-51 went out of control and hit the ground while flying a gunnery pattern over a train. Left, Lt. Arlen R. Baldridge was taken prisoner shortly after crash landing and then murdered. Baldy is seen here posing as if being debriefed by Lt. James T. Burgess. If it was an actual debriefing Baldy would have shed his flying helmet by now. Photo was taken on February 14, 1944.

Mustangs arrive over Ratzburg at 1234 and 10,000'. The ensuing action is broken down by squadrons.

370th FS at 1230 on an airfield near Schwerin, Lt. Robert M. Callahan, one Ju 88 destroyed and one damaged. Lt. Warren R. Newberg, two Ju88s damaged and Lt. Joseph E. Shupe, four Ju88s destroyed and three damaged. During the attack Shupe's ventral scoop strikes the ground and the Mustang is also hit by ground fire. Shupe gains enough altitude to bail out and is listed as MIA. Other 370th ground claims are: one twin engine trainer aircraft destroyed by Lt. George A. Doersch near Bruel, 2-2 locomotives, 0-2 switch houses, 0-1 water tank, 0-2 round houses, 0-2 railroad stations,

0-1 oil storage tank, 0-1 electric transformer, 0-1 small factory and 0-3 radar stations.

369th FS: at 1235 near Klutz, Capt. Richard H. Broach and Lt. Robert B. Sander share in the destruction of a single engine aircraft that crashes in a field. The two German airmen are then killed by strafing. From 1240-1325 between Lübeck and Scherwin, Lt. Eugene R. Orwig Jr. destroys a twin engine transport and damages another parked on a grass field. Lt. Homer L. Rodeheaver is killed while making a sharp turn after attacking a train near Reinfeld. Rodeheaver's Mustang goes out of control, noses in from 200' and explodes. It is believed that the fuselage fuel tank had not been sufficiently

During the mission of May 21, 1944 Lt. Glenn Carrol Bach, top left, destroyed two Fw190s while strafing an airfield and damaged four unidentified aircraft. Top right, Lt. Albert G. Homeyer strafed the same airfield and destroyed a Fw190 and damaged a second 190. Bottom, Lt. Eugene R. Orwig Jr. (Rumberto) and his crew chief S/Sgt. Emile V. Segond pose atop Orwig's P-51 which was named for his wife Loretta. On May 21 Orwig destroyed a twin engine transport and damaged a second while strafing.

depleted causing the tail heavy 51 to crash. Other ground claims for the 369th are: 14-0 locomotives, 0-10 tank cars, numerous boxcars and coach cars, 0-3 signal towers and 0-1 radar tower.

368th FS: from 1230-1330 north of Grevesmuhlen, White Flight strafes an airfield with these results, Lt. Glenn C. Bach destroys two Fw190s and damages four unidentified aircraft, Lt. Albert G. Homeyer, one Fw190 destroyed and one damaged, Lt. Robert B. Hatter, six unidentified aircraft destroyed and three damaged for a Group record, Lt. Thomas S. Lane, two unidentified aircraft destroyed and three damaged. Near Dassow Homeyer also destroys a docked seaplane with the last of his ammo. From 1245-1315 Red Flight led by Lt. Thomas J. McGeever attacks an airfield near Rehna. McGeever catches a Ju52 making a landing approach sending it down in flames and on his next pass destroys one unidentified aircraft. Lt. Gaston M. Randolph damages two unidentified aircraft on this field. Red Flight then moves on to Gadebusch and attacks rail targets. Near Wismar Lt. Clyde M.(Bunky) Hudelson Jr. is hit by flak and disappears over a hill with his engine trailing smoke. Bunky is listed KIA. From 1245-1330 Blue Flight, led by Lt. Benjamin M. Hagen III, begins attacking targets near Wismar. Hagen's radio fails and he becomes separated from his flight. Hagen then finds an airfield being attacked by another P-51 from the 359th and joining the gunnery pattern destroys one trainer and damages two others. Meanwhile the rest of Blue Flight, consisting of Lts. Olin P. Drake, Arlen R. Baldridge and John B. Hunter, attack an airfield in the Wismar-Rostock area. Drake damages a He111 and a Go242 and as the trio passes over an adjacent field Baldridge's P-51 is hit in the coolant system by flak and he makes a safe crash landing. Drake waits till "Baldy" is clear of his downed fighter then sets it on fire by strafing so it can't be salvaged by the Germans. The fire dies soon after and damage is confined to the area of the engine. Other claims for the 368th include: 2-2 locomotive, 0-1 railroad building, 0-1 radar tower, 0-1 flak gun and 0-1 powerline.

After his Mustang was strafed by Drake, Baldridge ran in the direction of a forest but was intercepted by a soldier on a borrowed motorcycle. Soon after surrendering to the soldier he was picked up by SS Sturmfuhrer Peters, who drove him to the courthouse at Bad Doberan. After being brutally beaten Baldridge was shot through the heart by Police Sgt. Gosch, supposedly while trying to escape. The body was taken directly to the cemetery morgue at 1800 and Willi Selk, the cemetery-caretaker, interred the remains (no coffin) the next morning, in the civilian cemetery.

On April 2, 1946, Willi Selk was questioned concerning the burial of two Allied flyers and a Pandora's Box was opened. The area in which Baldridge was shot down turned out to have the greatest concentration of atrocity cases involving flyers ever encountered by the Theater Graves Registration Command. By Sept. of 1948 the remains of twenty-two American and two British pilots had been found.

Arlen's remains were returned to his family in 1948.

99   May 22, 1944 (1004-1349)

Early in the morning a German intruder aircraft shoots down a RAF Lancaster which crashes near the 359th's Service Company area. Six of the seven man crew perish and only the tail gunner survives to be treated at the station's hospital.

Lt.Col. William H. Swanson leads the first mission today, a Type 16 controlled sweep of the Compiegne area of France, where B-24s are bombing Noball targets. The 359th crosses the coast at 1051 and 20,000' over Cayeux, France. No bombers are lost and no enemy fighters are encountered.

During the early morning hours of May 22, 1944 a RAF Lancaster which was returning from a night raid on Duisburg, Germany was caught over England and mortally wounded by an intruding German night fighter. The Lanc then crashed at East Wretham. Of the seven man crew only the tail gunner, who was found still clutching his guns, survived. Mechanics quickly salvaged any equipment and materials they could use, which upset the Brits. While the Lanc was considered the best heavy bomber the RAF had, it is evident from this photo it didn't hold up as well as Boeing B-17 usually did in similar crashes. The British sacrificed structural integrity and armor protection for the crew for increased bomb loads.

100   May 22, 1944 (1115-1500)

Lt. Ray S. Wetmore, of the 370th FS, leads a flight of four Mustangs on an ASR patrol, which begins at 1122 off the coast of Cromer, England. Stragglers are picked up at 1315 and escorted back until 1345, when the Mustangs turn for home.

101   May 23, 1944 (0713-1153)

Col. Tacon leads the Group as they provide penetration, target and withdrawal support for B-17s bombing the marshalling yards at Metz, France. R/V is made at 0830 and 23-25,000' over Reims, France. Two Forts are lost as seven enemy fighters make a single diving pass through the bombers near Lure and escape into cloud cover. Escort is dropped at 1040 and the 359th returns safely to East Wretham.

102   May 23, 1944 (1502-1753)

Lt.Col. William H. Swanson leads the days second mission, which is a dive bombing effort at Hasselt, Belgium. The target is a railway bridge and this will mark the first time the Merlin powered P-51 has been used as a dive bomber. The strike force is

A view of the May 24, 1944 takeoff crash of Lt. Charles H. Kruger, from the 369th FS. An oil leak developed obscuring Kruger's vision and when he set back down the impact caused the right drop tank to explode. Allowing for a minimum capacity drop tank of 75 gallons and multiplying by four we have the potential explosive power of 300 sticks of dynamite. Kruger was lucky to have escaped from this crate. His luck held and he completed his tour.

comprised of 103 Mustangs of the 359th and 361st FGs. Eighty-nine of the P-51s are hung with two 500 lb. bombs each, while the remaining fourteen provide escort. Seventy-five of the Mustangs drop their loads on the bridge, which is demolished. To achieve 84% accuracy on the first time out is an amazing feat. The 361st FG loses one Mustang.

103   May 24, 1944 (0829-1409)

Maj. Clifton Shaw, of the 368th FS, leads the 359th FG on an escort mission for B-17s blasting Berlin, Germany. Shortly after taking off, the P-51 flown by Lt. Charles H. Kruger, of the 369 FS, develops an engine oil leak that obscures his vision and he makes an emergency landing at East Wretham. The landing impact causes the right drop tank to explode enveloping the fighter in flames. Kruger rapidly exits his P-51 and escapes serious injury but the aircraft is a total loss. R/V is made at 1006 and 10,000' near Neumunster, Germany. The bombing

is done visually and thirty-three Forts are lost to flak. Escort is dropped at 1110 northwest of Berlin with the 368th and 369th soon engaging twenty-five plus Me109s. During this combat Lt. John B. Hunter, of the 368th and Lt. Virgil E. Sansing, of the 369th share in the destruction of a Me109. Lt. Thomas J. McGeever, of the 368th and three flights from the 369th then strafe from Stendal to south of Berlin. Claims include: 8-1 locomotives, 6-0 oil tank cars, 0-1 gas truck and trailer, 0-1 medium tank, 0-1 radar tower, 0-2 powerlines, 0-3 tugboats, 0-1 cargo ship and 0-3 barges.

104   May 25, 1944 (0735-1218)

The field order for this mission arrives so late the Group is thirty minutes behind schedule when they take off. Col. Tacon is in the lead as the 359th rushes to provide target and withdrawal support for B-24s raiding the marshalling yards at Mulhouse, France which is on the border with Germany. The target is

The 369th FS lost two pilots and their P-51s on May 29, 1944. Left, Lt. Lowell William Brundage, also known as One-Eye. Brundage is shown here posing for photo taken of all 369th pilots during training. Right, Lt. Myron Clinton Morrill Jr., alias "Moe." Both pilots were last seen chasing five Fw190s near Berlin.

bombed visually and two B-24s are lost to flak. The 359th arrives as the Libs are leaving the target and R/V is made over Sens, France at 1017 and 23,000'. No contact is made with the Luftwaffe today. Meanwhile Capt. Charles E. Ettlesen, of the 369th FS, takes a flak hit in the engine of his P-51C, at 25,000' over Sarrbrucken, Germany. Turning due south he covers twenty-five miles and bails out near Sarrebourg, France at 0925 from 3,000'. Ettlesen lands safely, evades capture and joins the Maquis (French underground). He returns in Aug. and learns his mother has commited suicide believing her son to be dead. Ettlesen is never the same man.

105   May 27, 1944 (1002-1521)

Col. Tacon leads again as the 359th furnishes escort for B-17s hitting the marshalling yards at Mannheim and the chemical industry at Ludwigshafen, Germany. At 1125 and 25,000' over Chateau Thierry, France the Group receives a vector and goes to investigate. No enemy aircraft are found and the 359th makes a sweep from Amiens to Metz, France before making R/V over Mannheim at 1315. The bombing is done visually and flak downs twelve B-17s while damaging ninety-eight others. The Forts are

taken out over Ostende, Belgium at 1437 and left over the English Channel.

106   May 28, 1944 (1155-1718)

Maj. Niven K. Cranfill, of the 369th FS, leads the Group as they fly penetration, target and withdrawal support for B-17s bombing oil dumps at Magdeburg, Germany. R/V occurs over Dummer Lake at 1333 and 25-30,000'. Good bombing results are noted and the Group encounters no enemy fighters. Escort is broken in the vicinity of Frankfurt, Germany at 1540 and the 359th returns to England without loss.

107   May 29, 1944 (0942-1525)

Lt. Col. William H. Swanson leads as the Group furnishes penetration, target, and withdrawal support for B-24s bombing Politz, Germany. At 1200 the 370th FS is in position at 30,000' escorting the Libs, with the 368th and 369th about fifteen miles behind, when about sixty German fighters attack the lead box of bombers. Two Libs are seen to go down as the bandits cut through the formation and continue on in a dive. All three squadrons of the

A lot of hard work went into construction of the base's 450 seat theatre which not only had a stage but was equipped with a state of the art movie projector. During May of 1944 Phil Consuelo and his USO troupe, shown in the left photo, dedicated the new theatre and put on a show titled *Boomps A Daisy*. The troope was duly impressed with the facility. Right, Doc Duennebier, flight surgeon for the 368th FS, and Maj. Jefferson James Fraley of headquarters judge a baby beauty contest held during May of 44. These events not only gave the men a break from the tension of war but helped to establish good Anglo-American relations.

359th FG engage the enemy in the vicinity of Stettin with these results: 370th, Capt. Raymond B. Lancaster, one Me109 destroyed, the pilot of which he circles back to and films in his chute, plus one probable, Lt. Howard E. Grimes, two Fw190s destroyed with one of the pilots bailing out, Lt.Col. John B. Murphy, one Fw190 destroyed and one destroyed/shared with Lt. George A. Doersch, Lt. Ray S. Wetmore, two Fw190s destroyed with one of the pilots bailing out and Lt. Robert W. Siltamaki, one Fw190 destroyed/shared with Lt. Doersch. 369th, Lt. Robert L. Thacker chases a Fw190 from 23,000' to the deck with an indicated airspeed of over 600 m.p.h. At 8,000' Thacker successfully begins pulling out of the dive using both arms on the control stick; the Fw190 fails to recover and augers in. Lt. Robert J. Booth hammers a Fw190 hard at close range and pieces from the disintegrating fighter put five dents in the Mustang's skin and crack the bullet proof windscreen. The 190 is left in a spiralling vertical dive, trailing grey smoke. The 369th loses two pilots during this fight. Lts. Lowell W. "One-Eye" Brundage and Myron C. Morrill Jr. are last seen chasing five Fw190s. Brundage is listed KIA and Morrill as MIA. 368th, Lts. Robert B. Hatter and Benjamin M. Hagen destroy one Me109 each, Hagen's kill being painted solid black. After the encounter ends part of the 359th FG resumes escort until relieved by P-38s near Schleswig, Germany at 1331.

108   May 30, 1944 (0900-1410)

Col. Tacon is in the lead as the 359th flies penetra-
tion, target and withdrawal support for B-17s pounding aircraft industry targets at Dessau, Germany. Thirty-nine Mustangs leave East Wretham but there are twelve aborts. R/V is made over Einbeck, Germany at 1048 and 25,000'. At 1100 the 369th FS engages ten Me109s fifty miles west of Dessau, with no claims being made. During the encounter the engine in Lt. Robert J. Booth's P-51 starts cutting out so he drops down low and heads for England. On his way out Booth chances across and damages the following targets: one Ju88, one locomotive and tank car plus one oil derrick. Booth then joins with a crippled B-17 on its way home and provides escort until the Fort is shot down by flak at 1215 near Lathen. Only two chutes are observed. At 1115, twenty miles west of the target, a large force of enemy fighters slash through the Forts and the 368th and 370th break into the bandits with the following claims being made: 370th FS: Lt. Howard E. Grimes, one Me109 destroyed/shared with Lt. Charles W Hipsher and Lt. Robert W. Siltamaki, one Me109 destroyed/shared with Hipsher. The German pilots bail out from both of these doomed fighters. 368th: Lts. Robert W. Hawkinson and John B. Hunter share in the destruction of a Me109 that breaks up while attempting to crash-land. One B-17 is seen exploding as a result of the attack made by the 109s. On the way home Capt. Richard H. Broach of the 369th strafes a barge near Tiel and leaves it burning. Broach then attacks a train but takes a 20mm hit in an oil line. He makes it back to just southwest of Amsterdam, Netherlands where a safe forced landing is accom-

Top, a small section of the French coast during D-Day. Note the right engine and prop arc of the F-5 photo ship in the upper right corner. ANDREW TREAT COLLECTION.

plished. After setting his P-51B on fire, Broach hides in the backyard of a nearby farmhouse, where he is found three hours later by the Germans and taken prisoner. Back at East Wretham Lt. Andrew T. Lemmens experiences locked brakes while landing and his Mustang is destroyed in the resulting flip. Lemmens escapes injury although it takes ten minutes to extract him from his inverted fighter.

109   May 31, 1944 (0910-1335)

Col. Tacon leads the Group as they provide penetration, target and withdrawal support for B-17s hitting the marshalling yards at Schwerte and Hamm, Germany. R/V is made at 1044 and one bomber is lost to flak at 1115. The Luftwaffe is not encountered and the 359th returns without incident.

A fine example of invasion stripes. This P-51D-5 belongs to the 368th FS and was flown by Col. Tacon, Benjamin H. King and David B. Archibald. Note the fuselage code letters CV-Z have been almost obliterated by the hastily applied stripes. Notice also the stripes are not uniform, parallel or plumb. This is a wartime paint-job, done within a limited time frame, not the slick mega-buck job today's warbird pilots decorate their Mustangs with. ROBERT HATTER PHOTO

110   June 2, 1944 (?   )

The first mission today is escort for B-17s bombing targets in northwestern France. At 1045 White Flight of the 368th FS dives on about twenty Fw190s in the vicinity of Chateau Thierry, France. After being fired on the enemy fighters dive into cloud cover and are lost.

111   June 2, 1944 (1905-2228)

Lt.Col. William H. Swanson leads the second mission today, which is penetration, target and withdrawal support for B-17s raiding marshalling yards near Paris, France. Forty-three Mustangs leave East Wretham and six abort. R/V is made at 2015 and 23,000'. One Fort is seen going down, trailing smoke, twenty miles north of Paris and another one going down with an engine on fire, south of Rouen. Bombing results are noted to be good with direct hits made on buidings and oil storage dumps. No enemy aircraft are encountered and the Group returns safely to base.

*   June 3, 1944

The Group is released for training and maintenance.

112   June 4, 1944 (1333-1616)

Lt.Col. William H. Swanson leads the first of two missions flown today, which is area support for B-17s and B-24s pounding coastal defences in the Pas de Calais region of France. Forty-three P-51s make it off and only one returns early. R/V is made over Gravelines, France at 1415 and 21,000'. Black smoke is observed over several targets and the flak is very light. No bombers are lost and no contact is made with the Luftwaffe. At 1452 a R/T is heard from Lt. Emer H. Cater, of the 368th FS, saying he has lost oil pressure and is bailing out. Cater bails out over the Strait of Dover, twenty miles southeast of Folkestone, England. Lt. Earl P. Perkins, of the 368th FS and Lt. John S. Marcinkiewicz, of the 370th FS, follow the chute down until it reaches the water. Three Spitfires, four Thunderbolts, a Warwick and two launches are on the scene almost immediately but all they find is an oil slick, seat cushion and a half inflated dinghy. A mysterious end for a former Navy man. The Group breaks off the patrol at Berck-sur-Mer and heads back to base.

113   June 4, 1944 (1916-2215)

The second mission today is penetration, target and withdrawal support for B-24s bombing airfields and a marshalling yard in the vicinity of Paris, France. Lt.Col. Swanson leads A group and Capt. Daniel D. McKee leads B group, the 359th FG being split into two units, as they will be on most of the succeeding missions. A total of forty-two Mustangs leave East Wretham and four return early. Visibility is good and excellent bombing results are noted. No enemy aircraft are seen and no bombers are lost.

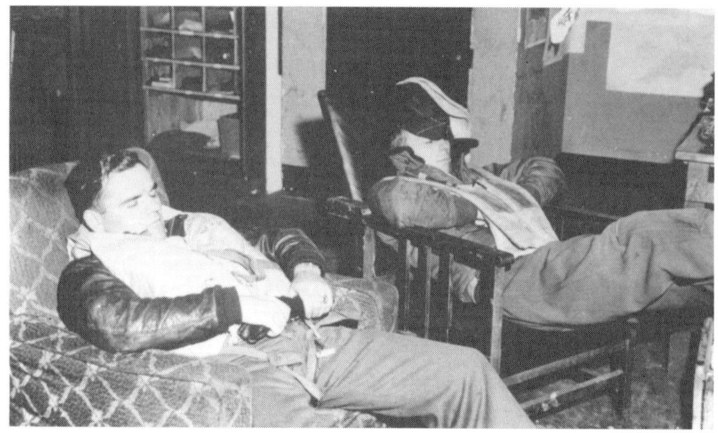

Capt. Robert Laughry Pherson of the 369th FS, in the foreground and Lt. Robert H. Addleman of the 368th FS catch a nap between missions on D-Day. Pherson was killed by the pilot of a Fw190 on June 12, 1944. He had amassed 240 combat hours. Addleman completed his tour in November of 1944. Right, Lt. Harry Frederick Cuzner Jr. of the 369th FS. On D-Day "Cuz" teamed with Oliphint and Pherson to destroy 30-40 ammo cars and damage 10 boxcars and 2 tank cars.

The raiders are escorted to the coast in a race against the gathering darkness.

*   June 5, 1944

The 359th is released for training and maintenance. All passes are stopped, phones leading off the base are cut-off and the civilians on the base are not allowed to leave. The ground crews begin painting 'zebra' invasion stripes on the Group's Mustangs.

D-Day   June 6, 1944

Today the long awaited invasion of France begins and the 359th FG flies six missions. The briefing for the first operation is called about 0200 and the pilots emerge ready to take care of business. Just before boarding the trucks that will take them out to their waiting Mustangs the pilots gather around Capt. Wilbur C. Zeigler, the Station Chaplain, for the pre-mission prayer. A rain that is falling suddenly stops and the clouds part, revealing a bright moon that lights up the entire base. Zeigler also notes there isn't a sound anywhere. In his monthly morale report he calls this "one of the holiest moments of my life." It is a sentiment not lost on those present.

114   June 6, 1944 (0242-0930)

'Plan Full House' is an area patrol of Normandy. A total of thirty- three P-51s take off with Col. Tacon in the lead and seven return early. This mission is flown by A group, consisting of fighters from the 368th and 369th FSs. No contact is made with the enemy.

115   June 6, 1944 (0554-1225)

This 'Plan Full House' is escort for bombers hitting targets on the coast of France. Lt.Col. John B. Murphy, of the 370th FS, leads B group consisting of eighteen Mustangs, representing all three squadrons, off and only one aborts. At 1045 while flying at 25,000' over Chateau Thierry, France, four Fw190s are sighted at 8,000'. White Flight of the 368th FS dives toward the bandits and discovers there are actually about twenty enemy aircraft. Capt. Wayne N. Bolefahr, Lts. Thomas J. McGeever and James R. Pino each fire a short burst at the 190s before the Germans escape by diving into cloud cover.

116   June 6, 1944 (1048-1450)

'Plan Stud'. Lt.Col. Albert R. Tyrrell, of the 368th FS, leads twelve P-51s on a mission to dive bomb railroads and highways in the vicinity of Le Mans, France. The following claims are made: 4-6 oil tank cars, 0-15 boxcars, 1-0 truck, 1-0 staff car and 0-2 stone arch bridges. Visibility was poor.

117   June 6, 1944 (1151-1603)

'Plan Stud'. Maj. Niven K. Cranfill, of the 369th FS, leads fifteen Mustangs on an identical mission to Le Mans.

118   June 6, 1944 (1318-1646)

'Plan Stud'. Maj. Daniel D. McKee, of the 370th FS, leads eleven of his squadron's P-51s on a dive

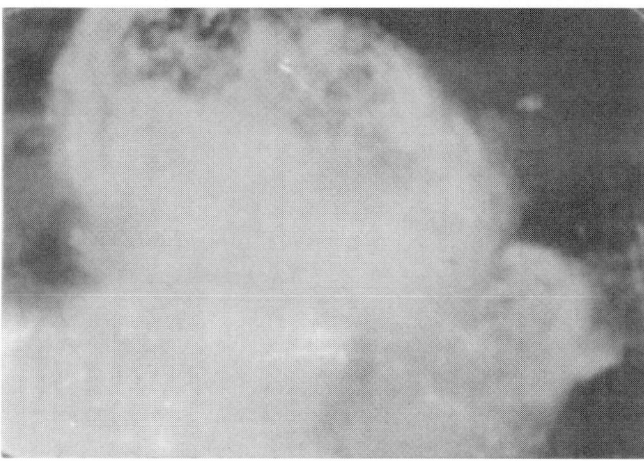

At left is a sequence taken from the gun camera footage of Lt. John H. Oliphint on June 6, 1945. In the top frame machine-gun fire has started a series of small explosions in a string of boxcars. In frame two a major bang has occurred. Frame three shows a series of secondary explosions brewing up. In the final frame a huge cloud of smoke and debris rises to meet Oliphint's speeding Mustang and somewhere in the fiery blast a wheel from one of the boxcars is arcing up and will pass over its wing.

bombing mission in the area of Le Mans. Eight of these Mustangs carry two 500 lb. bombs each, while the remaining three provide escort. Two railway bridges are hit west of Le Mans causing minor damage. Two of the bombs are duds. The escorts flown by Capt. Howard L. Fogg, Lts. Dick D. Connelly and William H. Hastings strafe and make the following claims: Fogg one locomotive damaged, while the trio shares in damaging a tank car.

119   June 6, 1944 (1805-2315)

'Plan Royal Flush'. The last mission of D-Day is led by Lt.Col. William H. Swanson. All three Squadrons participate in this effort launching thirty P-51s, three of which return early. West of Le Mans the 369th's Red Flight, consisting of Lts. Herbert C. Burton (Red 1), Robert J. Booth and Gilbert R. Ralston Jr., attack rail targets and file the following claims all shared: two locomotives destroyed, eight to ten oil tank cars destroyed, one German army truck damaged and one radio tower damaged. East of Le Mans Yellow Flight, of the 369th, also consisting of three P-51s but piloted by Lts. Robert L. Pherson (Yellow 1), John H. Oliphint and Harry F. Cuzner Jr., attack rail targets as follows: near Conlie at 2010 the flight makes several passes on ten boxcars that refuse to burn, evidently being empty. The ground fire becomes intense so they move on to Biele, where thirty to forty ammo cars are spotted on a rail siding. Oliphint and Cuzner explode two of these cars, which derail others, start fires and wreck the siding and mainline tracks. Strafing the remaining cars starts a series of explosions that completely destroy the adjacent tracks and near-by warehouses. An electric transformer station is also strafed and Oliphint destroys a two-ton truck.

During one of his passes Oliphint's Mustang is enveloped in the flames from an exploding boxcar and is hurled from an altitude of less than 100' to over 1,000', where he witnesses a wheel from the boxcar passing over his wing. On returning to base Oliphint's 51 is found to have the paint on its un-

These three pilots flew combat on June 7, 1944. Left, Lt. John S. Marcinkiewicz who became a POW that day. Center Capt. John W. McNeill Jr., who completed his tour in Nov. of 1944. Right, Lt. Richard O. Rabb, who was interned in Sweden on August 4, 1944.

derside singed by fire, dents in both wings and the tail plus pieces of a wood 2×4 lodged in the position formerly housing the landing light, which is on the leading edge of the left wing. This Mustang is back flying the next day!

Today the 359th's morale is at an all-time high but the worst is yet to come for Germany. 75% of the total bomb tonnage dropped by the 8th AF will be dropped after this date.

120   June 7, 1944 (0638-1000)

A dive bombing and strafing assignment in the Le Mans area is the first mission flown today. Sixteen Mustangs from the 370th take off at 0439 and return fifteen minutes later due to bad weather. At 0638 the 370th is off again with Lt.Col. John B. Murphy leading fifteen P-51s, two of which abort. At 0756 Lt. Robert M. Borg bombs a string of boxcars on a rail siding outside of La Fleche, France. Borg puts two 500 lb. bombs under the center car and all ten cars explode. Four minutes later Red, White, Blue and Yellow Flights attack an armored convoy north of Le Mans with the following results: 5-15 light tanks, 6-15 trucks and 2-0 signal trucks.

121   June 7, 1944 (1019-1530)

The second mission is a 'Plan Royal Flush' area

support assignment for B-17s and B-24s blasting targets in northwest France. This mission is flown by the 368th and the 369th FSs . Lt.Col. Albert R. Tyrrell, of the 368th, leads twenty-nine P-51s off and four return early. No bombers are lost and no contact is made with the Luftwaffe. The 368th strafes nine locomotives, 100 boxcars, a roundhouse and three trailers of ammunition which explode. Lt. John Stanley Marcinkiewicz's Mustang is damaged by one of the exploding trailers; his engine quits before reaching friendly territory and he bails out five miles southeast of Fecamp. John is taken prisoner and remains so until the end of the war.

122   June 7, 1944 (1739-2227)

The third and final mission today is an area patrol in the vicinity of Tours, France. Lt.Col. William H. Swanson leads thirty-one Mustangs off and there are three aborts. Fires are observed resulting from the B-17 and B-24 raids at Avranches, Argentan, Domfort, Flers and Falaise, France. One B-17 is observed exploding over Rennes at 1940 and no chutes are seen. Again no contact is made with the Luftwaffe.

123   June 8, 1944 (0628-1150)

The 359th FG flies three missions again, with the first being escort and area support for B-17s pound-

Right, Capt. Wayne N. Bolefahr lost his life while attacking gun positions so unarmed F5s could take photos of a marshalling yard. Above, Red Elders acting as crew chief for Bolefhar, as he prepares for a mission in his P-51B. Note ring and bead gunsight suspended next to the N-3B optical gunsight as a back-up.

ing targets in the vicinity of Tours, France. R/V is made over Tours at 0759 and 23,000'. Good hits are observed on four bridges. One Fort is lost and no enemy aircraft are encountered. The Group loses two pilots. Lt. Robert B. Sander, of the 369th FS, is killed while strafing a convoy of 40-50 ammo trucks and Lt. Benjamin M. Hagen III, of the 368th FS, is hit by flak while attacking a train. Hagen's P-51 catches fire and he receives burns to the face and right leg before bailing out. He is taken prisoner and taken to a hospital, where he is blind for a week due to burns. Hagen returns after the war. Claims for the 368th are: 1-2 locomotives, 0-3 boxcars and gondola cars and 7-3 trucks. For the 369th: 26-0 trucks and staff cars and 0-100 boxcars. The 370th claims one truck destroyed.

124   June 8, 1944 (1239-1643)

The second mission, led by Lt.Col. William H. Swanson, is a bombing and strafing assignment in the vicinity of Domfront, France. Thirty-two P-51s take off and three return early. Claims for this mission include: 368th FS: three cuts in railroad tracks, 0-1 electric locomotive, 8-0 boxcars, 3-0 trucks, 2-0 trucks, 2-0 cars, 2-0 light tanks, 4-0 armored vehicles and 35 troops killed. 369th FS: 0-3 armored vehicles, 1-0 truck and 1-0 radio tower. 370th FS: 0-1 locomotive, 10-8 boxcars and 3-4 trucks. The Group returns safely to East Wretham despite bad weather.

125   June 8, 1944 (1827-2245)

Mission number three is bombing and strafing in the area of La Fleche, France where the 370th raids another marshalling yard. Claims are: 370th FS, tracks bombed, 3-0 railcars, 1-0 half track and 0-1 bridge abutment. 369th FS, 2-0 locomotives, 10-12 boxcars and six bombs are dropped in the midst of 100 boxcars. 368th FS, 1-2 locomotives and 1-1 armored vehicles. Two pilots from the 369th FS are lost to flak during this mission, Lts. John H. Oliphint and Robert J. Booth. Both pilots are taken prisoner but return. The 359th returns to base to find the visibility is poor due to rain and lands with the help of flares.

Oliphint, who was one of the *Buzz Boys*, is nearing La Fleche when his P-51 is spotted losing coolant; he refuses to turn back and presses on to attack a train (this action will earn him a Silver Star). As the Mustang bores in the Merlin seizes and Oliphint begins strafing as 20mm fire rakes the fuselage of his fighter from nose to tail. The bombs are released at point blank range and the now lightened Mustang zooms up and over the train, glides silently over a German anti-aircraft gun and its wide eyed crew and crashes some distance further on. The impact tears off both wings, shears off the tail and buries the engine and cockpit in mud. The next morning Oliphint is dug out by the Maquis but due to his injuries they report his location to the German military in hopes he will get proper medical attention. Instead the Gestapo takes him prisoner. After being interrogated and brutally tortured, Oliphint, with the help of a few other inmates, one of whom carries him on his back, makes a daring escape and joins the Maquis. During his stay with the underground Oliphint is asked by British Intelligence to gather data on locations they specify periodically. Not all of his time is spent on cloak and dagger operations though. During one night raid Oliphint joins the Maquis as they sneak onto an enemy airfield. He gets into the cockpit of a Me109 and tries to steal it but in the dark and unfamiliar layout only succeeds in retracting the landing gear. His frustration in failing to make off in an enemy fighter is lessened somewhat as the raiders blowup nine aircraft. During August the British extract Oliphint in a Lysander and fly him to London. He later learns that the information he collected was used by Gen. George S. Patton during his famous breakthrough.

*   June 9, 1944 (1729-   ?   )

The Group is scheduled to fly a dive bombing mission west of Paris, France. The Mustangs are airborne twenty minutes when they are recalled due to poor weather.

126   June 10, 1944 (0708-1210)

The rigorous pace continues as the 359th flies four missions today. The first one, led by Lt.Col. William H. Swanson, is escort and area support for B-24s hitting targets in the vicinity of Rouen, France. Thirty-five P-51s take off and seven abort. After the escort is broken the Group drops down to strafe. Near Evreux, Capt. Howard L. Fogg, Lts. Robert M. Callahan and Warren R. Newberg, of the 370th FS, damage an electric train engine and five boxcars.

127   June 10 (1333-1521)

Eleven P-51s of the 368th FS, led by Lt.Col. Albert R. Tyrrell, provide escort for four F-5 Lightnings (photo-recon version of the P-38) on a photo reconnaissance mission to Antwerp, Belgium. The target is a heavily defended marshalling yard. After the Lightnings make several abortive attempts to photograph the yards and are driven away by ground fire, Capt. Wayne N. Bolefahr, a West Pointer, distracts the German gunners by making a daring attack on the main gun emplacements. As the F-5s make their runs Bolefahr's Mustang is hit countless times, crashes through a row of trees and disintegrates as it hits the ground. This action of a true warrior earns the fallen hero the Distinguished Service Cross. On the way out the squadron destroys four locomotives and damages a fifth. Tom McGeever's P-51 is damaged by flak but he puts it down safely at Manston.

This mission was considered, by many who flew it, to be a suicide job, especially since none of the recon aircraft previously sent to this area ever returned.

128   June 10, 1944 (1350-1810)

Before the 359th takes off again, a sudden rainstorm forces the 352nd FG to land at East Wretham. The third mission today is bombing and strafing in the vicinity of Domfront, France. Maj. Chauncey S. Irvine leads the 369th FS and Lt.Col. John B. Murphy leads the 370th. Twenty-six P-51s are launched and there are no aborts. South of St. Malo, near Dinan, the force dive bombs a railway bridge scoring several hits. At 1545 White Flight of the 370th attacks a convoy of medium tanks near Domfront. Two tanks are destroyed and two damaged. One of the damaged tanks is credited to Lt. Richard O. Rabb who pulls out of his strafing run too late and strikes some trees, causing considerable damage to his Mustang. The battered fighter brings Rabb safely back to base. Elsewhere claims are made for: 14-2 trucks, 2-0 staff cars and 2-0 boxcars. Lt. Daniel R. Tuchscherer, of the 370th, crash lands near Manston, England and returns to base several days later.

129   June 10, 1944 (1953-2235)

The fourth and final mission today is bombing and strafing in the vicinity of Paris, France. Maj. Niven K. Cranfill, of the 369th FS, leads twenty-one Mustangs off and there are no aborts. At 2115, between Elebuf and Louveres, the 370th FS bombs and destroys four railcars and numerous sections of track. Maj. Cranfill attacks a heavily defended railroad tunnel near Conches and skips both bombs inside. Just after these attacks Red Flight encounters a Me109 with its wheels down. The German pilot is very talented and evades being shot down by Capt. Raymond B. Lancaster and Lt. Vincent W. Ambrose, who only score a few hits. Lt. George A. Doersch, of the 370th's White Flight, receives a R/T that bandits are in the area and joins the battle. Doersch gets behind the 109 and fires several bursts hitting

Top left, Lt. Paul H. Bateman. On June 11, 1944 Bateman damaged a truck and a staff car. Top right, Capt. Howard L. Fogg flanked by his armorer, Sgt. Joe W. Creech on his right, and crew chief S/Sgt. Ira J. Bisher on his left. This photo was taken during May, while Fogg was still in the 368th FS. On June 11, 1944 while flying with the 370th FS, Fogg and Lt. William H. Hastings destroyed considerable yardage of railroad tracks with their bombs. Bottom left, a pair of British Walrus seaplanes. This was the type of aircraft that rescued Lt. Gilbert R. Ralston from the English Channel on June 11, 1944. Bottom right, Lt. Ralston playing solitaire.

the coolant system. The German pilot bails out but his chute is not seen to open. Meanwhile in the area of Evereux, Blue Flight of the 368th FS has just finished bombing a target when they engage three Me109s. During the ensuing fight Lt. Olin P. Drake causes two of the bandits to crash but the third one latches onto Drake's tail. 20mm fire from the 109 blows a large hole in the Mustang's left wing root and also explodes into the engine. In a chivalrous gesture the German pilot flies formation with Drake until he makes a safe crash landing and then circles before leaving. Drake then evades capture and is hidden by the French, along with Staff Sgt. Melvin Curry, a ball turret gunner from a B-17. Both are liberated by American forces and return to England in September.

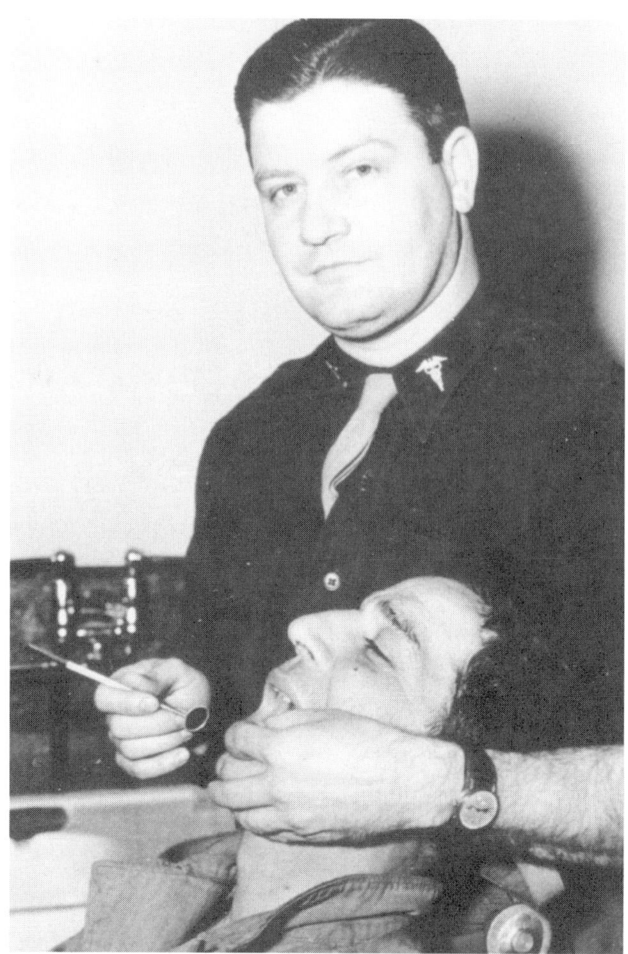

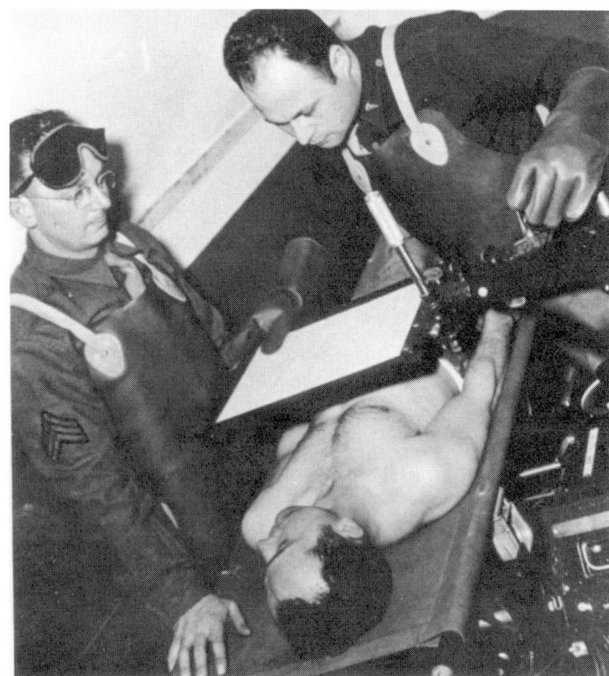

Health is a major concern for everyone but even more so for those who fly. Problems a pilot might consider minor or not be aware of can manifest themselves with a vengeance at high altitude. On this page are some of the doctors that kept the Group in top shape. Top left, Major Albert H. Hirshiemer the Station Surgeon at work in the laboratory. Top right, Capt. Alfred P. Jones the 359th's Dental Surgeon. Bottom right, the 85th Service Group's Dental Surgeon Capt. Morris J. Jacobson being assisted by Cpl. William J. Morris. Above, Sgt. James M. Carson on the left helps Capt. Milton M. Kendall examine a patient by use of a fluoroscope.

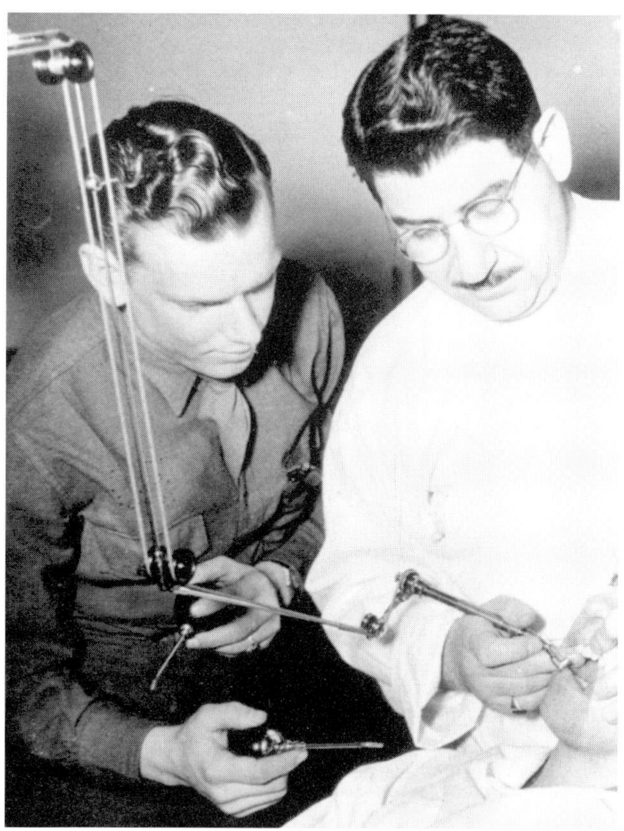

for B-26s headed for Paris, France to be followed by dive bombing and strafing in the vicinity of Herblay, France. Col. Avelin P. Tacon leads thirty-six Mustangs off and two return early. At 0935, southwest of Amiens, the 370th FS raids a marshalling yard where Lt. Charles V. Cunningham drops two 250 lb. bombs that destroy two oil tank cars and Lt. Charles W. Hipsher destroys a railway station with his load. Additional claims are: 4-0 oil tank cars, 1-0 staff car plus several bridges and viaducts damaged. On the return flight the P-51 flown by Lt. Gilbert R. Ralston, of the 369th FS, is hit by flak near Compiegne and he is wounded in the belly. Bailing out over the English Channel, five miles off the French coast, Ralston finds his dinghy is missing its inflation bottle, but his Mae West keeps him afloat until he is picked up by an ASR Walrus thirty minutes later. Fired on by coastal batteries and unable to take off, as it is overloaded, the Walrus is forced to taxi across the English Channel. Ralston has the distinction of being the first pilot in the Group to be rescued after ditching.

In 1962 while stationed at a German-American radar site at Freising, Germany Ralston became friends with the man he would find shot him down.

131   June 11, 1944 (1354-1718)

The second mission, led by Lt.Col. John B. Murphy, of the 370th FS, is bombing and strafing targets of opportunity in the area of Vire/St. Martin, France. Thirty-four P-51s leave East Wretham and two abort. At 1515, near Vire, the 370th FS begins attacks on transportation targets using 250 lb. bombs. Claims include: several sections of track destroyed, 2-3 railcars, 0-1 heavy tank, 5-7 armored vehicles, 17-21 trucks, 2-4 staff cars, 0-1 Jeep in German markings, 0-1 car, 0-2 bridges and 0-1 radar station. The 368th FS loses Lt. William R. Simmons, who dies when his P-51 is hit by flak. His Mustang crashes near Maltot, France.

132   June 12, 1944 (0638-1141)

Col. Tacon is in the lead as the 359th FG furnishes target and withdrawal support for B-17s raiding airfields in the vicinity of Paris, France. Thirty-six turns back to strafe targets of opportunity west of Paris. White Flight of the 369th FS passes over a light AA position and Lt. Leroy D. Hess' P-51 is hit. Heading home without an escort he is jumped by enemy fighters and scores two kills before being forced to bail out. Hess becomes a POW. Meanwhile the rest of White Flight strafes two light AA positions, then encounters a fight between P-51s and some Fw 190s (which are evidently taking off because their landing gear is still down). Maj. Chauncey S. Irvine fires a burst at a190 that is about to attack a P-51 that is on fire and bellying in. Two 190s then jump on Irvine's tail and begin firing. Firewalling the Mustang as he heads for home Irvine notices his pursuers have not yet retracted their landing gear. While exiting Irvine crosses an airfield where he strafes a hangar containing a Me109, then a light tower. With the Germans having given up the chase Irvine continues on toward base. After the 369th expends all their ammo strafing they are jumped by eight Fw190s. During the resulting melee Lt. Robert L. Pherson is killed and Lt. Howard A. Linderer is shot down and taken prisoner. Other claims include: 0-2 locomotives, 0-2 boxcars, 2-4 trucks and 0-2 staff cars.

133   June 13, 1944 (0632-1025)

Col. Tacon leads the 359th as they provide target and withdrawal support for B-17s bombing the marshalling yards at Nantes, France. Fifty-four Mustangs take off in the rain, under a grey sky and five return early. The bombing results are noted to be excellent. An airfield at Logne is also hit with good results. No Forts are lost and no contact is made with the Luftwaffe. When the Group returns to England they land at several bases because East Wretham is socked in. The sun comes out at noon and the 359th returns to their base.

134   June 13, 1944 (1808-2317)

Maj. Daniel D. McKee leads the second mission of the day, which is area support for B-24s bombing bridges at Ploermel and Montfort, France. The bombing results are not observed due to the weather and two B-24s are lost. Lt. Samuel J. Huskins, of the 370th FS, lands at an emergency strip on the

Top left, Lt. Leroy Donald Hess Jr. Hess' P-51 was damaged by flak on June 12, 1944 and while heading back to base alone he was jumped by German fighters. He scored two kills before bailing out and becaming a POW. Top right, Maj. Chauncey Stewart Irvine, who was assigned to headquarters at the time of June 12, 1944, forced a Fw190 to break off its attack on a P-51 and in turn was chased, full bore, by two 190s for several minutes at low level. On a heading for home and stretching his lead Irvine crossed an airfield and strafed a hangar containing a Me109, then hosed a light tower. Below, a P-51B damaged by flak during the invasion of Normandy. This aircraft was repaired and shows up in the Destruction Diary on Aug. 28, 1944 coded CV-H and flown by Billy D. Kasper.

French coast for an oil check and returns with four letters given him by RAF airmen. These letters are turned over to S. L. Watson of RAF security.

135   June 14, 1944 (0612-1015)

Today the Group flies an area support mission for B-17s hitting airfields at Le Culot, St. Trond and Florennes, Belgium. Lt.Col. William H. Swanson leads thirty-three P-51s off and seven abort. The bombing is done visually and fires are observed at Le Culot. One Fort is lost and no enemy aircraft are encountered.

136   June 15, 1944 (0720-1140)

With Col. Tacon leading, the 359th provides withdrawal support for B-17s raiding the marshalling yards at Angouleme, France. Thirty-seven P-51s leave East Wretham and five return early. The 359th arrives at the R/V point on time, to find the bombers were early and are heading back. At 0925 the Group makes R/V off St. Nazaire and shepherds the Forts across the English Channel to Portland Bill, England, where the escort is dropped. The weather today is magnificent!

At noon the four-plane alert flight, maintained

Left, Maj. Wayne R. Brown who died during a non-operational flight on June 17, 1944. Right, Lt. Joseph P. Kelsey chats with Lt. John C. Allen who suffered a broken ankle after bailing out over England on June 18, 1944.

since May, is abolished, the threat of a German paratroop attack during the invasion having passed.

137   June 16, 1944 (1547-1910)

The Group is briefed at 0915 for an escort mission that is scrubbed at 0945. Another briefing is held at 1500 for a penetration, target and withdrawal support mission, under MEW control, for B-24s blasting Noball targets in northern France. Forty-five P-51s take-off but eight return early. Lt.Col. William H. Swanson leads initially but aborts with a rough engine. Lt. Raymond B. Janney III, of the 368th FS takes his place. The 359th makes R/V with the bombers over Ypres, Belgium at 1630 and 25,000'. Overcast conditions prevent the bombing results from being observed and no enemy aircraft are encountered.

138   June 17, 1944 (1210-1540)

The 359th flies two missions today. The first is a scheduled penetration, target and withdrawal support job for B-24s bombing airfields in France. Due to a mixup in takeoff times the Group is late getting started. Lt.Col. John B. Murphy, of the 370th FS,

leads forty-five P-51s off and there are seven aborts. R/V occurs northwest of Paris at 1318 and 22,000'. The targets have already been hit using radar and no results are seen. Again no contact is made with the Luftwaffe. Twenty-eight Libs are escorted out at Coburg, France and left at Beachy Head.

139   June 17, 1944 (1854-2157)

Maj. Daniel D. McKee, of the 370th FS, leads the second mission which is an area patrol at Evreux, France under Type 16 control while B-24s bomb airfields at Tours and Laval. Forty-one Mustangs take off and four return early. The 369th FS shoots down a weather balloon over Evreux, the high point of a rather dull operation.

Maj. Wayne R. Brown, Group Operations Officer of the 368th FS is killed on a non-operational flight near Coafield, England.

140   June 18, 1944 (0728-1205)

Col. Tacon leads as the 359th provides penetration, target and withdrawal support for B-17s raiding an airfield at Lüneburg, Germany. Forty P-51s leave

Left to right, Lt. Harry L. Matthew and Lt. Robert C. Thompson celebrate finishing 300 hour tours on July 19, 1944. Dinghy-Butt refers to a physical condition fighter pilots developed by sitting for hours on a deflated dinghy and parachute.

East Wretham and six abort. R/V is made against a ninety m.p.h. headwind over Pellworm Island at 0919 and 26,000'. Lt. John C. Allen, of the 368th FS, aborts with engine trouble and using his escape kit compass navigates all the way back to England. Allen then bails out just inside the coast and suffers a broken ankle. The bombing is noted to be excellent and although all 8th AF fighter groups are operating not one enemy aircraft is shot down. However, four bombers are lost to flak. The 359th escorts the Forts back to the English coast without incident.

141   June 19, 1944 (0645-1147)

Col. Tacon leads again as the Group furnishes penetration, target and withdrawal support for B-17s blasting airfields in the vicinity of Bordeaux, France. The 359th FG puts up forty-two Mustangs today and eight return early. Two fighter groups turn back early because of cloud layers extending to 29,000'. The 370th FS and two flights from the 369th FS press on and R/V is made over Cholet, France at 0822 and 30,000'. The results of the bombing are noted to be excellent and one of the seven Forts lost today is observed going down over the Merignac airfield. Only one crewman is seen bailing out. Lt. George A. Doersch, of the 370th, looses the use of his flight instruments and after an amazing seven and one half hour flight returns to base by using his escape kit compass.

142   June 20, 1944 (0617-1146)

Lt.Col. William H. Swanson leads the 359th on the first of two missions flown today, a penetration escort for B-24s bombing the oil industry at Politz, Germany. Forty-eight Mustangs take to the air but ten abort. R/V occurs north of Heligoland Island, Germany at 0801 and 25,000'. At 0920, near Putbus, the bombers are attacked by about eighty rocket firing Me410s. Before the 359th can break up the attack four B-24s are in the waters of Griefswald Bay and a fifth is on fire and going down. No chutes are observed. After launching their air to air rockets the Germans dive for the deck. Lts. Grant M. Perrin and Herbert C. Burton, of the 369th FS, foil an attack on a lone B-24 by a Me410 and in a chase from 15,000' to the deck both score hits causing the 410 to belly-in, shedding its right wing in the process. Of the 358 Libs participating in the raid thirty-four are lost and 205 are damaged.

143   June 20, 1944 (1722-2051)

The second mission today is a strafing assignment east of Paris, France. Lt. Col. John B. Murphy, of the 370th FS, leads thirty-three P-51s off and five return early. The Group receives one vector, which turns up no enemy aircraft. When no ground targets are found in the assigned area the Group flies east to Chalons and hits a marshalling yard. Claims

Top left, Lt. Virgil Edward Sansing of the 369th. Sansing, who sported the bushiest mustache in the Group, bailed out near Versailles, France after his P-51 was hit by flak on June 20, 1944. He was picked up by the French underground and later returned to England in September. Top right, Lt.Col. Albert R. Tyrrell CO of the 368th FS. "Trigger" Tyrrell was taken prisoner on June 21, 1944, after bailing out near Berlin, Germany. Note this Mustang was equipped with a Malcolm Hood, which gave pilots of B and C model P-51s better visibility. Right, Bundesarchivs' photo of a Fw189 light reconnaissance aircraft, one of two types of German aircraft destroyed by Tyrrell on his last mission.

include: 1-7 locomotives, 3-8 oil tank cars, 3-2 vehicles and 0-1 flak tower. The 369th FS suffers the only loss today when Lt. Virgil E. Sansing's P-51 is hit by flak near Versailles. The cockpit catches fire, Sansing bails out at 5,000' and is picked up by the French underground. He returns in Sept.

144   June 21, 1944 (0719-1330)

Lt.Col. Albert R. Tyrrell, of the 368th FS, leads the Group as they fly penetration, target and withdrawal support for B-17s bombing Berlin, Germany. Forty-one Mustangs leave East Wretham but there are sixteen aborts. R/V occurs over Ratzeburg, Germany at 0930 and 29,000'. The bombing is done visually and black smoke is noted rising to 15,000'. No enemy aircraft are encountered by the 359th FG but the Luftwaffe does attack other sections of the bomber force, contributing to the loss of sixteen Forts. Escort is dropped near Wittstock and Lt.Col. Tyrrell and his wingman Lt. James J. Lubien, of the 368th FS, strafe an airfield east of Plau, Germany at 1100. Tyrrell destroys a Me410 and Fw189, while Lubien damages another aircraft despite his visibility being hampered by a windscreen cracked by ground fire. Tyrrell is also hit and forced

Top, 370th FS 'C' and 'D' Flights ground crewmen. Kneeling; Shuster, James Lammy and Bicheler. First row left to right; Morris Moskowitz, George Issac, Tom Purcell, Edward O'Brien, Roscoe Speziale, John Yetman, Harilaoso DeMos and K. Young. Second row; Kenneth Coleman, Bartley Conrad, Frank Purawic, Borden Ritchey, Dominick Buono and John Ricci. Third row; Charles McCrone, Robert Erickson, Cornelius McCaughery, Bruce Compton, Stan Smarkus, Edward Zuchowski, Lucien Ruel, Dorem and Locklyn Sangster. Mustang is a P-51D-5NA named *Pandemonium* CS-D 44-13529. Bottom, more 370th ground crewmen. Kneeling; Joe Marcy, George Thiehaud, Clair Harkless, Howard McElvania and Robert Gill. Standing left to right; Edward Moylan, William Haywood, William Kindolem, Charles Veasey, William Reynolds, Edward Schaeffer, Seger and Richard Matthew. On wing; Coffey, Roy Kendall, Emilio Peroni and Clifford Brown. On cowl; Elijah Taylor, Gregory Barone, Ray Martini and Emil Soda. Mustang is P-51D-10NA flown by Capt. Robert L. McInnes and named *Blondie II* CS-S 44-14192.

to bail out, becoming a POW. Command of the group goes to Maj. Daniel D. McKee for the remainder of the mission. At 1130, in the vicinity of Bad Oldesloe, a flight from the 370th FS strafes a train, damaging five boxcars. The Group then returns to England. Col. Tacon has a talk with the pilots that aborted and as a result the number of aborts drop significantly.

145   June 22, 1944 (1401-1725)

Col. Tacon leads today as the 359th flies a dive bombing mission against a railway bridge at Nanteuil, France, just north of Paris. Forty P-51s take off and five return early. The 370th FS drops twenty-four 500 lb. General Purpose bombs some of which bounce off the span without exploding. The 370th's bad day continues as Lts. Howard E. Grimes and Harold D. Hollis are both killed as a result of flak over the target. Lt. Vincent W. Ambrose reports seeing Grimes' Mustang catch fire, then hit the ground and explode. The P-51 flown by Ambrose is also damaged by flak but he makes it back to England and lands at Manston, where he is picked up by the Groups AT-6 hack.

146   June 23, 1944 (1810-2229)

Today the 359th provides area and withdrawal support for B-17s being sent to destroy the still standing bridge at Nanteuil, France. Col. Tacon leads forty-four Mustangs off and there are only two aborts. The Group arrives over its assigned area at 1930 and 24,000'. Only thirteen of the twenty-eight Forts sent to bomb the span actually drop their loads and they take so long doing it that the 359th's Mustangs are forced to return, due to low fuel, before providing withdrawal support for the B-17s. No contact is made with the Luftwaffe and the Group returns safely to England, where three P-51s from the 370th FS are forced to land at other bases because of low fuel. The 368th FS reports its P-51s were fired on three times by light bombers

147   June 24, 1944 (0613-1059)

Col. Tacon leads again as the 359th furnishes penetration, target and with-drawal support for B-24s blasting airfields in northern France. Forty-one Mustangs take off from East Wretham and four return early. Bomb dust obscures the results of the raid and one bomber is seen exploding over

Bretigny, after being hit by flak. Seven chutes are counted. One other Lib is lost today and no enemy fighters are encountered. The B-24s are escorted to St. Valery, on the coast, where the 359th turns back to strafe. One train is attacked south of Rouen by the 368th and 369th FSs, before the hunt is called off due to poor visibility. Claims are: 1-0 locomotive and 30-0 boxcars.

148   June 25, 1944 (0614-1225)

Maj. Daniel D. McKee, of the 370th FS, leads the first mission today which is penetration, target and withdrawal support for thirty-six B-17s dropping supplies and OSS personnel near Saillans, France. The code name of this mission is *Operation Zebra*. At 0920 each Fort drops twelve containers from 3,000' and four chutes are observed to not open. No enemy aircraft appear and no bombers are seen in trouble. Escort is broken north of Dijon, France at 1032.

149   June 25, 1944 (1717-2108)

Maj. Clifton Shaw, of the 368th FS, leads thirty-eight P-51s off on the days second mission, which is penetration and target support for B-24s scheduled to destroy the bridge at Nanteuil, France, there is only one abort from the 359th. R/V is made over Tronville at 1836 and 22,000'. The Liberators divert from their briefed course and fly directly across Paris, while the fighters skirt the area to avoid the flak. One B-24 is lost to the flak over Paris and no chutes are seen. The bombers then raid airfields to the south and west of Paris. The 359th returns without loss and the bridge at Nanteuil still stands.

*   June 26, 1944 (bad weather)

150   June 27, 1944 (1654-2055)

Lt.Col. William H. Swanson leads today and it's back to France as the 359th provides and escort and area support for B-24s bombing the marshalling yards at Criel. Thirty-five Mustangs leave East Wretham and three return early. R/V is made over Schouwen Island, Netherlands at 1740 and 24,000'. The Group is under MEW control. No bombing results are observable, other than black smoke over the target. One of five bombers lost today is seen hit by flak over Criel and there are no chutes. No contact is made with the Luftwaffe.

151 June 28, 1944 (0629-1054)

Lt.Col. Swanson leads again and the 359th flies penetration, target and withdrawal support for 378 B-24s heading for the marshalling yards at Saarbrücken, Germany. Thirty-seven P-51s take off and only one returns early. R/V occurs over Beaumont, Belgium at 0736 and 24,000'. The target is covered with black smoke after the raid making it impossible for the 359th to observe the results. One B-24 is lost and 125 are damaged by flak. Escort is dropped at 0943. No enemy aircraft are encountered and the Group returns without incident.

152 June 29, 1944 (0730-1234)

Maj. Chauncey S. Irvine is in the lead as forty P-51s take off to provide penetration, target and withdrawal support for B-24s bombing targets in the area of Hannover, Germany. Four of the Mustangs return early. R/V is made at 0835 and 26,000' over the Zuider Zee. Escort is specifically provided by the 359th for the Libs bombing Magdeburg but the bombers are strung out in poor formation, making effective escort impossible. Two bombers are seen lost to flak over the target, one exploding and the other one spinning down out of control. Several chutes are noted and three are fired on from the ground. An airfield north of Oscherleben is also bombed and several fires are observed there. At 1045 General Anderson orders the 359th to send out another flight of Mustangs to help escort stragglers back. The escort is dropped off the English coast and the 359th returns to base where Lt. James J. Lubien, of the 368th FS, makes an emergency landing and noses his P-51 over.

153 June 30, 1944 (1300-1650)

Today the 359th provides escort for B-17s bombing an airfield at Le Culot, Belgium, followed by dive bombing. As Lt. Harry F. Cuzner, of the 369th FS, is making his takeoff run; his P-51 loses power and he steers the faltering fighter onto a taxi-strip, averting a pileup. Of the forty P-51s making it off, four abort. Lt.Col. William H. Swanson leads today and R/V is made over Dixmude, Belgium at 1356 and 24,000'. Escort continues through the target, where no observations are made and out to the coast near Nieuport. The 359th then turns south to dive bomb a wooded area five miles northeast of Ypres, Belgium. The bombs are released from 7,000'

on a cluster of about twenty-five barracks, with what appears to be good results. Two Mustangs of the 370th FS receive minor flak damage.

By the end of June fifteen P-51D Mustangs have been delivered to East Wretham. Also only forty-six of the original eighty-six pilots remain on flying status.

* July 1, 1944 (bad weather)

154 July 2, 1944 (1129-1520)

Maj. Clifton Shaw, of the 368th FS, leads as the Group flies area support for B-24s blasting Noball targets in the Pas de Calais sector of France. While the patrol is maintained, from 1234-1420, two Liberators are seen exploding after being hit by flak near Abbeville. No chutes are seen coming from either bomber. Due to the cloud formations no bombing results are noted. No contact is made with the Luftwaffe and the 359th returns safely to base.

* July 3-4, 1944 (bad weather)

155 July 5, 1944 (0730-1059)

Col. Tacon leads today as the 359th flies support for B-24s hitting a Noball supply site in France. Forty-six Mustangs take off and six return early. The bombers are fifteen minutes late when R/V is made west of Le Harve, France. The bombing results are hidden by clouds and no enemy aircraft are encountered. Escort is dropped at 0947 over St. Valery and the Group makes a northeasterly sweep before exiting the French coast at Cayeux. No strafing is undertaken because of the fuel consumed while waiting for the bombers to arrive.

156 July 6, 1944 (0739-1437)

The first mission today is support for B-24s bombing the shipyards at Kiel, Germany. Col. Tacon leads forty-two P-51s off and only two return early. R/V is made west of Busum, Germany at 0915 and 25,000'. A heavy smoke screen hides the bombing results. The flak is heavy and three Libs are lost. No sign of the Luftwaffe. At 1030 on the return flight, thirty miles north of Borkum Island, one of the three B-24s lost on this mission is observed as nine of its crewmen bail out. Col. Tacon and his

Two photos showing P-51D CV-D 44-13762 being refueled. Left, S/Sgt. Ira J. Bisher fills the 92 gallon, left main fuel tank. Standing on his left is Cpl. John E. Conklin, the fuel truck operator. Right, S/Sgt. Kenneth S. Wilson fills the 85-gallon, fuselage tank. This tank (behind the pilot) was used early in the mission to eliminate the tail heavy condition it created. Modelers should look close at the mud splashed on the ventral scoop. This is what a Mustang operating from sod or PSP runways looked like when it rained or snowed. Mud also found its way inside the scoop clogging the radiator core. This led to overheating a situation remedied by converting a fuel truck into a water carrying decontaminator unit. By spraying water directly into the scoop a potential abort from a popped coolant plug was averted. This particular Mustang was flown regularly by Howard L. Fogg Jr. and John T. Gordon. Fogg named it *Moose Nose*; later it was renamed *Cookie*. This P-51 saw a lot of combat and the reader may find it interesting to trace the career of this and other fighters by checking the serial numbers in the Destruction Diary.

section circle the area for two hours and forty minutes calling ASR for help. The pilots drop their empty fuel tanks for the downed airmen to cling to, but by the time a British Wellington arrives and drops a dinghy all have perished. Meanwhile escort is dropped, forty miles off the English coast, at 1155 and the fighters return to base.

157 July 6, 1944 (1832-2202)

The second mission today, led by Maj. Clifton Shaw of the 368th FS, is area support under MEW control for B-17s and B-24s bombing Noball targets in the Pas de Calais sector and rail targets south of Paris, France. Forty-three Mustangs are put into the air but nine abort. R/V occurs over Cambrai, France at 1942 and 23,000'. The 359th FG is vectored three times but no contact is made with enemy aircraft. No bombing results are noted and no B-17s are lost. The 359th is released at 2100 and returns safely to East Wretham.

158 July 7 1944 (0650-1235)

Maj. Chauncey S. Irvine leads the Group on a scheduled penetration, target and withdrawal support mission for B-17s blasting the oil industry at Leipzig, Germany. The 359th fields forty-five Mustangs but fifteen return early. Visibility is poor as the Group nears the R/V point and the 368th FS joins up with B-24s to which they were not assigned west of Dummer Lake at 0830 and 26,000'. These bombers are headed for targets in the area of Asherleben, Germany and the 368th FS escorts them to and from their targets, where excellent bombing results are noted, with two oil dumps seen exploding. The 369th and 370th FSs R/V with the proper bombers at the same time and location of the 368th's R/V. These two squadrons observe good bombing results at Leipzig and several other targets. No contact is made with the enemy by the 359th FG and they return to base without incident.

Col. Tacon leads forty P-51s off on a scheduled penetration and withdrawal support mission for B-17s hitting targets in the vicinity of Auxerre, France. There are only two aborts today. R/V is made off the coast at St. Valery, France at 0629 and 24,000'. One minute later a Fort is hit by flak and explodes, with no survivors. At 0715, near Neufchatel, another B-17 is hit and no chutes are seen. A weather front is encountered about fifty miles inside France and the bombers elect to hit targets of opportunity. A bridge north of Rouen and an airfield northwest of Beauvais are hit with good results observed. Col. Tacon leads his section down to attack a train but it escapes into a tunnel. The last of the bombers are escorted out at 0815. No enemy aircraft are seen during the mission.

During the night the 359th's ground crews strip the invasion stripes from the upper surfaces of their Mustangs.

160   July 9, 1944 (1155-1530)

Today the 359th flies an area support mission under Type 16 control. Col. Tacon leads as forty-five Mustangs leave East Wretham. Only two of the fighters turn back. The Group begins its patrol in the area of Abbeville-St. Just-Rouen and Dieppe, France at 1305. Lots of RAF Lancasters and Spitfires plus 8th AF Mustangs and Thunderbolts are observed during the patrol, which ends at 1420. The 359th exits France at 1430, near Le Treport and arrive over East Wretham at 1527. Despite rain and poor visibility the Mustangs land safely.

Late in the evening a V-1 Buzz-Bomb flies over the base and explodes twelve miles to the north, at Ovington Parish, without inflicting any casualties.

*   July 10, 1944 (bad weather)

161   July 11, 1944 (1003-1622)

Col. Tacon leads as the 359th FG furnishes penetration, target and withdrawal support for B-24s raiding Munich, Germany. Forty-six fuel laden P-51s leave the turf at East Wretham and six abort. One hour and fifteen minutes into the mission Lt. Eugene F. Britton, of the 368th FS, becomes separated from his flight during an intense flak barrage and returns to base without an escort in his damaged P-51. R/V occurs over Germersheim, Germany at 1155 and 25,000'. The Libs are then taken to the target, where the bombing is done by radar. The flak is heavy and sixteen B-24s are lost. No enemy fighters are seen and the escort is dropped at 1451, near Helsen. Just prior to breaking escort Lt. Warren R. Newberg, of the 370th FS, has engine trouble and (his) Yellow Flight drops down to 10,000' to see if the Merlin will run any better. As they near Worms, Germany several trains are spotted in a marshalling yard. Lts. James H. O'Shea and Wilson K. Baker make one pass, with O'Shea destroying one locomotive and Baker damaging three more. While returning to base Lt. Bennie F. White, of the 370th, becomes lost in the undercast over the English Channel and fails to return. He is listed as MIA.

162   July 12, 1944 (1102-1722)

It's back to Munich again, providing penetration, target and withdrawal support for B-24s. Col. Tacon leads and forty-six P-51s take off, with six returning early. R/V is made once more over Germersheim, time 1252 at 25,000'. Red Flight from the 370th FS escorts an aborting B-24 from the R/V point and almost the entire distance back to England. After the target is hit Yellow Flight of the 370th escorts a damaged B-24 and P-51 back out. The 370th's Blue Flight escorts another crippled B-24 home from the vicinity of Aalen, Germany. White Flight of the 370th remains with the Libs until reaching a point east of Herson at 1610. The 359th FG encounters no enemy aircraft and returns safely to England, exiting the French coast near Dunkirk.

163   July 13, 1944 (0930-1424)

This is the third consecutive mission to Munich, Germany and the Group is scheduled to provide penetration, target and withdrawal support for the raiding B-17s. The base is completely socked in and the Group can't get off in time to furnish the penetration or target support. They do however get aloft in time to fly withdrawal support for the returning Forts. Maj. Clifton Shaw, of the 368th FS, leads the Group with four P-51s returning early out of the forty-one taking off. Shortly before R/V Lt. Thomas S. Lane, of the 368th FS, reports his Merlin is losing power and he turns back, with Lt. John S. Keesey as escort. Over the English Channel, near Bradwell Bay, Lane's engine begins smok-

The Royal Air Force operated high speed boats like the Sea Gull shown above left to rescue downed airmen from the English Channel and the North Sea. The similarity to the American PT Boat is apparent and top speed was on a par at 44 m.p.h. The three gun turrets contained two .303 caliber Browning machine guns each and were nearly identical to the turret mounted in the Lockheed Hudson bomber. In the right photo seated on the right is Lt. Jack H. Bateman of the 370th FS who was on detached service. Bateman transferred out of the 370th FS in May of 1944. Lt. Thomas S. Lane of the 368th FS was picked up by a RAF boat on July 13, 1944, after bailing out over the English Channel. BATEMAN

ing badly and he bails out at 800'. After twenty minutes Lane is picked up by an ASR launch. Meanwhile the Group makes R/V at 1105 and shepherds the bombers back to England. Lts. Wilson K. Baker Jr., Robert M. Callahan and James H. O'Shea, of the 370th FS, escort two straggling B-24s with wounded aboard, back to England. The trio runs interference to draw flak, then radio course changes to the bombers so they can avoid further punishment. O'Shea takes the B-24 he is escorting to the English mainland before he heads home, while Baker and Callahan take their crippled charge to Manston, England. The bomber crews later phone and write letters of appreciation to the trio of Mustang pilots, who are recommended for the Air Medal.

164   July 14, 1944 (0754-1255)

Maj. Chauncey S. Irvine leads the first mission today which is withdrawal support for B-17s dropping supplies and equipment to troops in southern France. Forty-three P-51s take off and seven return early. R/V is made at 1020 southeast of Vichy, France and the B-17s are escorted until they are just south of Beachy Head, England at 1220.

165   July 14, 1944 (1648-2015)

Capt. Raymond B. Janney III, of the 368th FS, leads a flight of four Mustangs on a weather reconnaissance mission, forty miles east of Paris. The mission is in preparation for a strike by the 364th FG. No enemy aircraft are encountered and the flight returns without incident.

* **July 15, 1944**

The 359th FG is released for maintenance and training.

166   July 16, 1944 (0638-1251)

Capt. Edwin F. (Fox) Pezda, of the 369th FS, leads today as the Group provides penetration, target and withdrawal support for B-17s going to Munich, Germany. Forty-five P-51s start out on this mission and fifteen return early. R/V is made at 0905, north of Aalen, Germany and the Forts are taken to the target and out. The visibility is poor and no bombing results are noted. The Luftwaffe is not encountered but the flak is intense and fairly accurate over Munich. On returning to base Lt. Donald S. Melrose, of the 369th FS, damages his P-51 slightly in a landing accident. The 359th's pilots report the worst weather yet encountered over the continent.

167   July 17, 1944 (0853-1407)

Col. Tacon leads today as the 359th flies area support for bombers hitting targets in northern France. Although forty-six Mustangs leave East Wretham eleven abort. The Group patrols in the Bray-sur-Seine area from 1030-1130 and then the 368th and 369th FSs provide top cover for the 370th FS, while they strafe. Claims are in the destruction diary. The Group then crosses out near Neiuport, Belgium at 1310.

168   July 17, 1944 (1905-2226)

The second mission today is area support for B-17s

Left, Lt. Lawrence Hector Bouchard of the 369th FS and his P-51B *Mary* IV-L 42-106906. Larry competed a 300-hour tour. Right, Lt. George F. Baker Jr. of the 368th FS and his P-51B *Little Liquidator* CV-H 42-106809. Baker destroyed 4.5 enemy aircraft in the air and picked up another 0.5 with a shared on the ground. Note the Invasion Stripes on his Mustang and those ragged edges.

and B-24s bombing Noball targets. Lt.Col. John B. Murphy, of the 370th FS, leads the Group and of the forty-nine Mustang taking off only seven return early, a noticeable improvement over the earlier mission. R/V is made over the Montdidier area at 2010 and the patrol, which is under MEW control, continues until 2145, when near Bruay a R/T is received stating that all bombers have left the area.

169   July 18, 1944 (0618-1052)

Col. Avelin P. Tacon leads the 359th as they provide penetration, target and withdrawal escort for B-17s hitting an oil refinery at Hemmingstedt, Germany. Forty-two Mustangs take off and only two abort. R/V occurs over Heligoland Island, Germany at 0808 and from 20-24,000'. Visibility is poor throughout the entire mission and the bombing is done by radar. No enemy aircraft are encountered and the escort is dropped at 1020 over the North Sea, near Great Yarmouth.

170   July 19, 1944 (0659-1310)

Lt.Col. William H. Swanson leads the 359th on a penetration, target and withdrawal support mission for B-17s bombing industrial targets at Ulm and Augsburg, Germany. Fifty-two P-51s set a course for Germany, but fifteen abort. R/V is made over Kemten, Germany at 0925 and from 25-28,000'. Four of the eleven bombers lost today are seen going down over the target area, one the victim of fighters and the other three falling to flak. Only one

chute is observed. Twenty-five enemy fighters make a single diving pass through the Forts and continue on to the deck, but in their haste to escape interception two of them collide. Two Me109s dive through the 368th FS and keep on going but the Mustangs maintain escort. A flight from the 368th observes a B-24, from the 466th BG, circling aimlessly, evidently on auto-pilot as no crewmen are seen. The 359th returns safely to base.

171   July 20, 1944 (0839-1411)

Capt. Edwin F. Pezda, of the 369th FS, leads fifty-four of the Group's Mustangs off on a penetration, target and withdrawal support mission for B-17s bombing the oil industry in the area of Leipzig, Germany. There are seventeen aborts today not related to combat, plus two early returns due to flak damage plus their escorts. R/V occurs at 1013, near Munstereifel and soon after Lts. John B. Hunter and Paul E. Olson, of the 368th FS, escort a flak damaged B-17 back to England. As the force approaches Leipzig from the south, about twenty-five enemy fighters attack the Forts from the rear. Five B-17s are lost and only one chute is seen. The 370th FS drops their tanks and dive after the bandits with the following results: Lt. Wilson K. Baker destroys a Me109 and the pilot bails out. Baker then damages a Fw190 that disappears into the clouds. F/O Luther C. Reese scores hits on a Me109 that begins smoking heavily before it too ducks into cloud cover. Reese is awarded a probable. Lt. Gordon M. Shortness is last seen near Gera, pursuing a Me109. He is listed MIA.

Lt. Elbert W. Tilton on the right and S/Sgt. George Dillard pose for the camera on *Mega Ann*, Tilton's Mustang. On July 24, 1944 Tilton shot down a German trainer, one of two air victories he would score before completing his tour.

172 July 21, 1944 (0734-1326, A) (0729-1324, B)
173

At the 0630 briefing Col. Tacon takes a hard line on aborts, affixing some very harsh names to those who shirk their duty. Today the 359th is divided into *A* and *B* groups for a double escort mission to Germany. *A* group provides target support for B-24s bombing Oberpfaffenhofen, with Maj. Niven K. Cranfill of the 369th FS leading, while *B* group furnishes penetration, target and withdrawal support for B-24s raiding Munich. Col. Tacon leads *B* group and of the twenty-eight Mustangs taking off in his group only two abort. *A* group fields twenty-four P-51s and has no aborts. R/V occurs near St. Wendel, Germany at 0924 for B group and 0926 for *A* group at 27,000'. One Lib is seen exploding over Munich, from flak, with no chutes. It is one of twenty-two lost today. At 1040, in the target area, seventy-five enemy fighters attack the bombers and Lt.Col. John B. Murphy, of the 370th FS, leads his section through the flak over Munich to intercept the bandits. All but one of the Me109s dive for the deck. The now lone 109 is intent on hammering a B-24, which it sets on fire before diving to escape the P-51s. Three chutes are counted from the stricken Liberator. Murphy follows the 109 in a high speed dive to below 10,000' and scores a victory, with the German pilot bailing out of his doomed fighter. On the way home, north of Landsberg, Germany at 1110, Yellow Flight of the 370th strafes an airfield with these results: F/O Walter W. Wiley one Ju88 destroyed and ten damaged plus two oil storage tanks and a locomotive damaged, Lt. Robert W. Siltamaki one Ju52 destroyed, three

He111s and two unidentified twin engine aircraft damaged, F/O Luther C. Reese one Ju88 destroyed. The P-51s flown by Reese and Siltamaki are both hit by 20mm fire during the attack. Siltamaki's P-51 is hit in the coolant system, then an oil line and the Merlin runs for one minute before it seizes. Siltamaki crash lands, striking his head on the gunsight during impact and is taken prisoner after hiding in the woods for two hours. Reese is not as lucky, he and his Mustang crash but Reese is listed as MIA. Wiley, the sole survivor of Yellow Flight, climbs to 30,000' and heads for base. On the way out he picks up a B-24 with two engines out and escorts it back to England. The B-24 is marked with green and white bands on the vertical stabilizers. Also during the trip out White Flight of the 368th FS strafes near Sedan, France claiming two locomotives destroyed and numerous railcars damaged. As White Flight passes over Lille, France Lt. Chester R. Gilmore's Mustang is hit during an intense barrage of flak. While crossing the English Channel the coolant gauge begins to fluctuate and the Merlin starts running rough. Over England the engine quits and catches fire and Gilmore rolls his 51 over and bails out near Wingham at 1315. He receives cuts to the head and a knee and ends up in a British hospital for observation until the end of the month.

* July 22, 1944 (bad weather)

174 July 23, 1944 (1645-2130)

Today the 359th FG furnishes penetration, target and withdrawal support for B-24s raiding airfields at Juvincourt and Laon, France. Col. Tacon leads the Group and of the fifty-three P-51s taking off seven abort. Due to 10/10 cloud cover no bombing results are observed. No B-24s are lost and no enemy fighters are encountered. On the way out a flight from the 368th FS, led by Lt. John B. Hunter, escorts a B-24 straggler, with yellow and black vertical tail stripes (93rd BG) and the name *Flying Fool* painted on the nose, out to the coast.

175   July 24, 1944 (0934-1457)

Col. Tacon leads the Group on a scheduled strafing mission to a jet airfield at Leipheim, Germany which is just east of Ulm. Forty-five Mustangs start out on this assignment. Visibility is poor and nine of the 368th FS's pilots fail to find their leader during assembly. These nine proceed to Germersheim, Germany where they fail to find the rest of the Group and return to England. Meanwhile the 359th arrives over the target area at 1155 and can't find the airfield due to a 10/10 overcast. After a twenty minute search the Group locates an opening in the overcast and drops down near Ulm, where they find a grass airfield. The 368th FS, led by Col. Tacon and supplemented by Yellow Flight from the 370th FS, executes an attack while the remaining P-51s provide top cover. Col. Tacon strafes a line of five glider/trainers during his first pass and damages a twin engine aircraft on his second pass. Lt. Joseph P. Kelsey damages a twin engine aircraft and a hangar, while Lt. Donald W. Chatfield damages two twin engine aircraft. F/O Emory C. Cook's P-51 is damaged by flak. Claims for the 370th FS include: Lt. Elbert W. Tilton, one hangar damaged and Lt. Warren R. Newberg, one hangar and several nearby railcars damaged. Five miles southwest of this target Yellow Flight encounters three biplane trainers over another airfield. Tilton flames one trainer while Newberg and Lt. Robert M. Callahan shoot down one each. Tilton then strafes the other two downed trainers, setting them afire.

*   July 25-27, 1944 (bad weather)

176   July 28, 1944 (0654-1303)

Col. Tacon leads as the Group flies penetration, target and withdrawal support for B-17s blasting the synthetic oil industry at Merseburg, Germany. Fifty-six Mustangs leave East Wretham and ten return

early. The Forts are twelve minutes late when R/V occurs north of Koblenz, Germany at 0835 and 26,000'. At 0932, near Sangerhausen, two B-17s are seen colliding, with one exploding and the other going down in a spin. Only three chutes are counted. At 0933 the target is bombed but no results are observed due to cloud cover. The force is south of Merseburg at 0940 when contrails are called in at 6 o'clock high. Col. Tacon identifies them as jet aircraft trails and becomes the first 8th AF pilot to observe a Me163. There are five 163s and two make a diving pass at the B-17s. Tacon leads his flight in an overhead frontal attack on the bandits, placing the Mustangs between the 'jetties' and the bombers. The Germans then turn into the Mustangs and quickly pass below them before a shot can be fired. One Komet continues in a dive while the other pulls up into the sun and ignites its rocket motor. This Komet is described as being rusty brown in color and highly polished. These Me 163s are part of J.G.400, making trial flights. Escort is dropped at 1030, south of Gotha and the Group strafes in the area of Hersfeld, about forty miles to the west. Claims are listed in the destruction diary. The 370th loses F/O Walter W. Wiley when his P-51 runs out of fuel ten miles south of Rotterdam, Netherlands at 1125. Wiley bails out safely but becomes a POW.

177   July 29, 1944 (0805-1232)

With Lt.Col. William H. Swanson in the lead the 359th provides penetration, target and withdrawal support for B-24s hitting Bremen, Germany. The Group puts up fifty-three P-51s and sixteen return early. R/V is made near Wangeroog Island at 0941 and 28,000'. Escort is maintained around the target but the bombing results are obscured by 10/10 cloud cover. The flak today is heavy but inaccurate and no Libs are seen to go down. The escort ends at 1150, just off the coast of England and due to the poor weather twenty-seven of the 359th's pilots are forced to land at other bases.

178   July 31, 1944 (1010-1615)

Maj. Niven K. Cranfill, of the 369th FS, leads the Group on an escort mission for B-17s raiding Munich, Germany where industrial sites are targeted. Of the fifty-one Mustangs to leave East Wretham thirteen abort. The R/V is made near Neustadt, Germany and the Forts are taken to Munich where the bombing is accomplished using

Top left, Capt. Robert W. Hawkinson of the 368th FS. On Aug. 2, 1944 he was forced to bail out over German occupied France. Hawkinson evaded capture, with the help of the French and was liberated several days later by advancing Allied troops. His P-51C, *Miss Janet* CV-N, 42-103386 is shown at the bottom. In the upper right is Lt. Ivan Brooks Hollomon "Rocky," of the 369th FS. Returning from the same mission on which Hawkinson was nailed Rocky gave the troops at East Wretham a show by making a precision one wheel landing after one of the main landing gear struts on his P-51 failed to extend. The Mustang suffered minor damage.

radar, due to 9/10 cloud cover. The flak is heavy and a B-17 is observed exploding over the target area at 1322. There are no chutes. No enemy fighters are encountered and White Flight of the 370th FS provides escort for a straggling Fort until 1415. Escort is broken by the group near Merzig, Germany at 1430.

179   August 1, 1944 (1200-1806, A) (1208-1836, B)

The 359th is divided into *A* and *B* groups with Capts. Edwin F. Pezda, of the 369th FS and William C. Forehand, of the 368th FS, leading. The job is to provide escort for 195 B-17s dropping supplies to the French underground in the southern part of France. The number of P-51s to take off increases to sixty-two but there are fourteen that return early. Lt. Cornelius J. Cavanaugh, of the 368th FS, has engine trouble on the way in over northern France and turns back. He bails out safely over Nuthampstead, England. *A* group makes R/V over Cruseilles at 1420 and 11,000' while *B* group makes R/V over Frangy five minutes later at 24,000'. No enemy aircraft are encountered and there is no flak over the target areas. No bombers are lost and *Operation Buick* is a success. As the 368th FS leaves the drop zone Lt. Elby J. Beal's Mustang develops a runaway prop at 11,000' and loses 2,000' while he tries to stall the prop into high pitch. With the Merlin running between 3,500 and 3,800 r.p.m. (redline is 3,000 r.p.m.) it begins to smoke heavily and Beal lands at a P-47 base in Normandy. While he stays overnight awaiting repairs to his P-51, German aircraft bomb the base and Beal spends most of the night in a foxhole. The following day the P-51 receives a new engine and prop governor. After testing is completed Beal returns to East Wretham.

180   August 2, 1944 (1422-1959)

Lt.Col. William H. Swanson leads today as the 359th furnishes escort for B-17s bombing fuel dumps near Paris, France to be followed by strafing at Rouen. Fifty-five Mustangs take off and eighteen abort. R/V is made over Coburg, France at 1551 and 21-24,000'. The results of the bombing are observed to be good. After escorting the bombers out to the coast the 359th turns back to carry out their strafing assignment. White Flight of the 368th FS, led by Capt. Robert W. Hawkinson, follows a railroad track looking for a target when they spot an army truck. As the flight attacks the vehicle, three flak positions cut loose on the them and Hawkinson's 51 is hit severely. He pulls up to 800' and bails out at 1840, northeast of Rouen. The landing results in a broken ankle which necessitates crawling to a nearby hedgerow for concealment. Hawkinson is amazed that he is not seen as several German soldiers pass within four feet of his hiding place on their way to inspect his crashed fighter. The next morning he hails a boy riding a draft horse, whose name is Gilbert Merriene, and asks (using his phrase book) for civilian clothing and help in hiding. Answering in the affirmative the boy leaves. Later a lad by the name of Rene Dehayes brings the change of clothes and directs him to a nearby wooded area where he hides until later that night. During the night the two boys return with their uncle, Monsieur Merriene, the mayor of Vieux Manoir. They carry Hawkinson to the farm of another family member where he is fed and bedded down in a barn. The next morning he is covered with hay in the back of a horse drawn cart driven by the mayor and after clearing a German checkpoint is taken to the farm of Madam Alexandrine Herbert, near Cauricourt. Here Hawkinson is provided with a place in a hayloft where he remains until mid-August, when retreating German troops begin filtering

On Aug. 4, 1944, three pilots from the 370th FS were interned in Sweden; Capt. Raymond B. Lancaster and Lts. Wilson K. Baker and Richard O. Rabb. Lancaster's P-51 began losing oil pressure over Schleswig and with Baker and Rabb as escort made for Sweden. This photo shows Lancaster posed with his P-51B *Galveston Gal*. Lancaster was of course a Texan. Col. Tacon was livid when informed three perfectly good aircraft and pilots were gone.

through the area. Fearing he might be discovered by these soldiers, Alexandrine moves the downed flier into her house. In late August the spearhead of a Polish armored division arrives and one of the tankers suggests that Hawkinson remain hidden until the main body of the division caught up. A couple of days later he is picked up by a Canadian Army medical unit. To end the mission of August 2, Lt. Ivan B. Holloman, of the 369th FS, arrives at base to find that one of his main landing gears will not extend. After two hours of unsuccessful attempts to force the gear down he makes a precise one wheel landing that results in very minor damage to the Mustang.

181   August 3, 1944 (1428-1925)

Lt.Col. John B. Murphy, of the 370th FS, leads the Group as they fly penetration, target and withdrawal support for B-24s scheduled to bomb V-1 storage dumps in the vicinity of Paris, France. Due to cloud cover over the primaries, targets of opportunity are hit. A good concentration of strikes are observed on an airfield at Evreux. No bombers are lost and no enemy fighters are encountered. Two 370th FS Mustangs are damaged while landing at base. Lt.Col. Murphy's P-51 noses over due to locked brakes, while the other P-51 is a total loss.

182 August 4, 1944 (1120-1725)

Lt.Col. William H. Swanson flies lead as the Group gives penetration target and withdrawal support for 401 B-17s raiding Peenemünde and Anklam, Germany. The 359th puts up fifty-two fighters today and only six abort. R/V is made over Kiel Bay at 1346 and 23,000'. Large clouds of smoke are observed rising from the targets and the flak is very light. Three Forts are lost today and no enemy fighters are encountered during the escort, which is dropped at 1540 near Eckernforde. Five minutes later, over Schleswig, Capt. Raymond B. Lancaster, of the 370th FS, radios his P-51 is losing oil pressure and that he is heading for Sweden. Lts. Richard O. Rabb and Wilson K. Baker escort Lancaster to the Swedish border and then turn for home. At 1600 Rabb and Baker are bounced by a Me110. Baker downs the 110, which crashes and burns. After the encounter Rabb and Baker's Mustangs are too low on fuel to get back to England and they too fly to Sweden. Lancaster's P-51 is destroyed in a crash landing after his engine quits, while Rabb and Baker land safely, with only fifteen gallons of fuel left in each of their fighters. All three pilots are sent back to the U.S. a few weeks later. On the way out Lt.Col. Swanson, plus the following pilots from the 368th FS, Lts. Donald W. Chatfield, Willis J. Cherry and John S. Keesey, strafe a twin masted schooner twenty miles north of Terschelling Island, Netherlands.

183 August 5, 1944 (1002-1447)

Today the 359th FG provides escort for B-24s blasting an airfield at Halberstadt, Germany. Maj. Edwin F. Pezda, of the 369th FS, leads forty-seven fighters off the turf at East Wretham and six return early. R/V occurs southeast of Cuxhaven, Germany at 1150 and from 24-27,000'. At 1210, between Bremen and Hamburg, Red Flight of the 369th FS engages six to eight Me109s with no markings. Lt. Frank W. Holliday damages a 109 while Lt. Harold R. Burt scores hits on another one that goes into a vertical dive. Burt follows it registering 630 m.p.h., as he pulls out at 500'. The 109 fails to recover, hits the ground and burns. At 1220 Red Flight spots about twenty Fw190s twenty miles off to the right of the bombers and they attack. Capt. Lester G. Taylor scores good hits behind the cockpit of a 190 that goes into an uncontrolled dive, its pilot probably dead. Meanwhile, also beginning at 1210, White Flight makes a diving attack on two Me109s. Maj.

Pezda chases a diving 109 and nails it. As he pulls up and over the fighter Pezda can see the pilot kicking the rudder pedals. The enemy pilot then bails out. Lt. Edwin L. Sjoblad also bags a 109 and its pilot bails out. The target is bombed visually and only one of the seventy-eight Libs dispatched is lost. On the way out Pezda strafes and destroys a locomotive between Linden and Sulingen.

184 August 6, 1944 (0933-1528)

Lt.Col. John B. Murphy, of the 370th FS, leads the Group today as they provide penetration, target and withdrawal support for B-17s bombing aircraft engine and diesel engine factories in the vicinity of Berlin, Germany. Forty-six P-51s take off but fifteen return early. R/V is made northeast of Berlin at 1230 and 26,000'. The Luftwaffe is up today but not engaged by the 359th. The bombing is done visually and with good results. Five B-17s are lost. Escort is broken at 1350, near Stade, Germany. The 369th and 370th FSs then strafe near Bucholz claiming 2-1 locomotives and 55-6 railcars. The Group exits the coast over Cuxhaven, Germany at 1415.

News is received by the Group that Lt. John H. Oliphint is back in England.

185 August 7, 1944 (1041-1735)

Lt.Col. William H. Swanson is in the lead as the 359th FG furnishes escort for B-17s blasting Montauban, France. Fifty-three Mustangs lift off from East Wretham and eight abort. R/V occurs south of Brive, France at 1310 and 20,000'. The bombing results are noted to be good, with hits made on thirty to forty wooden buildings and a huge oil fire started, sending black smoke to 15,000'. No bombers are lost and no enemy fighters are encountered. On the way out a flight from the 368th FS consisting of: Capt. William C. Forehand, Lt. Elby J. Beal and F/O Emory C. Cook, strafe a Tiger tank west of Le Mans. No vital hits are made on the heavily armored vehicle.

186 August 8, 1944 (1126-1609)

Today the Group provides area support for B-17s bombing enemy troop concentrations south of Caen, France, followed by strafing. Maj. Niven K. Cranfill, of the 369th FS, leads fifty-four Mustangs up and six return early. During the patrol, which starts at 1250, good bombing results are observed

Left, F/O Emory C. Cook, one of three pilots who strafed a Tiger tank near Le Mans, France on Aug. 7, 1944. On Aug. 8, 1944 Lt. Cornelius J. Cavenaugh, center, damaged a Fw190. On the same day Lt. Eugene F. Britton, right, shared in damaging 2 trucks.

at the Lisieux marshalling yards. Patrol has just been dropped at 1350 and the 368th FS is letting down to strafe, near Dreux, when they encounter twenty-five Fw190s. The 368th chases the Germans down to 3,000' and back to 15,000' when they are jumped by about thirty additional Fw190s. During the ensuing fight Lt. John S. Keesey destroys one Fw190, claims another as a probable and damages two more. Lt. Cornelius J. Cavenaugh claims one 190 damaged. The 368th loses two pilots, Lts. John C. Allen and Willis J. Cherry. Cherry receives severe burns to the right hand, left wrist and leg as his P-51 catches fire and crashes near Poix, where he is taken prisoner immediately. Allen is last seen near Dreux and is listed KIA. The ground claims for the 368th and 370th are listed in the destruction diary.

187   August 9, 1944 (0815-1340)

Lt.Col. John B. Murphy, of the 370th FS, is in the lead as the group furnishes penetration, target and withdrawal support for B-17s headed for Munich, Germany. Forty-five P-51s take off on this mission and eleven abort. R/V is made at Haguenau, France at 1006 and 27,000'. The weather progressively worsens as the force crosses Germany and many of the Forts hit targets of opportunity. At 1100, near Gunzburg just east of Ulm, the 368th

FS engages thirty enemy fighters that appear head-on out of the sun. Lt. John S. Keesey nails a Fw190 and its pilot jettisons the canopy before disappearing into the clouds. Keesey is awarded a probable. F/O Emory C. Cook expends 1,070 rounds of API on a Me109 to be awarded a damaged. At 1115 in the same area the 370th FS takes on twenty Me109s with the following results: Lts. Robert M. York, John W. Wilson and Frank O. Lux, one Me109 each destroyed, and Lt.Col. John B. Murphy, one Fw190 destroyed. Lt. Cyril W. Jones Jr., who is on his first mission, destroys a Me109 and damages another. Jones will have a meteoric combat record. In order for York to do battle today he has to secure the manual high blower switch in the *on* position with his neck-tie. The 369th FS destroys two locomotives and the Group returns without a loss.

188   August 10, 1944 (0911-1335)

Today the group is assigned a dive bombing mission against rail targets in the area from Bar-le-Duc to Strasbourg, France. Lt.Col. William H. Swanson leads the 359th, which puts up forty-nine P-51s, two of them returning early. The 368th FS attacks the marshalling yard at Bishwiller, France scoring twenty-five hits on the buildings and tracks. During the bombing Lt. Lester W. Hovden makes a quick 45° turn to line up with his target and over-

Brig.Gen. Edward W. Anderson of Wing selected East Wretham as the fighter base to be inspected by two Soviet officers on Aug. 9, 1944. Left to right beginning with the second man; Lt.Col. William H. Swanson, Maj.Gen. (Soviet A.F.) Ivan Skliarov, Brig.Gen. Anderson, Maj. (Soviet Army) T.T. Samarin, unidentified and Lt.Col. Grady L. Smith.

stresses his Mustang's bomb laden airframe. Both wings fold up and tear off. Hovden doesn't survive. Lt. Paul E. McCluskey is shot down by ground fire and dies as the 369th FS raids targets near Winden, Germany. The 370th FS attacks rail targets from 1120-1140 at Luneville, France and Lahr and Offenburg, Germany. Total claims for the day include: 16-11 locomotives, 3-30 railcars, 0-1 railway bridge, 1-0 highway bridge, 3-0 railway sheds, 1-0 switch tower, 1-0 truck and 2-0 warehouses.

The 369th FS suffers its second loss of the day as Lt. Lawrence A. Bearden, who is on a training flight, enters a dive from high altitude and fails to recover.

189   August 12, 1944 (0724-1358)

Maj. Chauncey S. Irvine leads the first mission today which is penetration, target and withdrawal support for B-17s raiding the marshalling yard at Metz, France. Forty-five P-51s leave East Wretham and six return early. R/V is made at 0916 over Fogeres, France at 25,000'. The bombing results are observed as excellent, no Forts are lost and the 359th FG makes no contact with the Luftwaffe. On the way out Lt. John T. Gordon, of the 368th FS, has engine trouble and makes an emergency landing in Normandy. Gordon returns after his P-51 is serviced.

190   August 12, 1944 (1536-1856)

The second mission today is dive bombing of the marshalling yard at St. Just, France. The Group manages to put up thirty-three Mustangs and four of them abort. Lt. Robert B. Hatter, of the 368th FS, leads after Lt.Col. John B. Murphy aborts over the English Channel with a radio problem. Time over the target is 1655 at 15,000'. The mission is a complete success with numerous strikes scored on the tracks and rolling stock. Claims include: 0-1 locomotives, 3-37 railcars, 3-1 trucks and 16 troops killed. The 359th returns intact.

Top left, Lt. John S. Keesey with groundcrew after returning from the mission of Aug. 8, 1944 during which he shot down a Fw190 and damaged three others. Top right, a profile of Keesey's P-51B *Tootser*, CV-V, serial number 42-106581. Middle right, assistant crewchief Sgt. Andrew Hardy poses with crewchief S/Sgt. Charles S. Doersom's charge. Note the red stripe on the wheel rim at the bottom. This mark should extend onto the tire and serves as a indicator for a tire that is slipping on the rim. Middle right, Ray Wetmore's P-51B shows its D-Day stripes to good advantage. Note the censor cut out the serial number (42-106894). Bottom left, Wetmore in his P-51B. A white "G" in the center of a victory cross denotes a ground kill. Bottom right, T/Sgt. Phillip Dupont (in vest) and S/Sgt. George M. Renaldi caught by the camera as Dupont services the radio equipment of a P-51B. Good aluminum drop tank details. DUPONT

Top left *Louisiana Heatwave* and immediately below *Heatwave* two of Captain Claude Crenshaw's three known Mustangs. Top right and immediately below two views of Lt. Charles H. Kruger's *Tojo-Peach*. Note this P-51C has a sliding Malcolm hood. Kruger is second from the left in the top photo and his crew chief S/Sgt. Roland Lutz is seated nearest the prop. Third row on the left Lt. Galen Ramser stands in the center of his ground crew posed in front of his second Mustang bearing the name *Zombie*. Third row on the right is Lt. Col. William H. Swanson's P-51B *Poison* with the code letters IV-Y. Bottom left is Flight Officer Thomas George Bur's P-51D *Big Noise from Winnetka*. Bottom right is F/O Bur.

On Aug. 10, 1944 the trio of 369th FS pilots above shared in damaging three loco's. Top left, Capt. Joseph W. Mejaski, also known as "Shoot everything that moves Mejaski". Top right, Capt. Jack Duane Stevens. Bottom right, Grant Michael Perrin.

191   August 13, 1944 (0808-1155, A)

The Group flies three missions today, two dive bombing and one escort. It is an auspicious day for the 359th, three missions with no losses and no aborts. The first effort is dive bombing directed at the rail system in the Paris, France area. Capt. William C. Forehand, of the 368th FS, leads twenty-five P-51s designated as *A* group on this mission. The marshalling yard at Haux and a tunnel east of Voissy are bombed and numerous targets strafed. Lt. Donald W. Chatfield, of the 368th makes a forced landing on the Normandy beachhead landing strip, but he returns later in the day.

192   August 13, 1944 (1110-1440, B)

The second mission today is flown by *B* group which also consists of twenty-five Mustangs. Maj. Niven K. Cranfill, of the 369th FS, leads this mission which is penetration, target and withdrawal support for B-17s bombing battle area targets at Rouen, France. R/V is made west of St. Aubin, France at 1219 and 21,000'. At least fifteen fires are observed in the target area as a result of the bombing. One Fort is seen going down, a victim of the flak, with five chutes counted. No contact is made with enemy aircraft.

193   August 13, 1944 (1704-2055)

Mission three has twenty-four Mustangs led by Lt. Charles V. Cunningham, of the 370th FS, returning to the Paris area for more dive bombing. A bridge over the railroad ten miles west of Rambouillet is hit along with tracks along the route. Cunningham has a 500 lb. bomb that fails to release and heads back to base. As he arrives over East Wretham, at 2015, the bomb falls harmlessly on the field. The base is then closed for three hours while the

On Aug. 16, 1944 the 370th FS made history by claiming the first two Me163s destroyed in aerial combat. A third 163 would fall before the guns of Ray S. Wetmore, also of the 370th FS, on Mar. 15, 1945 which also happened to be the only enemy aircraft shot down by VIII Fighter Command that day. Only five Komets were claimed by P-51 pilots and three of those going to the same squadron is quite an achievement. Top left, Lt.Col. John B. Murphy CO of the 370th FS from Mar. 16, 1943 to Sept. 1, 1944. Top right, Lt. Cyril W. Jones Jr. While both pilots were simultaneously engaging the enemy it was Murphy who scored the first kill. Murphy's gun camera footage was quickly sent to Wing for viewing and the press worldwide, Stars and Stripes included, who featured tremendous articles covering the combat. Almost unnoticed Lt. Jimmy Shoffit damaged a third Komet that day. Cyril Jones' combat career was short but glorious. In sixteen missions he destroyed six enemy fighters in the air and five aircraft on the ground. In stark contrast to this record, other pilots completed 300 hour tours without ever being in a position to score a single kill. Murphy in comparison completed his tour with 6.25 aerial kills and none on the ground. Jones also destroyed one locomotive and shared in the destruction of twelve more. Those who knew him said you could tell Jones wouldn't last long, he threw himself into battle with a total disregard of his chances of survival.

unexploded bomb is disposed of. Other claims are: 10-10 railcars, 2-4 vehicles, 0-1 tank, 0-1 water tower and 0-1 flak tower. No contact is made with the Luftwaffe.

The first seven P-51D-10 Mustangs are delivered to the 359th FG.

194   August 14, 1944 (0916-1506)

Today the 359th FG furnishes penetration, target and withdrawal support for B-17s blasting airfields in the vicinity of Stuttgart, Germany. Maj. Edwin F. Pezda, of the 370th FS, leads forty-eight P-51s off but thirteen return early. R/V is made over Commercy, France at 1110 and 23,000'. Good bombing results are observed on two airfields. On the way back a Mustang from the 368th FS makes a pass on

six trains, running end to end, fifteen miles east of Hirson, France and is driven off by heavy machine-gun fire. Claims made by the 368th FS include: 1-0 locomotive, 1-0 staff car and 0-1 truck. Lt. Milton S. Merry, of the 370th FS, claims four boxcars damaged near Beaumont and twenty more near Mons, France.

A B-24 on a training flight crashes near East Wretham. There are no casualties.

195   August 15, 1944 (0832-1337)

The 359th is divided into A and B groups to provide penetration, target and withdrawal support for B-17s bombing an airfield at Frankfurt, Germany. A group is led by Lt. Luster H. Prewitt, of the 369th FS, while Lt. Col. William H. Swanson leads

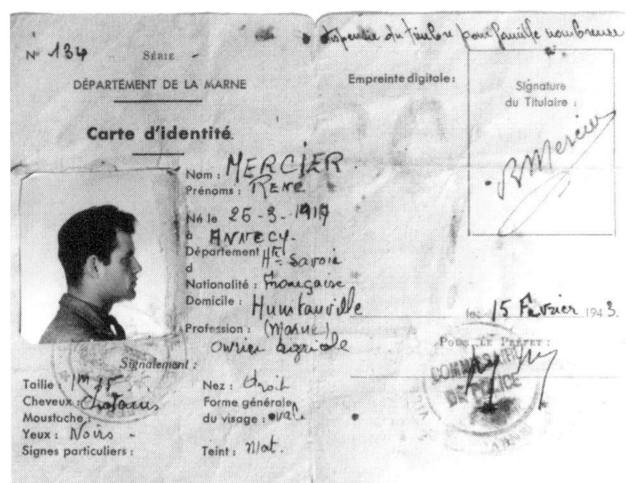

N° 134   Série —

DÉPARTEMENT DE LA MARNE

Empreinte digitale :

Signature du Titulaire :

Carte d'identité

Nom : MERCIER
Prénoms : René
Né le 25-3-1919
à ANNECY
Département d Hte Savoie
Nationalité : Française
Domicile : Humtauville
Profession : (Marne) ourrier agricole

Signalement :
Taille : 1m75
Cheveux : Chatains
Moustache :
Yeux : Noirs —
Signes particuliers :

Nez : droit
Forme générale du visage : oval
Teint : Mat.

le 15 Février 1943.

Pour LE PRÉFET :
COMMISSAIRE DE POLICE

Top left, Lt. Rene L. Burtner, of the 369th FS, a victim of flak while strafing on Aug. 18, 1944. Burtner was hidden by the French, liberated by Patton's 3rd Army and returned. Top right photo shows the inside of Burtner's bogus identity card which the underground made for him under the name Rene Mercier. Bottom left, MIA as a result of being nailed by flak over the same target that got Burtner was Lt. Donald Steward Melrose, also of the 369th. *Agony Wagon* was his P-51's name but what you see in the photo was applied to the negative. In the bottom right position is Lt. Theophalus T. Williams, of the 370th FS. Williams was KIA on Aug. 17, 1944.

B group. Of the forty-nine P-51s taking off this morning eleven abort. R/V occurs over Valenciennes, France at 0945 and 23,000'. The bombing results are observed as good. The Luftwaffe makes an appearance but the 359th FG maintains escort while other fighter groups counter the attacks. Lt. Frank A. Westall's Mustang loses manifold pressure near Namur, Belgium at 1000 and two other pilots, of the 370th FS, escort Westall out to a point twenty miles south of Dunkirk. With his P-51 only able to maintain 115 m.p.h., Westall then bails out, but is later reported killed. Escort is broken over Schouwen, Netherlands at 1250.

Because there were eleven aborts today Lt.Col. Swanson orders a meeting of the pilots that returned early to discuss their reasons for doing so.

At 1805 the air raid alarm is sounded as a buzz-bomb nears the base. It explodes harmlessly to the south.

196   August 16, 1944 (0757-1310)

Lt.Col. John B. Murphy, of the 370th FS, leads the Group as they provide penetration, target and withdrawal support for B-17s bombing the oil industry at Bohlen, an airfield at Delitzsch and aircraft industries at Halle and Schkeuditz, all in the same area of Germany. Forty-seven Mustangs leave East Wretham and fourteen return early. At 1000, near Einbeck, Germany White Flight of the 369th FS is flying at 28,000' heading for R/V at Erfurt, when three Me109s make a diving head-on pass at them. Maj. Niven K. Cranfill scores hits on one, follows it down and watches it hit the ground and explode. At 1020, just before R/V is made, Blue Flight of the 370th FS engages four Me109s. Lt. Frank O. Lux fires a long burst into a 109, which sheds some parts and begins loosing coolant. Lux follows the damaged fighter down and watches it go into aerial cartwheels, throwing the pilot clear. At 1045 southeast of Leipzig, as the Forts are being escorted out, Lt.Col. Murphy notices a contrail climbing rapidly towards the rear of a straggling B-17 named *The Outhouse Mouse*. Murphy overtakes the Me163 after it passes the B-17 and scores hits before he turns to avoid overshooting his prey. Lt. Cyril W. Jones Jr., Murphy's wingman, catches the 163 in a half-roll and fires a burst into the cockpit for the kill. Meanwhile Murphy engages a second Komet firing a long burst into its fuselage, causing an explosion that blows off the top of the fuselage from the cockpit back. Murphy's victory precedes Jones' and he becomes the first Allied fighter pilot to shoot down a Me163 Komet. Murphy follows the stricken rocket fighter down until he spots another one but opts to head for England since he is alone and low on fuel. During this time Lt. Jimmy C. Shoffit breaks into a 163 that is making an attack on a B-17 and during the brief engagement scores some hits on the Komet's right wing. The 163 escapes by making a power-on dive for the deck. Pilots of the 359th witness the destruction of four of the ten B-17s lost today and the bombing results are observed to be excellent.

197   August 17, 1944 (1240-1629, A)

Two missions are flown today, with the 359th split into *A* and *B* groups to carry out dive bombing and strafing assignments in France. *A* group, which starts out with twenty-six Mustangs and has four that return early, is assigned rail targets from Rouen

northeast to Amiens. Lt. Luster H. Prewitt, of the 369th FS, leads the group after Maj. Chauncey S. Irvine aborts. Lt. Will D. Burgsteiner, of the 370th FS, hits a tree while strafing a train and shears off a wingtip. Blue Flight, which he is leading at the time, escorts him back to base, landing at 1605. Mission claims include: 3-13 locomotives, 0-31 railcars, 9-10 trucks, 1-0 armored car, 1-1 bridges and 1-0 flak tower. An airfield at Grandvillers is bombed by the 368th FS.

198   August 17, 1944 (1231-1619, B)

The twenty-seven Mustangs of *B* group are given the area from Rouen southeast to Beaumont. Lt.Col. William H. Swanson leads this group and there is only one abort. Lts. Jimmy C. Shoffit and Theophalus A. Williams, both from the 370th FS, are jumped by four Fw190s, near Nogent, while making a pass on some trucks. Shoffit gets a quick shot at one of the bandits and then manages to shake a 190 on his tail, even though his bombs will not jettison. Williams is killed. Claims for this mission include: 0-12 boxcars and 1-5 trucks.

199   August 18, 1944 (1112-1753)

Maj. Niven K. Cranfill, now of the 368th FS, leads the 359th FG as they furnish penetration, target and withdrawal support for B-17s raiding an air field at St. Dizier, France. Fifty Mustangs take off on this mission and there are no aborts. R/V is made at 1245 and from 14-17,000' over Port-En-Bassin. The bomber formations are noted to be excellent, as are the bombing results, with ammo and fuel dumps seen exploding. No B-17s are lost and no contact is made with enemy aircraft. After the Forts have cleared the target area the 369th FS strafes an airfield with these results: Lt. Rene L. Burtner three Me109s destroyed plus one Ju88 and Ju52 damaged, Lt. Claude J. Crenshaw, one Ju88 and Ju52 destroyed plus one Ju88 damaged and Maj. Edwin F. Pezda, two Ju88s damaged. Lt. Donald S. Melrose is downed by flak on his second pass across the field and is listed MIA. As Burtner finishes his second pass and exits the target, he strafes a water tower, then turns to the right and rakes a factory. Burtner then starts to rejoin his flight and is hit in the coolant system by flak. Four to five gun emplacements are then strafed by Burtner before his P-51's engine begins to smoke and vibrate badly and he is forced to bail out twenty miles south of

St. Dizier. The French hide the downed pilot for more than a week before the lead elements of Gen. Patton's 3rd Army arrive and Burtner joins them for two days. On the second day a convoy is sent to the rear and Burtner is assigned the position of a machine-gunner on the top of an escorting tank. After spending the night in Troyes and then hitching a ride to Orleans, where B-24s are flying in shipments of flour from England, Burtner gets on a return flight.

***   August 19-23, 1944 (bad weather)**

200   August 24, 1944 (0900-1448, A) (0902-1443, B)
201

The 359th is divided into *A* and *B* groups today, with Majs. Edwin F. Pezda and Niven K. Cranfill leading respectively. Pezda takes his group on a penetration, target and withdrawal support mission for B-17s hitting Kolleda, Germany. Of the twenty-five Mustangs making up *A* group ten abort. Good bombing results are noted on an airfield near Kolleda. The bomber formations are poor today, making escort difficult. One of the sixteen Forts lost today is seen disintegrating over Gera. Four chutes are counted and one collapses after the crewman falls out of his harness.

Cranfill takes *B* group on a penetration, target and withdrawal support mission for B-17s blasting Weimar, Germany. Thirty Mustangs are in this group and only three return early. Excellent results are observed as the Forts wipeout an armaments and a radio factory plus causing substantial damage to a large number of barracks.

The 359th encounters no enemy aircraft at either target area. On the way out Lts. Merle B. Barth and Eugene F. Britton, of the 368th FS, share in the destruction of a locomotive south of Egmond, Netherlands and Barth leaves an armed trawler sinking in the North Sea.

202   August 25, 1944 (1003-1557)

Lt.Col. John B. Murphy, of the 370th FS, leads the Group on a penetration target and withdrawal support mission for B-17s bombing Peenemünde, Anklam and Neubrandenburg, Germany. Fifty-three P-51s leave East Wretham this morning and eight return early. R/V is made off Hjaeln Bay at 1210 and 27,000'. Good bombing results are noted at all of the targets, especially the airfield at Neubrandenburg. No enemy aircraft are encountered. On the way out Lt. David B. Archibald, of the 368th FS, drops to the deck because his Merlin is cutting out at high altitude. In the vicinity of Güstrow, Germany from 1300-1345 Archibald first strafes and destroys a single engine, high wing monoplane on an airfield and then destroys a locomotive on a nearby track. A few minutes later heading out over Weeklenburg Bay, still on the deck, he strafes a Maasz class destroyer scoring numerous hits on the bridge and as he pulls up and over the ship his Mustang's left wing severs a radio mast.

203   August 26, 1944 (1013-1430)

Today the Group furnishes penetration, target and withdrawal support for B-17s raiding Gelsenkirchen, Germany. Out of fifty P-51s taking off on this mission six abort. During takeoff Lts. John W. McAllister and Emory G. Johnson, of the 370th FS, taxi into each other, with minor damage resulting. Lt.Col. William H. Swanson leads the Group and R/V is made, with the help of MEW control, over Alkmaar, Netherlands. The bombing results are not observed although the drop was made visually. There is no sign of the Luftwaffe reported by any operating 8th AF fighter group. Three Forts are lost to flak, which is intense but mostly inaccurate. The 368th FS escorts several crippled B-17s out to Egmond, Netherlands.

204   August 27, 1944 (1150-1735)

Maj. Edwin F. Pezda, of the 370th FS, leads fifty-three Mustangs off today and only three return early. The Group is scheduled to fly penetration, target and withdrawal support for B-17s bombing Berlin, Germany but due to heavy cloud formations over northern Germany the bombers are recalled before R/V is made. Of the 371 Forts dispatched to Berlin only 144 manage to bomb targets of opportunity, in the vicinity of Wilhelmshaven, before returning to England. The 359th FG proceeds to the Münster-Osnabruck area of Germany, where the following claims are made from 1500-1600, 368th FS: 5-10 locomotives, 0-5 coach cars, 0-5 boxcars and 0-1 tugboat. 369th FS: 4-0 locomotives, 0-5 coach cars, 0-1 tugboat and 0-1 barge. 370th FS: 7-1 locomotives, 0-68 railcars, 0-1 switch house, 2-0 trucks and 0-1 tug- boat. Lt. Lawrence A. Zizka, of the 370th, scores the only aerial victory made by any 8th AF fighter group today when he bags a twin

Aug. 27, 1944, was a good day for strafing and most of the pilots on this page added to the score. Top left, Maj. Edwin Felix Pezda, "Fox" or "Swami" to his friends, one loco destroyed and one barge damaged. Top center, Lt. Roger Winston Porter, shared in the destruction of two locos, a tugboat, and damaged three more tugboats. Top right, Lt. James H. O'Shea shared in the destruction of five locos and damaging 39 boxcars. Bottom left, Lt. John W. McAllister Jr. on the left, (Capt. Rene L. Burtner on the right) shared in the destruction of two locos, two trucks and damaging 15 boxcars. Bottom right, Lt. Harold Ralph Burt, shared in the destruction of two locos. Burt would be KIA on Sept. 17, 1944.

engine aircraft near Münster. One crewman escapes the aircraft after it crash-lands and starts to burn. The 370th also suffers the Group's only loss today, when Lt. Paul E. Sundheim becomes separated from Green Flight near Münster and is later shot down by ground fire over the Netherlands. Sundheim is quickly taken prisoner and ends up in Stalag Luft 1.

205   August 27, 1944 (1023-1530)

The second mission today is escort for three RAF Warwick ASR aircraft, that are searching for a downed bomber crew. Lt. Chester R. Gilmore, of the 368th FS, leads four P-51s from his squadron on the mission, which is over the North Sea. Visibility is poor and the flight is uneventful.

206   August 28, 1944 (0723-1130)

Lt.Col. William H. Swanson leads the Group on a strafing mission in the area from Bar-le-Duc, France to Sarrbrücken, Germany. Fifty Mustangs lift off from East Wretham and only two abort. One of those to abort is Lt. John W. McAllister of the 370th FS, who makes a dead-stick landing at Bentwaters, England after his engine seizes. The Mustang sus-

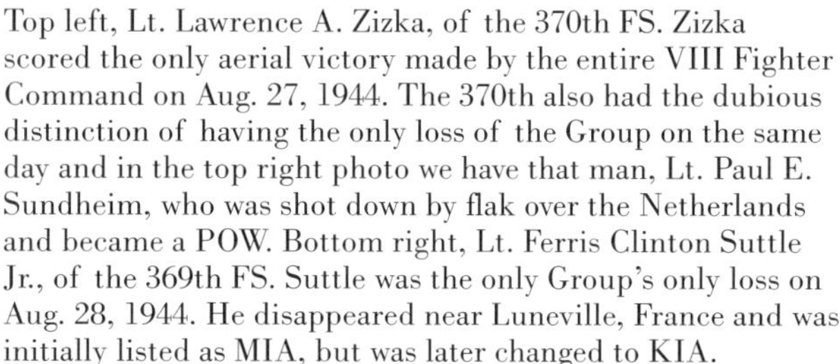

Top left, Lt. Lawrence A. Zizka, of the 370th FS. Zizka scored the only aerial victory made by the entire VIII Fighter Command on Aug. 27, 1944. The 370th also had the dubious distinction of having the only loss of the Group on the same day and in the top right photo we have that man, Lt. Paul E. Sundheim, who was shot down by flak over the Netherlands and became a POW. Bottom right, Lt. Ferris Clinton Suttle Jr., of the 369th FS. Suttle was the only Group's only loss on Aug. 28, 1944. He disappeared near Luneville, France and was initially listed as MIA, but was later changed to KIA.

tains moderate damage. Time over the target is 0915 at 22,000'. Claims are, 368th FS: 17-0 locomotives, 0-109 boxcars, 0-37 coach cars, 0-4 oil tank cars, 2-3 trucks, 0-1 armored car and two soldiers hiding in a field killed. Lt. Oscar R. Faldmark destroys the only aircraft today when he strafes a Ju88 and leaves it burning near Saarbrucken. Claims made by the 369th FS include: 16-4 locomotives, 2-35 boxcars,1-0 truck and trailer and 1-0 flak gun. The 369th suffers the days only loss when Lt. Ferris C. Suttle disappears near Luneville, France and is listed MIA, later amended to KIA. The 370th FS claims include: 12-2 locomotives, 10-72 boxcars, 0-1 roundhouse, 0-1 switch tower, 1-0 oil storage tank and 5-0 trucks. On returning to England Blue Flight from the 370th FS stops at Martlesham Heath because of the bad weather reported at base. Before leaving Lt. Frank O. Lux has the tailwheel on his P-51 repaired. While

taking off he crash-lands, totaling the Mustang and getting badly shaken in the process. Lux returns to East Wretham the next day.

207   August 30, 1944 (1424-1922)

Today the Group flies penetration, target and withdrawal support for B-17s raiding Kiel and Bremen, Germany. Forty-seven P-51s take off and nine return early. Maj. Chauncey S. Irvine leads the Group and R/V is made over the North Sea at 1545 and from 23-28,000'. Dense layers of cloud cover the route making observation of the bombing results impos-

Top left, Capt. Howard Fogg Jr's. P-51D-5NA *Moose Nose* CV-D 44-13762 (note moose painted on fuselage just forward of the canopy). Bottom left, Lt. John T. Gordon poses with *Moose Nose* now named *Cookie*. Gordon came to the 368th FS a month after Fogg went to the 370th FS. This photo must have been taken early in November of 1944 for if you look next to Gordon's right hand there sits a full green nose P-51. Above, part of the ground crew of *Pegelin* P-51D-5NA IV-I 44-13669. Left to right are; crew chief S/Sgt. Walter W. Wadley, line chief M/Sgt. Lloyd S. Beck, assistant crew chief Pvt. John P. Babola and fueler M. Rhiensheld. *Pegelin* was one of the first D models acquired by the group and saw action during the Normandy Invasion. This Mustang was flown by Capt. Glenn C. Bach who became the CO of the 101st FS, Mass. ANG from March 1949 to November 1951and then became a test pilot for Republic Aviation. The name *Pegelin* and the shamrock is repeated on the opposite side of the nose in the same location and sequence.

sible. No Forts or escorting fighters are lost and the Luftwaffe is a no-show. Escort is dropped at 1805.

* August 31, 1944 (no combat mission)

Capt. Benjamin H. King, of the 368th FS, leads six pilots from his squadron to a practice escort with two boxes of B-17s (36). The fighters are ten minutes late and the Forts are not on course. Radio contact is made with the B-17s but no R/V.

208 September 1, 1944 (0855-1355)

Lt.Col. John B. Murphy, of the 370th FS, leads the Group on an escort mission for B-17s scheduled to bomb Ludwigshafen, Germany. The 359th FG puts up fifty-two Mustangs, most of which are now 'D' models, with only one abort. Two of the three bomber boxes abort in response to a recall, due to 10/10 cloud cover. The third box presses on while the 359th conducts a futile search for them. The Group is then recalled and on returning the P-51 flown by Lt. Edward G. Kaloski, of the 368th FS, develops a runaway prop, followed by a loss of oil pressure. Kaloski crosses out over the French coast near Cayeux at 1150

and 9,000'. His wingman, Lt. Ray A. Boyd, looses sight of the doomed fighter as Kaloski bails out over the English Channel.

209 September 2, 1944 (1117-1500)

Capt. Benjamin H. King leads, as he and five other pilots from the 368th FS carry out an ASR search for Lt. Edward G. Kaloski. Visibility is hampered by rain during the four hour flight but Kaloski's dinghy is found and a fix is made on its location. It is later learned he sustained a broken leg while bailing out, paddled his dinghy five miles back to the French coast and lay on the beach three days, before being discovered by fishermen. He was then reported hospitalized in Kingston, England.

The petro-chemical industry at Ludwigshafen, Germany. Cities producing fuels were top priority targets and Ludwigshafen received the attentions of the 8th AF three missions in a row on Sept. 1, 3 and 5 of 1944. Another raid was flown against this target on Oct. 19, 1944. Gasoline refineries are not as easy to destroy as you might imagine. Many facilities like the one shown above were bombed and back at almost full capacity within a week or two. Merseburg, Germany was another city producing fuel for the Reich and the 359th FG provided escort for bombers striking that target seven times, a clue to the importance assigned to destruction of fuel production.

210   September 3, 1944 (0900-1455)

Today B-17s are headed for Ludwigshafen, Germany again, to hit the oil industry. Capt. William C. Forehand, of the 368th FS, leads the Group as they furnish escort. Of the fifty-one Mustangs leaving East Wretham today five return early. The 359th crosses in near Dunkirk at 0950 and makes R/V over Meaux at 1022 and 22,000'. Due to cloud cover the bombing results are obscured. No enemy aircraft are encountered and the flak is light. Lt. Albert E. Wolfe, of the 370th FS, lands in Normandy and returns on the 9th of September, after having fuel lines repaired.

*   September 4, 1944 (bad weather)

211   September 5, 1944 (0842-1411)

Lt.Col. William H. Swanson leads as the 359th FG furnishes escort for B-17s bombing Ludwigshafen for

The P-51B of Lt. Oscar R. Faldmark didn't make the mission of Sept. 5, 1944, because of this takeoff accident.

this the third mission in a row. Lt Oscar R. Faldmark of the 368th FS crashes during takeoff and his P-51 sustains minor damage. Lt. Eugene F. Dauchert, also from the 368th, cracks up at the end of the runway but escapes injury. Of the fifty Mustangs that do become airborne only three abort. While crossing the French coast, near Dunkirk, the Mustangs flown by Lts. Elby J. Beal and George J. Kosc, once again from the 368th, are hit by flak but continue on. R/V occurs north of Chalons-sur-Marne, France at 1032 and 25,000'. The B-17s are taken to the target, where three Me262s are sighted, then back out as far as Reims, France where the escort is broken at 1215. Lt. John S. Keesey, of the 368th, escorts a flak damaged B-17 out, until his fuel runs low. Other Mustangs then shepherd the Fort to the coast.

* **September 6,7, 1944 (bad weather)**

212   September 8, 1944 (1300-1723)

Today the Mustangs of the 359th and 352nd FGs are scheduled to provide escort and top cover for the Thunderbolts of the 56th and 353rd FGs, which are to strafe transportation targets in western Germany. Maj. Edwin F. Pezda, of the 369th FS leads the Group today and of the fifty-one P-51s leaving East Wretham only one returns early. A R/T from the 56th and 353rd relates that they have encountered a heavy storm and cannot make the R/V. At 1500 the 359th FG begins hunting targets and two flights from the 368th FS strafe an airfield near Cronberg, Germany. Lt. Joseph M. Ashenmacher destroys one Ju52 and damages a second, Lt. Chester R. Gilmore burns a Ju52 and Lts. George F. Baker Jr., Clifford L. Bartlett and Robert E. Benefiel share in the destruction of a

third Ju52. Other claims include: 33-14 locomotives, 3-68 railcars, 22-19 trucks, 0-6 staff cars, 1-1 motorcycles, 2-2 half-tracks, 5-0 vehicles, 1-0 cannon and 0-1 radar station. Lt. Lawrence A. Zizka, of the 370th FS lands at Amiens, France with a cable dangling from his P-51s wing, after being hit by flak. Zizka flies back to England on a C-47 and returns to base the next day.

Although the 359th FG suffers no losses today, Fighter Command is going to ban freelance strafing by P-51s. Losses while strafing have become unprofitable.

213   September 9, 1944 (0844-1350)

The 359th FG furnishes escort for B-24s bombing the marshalling yard at Mainz, Germany. Lt.Col. William H. Swanson leads today and fifty-two P-51s take off with only one returning early. R/V is made southeast of Namur, Belgium at 1000 and 25,000'. At 1045 a Lib is seen hit by flak over the target and goes down in flames. The 370th FS notes the bombing results to be good. Another B-24 goes down east of St. Hubert , Belgium at 1145 and six chutes are counted. No enemy aircraft are encountered today.

214   September 10, 1944 (0908-1438)

Today's mission is penetration, target and withdrawal support for B-24s going to Stuttgart, Germany. The Group puts up forty-nine P-51s and five return early. R/V is made at 1120 just after the bombers have hit their targets. At 1140, northwest of Stuttgart, Lt. Kenneth L. Hobson, of the 369th FS, is diving through a light over-cast at 5,000' in search of reported bandits, when he spots two fighters. Despite being unable to jettison his drop tanks, Hobson bounces them as they break in two directions. As he

While death and destruction were confronted at East Wretham life went on and as a part of that celebration there were several weddings. Left, Sgt. Edwin J. Slusser of the 370th FS wed Cpl. Anne H. Augusta, a WAAF, on Sept. 3, 1944. The ceremony was performed by Chaplain Wilbur C. Zeigler at St. Ethelbert's Church. (Right) In an earlier ceremony Sgt. James R. Underwood, a 370th photographer, married Miss Freda Newton of Thetford on April 8, 1944. They were blessed with a daughter before sailing to the U. S. Other marriages include:

Sept. 1944 Sgt. Paul Chester of the 370th wed Miss Mary C. Bergin of London in St. Mary's Catholic Church.

Nov. 3, 1944 Pvt. George W. Wilkes of the 369th wed Miss Mary Ann McKenzie.

Nov. 11, 1944 Sgt. Harold K. Stewart of the 369th wed Miss Betty Mable Marco while Sgt. Mathew Babola of the 370th wed Miss Sadie Harris in London.

Nov. 12, 1944 Cpl. Donald M. Black of the 369th wed Cpl. Nora M. Wright, a WAAF serving in Her Majesties Forces.

Mar. 1945 Cpl. Edward A. Johanson of the 370th wed Miss Mary Ann Landers in Our Lady of the Rosary Church in Marylebone, London. Father J. P. Murphy performed the rite. Pvt. Robert W. Macigewski of the 370th wed Miss Olive Maud Sturgeon in The Parish Church in Wretham.

Mar. 31, 1945 S/Sgt. Francis E. Davis of the 370th wed Miss Marion Watson in the Nanse of Cockpen, Midlothian County, Scotland.

scores hits on his first prey the other fighter crosses in front of the P-51. Hobson then breaks after the second fighter and again scores hits as the bandit makes evasive moves, following the terrain. While attempting to shake the Mustang the bandit clips a tree with his right wing and crashes. Intent on his pursuit Hobson now finds he is being fired on from the left by the remaining fighter. He breaks and then receives a head-on attack, the bandit pulling up and over. When Hobson next spots his opponent he is 45° to the P-51's stern. Turning as hard as possible, still carrying those drop tanks, Hobson continues an evasive turn for two or three minutes until the bandit disappears, then clears his tail and rejoins the Group. The 359th also does some strafing with the following claims made: 3-1 locomotives, 1-1 trucks, 1-0 automobile and 0-1 trailer. The only loss today occurs when the 370th's Yellow Flight attempts to strafe an airfield near Wurzburg, Germany. Intense flak drives them off but not before Lt. Benjamin J. Vos Jr's. P-51 is hit and crashes and burns on the enemy airfield. Vos is listed MIA.

This mission is significant due to the nationality of the fighters Lt. Hobson engaged. His combat report stated that the aircraft involved were painted black and looked similar to a P-40 Warhawk but with twin rudders. The aircraft's markings were described as white crosses on a red background. Clearly these were Swiss fighters, specifically Fabrique Federale C-3603 types.

At this point in the war Germany was not yet a clear loser and while Switzerland was technically a neutral country, there were a number of Swiss people sympathetic to the Germans. The fact this combat took place over seventy miles inside the German border leads one to speculate on the intentions of these errant Swiss pilots. Let it also be remembered that the treatment of American airmen interned by the Swiss improved noticeably when it became evident Germany had lost the war!

215   September 11, 1944 (0921-1430)

This is the mission referred to by the 359th FG as their "Greatest Day". For their outstanding performance engaging superior numbers of enemy fighters, while protecting the bomber formations, the Group is awarded a *Distinguished Unit Citation.* Capt. William C. Forehand, of the 368th FS, leads the Group as they provide penetration, target and withdrawal support for B-17s raiding the synthetic oil plants at Merseburg, Germany. The day begins on a good note as forty-nine P-51s take off and only one aborts. R/V is made near Blankenheim, Germany at 1050 and 22,000'. As the forty-eight Mustangs approach Giessen, fifty plus Me109s are spotted flying a formation identical to that used by 8th AF fighters, a tactic used in hope of getting closer to the bombers before being recognized. Before the bandits can make an attack the 368th FS breaks into them and the Germans dive for the deck. During this combat the following claims are made: Lt. Robert E. Benefiel damages two Me109s while separated from his (Yellow) flight. Low on fuel Benefiel then heads for home. Lts. Clarence M. Lambright and Jack O. Flack share in the destruction of a Me109 and notice the other German pilots are reluctant to do battle. Down on the deck Lambright destroys one locomotive and shares in the destruction of two more with Flack. Flack also destroys an oil tank car before the pair head back to England, low on fuel and ammo. Lt. Wilbur H. Lewis, of Yellow Flight, scores hits on a 109, which he follows in a dive that opens the P-51's canopy slightly, blowing out the rear plexiglass panels and breaking the airspeed indicator. Busy pulling out of the dive Lewis loses sight of his prey and is awarded a probable. Lewis then rejoins his flight and they return to England. At 1130, near Weimar, Lt. Arvy F. Kysely destroys a locomotive and while pulling up from his firing run encounters a Fw190. During a brief dogfight Kysely scores hits on the 190's engine and prop, in a head-on pass. Alone and low on fuel Kysely turns for home and on the way out destroys two locomotives near Treysa, Germany. The next action takes place near Mulhausen at 1140, when Red Flight of the 370th FS, takes on thirty Me109s and Fw190s effectively breaking their formation and preventing an attack on the bombers. F/O James J. O'Shea bags a Fw190 from which the pilot bails out, and damages a second. Lt. John W. Wilson destroys a Me109, scoring hits around the cockpit and probably killing the pilot. O'Shea and Wilson are separated, Wilson returns to base and O'Shea is listed as MIA. Beginning at 1140, in a parallel action, Yellow Flight of the 369th FS tangles with some bandits north of Erfurt, which nets these results: Lt. Frank Holliday downs one Me109, its belly

tank exploding and engulfing the fighter in flames. Holliday is missing after this combat and is assumed KIA. Lt. John H. Keur destroys a Me109, then films the pilot in his chute. Keur then joins with some P-51s from the 357th FG and they return to England. Near Kolleda, at 1145, the 369th FS observes over 100 enemy fighters five miles north of bombers and goes directly after them, with these claims being made: Lt Grant M. Perrin destroys two Fw190s and scores hits on the cockpit of a Me109 for a probable. Lt. Gilbert R. Ralston bags one Fw190 and Me109, with the 190 pilot bailing out. The 369th loses Lt. James F. Hutton and F/O Charles R. Bruening during this fight, both are listed as MIA. Lts. James R. Parsons and Joseph W. "Shoot everything that moves" Mejaski become separated from Red Flight of the 369th and while searching for their flight find a small grass field south of Merseburg, with about fifty aircraft parked there. The pair makes five passes and files these claims: Mejaski two Ju88s destroyed and five damaged. Parsons one Ju88 and Ju188 destroyed plus two Ju88s and three Ju188s damaged. During the same time frame the 369th's Yellow Flight has engaged the enemy, with Lt. Claude J. Crenshaw downing two Me109s. One rolls over and explodes as it hits the ground, while the other 109 crashes after the pilot bails out. Crenshaw then destroys a single engine aircraft on the field Parsons and Mejaski hit. Lt. Robert S. Gaines Jr. claims a Me109 as a probable and a second damaged during a dogfight, while Lt. Thomas J. Klem damages a 109 by scoring hits on its left wing. Meanwhile starting back at 1145, just south of Gotha, Blue Flight of the 370th FS spots two Me 109s taking off from an airfield and drops down to engage. Three 109s are destroyed in the air by Lt. Cyril W. Jones Jr. and a fourth is destroyed/shared with Lt. William E. Buchannon. The flight then strafes the field, with Jones destroying one Ju88 and He 177 plus damaging two Ju88s and two Me210s. Lt. Wallace C. Murray is credited with two Ju88s destroyed on the ground. While the aforementioned action takes place, Blue Flight of the 368th FS encounters a few bandits near Halberstadt, just before the bombers unload on Merseburg and Lt. George F. Baker bags two Fw190s before heading home, low on fuel. Lt. Ivan B. Hollomon, who is leading the 369th's Red Flight, experiences a loss of power at high altitude during the major engagement near Kolleda and drops to the deck, looking for targets as he heads out. Holloman destroys a locomotive and damages another, along with three boxcars, near Kassel, Germany at 1300. As he passes near an air-

While Sept. 11, 1944, is remembered as the 359th's " Greatest Day" it came with a price paid in blood. For their claims of twenty-six destroyed in the air and nine on the ground the Group had four pilots listed as missing in action and one that bailed out over enemy territory, but evaded and later returned. Top, left to right F/O Charles Robert Bruening, Lt. James Franklin (Hut Sut II) Hutton and Lt. Frank W. Holliday, all from the 369th FS. Bottom photo is of Lt. Ivan Brooks Hollomon, also from the 369th, posing with his P-51B, Traveler. Hollomon was flying a P-51D the day he bailed out. Note oil pattern coming from the oil-breather vent tube. Inverted flight while doing slow rolls or loops will cause oil to gather in the heads and be vented as seen here. This Mustang hasn't been on the ground long for the oil is still running down its cowling.

field Hollomon's 51 is hit in an oil line by ground fire. The Merlin seizes near Utrecht, Netherlands, where he bails out safely, evades capture and later on returns to England. At 1202, in the vicinity of Eisleben, Capt. Benjamin H. King, who is leading the 368th FS's Red Flight, spots fifty bandits preparing to attack a group of B-17s from the rear. Blue Flight jumps these fighters from the rear and King quickly downs one Me109 and two Fw190s. Two of the German pilots are seen bailing out of their stricken fighters. This combat has taken Red Flight from 27,000' to the deck, where King then chases a Fw190 only to discover he is out of ammo. King hands the 190 off to Lt. Chester R. Gilmore who makes the kill.

The mission account you have just read was pieced together from the pilots reports and gives a good, although incomplete picture of the combat that took place. Total claims for the day were: 26-4-5 in the air and 9-13 on the ground. For these victories the 359th lost five pilots and six P-51s. Of the 351 B-17s dispatched to Merseburg, thirteen were lost. The low number of bombers lost is testimony to the excellent protection provided by their escorts.

216   September 12, 1944 (0834-1422)

Today the Group furnishes escort for B-17s bombing the oil industry at Brux, Germany (Czechoslovakia after WWII). Maj. Chauncey S. Irvine leads the 359th off but aborts early on and is replaced by Lt. Jack D. Stevens of the 369th FS. Lt. David B. Archibald aborts over the Frisian Islands because of a rough engine and crashes at East Wretham when the engine quits as he attempts to land. The right main landing gear strut snaps off on touching down, causing the P-51 to do a cartwheel that tears off the prop. Archibald is not injured. There are a total of ten aborts from the forty-four P-51s that take-off. R/V occurs from 1020-1045, by squadron, north of Hamburg, Germany at 25,000'. At 1130, northwest of Berlin, Red Flights of the 368th and 369th FSs engage about fifty enemy fighters making a diving attack on the B-17s. Claims for the 368th are: Capt. Benjamin H. King, one Me109 destroyed at such close range its coolant covers King's windscreen. During this combat two of his four machine-guns jam and King joins with another Mustang from his flight and returns to base. Lt. Merle B. Barth nails a Me109 and its pilot hits the silk. Lt. Leonard D. Carter damages a Fw190, then latches onto another 190's tail and continues firing until it crashes. Lt. Robert B. Hat-

On Sept. 12, 1944 Lt. David B. Archibald aborted over the Frisian Islands and made it back to base, only to have the engine quit seconds from landing. Note prop stuck in fuselage, after being torn off during a cartwheel. All 24 spark plugs were found to be fouled.

ter damages a Me109, then scores heavily on a Fw 190. Pulling alongside the 190 he notices the pilot is slumped over the controls. The 190 then crashes. Hatter catches a second 190 with a solid burst sending it crashing into the ground along with the pilot. Lt. Elby J. Beal fires 480 rounds of API and scores only a few hits on a Me109; surprisingly the pilot then bails out. Lt. James H. Haas, of the 368th FS, bags a Fw190 but as he pulls out of his dive a wing snaps off and crushes the canopy. Haas bails out through the broken canopy and is taken prisoner. Lt. Louis E. Barnett is listed as MIA and assumed killed. The 369th FS also scores during this fight, with Lt. Grover C. Deen, who is leading Red Flight, and his wingman Lt. Kenneth L. Hobson, engaging the bandits. Deen destroys a Fw190 then chases and scores hits on a Me410 headed for an airfield near Berlin, before being driven off by flak. Deen, now alone, heads back to England but is forced to stop at Ghent, Belgium for fuel. Hobson's P-51 has a structural failure during a dive and he bails out near Berlin, where he is quickly taken prisoner by local authorities. Hobson spends the rest of the war in Stalag Luft 1 at Barth, Germany. Lt. John E. Hughes is last seen strafing a locomotive near Wittenberge and is listed MIA. Lt. Harold R. Burt blasts the wing off a Fw190, then joins with Hatter, of the 368th FS, to head home. Both are obliged to land at Ghent for fuel. At 1200 the 370th FS tangles with enemy fighters about twenty miles south of Berlin. Lt. Dick Connelly dives after a Me 109 and is cut out by an aggressive P-47, which fails to score any hits and breaks off at 6,000'. Connelly then nails the 109 which crashes and explodes. Low on fuel he heads for base and twenty minutes later spots a Fw190 below him at 3,000' and sends it exploding into the ground. At 1250 Red

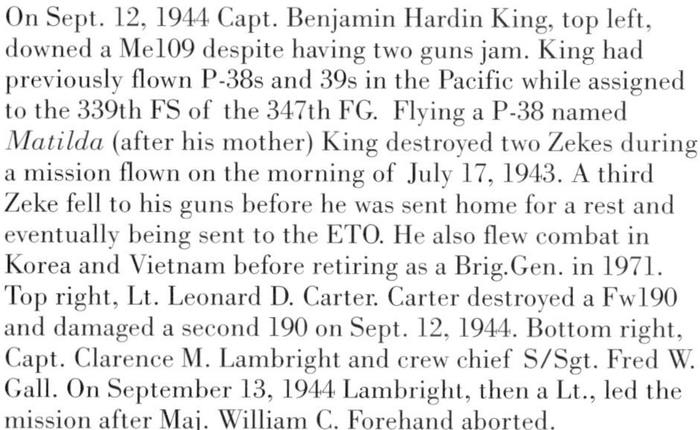

On Sept. 12, 1944 Capt. Benjamin Hardin King, top left, downed a Me109 despite having two guns jam. King had previously flown P-38s and 39s in the Pacific while assigned to the 339th FS of the 347th FG. Flying a P-38 named *Matilda* (after his mother) King destroyed two Zekes during a mission flown on the morning of July 17, 1943. A third Zeke fell to his guns before he was sent home for a rest and eventually being sent to the ETO. He also flew combat in Korea and Vietnam before retiring as a Brig.Gen. in 1971. Top right, Lt. Leonard D. Carter. Carter destroyed a Fw190 and damaged a second 190 on Sept. 12, 1944. Bottom right, Capt. Clarence M. Lambright and crew chief S/Sgt. Fred W. Gall. On September 13, 1944 Lambright, then a Lt., led the mission after Maj. William C. Forehand aborted.

Flight, led by Lt. Cyril W. Jones Jr., despite orders not to do so, strafes an airfield south of Meindingen. Results: Jones has three single engine aircraft destroyed, Lt. John W. Lamont, two single engine aircraft destroyed and Lt. Robert L. McInnes, one Ju52 destroyed plus two single engine aircraft destroyed and six damaged. Jones is shot down and dies while making a pass and the wreckage of his fighter is seen burning about 1,000 yards from the airfield. Other claims for the day are three locomotives destroyed. On the way out Lt. Eugene F. Britton, of the 368th, runs out of gas while making a landing approach at Abbeville, France. The Mustang's landing gear is sheared off by bomb craters and Britton spends the next three days hitching rides back to base. During an engagement near Berlin Lt. Robert E. Benefiel's P-51 sustains damage to the left aileron, when struck by the prop of a Mustang from the 352nd FG. Benefiel returns to England with the control stick pushed full right and makes a perfect wheels-up landing at the emergency airfield at Woodbridge, sustaining minor damage.

As today's accidents and combat losses cause an aircraft shortage for the 359th, Lt.Col. Swanson orders all P-51s being used for training to be made ready for combat.

The pilots shown above participated in the mission of Sept. 18, 1944, and all were from the 369th FS. *(From left to right)* Lt. Edwin Leonard Sjoblad listed as MIA. Lt. Grover Chester Deen who became a POW. Lt. Claude James Crenshaw added a Me109 to his list of victories. Lt. John E. Keur who shared in the destruction of a Me109 with F/O Thomas G. Bur.

217   September 13, 1944 (0822-1433)

Today the 359th provides escort for B-24s raiding the synthetic oil industry at Merseburg, Germany. The Group manages to get forty-four P-51s up, but thirteen abort. The increase in early returns is probably due, at least in part, to the pressing into service of war weary Mustangs relegated to training. Capt. Benjamin H. King, of the 368th FS, leads today after Lt.Col. William H. Swanson aborts. R/V occurs southwest of Huy, Belgium at 0950 and 24,000'. The bombing results are observed to be excellent but the B-24s don't leave the target area in formation, making it difficult to escort assigned units. There are numerous stragglers and the 359th stays in the target area giving support to the last combat wings of bombers. While escorting two crippled B-17s out, Capt. King's flight spots fifty-plus enemy fighters climbing up from 16,000', in the vicinity of Frankfurt. These bandits are not engaged so as to maintain cover for the cripples. The Group returns without loss.

*   September 14, 15, 1944 (bad weather)

218   September 16, 1944 (1443-1820)

The mission today is a scheduled area patrol to be followed by strafing in the Quedlinburg-Erfurt section of Germany. Maj. William C. Forehand, of the 368th FS, leads initially, but aborts and is replaced by Lt. Clarence M. Lambright, also from the 368th. Forehand is one of eleven aborts out of forty-nine P-51s taking off. Due to poor weather the 359th FG doesn't reach its assigned area. A R/T is received stating that the bombers have hit the target and that the Group is cleared to return.

219   September 17, 1944 (0825-1306)

Today the Group furnishes area support, under MEW control, for B-17s bombing strategic targets in the Netherlands. After a delay, due to ground haze, fifty-three P-51s take off and eight return early. The remaining forty-five Mustangs, led by Maj. Chauncey S. Irvine arrive over their assigned area, Steenbergen, at 0930. While patrolling the 370th FS notes good bombing results on airfields and bridges. No enemy fighters are encountered and the patrol ends at 1200. Lt. Harold R. Burt, of the 369th FS, bails out eight miles northwest of Antwerp after his P-51 loses its coolant. Burt is later reported killed.

As the Group returns to England, hundreds of gliders carrying troops for the invasion of the Netherlands are seen being towed by C-47s and British Stirlings. *Operation Market Garden* is in full swing.

220   September 18, 1944 (1157-1804)

Maj. William C. Forehand, of the 368th FS, leads the 359th on another area support mission, under MEW control, this time for B-24s dropping supplies to troops in the Netherlands. Fifty-seven P-51s leave East Wretham and aborts drop to three. R/V is made near Harderwijk at 1320 and 7,000'. At 1513 near Dieren, just north of Arnhem, Blue Flight of the

Top left, the Thunderbolt Dance Band organized by Cpl. Miles Gottschall, second from the left with saxophone. Top right. Sgt. Edward F. Palika points to the winner of a beauty contest, right, held on Oct. 4, 1944. Bottom left, one of the many squadron parties, this one a 368th FS gala held during Aug. of 1944. In the foreground with his right hand cupping a cigarette is Master Sgt. Herman F. Senter. Bottom right, the Red Cross sponsored Aero Club on what was described as "a stale night."

369th FS spots a Me262 at 9 o'clock, and jettisoning their drop tanks give chase. While searching for the jettie, which has flown into a thick haze, Blue Flight is jumped by about thirty Fw190s. Lt. James R. Parsons dives on a 190 scoring hits on the left cowling and cockpit. After another burst the 190's canopy pops off. Pulling out of his dive at tree top level and banking left Parsons observes the crashed 190, with the pilot's body nearby. The 369th loses two pilots, Lt. Edwin L. Sjoblad is listed MIA and Lt. Grover C. Deen becomes a POW. At 1520 Yellow Flight of the 369th is vectored to Dusseldorf, Germany and joins with P-51s of the 4th FG engaging some Me109s. Lt. Claude J. Crenshaw downs a109, from which the pilot bails out. At the same time, in the area of Munster, Germany Lt. John E. Keur and F/O Thomas G. Bur team-up to destroy a Me109. On returning to England Lt. John F. Lauesen, of the 368th FS, crash lands at Fersfield and his P-51 is declared Category E.

221 September 19, 1944 (1105-1709)

Today the 359th puts up fifty-seven Mustangs to pro-

vide penetration, target and withdrawal support for B-17s heading for Hamm, Germany. Lt.Col. William H. Swanson leads initially but aborts, as do a dozen others, and turns command over to Capt. Benjamin H. King, of the 368th FS. R/V occurs over the English Channel at 1150 and 10,000'. The force then crosses the Netherlands coast south of Ostende, at 1210. Ten minutes before reaching the target poor weather is encountered and the Forts turn south to bomb railway targets in the Koblenz area. During the strike the 359th provides area support under MEW control. Dust and fires are observed but specific targets are not visible. No enemy aircraft are encountered but three Forts are lost to flak. Escort is dropped at 1500 and the 359th returns safely to England.

222 September 20, 1944 (1518-1936)

Maj. Chauncey S. Irvine leads today as the 359th flies area support for 9th AF Thunderbolts hitting targets at Wessel, Germany. Fifty-six P-51s leave East

If any photograph proves the case of precision bombing this is it! This magnificent cathedral at Cologne, Germany escaped destruction while the surrounding buildings are roofless or heaps of rubble. Not many targets received this kind of careful attention. Sceptics claim the cathedral was used as a drop point hence its escape from destruction. The Norden Bombsight in the hands of a good bombardier on a clear day could achieve the results shown here. Twenty years later the Norden's sophisticated replacements proved unsuited for some operations in Vietnam and the Air Force had to bring back the Norden to achieve the desired results.

Wretham and only three return early. Time over the target is 1647, with the recall coming at 1750. No enemy aircraft are encountered and the Group exits Germany at Venlo, Netherlands. Lt. John E. Keur, of the 369th FS, has engine failure and bails out three miles off the coast from Lowestoft, England. Keur gets into his dinghy and is picked up by ASR thirty minutes later. The Group lands safely in a terrible fog.

223   September 21, 1944 (1449-1655)

Maj. Irvine leads again as the Group is off on a MEW controlled, area support mission for the 1st Airborne at Nijmegen, Netherlands. Twenty Mustangs take off and there are no aborts. The 368th FS is unable to assemble with the leader due to the weather. At 1600 just after joining with two flights of fighters, from another group, the mission is recalled.

224   September 22, 1944 (1123-1647)

Maj. Irvine leads the Group for the third consecutive mission as they provide area support for B-17s bombing the Henschel tank factory at Kassel, Germany.

Maj. Fred S. Hodges of the 369th FS. Hodges was a former Flying Tiger (American Volunteer Group) and scored one kill while serving with the 3rd Pursuit Squadron. Hodges' determination to complete the mission of Sept. 27, 1944, shows the mind-set of the AVG. Always outnumbered and flying "also ran" equipment, they approached battle with total commitment knowing every P-40 that aborted seriously weakened their already small group. Note the last four digits of his P-51D serial number 44-14313 applied to the nose above the third "e" in Jeepers. This was commonly done to avoid mixing panels when several aircraft were being serviced. Jeepers soon got a shark mouth painted on the nose.

Fifty-three P-51s leave East Wretham this morning and only four return early. R/V is made over Liege, Belgium at 1240 and 27,000'. The Forts bomb Kassel at 1410 and flak claims three of the raiding bombers. There is no sign of the Luftwaffe. As Lt. Raymond E. Magee, of the 369th FS, lands at East Wretham his P-51 noses over as a result of frozen brakes. Magee emerges uninjured.

*** September 23, 1944 (bad weather over the continent)**

Lt.Col. William H. Swanson leads a flight of four P-51s from the 368th FS to the RAF base at North Weald, to show off the Mustang to the British and Polish pilots there who are scheduled to transition to the type.

A practice escort mission is led by Capt. George A. Doersch of the 370th FS. On returning Lt. Frank R. Marshall dislodges a stuck landing gear by diving his P-51.

As night approaches the base's gun crews are put on alert for V-1s being launched by He111 bombers, off the Netherlands coast.

*** September 24, 1944 (bad weather)**

225 September 25, 1944 (0840-1403)

Capt. Benjamin H. King, of the 368th FS, leads as the Group furnishes penetration, target and withdrawal support for B-17s hitting industrial targets at Frankfurt, Germany. Fifty-one Mustangs take off and five abort. The assigned R/V is not made and the 359th proceeds on to Frankfurt. At 1015 near Weisbaden, Germany, Yellow Flight of the 368th encounters flak and as they make an evasive turn, Lt. John F. Lauesen is seen going down in a vertical dive from 26,000'. Lauesen, one of eleven brothers, is listed KIA. R/V is made at the target and the 359th orbits until the last B-17 passes through. Two Forts are lost to flak and its a no-show for the Luftwaffe.

226 September 26, 1944 (1247-1653)

Maj. Daniel D. McKee, who is beginning his second combat tour, is in the lead as the Group provides penetration, target and withdrawal support for B-17s blasting the marshalling yards and steel mills at Osnabruck, Germany. Of the forty-nine P-51s taking off six abort. R/V occurs near Egmond, Netherlands at 1345 and 22,000'. The bombing is done visually and great clouds of dust and smoke cover the target area after the raid. A "Big Ben" contrail is spotted near the target headed for England. The Luftwaffe is reported in the area but is not found. At 1535, on the way home, one of two B-17s lost to flak is seen crashing north of Lisse, Netherlands. Five chutes are noted. Four minutes later escort is dropped south of Egmond and the 359th returns to base without incident.

227 September 27, 1944 (0755-1250)

The 359th furnishes penetration, target and withdrawal support for B-17s hitting Dusseldorf, Germany. Capt. James K. Lovett, of the 370th FS, leads today and only three Mustangs of the fifty-one taking off return early. Capt. Fred S. Hodges, of the 369th FS, a former *Flying Tiger* (AVG) pilot, aborts soon after becoming air-borne. Hodges lands, has his P-51 fixed, takes back off and catches up with the Group over the continent. R/V is made 23,000' over Eindhoven, Netherlands at 0903. The Forts break into six ship elements during the bomb run and re-form afterwards. The Bombs are dropped with the aid of radar-equipped pathfinder aircraft. No enemy fighters are encountered and no bombers are lost to flak, which is moderate. The 359th escorts stragglers until reaching Ostende, Belgium.

228 September 28, 1944 (0854-1550)

Lt.Col. William H. Swanson flies lead as the Group escorts B-17s bombing Magdeburg, Germany. Fifty-three Mustangs leave East Wretham and six abort. The Forts are fourteen minutes late for R/V, which is made at 1130 and 27,000' over Witzenhausen, Germany. While the 359th maintains close and effective escort for its assigned bombers, the Luftwaffe makes heavy attacks on the other formations. The enemy fighters are engaged by other 8th AF fighter groups. Twenty-three Forts fall to fighters and flak, with one observed going down over the target at 1150. The bombing results are obscured by clouds. Green Flight of the 368th FS, consisting of Lt. Robert E. Benefiel (Green 1) and F/O Emery C. Cook, drop escort after leaving the target to investigate reported bandits. Finding the reported aircraft are friendly, the pair strafes extensively between Suhl and Fulda, Germany, destroying seven locomotives and a gasoline truck with a trailer. At 1215 two B-17s are seen colliding north of Halberstadt, Germany at 23,000'. No chutes are observed. A B-17 is observed exploding over Liege, Belgium at 1310. Lt. Howard E. Steussy, of

Lt. Galen E. Ramser of the 370th FS, crash-landed *Zombie* after the Merlin cut out during takeoff. Needless to say this bird never flew again.

the 370th FS, is last seen near Koblenz, Germany as Blue Flight picks up some straggling bombers. He is later reported a POW.

229 September 30, 1944 (1156-1607)

Maj. Chauncey S. Irvine gets the Group up on a penetration, target and withdrawal support mission for B-17s bombing an airfield at Münster, Germany. During takeoff Lt. Galen E. Ramser, of the 370th FS, crash-lands after his engine cuts out. Ramser escapes injury but his P-51B is totaled. Maj. Irvine aborts early into the mis-sion and is replaced by Capt. Benjamin H. King, of the 368th FS. Irvine is one of ten aborts out of the forty-nine pilots taking off today. R/V is made over Herenthals, Belgium at 1309 and 27,000'. The bombing results are obscured by clouds of smoke and dust. The 370th FS spots three jets and give chase, but are not able to catch them. Three bombers are lost today. The 359th FG returns to base without loss.

All fifteen 8th AF fighter groups are operating today but there are no claims or losses.

* October 1, 1944 (bad weather)

230 October 2, 1944 (0807-1400)

Capt. Benjamin H. King, of the 368th FS, flies lead as the Group furnishes penetration, target and withdrawal support for B-17s blasting Kassel, Germany. Fifty-three Mustangs leave East Wretham this morning and six abort. R/V is made over Brussels, Belgium at 0925 and 24,000'. Lt. Donald E. Cannon, of the 369th FS, turns back because of a dead radio and soon thereafter his P-51 develops a rough running engine. He makes it to friendly territory in France before bailing out safely. Cannon returns two days later by hitching a ride in a B-24. At 1110 Blue Flight of the 370th FS dives to investigate reported bandits that turn out to be P-51s. While climbing back to resume escort they spot five Me 109s at 5,000'. Diving from 20,000' proves futile, for by the time Blue Flight reaches the area the enemy fighters have disappeared into low cloud cover. As Blue Flight approaches Wabern, two trains are observed and during a series of running attacks that stretch several miles, Lts. Dick D. Connelly, John W. Lamont, Galen E. Ramser and Lawrence A. Zizka destroy twelve locomotives and fifty railcars. Zizka and Connelly run low on fuel and land in a pasture north of Verdun, France. Connelly is refueled and returns to base but Zizka damages his prop and a flap, which delays his return. Meanwhile escort is dropped at 1200 near Essen, Germany.

After the Group lands, Lt.Col. William H. Swanson makes the pilots involved in today's strafing sign a statement that they are aware of the current ban on *opportunity* strafing by Mustangs.

231   October 3, 1944 (0914-1506)

Maj. Daniel D. McKee, of the 370th FS, leads as the Group provides penetration, target and withdrawal support for B-17s headed for Nürnburg, Germany. Forty- five P-51s start out on this mission and four return early. R/V is made at 1044 near Vielsalm, Belgium. Bombing is done using pathfinder aircraft and the results are observed as good, with black smoke rising to 15,000'. No enemy fighters are encountered and escort is dropped at 1325, near Saarburg, Germany. Lt. Donald W. Chatfield, of the 368th FS, bellies his P-51 in near Possons, France and returns the next day. The Mustang flown by Capt. George A. Doersch, now with the 370th FS and flying the first mission of his second tour, is hit in the wing by flak, over Dunkirk, the only place on the French coast still held by the Germans. "Pop" lands safely at base.

232   October 5, 1944 (0945-1345)

Capt. Benjamin H. King, of the 368th FS, leads as the Group flies penetration, target and withdrawal support for B-17s bombing Dusseldorf, Germany. The 359th puts up forty-five Mustangs today and nine abort. R/V is made east of Herenthals, Belgium at 1110 and 26,000'. Bad weather splits the bombers

During the mission flown on Oct. 7, 1944, Bob York damaged a BV 138 seaplane and "Pop" Doersch and Jack McCoskey shared in the destruction of a second BV 138 as shown in the top photo. The engines were six cylinder, horizontally opposed, two-stroke diesels rated at 880 h.p. Barely visible inboard of number 3 engine is a depth charge. Below, on the same mission Emory Johnson damaged an Ar196 floatplane, like the one shown here. This particular Arado's engine is running. BUNDESARCHIV

up near the target and attacks are made on Cologne and Dortmund, Germany. No enemy aircraft are encountered. On the way out, near Tirlemont, Belgium, where escort is broken at 1230, Lt. Billy D. Kasper, of the 368th FS, sees Lt. Clifford L. Bartlett drop his tanks and enter a tight downward spiral from 30,000'. After an attempt to raise Bartlett on the radio fails, Kasper drops to 8,000' but fails to find any sign of him. Bartlett is later listed as KIA. Northwest of Ostende, Belgium Lt. Eugene F. Britton, of the 368th FS, spots a B-17 going down, smoking. Nine chutes are counted but by the time three ASR launches arrive there is only one survivor.

233   October 6, 1944 (0936-1530)

Maj. Daniel D. McKee leads as the Group flies penetration, target and withdrawal support for B-17s scheduled to bomb Politz, Germany. The 359th has one more fighter take off than yesterday and one more abort. R/V occurs near Rostock, Germany at 1135. Lt. Donald W. Chatfield, of the 368th FS, is over Rostock when his P-51 is hit by heavy and accurate flak. Chatfield returns safely to base. The primary target is covered by a 10/10 overcast so the Forts bomb Stangard Airfield and Stettin, Germany. At 1310, south of Stettin, the 370th FS jumps thirty Fw190s headed for the bombers. The 190s try to escape by diving but are overtaken inside Poland. The following pilots score: Capt. George A. Doersch, who led the chase, two destroyed and one damaged, F/O Jack E. McCoskey and Lt. Robert L. McInnes each claim one destroyed and one damaged.

234   October 7, 1944 (0931-1539)

With Capt. George A. Doersch of the 370th FS leading, the Group is off once more to Politz, Germany, providing escort for B-17s. Forty-eight P-51s lift off from East Wretham and eight return early. R/V with the Forts is made over the North Sea at 1045 and 20,000'. Escort is provided through the target, where the bombing results are noted to be good. Although no enemy aircraft are encountered flak takes its toll on the 141 Forts. Seventeen are lost and 106 are damaged. Meanwhile the 370th FS, which failed to find the bombers, strafes a seaplane base near Dievenow, Germany with the following results: Capt. Doersch and F/O Jack E. McCoskey share in the destruction of a Blohm & Voss BV 138, Lt. Emory G. Johnson claims an Ar196 and Lt. Robert M. York claims a second BV 138. Johnson and York's claims are awarded as damaged. Lt. Wallace C. Murray's P-51 is hit by flak and catches fire. Murray hits the silk two miles off the coast and is MIA.

*   October 8, 1944 (1247- ?)

After being put on stand-by the 359th is briefed for an area patrol and support mission in the vicinity of Nürnberg, Germany. Lt.Col. William H. Swanson leads the Group off at 1247 but due to the weather the mission is recalled at 1302, while the fighters are still circling the base.

235   October 9, 1944 (1137-1721)

Today the 359th flies a penetration, target and withdrawal support mission for B-17s bombing the ball bearing industry at Schweinfurt, Germany. Capt. Benjamin H. King, of the 368th FS, leads and there

are twelve aborts out of the forty-nine fighters that leave East Wretham. R/V is made near Huy, Belgium at 1303 and 24,000'. Due to 10/10 cloud cover no bombing results are noted. No bombers are lost and no enemy fighters are encountered. Today is a far cry from the "Black Thursday" mission of October 14, 1943 when sixty B-17s were lost, as the result of a raid on this target. Escort is dropped at 1630, near Leuze.

*   October 10-13, 1944 (bad weather)

236   October 14, 1944 (1088-1453)

Lt.Col. William H. Swanson is in the lead as the Group furnishes penetration, target and withdrawal support for B-17s raiding the marshalling yards at Cologne, Germany. Fifty-four P-51s take off on this mission and seven abort. R/V occurs near Liege, Belgium at 1115 and 24,000'. At 1150 one of two Forts lost today is observed going down in flames near the target. This B-17 is the victim of flak for no enemy aircraft are encountered. The escort is terminated at 1341, south of Bruges, Belgium.

237   October 15, 1944 (0744-1157)

It's back to Cologne again with the 359th FG escorting B-17s whose targets are industrial sites, oil facilities and the marshalling yards. Maj. Daniel D. McKee leads the Group off fifteen minutes early, to escape a rapidly closing fog. The 359th fields fifty-three Mustangs today and there are no aborts. R/V is made in the vicinity of Eindhoven, Netherlands at 0908 and 26,000'. Four bombers are lost today but only one is seen hit by flak over the target. Good bombing results are observed. Once more the Luftwaffe fails to show and escort is dropped near Ghent, Belgium at 1040.

*   October 16, 1944 (bad weather)

238   October 17, 1944 (0753-1247)

With Capt. Benjamin H. King, of the 368th FS, leading, the Group flies penetration, target and withdrawal support, for the third consecutive day, for B-17s hitting Cologne, Germany. This is the first mission of Capt. Ray S. Wetmore's second tour. The 359th puts fifty-six P-51s up and only one returns early. R/V occurs near Hellenthal, Germany at 0903 and 26,000'. At 0930 a B-17 is seen exploding over

Left, Lt. Robert J. Guggemos poses with Capt. Joseph W. Mejaski's P-51D-10NA *Stinky* IV-M 44-14117. Guggemos joined the 369th in Oct. of 1944 and the green nose band dates this photo as having been taken during that month. After Nov. 1, 1944, most of the nose was painted green and helps establish a time frame for the crash shown in the bottom photo. Since *Stinky* was Mejaski's aircraft and he left the Group in Feb. of 1945 that narrows the crash date some. In the right photo an armorer is clearing the guns which would have been hot during the takeoff attempt. Check the buckled fuselage panels aft of the wing. The left main landing gear strut has been wrenched to an odd angle, the right main has collapsed, the prop is bent meaning the engine will have to be pulled for inspection of the reduction gears and crankshaft.

the target, it is the only bomber lost today although another 263 are damaged by flak. Two Me163s are spotted east of Cologne and *Big Ben contrails* are seen at 1000 and 1010, passing through 40,000' near Weisbaden, Germany. Wetmore is given the lead when King drops down to look for a straggler. Backing up a bit, Lt. Carl M. Anderson, of the 368th FS, experiences an extreme engine vibration near Cologne and unable to raise his flight leader by R/T, drops his tanks and heads back, dodging heavy and accurate flak. After eluding five bandits and a forty-five minute flight across France, Anderson lands at two airfields before finding fuel. Villacoublay has only one fuel truck and it's 1515 before the Mustang is serviced. Now the weather will not permit departure, requiring an overnight stay in Paris. The following day while attempting a takeoff the radiator shutter fails to open and the P-51 pops its coolant. Mechanics are in short supply and the repairs are slated for the next day. Anderson spends another entertaining night in Paris and returns to base on the 19th.

239   October 19, 1944 (1118-1630)

Lt.Col. William H. Swanson leads the 359th on this the final mission of his tour. The Group provides penetration, target and withdrawal support for B-17s bombing Ludwigshafen, Germany. Fifty-seven Mustangs leave East Wretham and five abort. R/V is made near Luxembourg, Belgium at 1245 and the Forts are taken to Ludwigshafen and Mannhiem. No bombers are lost and no contact is made with enemy aircraft.

Escort is broken near Ostende, Belgium at 1525. Lt. Warren R. Newberg, of the 370th FS, lands at Florennes, Belgium with generator trouble.

*   October 20, 21, 1944 (bad weather)

The 359th FG is released for maintenance and training.

240   October 22, 1944 (1145-1626)

The Group flies another penetration, target and withdrawal support mission, with Maj. Daniel D. McKee leading. The target of the Forts are military vehicle plants at Hannover, Germany. Sixty-two Mustangs take off and six return early. Lt. James H. O'Shea, who is leading the 370th's Green Flight, crashes through a fence during take-off and escapes injury but the P-51 is Category E. R/V is made north of Lingen, Germany at 1327. Two Forts are lost to flak, and the Luftwaffe fails to show. No bombing results are observed. Escort is maintained until 1530, near Hoorn, Netherlands.

*   October 23, 1944 (bad weather)

241   October 24, 1944 (1219-1702)

Today the Group flies the month's only *authorized* strafing mission, which is to the southeast of Hannover, Germany. Maj. James K. Lovett, of the 370th FS, leads as fifty P-51s take off, with nine re-

October 24, 1944, was the month's only authorized strafing mission and the 359th made the most it by seemingly attempting to machine gun Germany into submission. Some of the scorers are shown above. Left to right and starting at the top; Lt. Robert V. Beaupre, Lt. Ray A. Boyd Jr., Lt. Jack O. Flack, Lt. John T. Gordon, Lt. Thomas J. Klem and Lt.Col. James R. Parsons Jr. The destruction diary lists their contributions to the day's tally. Beaupre would die in a fiery take-off crash on Jan. 6, 1945. Boyd was shot down by a Fw190 and became a POW on Dec. 24, 1944. Flack completed his tour in Dec. of 1944. Gordon completed his first tour in Feb. of 1945. Klem transferred out in July of 1945. Parsons was killed in a flying accident on Dec. 29, 1944.

turning early. The 359th arrives over the target area at 1430 and the hunt begins. Visibility is only one to three miles but it turns into a fruitful day, with these claims being made: 53-2 locomotives, 5-95 boxcars, 0-14 tanks on flatcars, 16-18 trucks, 0-19 tanks,0-1 barge, 1-0 flak gun and its five man crew, 0-2 switch houses and 2-0 flak towers. At 1445 Lt. Merle B. Barth, of the 368th FS, who is flying wing for Lt. Paul E. Olson, is pulling up from a strafing run on a truck, when he loses sight of Olson in the overcast. Barth then spots an aircraft he assumes to be Olson's and slides in close before noticing it's a Fw190. Before the German is aware of his presence Barth slips in behind him and fires two short bursts. The 190

A big time strafer on Oct. 24, 1944 was Lt. Harry Lee Matthew from West by God Virginia. Matt shared in the destruction of 10 locos with various teams from the 369th. He was well into his second tour and a Captain when he flew through power lines while attacking a train on Feb. 28, 1945. The Mustang Matt was flying lost its coolant and he was forced to bail out. The Germans took him prisoner but his captivity lasted only three weeks before being liberated by American ground forces. Matt is exiting *Pistol Packin' Mama II*, which was a P-51B IV-T, serial number 43-24798.

breaks left and the pilot bails out. The pilotless fighter dives into the ground and explodes. Flak then drives Barth away. During this time period F/O Boyd N. Adkins, of the 368th FS, who has become separated from his flight in the haze, has just pulled up from strafing a train when he spots an aircraft he believes to be part of his flight. Like Barth, Adkins identifies the aircraft as a Fw190 before the enemy pilot is aware of his presence, drops his flaps, pulls in behind the 190 and fires a three second burst at close range. The bandit enters a left turn that ends in a terminal dive. At 1510 the Group heads back to England and during the flight three pilots from the 368th FS land in France, returning to base the following day. Lt. Robert W. Davison, of the 369th FS, is down to less than ten gallons of fuel when he picks a field in France to land on. Just after touching down, he notices some farmers are in the path of his fighter and pulls up and over them. Davison bends two blades on his prop as he settles back onto the field, forcing him to catch a ride back to England, in a C-47, the next day.

From 1430-1600, four P-51s from the 370th FS fly a practice escort mission with some bombers.

The two kills scored by the 368th FS today are the only air victories scored by the nine 8th AF fighter groups operating. The fifty-three locomotives destroyed by the 359th FG constitute 39% of the days total for those nine groups.

The 359th also encounters "jack-in-the-box" barrage balloons for the first time. These balloons are carried on trains and are designed to deploy to an altitude of 300' when released, to provide protection against strafing fighters.

242 October 25, 1944 (1108-1542)

Capt. Benjamin H. King, of the 368th FS, leads today as the Group provides penetration, target and withdrawal support for B-17s blasting an oil refinery at Rheinbeck, Germany near Hamburg. R/V occurs at 1242, off Terschilling Island. One B-17 is observed lost to flak, with no survivors. The bombing results are noted as good. The Luftwaffe fails to show and escort is dropped twenty-five miles north of Schiermonnikoog Island. The 359th returns without incident.

243 October 26, 1944 (1252-1652)

On the left, Capt. George F. Baker Jr. who shared the destruction of a Me109 with Lt. Oscar Faldmark and damaged another on Nov. 2, 1944. Center, Lt. Ralph R. Klaver who damaged a 109 on the same day. Right, Lt. Edward James Thorne sports a Cheshire Cat grin. Thorne's P-51 was hit in the coolant system by flak while strafing an airfield on Nov. 4, 1944. He bailed out and became a POW.

The Group flies another penetration, target and withdrawal support mission for B-17s, with Maj. James W. Parsons, of the 369th FS, in the lead. Fifty-five Mustangs begin the mission and three return early. The targets are an aircraft repair depot and the marshalling yards at Münster, Germany. R/V is made over Egmond, Netherlands at 1416 and 26,000'. No Forts are lost and no enemy aircraft are encountered. Escort is broken near Enschede, Netherlands at 1455 and the 359th returns intact.

*   October 27-29, 1944 (bad weather)

244   October 30, 1944 (1035-1403)

Maj. James K. Lovett, of the 370th FS, leads the Group on a scheduled escort for 459 B-17s sent to bomb the synthetic oil industry at Merseburg, Germany. Out of the fifty-five P-51s taking off six return early. At 1215, just inside the German border, near Rheine, a R/T is received from the Forts stating they can't get above the weather and they are turning back. The 368th turns back but the 369th and 370th continue on their assigned route for thirty minutes before also turning for home. Three "Big Ben" contrails are observed during the mission but the pilots are still uninformed as to what these trails are. Lt. Robert D. Erwin, of the 369th FS, experiences engine trouble and is escorted to St. Trond, Belgium where he makes a safe landing. Erwin's escort, Lt. Russell H. Jenner, never drops below the overcast to land and is not seen or heard from again. Jenner is later listed as KIA.

During the month of October the mysterious "Big Ben" contrails were observed by the pilots of the 359th FG on almost every mission. Censorship however keeps them from being told that these are the vapor trails left by Germany's new V-2 rocket.

245   November 1, 1944 (1202-1544)

Maj. Daniel D. McKee leads the first mission of the month which is escort for B-17s bombing two synthetic oil plants at Gelsenkirchen, Germany. Forty-two P-51s leave East Wretham and only two abort. R/V is made over Egmond, Netherlands at 25,000'. The bombing is done by radar, due to the weather and no Forts are lost. The only action of the day occurs when a Me262 attempts to bounce the 369th FS but is driven off. While returning to base, Lt. David B Archibald is forced to bail out ten miles northeast of Norwich, England. It is believed the coolant shutter stuck in the closed position, causing the engine in P-51D ser. no. 44-14854 to overheat and catch fire. Archibald returns to base later in the day.

The 385th FS, of the 364th FG, is temporarily based at East Wretham for a week, while the runways at Honington are repaired.

During this month all 8th AF fighter groups receive 'G' suits.

246   November 2, 1944 (1013-1607)

Maj. James A. Howard, of the 369th FS, flies lead today as the Group provides penetration, target and withdrawal support for B-17s pounding the synthetic oil plants at Merseburg, Germany. Fifty-four Mustangs begin this mission and seven return early. R/V occurs east of Zwolle, Netherlands at 1136 and 30,000'. The force arrives over the target at 1236 and one Fort is seen on fire, spinning down over the target at 1243, with no chutes. Two minutes later, as the force is exiting the target, thirty Me109s attack the bombers and down six. The 370th FS dives after the 109s and catches them at 12,000'. Capt. Ray S. Wetmore draws first blood by sending a 109 into a spin, from which it doesn't recover. Now alone and with only two functioning guns, Wetmore finds himself set upon by fifteen to twenty Me109s. Firing a short burst, with about 70° deflection and using the new K-14 gunsight, he nails his second victim in the cockpit. The German fighter stalls, then tumbles to earth. The remaining bandits scatter. For his heroic action today Wetmore is awarded the Distinguished Service Cross. Capt. Ralph R. Cox shoots off one-third of the right wing on a Me 109 for a kill. Capt. Sam J. Huskins Jr. shares the destruction of a 109 with a Mustang pilot from the 353rd FG (yellow and black checker nose markings). Capt. Dick D. "Dee Dee" Connelly destroys a 109 that hits the ground and explodes before the pilot can escape. At 1300 a B-17 is seen exploding near Weimar, Germany. At 1315 near Quedlinburg, Capt. George F. Baker Jr. and Lt. Oscar R. Faldmark, of the 368th FS, share in the destruction of a Me109 and Baker damages a second. Two B-17s are observed being shot down by fighters during this period. At 1330 southeast of Merseburg, Lt. Ralph R. Klaver, of the 369th FS, engages a single Me109 while separated from White Flight and scores a few hits in the left wingroot before being fired on by another bandit. Klaver breaks hard, stalls, then recovers just before entering a low overcast. He then joins with two P-51s from the 20th FG and they return to England.

*   November 3, 1944 (bad weather)

247   November 4, 1944 (1003-1539)

The 359th FG flies penetration, target and withdrawal support for B-17s raiding the synthetic oil industry at Hamburg and Harburg, Germany. Maj. Daniel D. McKee leads fifty-five Mustangs up and seven abort. R/V is made north of Norden, Germany at 1130 and 27,000'. At 1145 a Fort is seen hit by flak near Cuxhaven and it explodes with no chutes observed. 9/10 cloud cover obscures the bombing results and no enemy aircraft are encountered. At 1250 the escort is dropped and the 359th hunts for targets to strafe. Maj. James A. Howard and Lt. Edward J. Thorne, of the 369th FS, pop out of the overcast above an airfield at Quackenbrück, Germany and immediately come under fire from the field defences. Thorne's P-51 is hit in the coolant system and he radios he is bailing out. The Mustang is seen crashing but no chute is observed. Thorne is later reported to be a POW. At 1345 in the vicinity of Rheine-Lingen, Germany White Flight of the 370th FS consisting of Maj. McKee, Lts. Homer A. Staup and Lawrence A. Zizka destroy a locomotive before being driven off by ground fire. Lt. James H. O'Shea, of the 370th's Yellow Flight, also destroys a locomotive and damages two boxcars in the same area. Intense flak prevents further attacks by this flight. One other locomotive is destroyed by the Group today.

248   November 5, 1944 (0920-1425)

Maj. James A. Howard, of the 369th FS, leads this escort mission for B-17s blasting the marshalling yards at Frankfurt, Germany to be followed by strafing. The weather is so bad today that only thirty-six of the Group's best pilots are allowed to fly on this assignment. Two of the thirty-six abort. R/V is made over Liege, Belgium at 1035 and 23-24,000'. The visibility is poor in the target area and the bombing is done with the help of radar. No enemy fighters are encountered and the escort is broken southwest of Koblenz, Germany at 1150. Just after leaving the Forts the 368th FS runs into an intense flak barrage and splits up during violent evasive action. Due to poor visibility the 368th can't reform and White Flight escorts some crippled B-17s out, while Blue Flight strafes, making claims of two locomotives and five trucks destroyed. Lt. Maurice M. Haines, of the 369th FS, is strafing a train near Wendelsheim when his P-51 is hit by ground fire, forcing him to crash-land near Darmstadt where he becomes a POW. Other claims for the day include: 10-0 locomotives, 2-41 boxcars, 6-0 trucks, 1-0 bus

Top left, 395th Service Squadron personnel service a P-51 from the 359th FG. Left to right, Lt. Clarence L. Steele engineering officer, Cpl. Palmer Dappen, Pvt. James L. Bryan and Master Sgt. Harmon Doyle. Bottom left, Major Montimore C. Shwayder, Assistant Station Surgeon has his picture taken with one of the Group's Mustangs on Sept. 12, 1944. Right, the 368th's First Sgt., Master Sgt. Herman F. Senter. During WW I while serving as a platoon sgt. of Company "G", 60th Infantry, 5th Division Senter was cited for conspicuous bravery in action. Senter mentioned he thought he had won a medal to officers of the 368th FS who in turn submitted an inquiry on his behalf. During November of 1944 Senter received the Silver Star he had been awarded 26 years previously.

loaded with troops, 0-1 switch tower and 0-1 factory. Capt. Ralph L. Brown, of the 368th FS, crash-lands on returning to base but emerges unhurt.

The twelve locomotives destroyed by the 359th today represents one third of the total destroyed by 8th AF fighter command, with all fifteen groups operating.

249   November 6, 1944 (0847-1352)

The 359th flies escort for B-17s hitting oil refineries at Hamburg, Germany. Maj. Daniel D. McKee leads and the Group puts up fifty-two Mustangs, with four aborts. R/V occurs over Assen, Netherlands at 1000 and 27,000'. Red barrage balloons and zig-zag defences are observed at the German-Netherlands border. The bombing is accomplished by radar and four

bombers are lost to flak. Bandits are reported south of the target but none are encountered by the 359th, which returns to East Wretham without incident.

*   November 7, 1944 (bad weather)

250   November 8, 1944 (0853-1455, A) (0853-1500, B)
251

Today the 359th is split into *A* and *B* groups, with Col. Avelin P. Tacon and Maj. Roy W. Evans leading respectively. The mission is to provide support for B-17s raiding the synthetic oil industry at Merseburg, Germany. *A* group has thirty P-51s that take off, with two aborts, while *B* group takes off twenty-seven

On Nov. 8, 1944, pilots of the 359th FG witnessed the loss of three B-17s, one going down over the target in flames, with only four of the ten man crew escaping. That particular Fort was from the 384th BG illustrated in the left photo. Notice the de-icer boots have been removed from the wing and tail leading edges of these B-17s. It was found that the boots were seldom needed and when shredded by flak caused a considerable reduction in speed, an undesirable handicap over enemy territory. Right, Col. John P. Randolph CO of the 359th FG from November 12 to April 8, 1945. Randolph came from the 20th FG where he scored the five victories denoted on the canopy frame.

strong, with two aborts. R/V is made by *A* group south of Meppen, Germany at 1025 and 23,000'. *B* group makes R/V east of Dummer Lake at 1020 and 24,000'. The weather is so bad one bomber force abandons the mission because they can't assemble and two wings of B-17s abort on the way in. Bandits are reported in the vicinity of Dummer Lake but not found. Three Forts are lost to flak, one of which is seen going down in flames over the target, with only four crewmen escaping. The tail code on this Fort is noted to be a black triangle with a P inside (384th BG). On the way out the 369th FS strafes targets of opportunity. Maj. James A. Howard's P-51 is hit by small caliber AA fire while making a second strafing run on a train, in the station at Meppel, Germany. The 51 begins to smoke, falls off on one wing and crashes from fifty feet up, exploding on impact. Howard is assumed KIA. Lt. Rene L. Burtner destroys a locomotive and Lt. Harold Tenenbaum damages fifteen railcars.

252   November 9, 1944 (0814-1313)

Col. Tacon leads the 359th FG for the last time as they provide penetration, target and withdrawal support for B-17s raiding transportation targets in the area of Metz, France. Fifty-two Mustangs leave East Wretham this morning and only one returns early. R/V is made over Montcornet, France at 0924 and 28,000'. The bombers are strung-out, with B-17s and B-24s trying to hit the target at the same time. The 359th circles the target area until the bombers have finished, then

escorts them out to the coast. No bombers are lost and no enemy fighters are encountered.

253   November 10, 1944 (1105-1601)

Maj. James K. Lovett, of the 370th FS, leads as the Group flies escort for 203 B-17s bombing airfields at Cologne, Germany to be followed by strafing. In a repeat performance of yesterdays excellent record the 359th puts up fifty-two fighters and only one aborts. R/V occurs southeast of Eindhoven, Netherlands at 28,000'. The bombing results are obscured by low laying clouds. No enemy fighters are encountered but the flak claims one Fort and damages ninety-five more. Because of the limited visibility no strafing is undertaken. "Big Ben" contrails are sighted near the Ruhr Valley. Lts. Eugene F. Britton and Leonard D. Carter, of the 368th FS, escort a crippled bomber out of enemy territory and as a result have to land at St. Trond, Belgium for fuel, before returning to base at 1825.

*   November 11-19, 1944 (bad weather)

On November 12, Lt.Col. John P. Randolph, from the 20th FG, officially assumes command of the 359th FG and Col. Tacon moves up to take the position of chief of staff to Brig.Gen. Edward W. Anderson, commanding the 67th Fighter Wing.

Also on the 12th the 368th FS has a serious preflight accident that damages P-51B serial no. 42-106929. Sgt. Anderson starts the Merlin in the usual

While lousy weather precluded operations against the enemy On November 14, 1944, the 359th got in some formation flying. Above is a flight from the 370th FS. P-51D *Daddy's Girl*, coded CS-L, serial number 44-14733 is Capt. Ray S. Wetmore's mount. P-51D *Rayner Shine*, coded CS-A, serial number 44-14521 flown by Lt.Col. Daniel D. McKee. The other two Mustangs are identifiable in another photo as CS-G, serial number 44-14773 and CS-S, serial number 44-14192. The pilots of these two aircraft are not known.

manner but when the engine catches, the throttle sticks in a high r.p.m. setting, the 51 jumps its chocks, noses over, then falls back on the tailwheel. With the fuselage tank being full, the drop back bends the tailwheel strut and springs the tail empennage. The prop is obviously damaged, as is the engine. It is found that the throttle linkage stuck on a cable going to the K-14 gunsight's voltage regulator. A recommendation is made to move the regulator from the left to right side of all K-14s.

During this month the 359th's service squadron makes the landing gear up-lock modifications to their early P-51Ds. This change is the result of two fatal crashes involving the first 100 'D' models built. The main gear doors on these aircraft would sag open during high 'G' pullouts, letting a wheel drop down, which in turn caused catastrophic wing failure. These modifications are finished in Dec.

254   November 20, 1944 (1024-1337)

Lt.Col. John P. Randolph leads the 359th on a sched-uled escort for B-17s heading for Bonn, Germany. Fifty-seven P-51s leave East Wretham and there are no aborts. Due to poor weather encountered over the continent, the bombers turn back. The 359th is advised by R/T that they can either return or strafe targets of opportunity. The decision is to return since the Group is not carrying the required maps to strafe. At 1100 Lt. Merle B. Barth, of the 368th FS, broadcasts his engine is on fire and he is going to bail out. F/O Emory C. Cook drops down to search for Barth and is soon joined by ASR aircraft. An oil slick and overturned dinghy are found but no pilot. Barth is listed MIA.

255   November 21, 1944 (0917-1557)

Maj. Roy W. Evans leads the 359th as they fly penetration, target and withdrawal support for B-17s bombing the synthetic oil industry at Merseburg, Germany. The Group puts up fifty-nine fighters this morning and four return early. R/V is made over Hasselet, Belgium at 1035 and 24,000'. The first action occurs west of the target at 1135. The leader of the 369th's Green Flight, Lt. Claude J. Crenshaw and his wing-man, Lt. Harold Tenenbaum are alone, Green 3 and 4 having aborted due to poor visibility, when bandits are called in over the radio. Flying at 31,000' Crenshaw spots about 100 Fw190s, with a top cover of about thirty-five more, trailing above a formation of bombers. The pair drop down behind the

Two more photos taken on Nov. 14,1944, these being of Mustangs from the 369th FS, at the left and a mix from the 369th and 370th FSs in the right picture. Left threesome of P-51Ds are; *Precious Pat*, IV-P, serial number 44-14543 flown by Capt. Gilbert R. Ralston, IV-Z, serial number 44-15007 flown by Lt. Thomas J. Klem and IV-D, serial number 44-15394, piloted by Rene Burtner. Positive identification of who is flying any of the Mustangs in the right photo is impossible but the aircraft are; IV-X the *X-Terminator*, P-51D serial number 44-14218, CS-C P-51D serial number 44-14096, CS-V, P-51D serial number 44-14096, IV-T, P-51D serial number 44-15081, IV-G, P-51C serial number 42-103793 and IV-H, P-51B serial number 42-106476. Note IV-G and IV-H have dorsal strakes added in the field and IV-G has a Malcolm Hood canopy.

bandits and observe eight P-51s from the 352nd FG closing in. Crenshaw lines up on a 190 but a 352nd P-51 cuts in, forcing him to select another target. After a second burst of fire the bandit rolls over and the pilot bails out. Victim number two is hit with a short burst, from seventy-five yards and again the pilot bails out. Popping out of a haze, Crenshaw finds fifty Fw190s firing on the bombers. Slipping behind one of the attacking enemy fighters he fires two short bursts into the engine. The190 rolls over, with fire trailing from its engine and goes down. Climbing back through the haze Crenshaw engages about thirty Bandits and scores hits on one, in the cockpit. He is then forced to break combat with the smoking bandit since two Germans are on his tail firing at him. After clearing his tail Crenshaw jumps two bandits and they head for the deck. While firing on one of these fighters the second one gets behind Crenshaw and a Mustang from the 352nd FG nails it. Continuing his attack Crenshaw watches his prey dive into the ground at 600 m.p.h. On reaching base it is found that only three of the Mustang's six guns were working, the others had jammed. Crenshaw later attributes his four confirmed kills to the K-14 gunsight and G-Suit. Tenenbaum, his wingman, engages a 190 on Crenshaw's tail, at the beginning of the fight scoring hits in the wing roots. The German jettisons his canopy but Tenenbaum continues firing until the 190 wings over in a spiral, the pilot apparently dead. At 1145 Lt. Carl M. Anderson reports that his Merlin is losing oil pressure and vibrating. The engine then

catches fire, forcing him to belly his fighter in on a muddy field, near Sonderhausen. Anderson is taken prisoner. The target is hit, with the help of radar, just before 1200 and the flak is heavy. At 1200 the 370th FS engages large numbers of enemy fighters, roughly half way between Kassel and the target and to the south. Capt. William R. Hodges, who is leading Red Flight at 31,000', spots about fifty Fw 190s 2,000' below, flying west. Hodges leads the bounce, pulling in behind the enemy formation. His first burst damages a tail-end charlie, just as the rest of the formation dips into a haze. Hodges follows blindly, then climbs out of the mist to find the Germans have also risen. His first kill is made from 300 yards and the bandit begins smoking before entering a high speed spin. The rest of the formation is still unaware of the Mustangs as Hodges pulls in behind two bandits flying a tight wing and his first burst hits one in the canopy. As he hammers the 190 again, it makes a slight left turn while the 190 on the left moves to the right. Holding down on the trigger Hodges riddles both enemy fighters, with one going down in a spin and the other straight down in flames. White Flight joins the battle and their leader, Maj. Daniel D. McKee, fires on a 190 but a P-51 cuts in, blocking his aim. McKee slides over behind another bandit, fires a short burst but observes no hits. Moving on to a third enemy fighter he does get some strikes and continues shooting until the 190 begins to burn. Lt. Thomas P. Smith blasts some large pieces off a 190 causing it to snap down to the right for kill number

Modelers will be glad to see the markings of fighters other than those flown by the aces and covered so often. Here are three P-51Ds from the 368th FS that will confirm two things; one, the commander always gets a good paint job. Two, it's foolish to argue about so called standard stencilling. Top left, crew chief Sid Wheeler's *Gruffie*. Note CV appears to be of the proper size and shape while the E's horizontal legs are too long. Bisher. Top right, crew chief Ken Wilson's *Irish*. The letters "CV-O" are equally proportioned but squat in comparison to CV-E. Bisher. On the bottom Col. John P. Randolph poses with his personal P-51D *Nancy*. Stencilling is by the book and the curvature at the edge of the green paint on the nose is very well executed.

one. As the first victim is on the way down, another 190 slides in front of Smith from the right and a four second burst tears off sections of the fighter that zip back past the P-51. This bandit also snaps down to the right, becoming kill number two. Smith then banks to the right and blasts a 190 from 200 yards. This one is hit in the left wing root and is awarded as a probable. Leveling out Smith pulls in behind another bandit scoring hits in the left wing root. The enemy fighter rolls over to the right and goes down, to also be awarded as a probable. Lt. Vernon L. Caid, also of White Flight, pulls in behind the enemy formation damaging his first target before having to break off. Moving back into firing position Caid scores hits in the cockpit of a second fighter and the pilot bails out. Caid then chases his next victim in a dive, scoring with several long bursts, before pulling out at 4,000', while the 190 augers in at almost 600 m.p.h. The battle is not one sided though, for during this combat pilots of the 370th FS witness six B-17s being shot down, with only one chute seen. The 370th loses Lt. Stanley F. Stegnerski who is listed as MIA. Meanwhile Blue Flight, led by Capt. Will D. Burgsteiner, enters the fray, with Burgsteiner scoring hits on a 190 as his three left side guns jam. This enemy fighter is hit in the left wing, across the fuselage and out into the right wing for a probable. Burgsteiner climbs back into the battle and fires several bursts at another 190 but observes no strikes. Lt. John W. Lamont damages a 190 before losing it in the haze. Lt. Homer A. Staup closes in with his (Blue) flight, fires on a bandit from 6 o'clock and notes strikes on it and the 190 directly ahead of his intended target. Moving into 100 yards Staup fires again and the nearest 190 explodes, while the second 190 pulls up in a chandelle and the pilot bails out.

Capt. Ralph L. "Slick" Cox, the leader of and last remaining pilot from Black Flight, which was used to fill slots caused by pilots that returned early, takes on about fifty enemy fighters. Singling out one on the left flank he fires two long bursts from 45°, scoring a few hits. Before Cox can get off another shot the pilot bails out. Now flying at 20,000', Cox spots another gaggle of fifty enemy fighters attacking the bombers. As he levels out of a climb to 35,000' three more gaggles of about fifty each are seen. Cox then climbs to 40,000' screaming for help over his radio. Ten minutes later, as he positions himself to bounce the last gaggle, six P-51s are observed climbing in his direction. Cox makes his dive, swoops down in front of the approaching Mustangs and calls over his radio for them to follow. Thinking his tail is covered, Cox singles out a Fw190 and after firing two long bursts, from dead astern, the pilot hits the silk. Pulling in behind victim number two Cox hammers it until it explodes. Now tracers burn past his Mustang and Cox discovers he has eight bandits on his tail. He then pulls away in a climbing spiral and heads for home, still very much alone. Cox later reports having seen a total of approximately 250 enemy fighters, none being aggressive, except the eight that latched onto his tail. This is perhaps due in part to the fact that many of the Fw190 pilots pressed into service today, in an attempt to crush the bombing force, were from ground attack units and as a result not well versed in the type of fighting they encountered. At 1230, near Erfurt, Yellow Flight of the 368th FS, spots about 100 Fw190s 5,000' below, parallel to and beneath the bombers. As they bounce the bandits, Lt. John S. Keesey selects a target and gives it a squirt. There is a flash and a puff of smoke just before the 190 goes into a turn. Following the damaged fighter down Keesey pulls the trigger several times but all six guns are jammed. On returning to England it is found that only three guns had fired. Keesey is credited with a damaged. Another flight from the 368th, led by Capt. Thomas J. McGeever, is near Gotha when the fighting begins in the vicinity of Erfurt, which is about fifteen miles away. McGeever leads his flight down to look for an airfield and do some *goal tending*. Lt. Emory C. Cook spots a well camouflaged Fw190 base and the flight makes a pass, as the Germans put up the heaviest hail of fire ever seen at an airfield. McGeever destroys a 190 but in turn his Mustang is hit in the coolant system and at 1238 he radios he is bailing out. He is later reported as KIA. The total aerial score for the day is 18-3-3, all Fw190s.

The 359th FG is placed on standby as a replacement group, should the 352nd FG at Bodney, or the 20th FG at Kingscliffe be unable to take off due to weather.

256   November 25, 1944 (0951-1540, A) (1000-1540, B)

Maj. James K. Lovett, of the 370th FS, leads *A* group and Lt.Col. John P. Randolph leads *B* group as the 359th provides support for B-17s that are hitting the synthetic oil facilities at Merseburg, Germany. *A* group puts up thirty-two P-51s and of that number five return early. *B* group has twenty-seven Mustangs take off and four that abort. The 359th is under MEW control on this mission. R/V occurs for *A* group at 1110 and 28,000' over Stavelot, Belgium, while R/V is made by *B* group at 1130 and 26,000' over Bad Nauheim, Germany. The bombing is done by radar and no B-17s from the force escorted by the 359th are lost even though the flak is wicked, in fact the worst ever witnessed by the Group. On the way out Lt. Eugene F. Britton, of the 368th FS, lands on the continent, returning the following day. "Big Ben" contrails are observed today.

257   November 26, 1944 (0954-1327)

Today the 359th provides penetration, target and withdrawal support. for B-17s raiding an oil refinery at Misburg, Germany. The mission is lead by Maj. Roy W. Evans, with forty-five P-51s taking off and two returning early. R/V is made over the Zuider Zee at 1110 and 24,000'. The bombing is done by radar because of a smoke screen over the target. Several oil fires are observed as a result of the raid. The other escorting fighter groups engage the Luftwaffe but the 359th encounters no enemy aircraft. Of the 406 Forts dispatched on this mission ten are lost, four are declared Category E and 160 are damaged.

258   November 27, 1944 (1021-1456)

Maj. Roy W. Evans leads the Group on a scheduled strafing mission to an airfield at Ehem, Germany located just north of Brunswick. Fifty-three P-51s leave East Wretham and four abort. R/V occurs over Egmond, Netherlands at 1115 and 29,000'. Prior to reaching Dummer Lake bandits are reported to the south (north of Münster, Germany). Most of the Group drop their tanks and divert to investigate. Heavy flak is encountered along the way and the

Nov. 27, 1944, was a memorable day for Capt. Ray S. Wetmore (Smack) and Lt. Robert Miles York (Rudy) of the 370th FS. When the pair, who were shadowing 200 enemy fighters and waiting on reinforcements to arrive, were discovered, Wetmore told York, "You take the hundred on the right and I'll take the hundred on the left." Then ensued one of the finest dogfights of WW II. When the smoke cleared Wetmore was credited with three kills and York with three kills and a probable, all Me109s. Left, Wetmore posed for this publicity shot on Jan. 24, 1945. Right, York and his P-51D. Note curved sheet metal deflector on the top cowling's forward edge. This simple device kept oil, which often leaked from prop seals, from obscuring the windscreen.

359th breaks into flights to evade the barrage. The reported bandits turn out to be another Mustang group and the 359th is now scattered, with some flights having to return because of limited fuel. Red Flight of the 370th FS, led by Capt. Ray S. Wetmore, is headed for Ehmen when he spots two gaggles of enemy fighters southeast of Hannover. One gaggle consists of about 100 Me109s and the other a like number of Fw190s. At 1300 Wetmore radios the remnants of the Group giving them his location and altitude. Lt. Robert L. McInnes (Red 4), reports engine trouble and Wetmore orders Lt. Jimmy C. Shoffit to escort McInnes back to base. Three minutes later, as Wetmore and his wingman Lt. Robert M. York, are shadowing the rear gaggle of Me109s at 6 o'clock high, they are discovered and several four ship flights turn to engage the two Mustangs. With no help in sight and trouble on the way Wetmore and York attack, despite odds of 100 to 1 against them. Closing to 600 yards and using his K-14 gunsight, Wetmore scores his first kill, sending a 109 spinning down in flames. York follows up by sending another 109 spinning down, billowing black smoke. Now turning to meet the 109s sent to attack them, Wetmore scores hits from 300 yards, at 20° deflection and sends the third 109 tumbling down, emitting black smoke. As yet another 109 attacks Wetmore, he turns into the attacker and they turn down from 30,000' to the deck, with the advantage changing several times, the German pilot being very adept at his trade. Wetmore scores hits several times before running out of ammo. Then playing a gambit he gets into firing position and the enemy pilot bails out. During this combat, which has taken twenty-five minutes, Wetmore's P-51 has taken two 20mm rounds in the left gun bay. For the next ten minutes he is repeatedly attacked by 190s and manages to out maneuver them until they break off and then he heads back to base. Meanwhile York presses his attack, sliding in behind a Me109 and scoring heavily, sending the enemy fighter tumbling

Top left, Maj. Niven Kendall Cranfill, of the 368th FS, destroyed two Me109s and a Fw190 on Nov. 27, 1944, which earned him a second Silver Star. "Cranny" completed 133 missions totaling 506 combat hours. Top right, Capt. Donald L. Windmiller, of the 370th FS, bagged two Me109s and while engaged with his second kill received a R/T from Lt. Dick D. Connelly saying, "The son of a bitch has shot me down Windy. I'm bailing out." Right, D.D. Connelly and his namesake P-51D. Connelly had a premonition the last mission of his tour would literally be his last. He was correct.

out of control, shedding parts and smoking. Suddenly another 109 passes about 800 yards in front of him, in a slight dive. Closing in, the K-14 gunsight aids York in making a long range shot that causes the bandit to explode. York then spots a 109 slightly above and turning into him. Cutting the German off in the turn he begins firing at 500 yards and holds down on the trigger until pulling up and over the 109. Just then he notices tracers passing over his P-51's wing and does a quarter snap and spin to evade the attacker. During this move York almost collides with the 109 he has just hammered, noting the pilot is in the process of bailing out. York dives past the now pilotless fighter, picking up speed in a spiral to keep his tail clear, levels off in a cloud layer and heads for England. By now Blue Flight of the 370th FS has joined the battle, diving on a gaggle of Me109s from 34,000'. Leveling out at 28,000', Lt. Dick D. Connelly (Blue 3) and his wingman Lt. Donald L. "Windy" Windmiller (Blue 4) pull in behind the Germans and

"Windy" nails a 109 from 500 yards, sending it down in flames. Looking back to clear his tail "Windy" notices a bandit moving into firing position. He pulls the Mustang up in a sharp 180° turn the 109 can't match; it stalls and drops its nose. "Windy" then sees a 109 attacking him from 90°. He turns to meet the attacker, gets on his tail and fires a long burst from 500 yards scoring a few hits. Closing in to 300 yards he fires again and this time the 109 noses over in flames. While making his second kill, Windmiller receives a R/T from Connelly saying "The son of a bitch has shot me down, Windy. I'm bailing out". Connelly, who had a premonition he would be shot down, on this the last mission of his tour, is later listed as KIA. Alone and low on fuel "Windy" heads for England. As Maj. Roy W. Evans, of the 369th FS, is leading his flight in response to Wetmore's R/T for help he is joined by Maj. Niven K. Cranfill and his wingman, Lt. Richard H. Daniels, White1 and 2 respectively, of the 368th FS. These six Mustangs arrive on the scene at 1305 and 31,000'. Making a diving attack, from out of the sun, on the rear of the enemy formation, Evans fires a burst from 50ø that takes off one and a half feet of a 109's wing , before breaking off with a bandit on his own tail. Moving back into a firing position Evans nails another 109 at 30 to 35°, from 250 closing to 200 yards and sees strikes on the left side of the fighters engine and fuselage. This 109 turns left, rolls over and spins down on fire. Evans is credited with one damaged and one destroyed. Lt. Robert T. Lancaster scores a victory when a 109 crosses in front of and below him. Firing from 70° he observes strikes on the wing roots and the fuselage near the cockpit. The 109 begins to smoke then snaps into a spin. Maj. Cranfill fires on a 109 during a violent evasive action but notes no hits. As he follows the German in a vertical dive, the 109's canopy comes off, the fighter then zooms up in a sharp climb and the pilot jumps, sailing past Cranfill's P-51 before opening his chute. Cranfill is now at 8,000' and seven minutes have elapsed since the battle began. Latching onto a Fw190 he chases it over a small town, where his Mustang draws some inaccurate ground fire. Looking back to clear his tail Cranfill finds a red and yellow checker nose P-51 (357th FG) following him and is grateful for the cover. Cranfill's windscreen has become iced over and he brushes it with his glove to clear the view. Despite this handicap he manages to track the 190 and fire several effective bursts, but due to a haze and the slate grey paint on the enemy fighter, he loses his prey. However F/O Thomas W. Jackson, pilot of the

357th P-51 covering Cranfill's tail, witnesses the Fw190 crash and confirms it as a kill. Now below 500', Cranfill spots a Me109 crossing over him from left to right and pulls in behind the bandit. The warmer air at this altitude is now melting the ice off the windscreen, making it easier for Cranfill to keep with the German fighter. Both fighters now have their flaps in combat position, but Cranfill is able to turn inside the 109, scoring hits several times, from about 300 yards. Finally the 109 pulls up, stalls and dives straight into the ground and explodes. Jackson is still there and confirms Cranfill's third kill. It is later found that only two of his guns were functioning and only 588 rounds of API were expended in the destruction of the three German fighters. Lt. Richard H. Daniels engages a Fw190 during the initial bounce and scores hits in the fuselage near the canopy. The pilot of the 190 then rolls it over and heads for the deck, kicking the fighter from side to side making it a difficult target. Daniels loses the 190 which is trailing black smoke, in the haze. On returning to base it is discovered that only his left outboard gun had fired and that a mere sixty-five rounds of API were expended. Daniel's claim of a Fw190 destroyed is later amended to a probable.

259   November 29, 1944 (1045-1626)

Lt.Cols. John P. Randolph and Daniel D. McKee lead *A* and *B* groups respectively today as the 359th provides escort for B-17s hitting an oil refinery at Misburg, Germany. *A* group has thirty-two P-51s get airborne with five returning early, while *B* group puts up thirty Mustangs with only one abort, Maj. Niven K. Cranfill, of the 370th FS. R/V is made over Egmond, Netherlands at 1140 and 25,000'. The 359th flies a MEW controlled sweep in the target area but encounters no enemy aircraft. No bombers are lost but the results of the raid are obscured by clouds. Lt. Frank O. Lux, of the 370th FS, lands at St. Trond, Belgium and returns to base on the 30th. The remainder of the 359th returns safely to England.

260   November 30, 1944 (1035-1639)

Maj. Roy W. Evans and Lt.Col. Daniel D. McKee lead *A* and *B* groups respectively as the 359th furnishes escort for 451 B-17s bombing the synthetic oil plants at Zeitz, Germany. *A* group has three P-51s that abort out of thirty-seven taking off, while *B* group gets thirty-two up and also has three return early. R/V is made over Leige, Belgium at 1205 and 20,000'. Ban-

Model builders have long pondered the application sequence of kill markings on Ray Wetmore's *Daddy's Girl*. The two photos on this page give some good clues to help make an educated guess. Look closely at the left photo and note the serial number has been applied using a stencil and the blue areas of the star and bar insignia are masked off with tape in preparation for spraying on a fresh coat of white paint. In the right photo the serial number has been touched up and the breaks in the lines caused by a stencil have vanished. Now look at the star, its points no longer touch the perimeter of the circular blue field. Notice the kill markings are on the side and the canopy frame before the paint job and have been removed from the canopy frame. In my opinion the kill markings on the canopy frame came first and since Wetmore and all of his ground crew have passed beyond the veil this is all we have to draw on.

dits are reported south of Frankfurt, Germany but none are found and the 359th returns to escort the bombers. The target is heavily defended by flak and eleven Forts are lost, four declared Category E and 287 damaged. The bombing results are noted to be excellent.

*   **December 1, 1944 (bad weather)**

261   December 2, 1944 (1118-1526)

Lt.Col. John P. Randolph leads the Group as they provide escort for B-17s raiding the marshalling yards at Oberlahnstein, Germany. Fifty-six Mustangs take off and three abort. R/V is made over Huy, Belgium at 26,000'. Over the target the 359th is vectored, by MEW control, to an area southeast of the target. No enemy aircraft are found and the Group returns to the target where they give escort to two squadrons of Forts that were forced to make a second bombing run due to poor visibility. It is an outstanding operation with no bombers being lost or damaged. Lt. Milton S. Merry, of the 370th FS, lands at St. Trond, Belgium returning when the weather permits. The remainder of the Group returns safely to England.

*   **December 3, 1944 (bad weather)**

262   December 4, 1944 (1000-1558)

Majs. Roy W. Evans, of headquarters, and James K. Lovett, of the 370th FS, lead *A* and *B* groups respectively as the 359th furnishes escort for B-17s blast-

ing the marshalling yards at Kassel, Germany. A total of sixty-two P-51s leave East Wretham on this mission and there is only one abort! R/V occurs over Leige, Belgium at 1114 and 24,000'. Although the Forts are twenty-two minutes late when they arrive over the target, the results of the bombing are observed to be excellent. No bombers are lost and no enemy fighters are encountered. Lt. Donald G. Page, of the 370th FS, lands at Brussels, Belgium for fuel and returns later in the day.

263   December 5, 1944 (0838-1435)

Lt.Col. John P. Randolph leads *A* group as they provide roving support and Maj. Roy W. Evans leads *B* group as they provide close support for B-17s hitting the munitions and tank industries at Berlin, Germany. Sixty-one Mustangs take off and six return early. R/V is made by *A* group at 0942 over the Zuider Zee and by *B* group at 0948 over Zwolle, Netherlands. The bombing is done by radar and the flak over the target is heavy. Nine Forts are lost and 105 are damaged. A single Me163 is the only enemy aircraft seen, fleetingly, by the 359th. Capt. William R. Hodges and Lt. Emory G. Johnson, of the 370th FS, land at St. Trond, Belgium and return when the weather permits. The remainder of the Group returns safely to England.

264   December 6, 1944 (0937-1500, A) (0945-1447, B) (1047-1450, C)

Majs. Daniel D. McKee, Niven K. Cranfill and William R. Hodges lead *A*, *B* and *C* groups respectively

Left, Capt. Wilbur C. Zeigler the Station Chaplain. Top right, Father Hewitt distributing Holy Communion to the Roman Catholics of the 359th FG. Bottom right, Chapel Choir which was directed by Cpl. Miles Gottschall top row on the left. Gottschall was the Chaplain's assistant and also formed the Thunderbolt Dance Band. He was awarded the Bronze Star for his many activities. The base chapel was used by all denominations.

as the 359th furnishes support for B-17s bombing the synthetic oil plants at Merseburg, Germany. The Group puts up a total of sixty-six P-51s and six return early. *A* and *B* groups make R/V over Egmond, Netherlands at 1033 and 22,000', while *C* group makes R/V over Hildesheim, Germany. The bomber formations are observed to be very good. The target is hit with the help of radar and, despite intense flak, no Forts are lost. The Luftwaffe is not encountered. Lts. Elby J. Beal and Ray A. Boyd, of the 368th FS, land at St. Trond, Belgium and return later in the day.

***   December 7-9, 1944 (Bad weather.)**

265   December 10, 1944 (0858-1304)

Lt.Col. John P. Randolph leads the Group today as they fly penetration, target and withdrawal support for B-24s raiding the marshalling yards at Bingen, Germany. Lt. Galen E. Ramser, of the 370th FS,

ground loops when his fighter's engine quits during take-off, but he escapes serious injury. The Mustang, however, is a total loss. Of the fifty-six P-51s that do take off, three abort. R/V is made over the English Channel at 0930. The bombing is accomplished using radar equipped pathfinder aircraft, with no results being observed. The flak is light. No enemy aircraft are encountered.

266   December 11, 1944 (0944-1448)

Maj. Roy W. Evans leads *A* group and Maj. James K. Lovett, of the 370th FS, leads *B* group as the 359th flies penetration, target and withdrawal support for B-17s bombing the marshalling yards at Frankfurt, Germany. The Group puts up sixty-two Mustangs and six return early. R/V occurs at 1053 and 26,000' over Leige, Belgium. The bomber formations are noted to be poor but improve after the target is hit. The Luftwaffe is not encountered and no Forts are lost.

The 368th FS can claim two pilots that became aces on the same mission Lts. Archibald and Olson (read mission text for Dec. 18, 1944). Left, Lt. David B. Archibald. Right, close-up of the P-51D flown by Lt. Olson on the day he became an ace.

On the way out, near Verdun, France a gunner on a B-24 fires at some P-51s from the 368th FS but his marksmanship is as bad as his aircraft identification and no hits are taken.

267 December 12, 1944 (0938-1530)

The 359th furnishes penetration, target and withdrawal support for B-17s hitting the synthetic oil plants at Merseburg, Germany. Lt.Col. John P. Randolph leads *A* group and Maj. Daniel D. McKee leads *B* group. The number of Mustangs to take off each day is gradually rising and sixty-seven make it off this morning, with four returning early. R/V is made over Huy, Belgium at 26,000'. The bombing results are observed to be excellent and only one B-17 is lost. A R/T is received stating RAF Lancasters are being attacked near Dortman, Germany and the 370th FS goes to the bombers aid. The 370th chases off about thirty Me109s but not before five Lancs have been shot down. While giving chase to these 109s the 370th is jumped by an even larger force of bandits that are flying as top cover. The entire enemy force is then lost in the clouds and the 370th returns to base without having fired a shot.

* December 13, 14, 1944 (Bad weather.)

On December 13, M/Sgt. Arthur E. Newman and T/Sgt. Lawrence F. Haas, of the 368th FS, are awarded the Bronze Star for inventions that increased the operational efficiency of the Group. Newman designed and constructed an engine pre-oiler that increased the life of Merlins three hours. Newman's contribution to increased efficiency in maintenance and an 87% in service rate for the 368th's aircraft are also cited. Haas designed new sway braces for drop tanks after the factory supplied units began breaking and puncturing the tanks. The braces designed by Haas had larger pads and failures were eliminated. The braces were manufactured by the Group's service squadron and were adopted by the VIII Fighter Command. Haas also designed new pressurization fittings for the drop tanks. By the end of December about 8,100 drop tanks using these fittings had been used without a failure. Haas made the required modifications to turn a fuel trailer into a ethylene glycol dispenser, making it possible to

Lt. Paul E. Olson on the right and his crew chief S/Sgt. Woodrow J. Wilson pose next to *Supermouse*, which was his aircraft at the time.

quickly service the entire squadron and eliminate waste.

268   December 15, 1944 (1006-1437, A) (1003-1425, B)

Majs. Roy W. Evans and Daniel D. McKee lead *A* and *B* groups respectively as the 359th flies penetration, target and withdrawal support for B-17s bombing the marshalling yards and a tank factory at Kassel, Germany. The Group manages to get forty-six fighters up for this mission but eight abort. R/V for *A* group is made over Hasselt, Belgium and Egmond, Netherlands for *B* group. Escort is difficult due to dense clouds, rising to 33,000' and the bombing is done in conjunction with radar equipped pathfinder aircraft. No bombers are lost today but six are listed Category E, as a result of flak. No enemy aircraft are seen. Lt. Donald W. Chatfield, of the 368th, is forced to land at St. Trond, Belgium when his P-51's engine catches fire.

*   December 16, 17, 1944 (bad weather)

On the 17th the pilots are finally told about the German V-2 rockets and that the mysterious "Big Ben" contrails they have been observing are made by these weapons, against which there is no defence.

269   December 18, 1944 (1124-1607)

This is another red-letter day for the 359th FG, as two pilots from the 368th FS, Lts. David B. Archibald and Paul E. Olson, both become aces in one day, a feat duplicated only once in the history of the 8th AF.

Lt.Col. John P. Randolph leads the Group as they provide penetration, target and withdrawal support for B-17s raiding the marshalling yards at Cologne, Germany. Out of the fifty-three Mustangs to leave East Wretham there is only one abort. R/V is made with the assigned bombers at 1240 and 26,000' over Hannut, Belgium. The weather is so terrible today that over 500 of the 985 bombers sent out abort. Due to 10/10 cloud cover the Forts being escorted by the 359th do not hit their primary target and look for targets of opportunity. After twenty minutes the Forts turn for home, without dropping their loads. The 359th is then ordered to stay with the remaining bombers. At 1300, while flying at 32,000', Lt. Paul E. Olson experiences freezing aileron controls and escorted by Lt. David B. Archibald drops to 10,000' so the controls will thaw. At 1340 a R/T is received stating that sixty plus bandits are between Kassel and Cologne, Germany but the 359th is ordered to remain with the bombers. Archibald and Olson head in the direction of Cologne to check out the report and soon notice a B-17 that has apparently crash landed. Archibald radios Olson that he will drop his fuel tanks on the bomber and for him to strafe the Fort and set it on fire. As they approach their target someone is seen exiting the bomber and the attack is called off. As Archibald starts to circle the bomber for another look, camouflaged 20mm flak guns open fire and he is hit in the left thigh by a shell fragment. The pain however is dulled because his legs are still numb, from the time spent at 32,000'. Five minutes later Archibald and Olson chance upon the enemy fighters. Approaching from the rear, they use the element of surprise and attack. Engaging the formation of Fw190s from an angle of 30°, Archy downs two and Olson one. Strangely, the formation doesn't break, so the two Mustangs swing around for another pass. This time they overshoot the last flight of 190s and Archy bags the leader of the next flight, while Olson downs the leader's wingman. Now the 190s break in confusion and during their third pass Archy explodes another bandit, while Olson gets good hits on one, causing the pilot to bail out. The now pilotless 190 collides with another bandit and they both explode. Maneuvering for a fourth strike Olson notices flak behind them but they continue to press the attack. Two Fw190s attack the Mustangs from the left and right and they collide head-on, becoming victims nine and ten. Archy then scores good hits along the fuselage of a 190 but the flak gunners now have their range and both P-51s are hit. Olson's P-51 explodes, throwing him clear but at the same time covers him with flaming fuel and oil. He manages to beat out the flames, just in time to pull the rip chord and get a good canopy. Due to his burns Olson is not able to evade capture and is soon taken prisoner by a flak guncrew at Vohn, which is just east of Cologne. The Germans take him to a local doctor, then place him in an ambulance for transport to a front-line hospital named Hoffmonstahl. Meanwhile, Archibald has passed out from loss of blood, and his Mustang crashes and explodes, hurling his body 100' from the wreckage. He is found seven hours later, still unconscious, and loaded onto the same ambulance that is taking Olson to the hospital. Archibald is in Hoffmonstahl for two weeks with only fleeting moments of lucidity, remembering only someone mentioning Christmas, then "Happy New Year." During

Archibald's next time of awareness he is shocked to discover that he is a POW. The pain from his injuries, a spine that is fractured in five locations, eight broken ribs, broken left shoulder blade, right wrist, two bones in the right hand and a fractured skull, cause him to pass out once more. The next time he awakens there is an air raid in progress, and a hot piece of shrapnel has come through the window, which is open to prevent the glass from being blown into the room, landing on his bad leg. Archibald is then moved to a room where Olson shares the cot next to him and learns that Olson is leaving. It is the last time he sees Olson until returning to the U.S. On March 3, 1945, Archibald and 220 other Allied fliers are packed into boxcars and taken to Stalag 11B, in Fallingbostel. During the trip their train is strafed by Mustangs from the 368th FS. Archibald, who is having to stand in shifts with the other men because there isn't room for them all to sit at the same time, has the prisoners wave their handkerchiefs out of the openings in the boxcar to signal the fighters; this evidently works, as the strafing ceases. The prison camp is liberated on April 16, 1945 and Archibald hobbles to freedom on two canes, but with several years of medical treatment ahead of him. The combat of Dec. 18, 1944, was witnessed by Pvt. Hunt, a captured American medic caring for the American wounded at Hoffmanstahl. Hunt stood on the hospital grounds watching the *Archibald & Olson vs. the Luftwaffe* show and confirmed their kills. The rest of the mission is mundane in comparison, no bombers being lost, only one damaged and the remainder of the 359th FG returning to base without incident.

*   **December 19-22, 1944 (bad weather)**

270   December 23, 1944 (1039-1529, A) (1034-1520, B)

Maj. Roy W. Evans leads *A* group and Maj. Daniel D. McKee leads *B* group as the 359th flies penetration, target and withdrawal support for B-17s bombing a rail junction and the marshalling yards at Homburg, Germany. Fifty-six P-51s take-off on this mission and three abort. R/V occurs north of Trier, Germany at 1220 and 28,000'. Five minutes later White Flight of the 368th FS receives a R/T stating bandits are seen climbing in the vicinity of Koblenz. As they head toward Koblenz a straggling B-17 is seen being attacked by a Me109. As Lt. Robert E. Benefiel (White 1) turns to attack, a second 109 appears from behind his flight and is engaged by Lt. Emory C. Cook. Cook

Lt. John J. Kelly III, top left, scored a victory over a Me109 on the mission of Dec. 24, 1944. Lt. Bryce H. Thomson, top right, scored a kill on the same mission when Lt. John Edwin Keur, below, handed off the Me109 he was attacking due to jammed machine-guns. The following information comes from a French magazine article translated by Ms. Anne Scheerer the French teacher at North Hagerstown, Maryland HS The article was also a class project. Thomson's P-51D, *Lil Audrey* (named for his wife), was damaged by debris from the 109 he shot down causing the Merlin to catch fire and Thomson to abandon ship.

nails his quarry and the pilot bails out. Benefiel then follows his target through a series of maneuvers before getting in a good burst that sends the 109 in a smoking, vertical dive into the ground. The pilot doesn't escape from this one. Later on, a 368th flight, led by Capt. Wilbur H. Lewis, spots a He280 jet fighter but they are unable to engage it. This is the first sighting of the type. The bombing results are observed to be excellent.

The He280 sighted today is probably the last flyable example of the type, the others having been either damaged or destroyed during testing, or by air raids, making this a very chance encounter.

271　December 24, 1944 (1135-1641, A) (1140-1639, B)

This is the biggest mission of the war in terms of the number of aircraft involved. The 8th AF will launch 2,046 heavy bombers and 853 fighters. The 359th will also set a record, for the Group, by sending off seventy-six Mustangs, with only four returning early. Lt.Col. John P. Randolph leads *A* group and Maj. Niven K. Cranfill, of the 368th FS, leads *B* group as the 359th furnishes penetration, target and withdrawal support for B-17s raiding airfields in Germany. R/V is made southeast of Brussels, Belgium at 1245 and 22,000'. At 1345, near Vogelsand, Yellow Flight of the 369th FS, led by Lt. John E.

Top, cooks of the Purple Shaft Club pose with some turkeys being served for Christmas 1944. The tonnage of food required to keep the 359th FG fed for a single month is reflected in these Jan. 1944 figures; chicken 3,807 lbs., turkey 1,000 lbs., steak 6,644 lbs., other beef 20,409 lbs., pork 6,134 lbs. frankfurters and luncheon meats 3,363 lbs. and 27,900 lbs. of bread. Bottom, the Group fed, entertained and gave gifts to about 200 local orphans during Christmas.

Keur, is apprized of a Me109 near the bomber stream. On being intercepted the 109 enters a dive, pulling out at 18,000'. Keur fires two bursts, observing strikes on the fuselage before overshooting his prey. He then chases the enemy fighter in another dive, scoring only a few hits before his guns jam. Keur then calls on his wingman, Lt. Bryce H. Thomson, to take over the attack, as the bandit climbs back to 15,000', where he is caught. Thomson fires a five second burst into the 109's cockpit and engine; it catches fire and crashes with the pilot still aboard. As this is happening, Lt. John J. Kelly III (Yellow 3) spots another Me109 starting to attack a straggling Fort. Firing a long burst from 30 down to 0° deflection he scores hits on the 109's right wing, tail and fuselage. The bandit rolls over and goes down trailing white smoke, then tumbles out of control into a forest where it explodes. Meanwhile Thomson's P-51 catches fire and he heads back to base. Forced to bail out near Dinant, Belgium, his chute luckily carries him to the west bank of the Meuse river, which is friendly territory. Good bombing results are reported by the 370th FS, on an airfield at Giessen, Germany, with enemy aircraft seen exploding. The 369th FS reports good hits made on an airfield at Hattenrod, Germany and several other targets in the vicinity. Two Forts are lost, one is seen exploding north of Dorsel, Germany with no survivors. On the way out the 359th is vectored from northeast of Giessen to the vicinity of Bonn, Germany and the 368th and 370th FSs intercept enemy fighters at 20,000' over Cologne at 1520. There are two formations of bandits, one consisting of twelve plus Fw190s and the other of fifteen to twenty Me109s. About fifteen miles to the south, about 100 9th AF B-26 Marauders are also observed, the probable target of the enemy fighters. Black Flight of the 368th FS, led by Lt. Elby J. Beal, jumps the 190 gaggle. Beal gets into a Lufberry (a defensive circle) with four 190s, only to find his guns will not fire. Eventually the guns fire erratically and Beal sends two of the enemy fighters crashing into the city of Cologne. A Me109 then gets on the tail of Beal's Mustang and while firing on him almost rams the P-51. As the 109 mushes by in the Mustang's prop wash, Beal tries to get a shot at it but a Fw190 gets between them. Switching targets Beal fires several bursts from twenty-five yards dead astern of the 190. Pieces fly off the bandit, which begins trailing black smoke and then enters a steep dive, the pilot likely dead. Lt. Ray A. Boyd (Black 3), gets behind a 190 scoring hits on the left wing and fuselage, but intent on his kill, fails to notice another 190 has slipped in behind him. The

Mustang is fatally hit and Boyd is wounded in the left leg and foot. Lt. Leonard D. Carter tries to raise him on the radio, to no avail. It is later learned Boyd became a POW. Meanwhile the 370th FS has joined the fight and Lt. John W. Wilson sees Boyd being nailed. Cutting out four checker nose Mustangs that are chasing the victorious Fw 190, Wilson gives it a long burst from 150 yards and 70 to 80° deflection. The 190 bursts into flames and the canopy pops off but the pilot doesn't bail out. The doomed fighter then enters a slow downward spin. Capt. Andrew T. Lemmens credits his K-14 gunsight with an 800 yard shot that hits a 190 in the area of the cockpit, causing an explosion that sends flames halfway out on the wings (the fuel tank is located under the cockpit floor). The 190 then enters a 75° dive and explodes as it hits the ground. The pilot doesn't escape. Wilson then joins with Lemmens and they return to England. Lt. Robert G. Oakley follows a 190 from 10,000' in a dive that reaches over 500 m.p.h., scoring hits that cause the bandit to emit brown smoke. Both fighters start to pull out of the dive but only Oakley succeeds, as the 190 plows into the ground and explodes. Lt. Emory G. Johnson (White 2) damages a 190 with strikes on its wing but is forced to break when a bandit gets behind him. Shaking the 190 on his tail, Johnson jumps another 190, scoring hits around the canopy and this one goes straight into the ground. Turning right, he fires on another190 registering hits on the right wing. Johnson's second kill is scored when he bounces a 190 flying at 2,000', fires a burst into the fuselage aft of the cockpit causing an explosion and throwing the fighter into a spin. Capt. William R. Hodges (White 3) hammers a 190 from astern, at 15,000', sending it down in flames. The score today is 10-2-4.

At 1900 a Christmas Eve Candlelight Service is held at the station theater. It is dedicated to those pilots who have fallen in battle.

***   December 25, 1944 (bad weather)**

272   December 26, 1944 (1007-1452)

Lt.Col. Roy W. Evans leads the 359th today as they furnish escort for B-24s bombing a railway bridge and the marshalling yards at Niederlahnstein, Germany which is near Koblenz. The weather is so bad that only volunteers are asked to fly the mission. Sixty Mustangs leave East Wretham and five abort. R/V is made over the target area at 1155. The bombing is

Top, the Douglas A-20 Havoc flown by the 359th and no doubt belonging to the 3rd Gunnery and Tow-Target Flight. This aircraft was used to take operations personnel to Reims, France for the Dec. 27, 1944 mission staged from there. The A-20 was later destroyed in a crash at East Wretham on April 19, 1945. Right, a group shot of the pilots who staged out of Reims; 369th FS unless noted otherwise, standing left to right: Lt. James R. Parsons Jr., Lt. Robert T. Lancaster, Lt. Vernon T. Judkins, Capt. Jack Duane Stevens, Capt. Ralph L. Brown (368th), Lt. George M. Givan and Lt. Cornelius J. Cavenaugh (368th). Kneeling left to right: Capt. Robert L. McInnes (370th), Maj. James W. Parsons, Capt. Harry Lee Matthew, Lt. Roger Winston Porter and Capt. Lewis G. Crane.

done both visually and by radar. No bombers are lost and no contact is made with the Luftwaffe. On the return flight twenty-one of the Group's Mustangs land at Reims, France. They are met by Lt.Col. John P. Randolph, Maj. John R. Fitzpatrick and Capt. Clarence Steele, who arrived in an A-20 Havoc, taking off right after the Group left for Germany. Their job is to organize a mission to be flown from Reims, the next day. Ten of the P-51s are damaged, mostly the tail wheels, while taxiing on the frozen and rutted turf. Over 500 C-47s are seen south of Charleroi, Belgium, headed east at 3,000', probably to drop supplies.

273   December 27, 1944 (0956-1444, A & B)

The 359th is divided into *A*, *B* and *C* groups today and two missions are flown. *A* and *B* groups are launched from East Wretham, with Majs. Niven K. Cranfill and Daniel D. McKee leading respectively. This force provides penetration, target and withdrawal support for B-24s bombing the marshalling yards at Kaiserslautern, Germany. R/V is made by *A* group over Mons, Belgium at 1055 and 1100 for *B* group. Excellent bombing results are observed at

Cologne, Fulda and Kaiserslautern. No enemy aircraft are encountered and one Liberator is lost to flak. With the exception of Lt. Robert E. Benefiel, of the 368th FS, who lands on the continent with a surging engine, *A* and *B* groups return safely to base.

274   December 27, 1944 (? -1444, C)

This is one of the missions the 359th FG doesn't receive credit for and can easily escape the researcher's eye. Lt.Col. John P. Randolph leads the second mission of the day, which is a free-lance fighter sweep in the Frankfurt-Koblenz area. Eleven Mustangs, designated as *C* group, take off from Reims, France and three abort with low oxygen. The remaining eight fighters complete their mission, encountering no enemy aircraft. They then join with *A* and *B* groups and return to base.

Lt.Col. Roy W. Evans leads *A* group, while Majs. James K. Lovett, of the 370th FS and Niven K. Cranfill, of the 368th FS, lead B and C groups respectively as the 359th FG flies penetration, target and withdrawal support for B-17s bombing the marshalling yards at Siegburg, Germany. The Group puts up fifty-four P-51s with only two returning early. R/Vs are made over Belgium at the following times and locations: *A* group- Hannut at 1232, *B* group- Eupen at 1250 and *C* group- Brussels at 1235. At the I.P., approaching the target, sixteen P-51s of the 368th FS pull ahead of the bombers and drop chaff to blind the enemy radar. No Forts are lost and the Luftwaffe fails to show. In fact not one enemy aircraft is shot down, despite the fact all fifteen fighter groups of the 8th AF are operating.

***   December 29, 1944 (bad weather)**

While no combat mission is flown today the 369th FS loses two pilots and their fighters, on a training flight. Four Mustangs piloted by Lts. James R. Parsons Jr., George M. Givan and Robert T. Lancaster, of the 369th FS and John W. Wilson, of the 370th FS, are returning to East Wretham from Reims, France when Parsons and Givan drop through the overcast above the Thames Estuary in England. Lancaster loses sight of them as they drop below 1,000'. On landing, Wilson's altimeter is found to be giving a false reading and it is assumed Givan and Parsons crashed into the River Thames while relying on faulty altimeters in the overcast.

Also today the A-20 and eight remaining Mustangs involved in the *C* group mission of the 27th, return to East Wretham. Aboard the A-20 are fifty bottles of 1937 vintage champagne, destined to brighten the holiday season.

276   December 30, 1944 (1049- 1550)

Lt.Col. John P. Randolph leads *A* group and Maj. Daniel D. McKee leads *B* group as the 359th furnishes escort for B-17s bombing Limburg, Germany. Fifty-nine Mustangs take-off on this mission and there are no aborts. The 359th makes R/V at 1140 in the area of Formies, France. 10/10 cloud covers most of the route and the bombing is done with the help of radar. The Luftwaffe is not encountered and only one Fort is lost. The 359th returns without incident.

277   December 31, 1944 (0845-1458)

Once again the 359th is split into *A* and *B* groups as they provide penetration, target and withdrawal support for B-17s blasting an oil refinery at Misburg, Germany and an aircraft factory with the adjacent airfield at Wenzendorf, Germany. Capt. Ray S. Wetmore, of the 370th FS, leads *A* group and Maj. Niven K. Cranfill, of the 368th FS, leads *B* group. The 359th puts up a total of fifty-four P-51s and five abort. R/V occurs over Langeoog Island, Germany at 1040. A B-17 is seen exploding, when hit by flak, off the coast from Bremerhaven. Six chutes are counted, one is on fire and it lands in the water. This is one of twenty-seven Forts lost today. Excellent bombing results are noted at Wenzendorf, the first target. At 1145, northwest of Hamburg, the leader of the 369th's Blue Flight, Lt. William F. Collins and his wingman Lt. Arthur B. Morris are flying above the bomber stream, at 27,000', when two Me262s are spotted approaching them from 6 o'clock level. Collins and Morris turn right and manage to get fleeting shots at the passing jets. Morris then observes one of the jets shooting down a P-51, before passing out of range. The pair then chase a Fw190 that is attacking the bombers and the gunners on the Forts bag the 190. Again two jets are seen approaching the bombers and once more the Mustangs drive them away. As the jets leave, four Fw190s fly past the Mustangs and Collins breaks after them. Then Morris sees fifteen 190s diving for the deck. As they pursue the diving Germans, one goes into a spin and crashes. Collins and Morris then share in the destruction of two additional 190s, from which the pilots bail out. At 1150 Red, White and Blue Flights of the 370th FS are over Hannover at 32,000', on their way to the second R/V, when ten plus Me109s are sighted, at 12 o'clock low (31,000'). The 370th bounces the bandits and Lt. Frank O. Lux gets into a tight turn with a 109 scoring numerous hits that sets it on fire. The 109 then enters a spin and the pilot fails to escape. Lux then latches on the tail of another 109 and scores good hits. Lt. Lawrence A. Zizka also scores hits on this 109, puncturing the drop tank, which envelopes the bandit in flames. The blazing fighter then dives straight into the ground. Meanwhile Lux's wingman, Lt. Emory G. Johnson takes on two Me109s. Johnson and a Mustang pilot from the 4th FG (red nose), share in the destruction of a Me109, which bursts into flames and spins down. Lt. Jack E. McCoskey drives off a 109 that is attacking Lux, scoring hits twice before two Mustangs and two Thunderbolts cut him

Scenes from the dreadful winter of 1944-45. Left, the YMCA tea wagon which was run by Helen Moore. In the background is P-51B CV-M 42-106693. This Mustang was flown by F/O Boyd N. Adkins Jr. when he shot down a Fw190 on Oct. 24, 1944. Note this aircraft is equipped with a Malcolm Hood and is carrying teardrop shaped 75-gallon drop tanks instead of the usual 110-gallon paper tanks. Photo taken during January of 1945. Right, posing at the tea wagon from left to right; Lt. Warner C. Jennings, Lt. Col. Daniel D. McKee, Lt.Col. Roy W. Evans, Helen Moore and Maj. Fred S. Hodges. The two pilots on the right are not identified. Lt.Col. Evans flew 15 missions in the RAF Eagle Squadron, then joined the 4th FG and scored five kills before joining the 359th.

out of the action. McCoskey then returns to base. Capt. Ray S. Wetmore hits a 109 fatally, with his third burst of fire, sending it into a violent spin, trailing smoke. His second victim is caught at tree top level over Hannover and this 109 is hit from dead astern, at 300 to 500 yards. As the German bellies in on a snow covered field, Lt. Werner J. Rueschenberg clobbers him, causing the 109 to cartwheel and disintegrate. Capt. Andrew T. Lemmens riddles a 109, starting a fire in the cockpit and follows it down for 10,000' before breaking off. Lt. Galen R. Ramser bounces a 109 firing several bursts from 300 yards at 20ø deflection during a turn, scoring hits on the left wing and fuselage. Ramser then follows the damaged fighter in a dive, getting strikes near the cockpit as they level out at 6,000'. Again he hammers the enemy fighter, this time from only fifty feet dead astern. The German's engine begins to smoke and he lowers his landing gear (an accepted sign of surrender). Out of ammo, Ramser breaks off combat. At 1215, southeast of Stade, Germany, Capt. George F. Baker Jr. is leading the 368th's Blue Flight, just after attempting to intercept two Me262s, when eight Fw 190s slice head-on through a bomber formation taking out four B-17s. Blue Flight engages the bandits as they begin a second attack on the rear of the Forts. Baker gets behind a 190 causing it to make a steep diving turn in an attempt to escape. After firing four bursts Baker scores hits in the 190's canopy, fuselage and wing roots. The 190 then slips sharply to the left and enters a spin, the pilot probably dead. Baker follows the smoking fighter down to 4,000', before breaking

off to engage another 190 that is coming at him head-on. He fires a short burst at this bandit, then loses sight of it. Climbing back to 10,000' Baker notices his wingman in a fight with a 190 and joins the battle. As the 190 enters a diving turn it is hit by two bursts from Baker's P-51, levels out at 2,000' and the pilot hits the silk. The now pilotless 190 gradually loses altitude, bounces off the ground and continues to fly over a wooded area. Two yellow nose Mustangs (361st FG) make passes on the 190 before it bellies in on a second field, slides into a line of trees and catches fire. For their twelve and one-half victories today the 359th FG suffers one loss, Lt. Donald L. Murphy of the 368th FS fails to return, cause unknown.

278   January 1, 1945 (0919-1525)

Lt.Col. Roy W. Evans leads *A* group and Maj. Daniel D. McKee leads *B* group as the 359th sets out to provide penetration, target and withdrawal support for B-17s hitting the oil industry at Magdeburg, Germany. *A* group starts out with thirty-two P-51s and four abort. *B* group gets twenty fighters up and three abort. *B* group makes R/V east of Meldorf, Germany at 1115 and a few minutes later they are attacked by two Me262s and six Me109s, with the only result being that *B* group loses contact with the bombers. At 1131, near Lüneburg, about thirty Fw190s and Me109s, plus four Me262s are engaged. The 370th FS makes the only claims during this combat, with Capt. Ray S. Wetmore chasing down and destroying a Me109, while Capt. Robert M. York does the same

In this photo we see the P-51D F/O Benjamin D. Schwartz Jr. landed so skillfully on Jan. 6, 1945 after the left main landing gear failed to extend. The serial number on this bird was 44-13966. Note the scoop escaped serious damage a fact at least partly due to the snow on the ground.

to a Fw 190. This is York's last victory and with it he becomes an ace. Part of *A* group makes R/V near Ratzeburg, Germany at 1145 but they break escort five minutes later when Lt. Billy D. Kasper, of the 368th FS, meets a Me109 head-on at 32,000' while searching for reported bandits. Kasper stalls his P-51 while trying to get into firing position, then his canopy fogs up. After clearing the canopy, Kasper cuts out three Mustangs now chasing the 109, firing from 30° and closing to twenty-five yards. The German fighter catches fire, starts disintegrating, then tumbling as the pilot bails out. Kasper and Capt. Ralph L. Brown are low on fuel and Lt. John A. Denman's guns are jammed, so the trio heads back to England. At 1155, in the vicinity of Havelberg, Germany Lt. Leonard D. Carter and F/O Boyd N. Adkins Jr., of the 368th FS, engage a Fw190. Carter makes the initial attack, scoring hits before his canopy fogs up. Adkins then moves in and makes the kill. At 1200 a Me262 makes a diving attack on part of *A* group, near Hamburg, with no results.

279   January 2, 1945 (1209-1603)

Lt.Col. John P. Randolph leads the Group on a fighter sweep in the area of Aachen, Germany. Forty-nine P-51s leave East Wretham and four return early. The 359th arrives over the target area at 1315 and patrols uneventfully until 1430 then turns for home. The 56th FG is observed dive bombing near Koblenz, Germany.

280   January 3, 1945 (0910-1348)

The 359th is back to escorting today as they furnish penetration, target and withdrawal support for B-17s blasting tactical targets at Cologne, Germany. The 359th is split into *A*, *B* and *C* groups, with Maj. Daniel D. McKee, Lt.Col. Roy W. Evans and Maj. Fred S. Hodges leading respectively. *A* and *B* groups put up eighteen Mustangs each and have no aborts, while *C* group starts out with fourteen and has only one return early. *C* group is to drop chaff. The assigned bombers are not at the R/V point and after a brief search the 359th proceeds to the target, giving area support. Lts. William F. Collins and Arthur P. Morris, of the 369th FS, break up several attempts to attack the bombers made by Me262s. The pair then bounces four Fw 190s and during the ensuing chase, to the deck, they destroy one each and share in the destruction of the others. The P-51 flown by F/O Boyd N. Adkins, of the 368th FS, has mechanical failure and he lands on the continent, returning later in the day.

Also on this day a Buzz-Bomb, launched from a He111 bomber, flies over East Wretham headed north.

*   January 4, 1945 (bad weather)

281   January 5, 1945 (1043-1503)

Today the 368th FS is assigned escort for twelve chaff-dropping B-17s. The targets for the bombing force are an airfield at Niedermendig and a communications center at Mechernich, Germany. Maj. Niven K. Cranfill leads the Squadron and fifteen Mustangs take-off, with one returning early. Once again the bombers are not at the R/V point, so the 368th provides escort for another group of bombers. A tail gunner on one of the Forts fires on the leader of Blue Flight, but misses. No bombers are lost and it's another 'no show' for the Luftwaffe.

Left, a Mustang from the 368th FS taking off during Jan. of 1945. Besides being bitter cold visibility isn't very good. Note the P-51 rolling toward the camera located between the wing tip of the P-51 in the foreground and the signalman. Operating from perforated steel plank runways was treacherous during anything but dry weather. Rain or snow turned PSP into the slickest surface imaginable. Right, 368th FS armorers. Left to right; Sgt. Russell Beamesderfer, Cpl. Calvin Fair, Larry Lovell, unidentified crew chief and S/Sgt. Neal Cadwalader. The canvas nose cover on the P-51 kept moisture from forming in the cylinders and made starting easier on cold mornings.

282   January 6, 1945 (0943-1347)

Lt.Col. Roy W. Evans leads *A* group and Capt. Andrew T. Lemmens, of the 370th FS, leads *B* group as the 359th flies escort for B-17s bombing communications targets at Kempernich, Germany. Lt. Robert V. Beaupre, of the 368th FS, crashes during take-off and perishes in the resulting fire. *A* group leaves East Wretham twenty strong and has no aborts. *B* group starts out with forty Mustangs and three return early. R/V occurs over Leige, Belgium at 1030 and 24,000'. The bombing is done by radar and one B-17 is lost. No enemy fighters are encountered. Three pilots from the 368th FS Capt. John B. Hunter, Lts. James J. Ferris III and Cornelius J. Collins land on the continent, but return later in the day.

283   January 7, 1945 (1011-1410)

Today the 359th flies penetration, target and withdrawal support for B-17s raiding the marshalling yards and a nearby communications center at Euskirchen, Germany. Capt. Ray S. Wetmore, of the 370th FS, and Maj. Ralph L. Brown, of the 368th FS, lead *A* and *B* groups respectively. *A* group has thirty-six P-51s take-off with one abort, while *B* group consisting of eleven Mustangs has no aborts. R/V is made southeast of Brussels, Belgium at 1120. The bombs are dropped at 1200 but an overcast obscures the results. No enemy aircraft are encountered and one Fort is lost. The 359th returns to base without incident.

*   January 8, 1945 (bad weather)

A B-24 named *Sweet Sue* crashes near East Wretham but the crew escapes serious injury.

*   January 9-12, 1945 (bad weather)

On January 9 F/O Benjamin D. Schwartz Jr., of the 370th FS, makes a successful one wheel landing at East Wretham after repeated attempts to get the other landing gear strut to lock in place fail.

284   January 13, 1945 (1050-1615)

Lt.Col. John P. Randolph leads the Group as they provide penetration, target and withdrawal support for B-17s bombing a railway bridge at Maximiliansau, Germany. Just after taking off, Capt. Karl K. Shearer, of the 369th FS, is killed as his Mustang crashes at Ashill, eight miles north of the base. Shearer, a veteran B-24 pilot of thirty-three missions, is believed to be the victim of icing. Of the forty-one Mustangs taking off only two return early. R/V occurs over Maubeuge, France at 1153 and 25,000'. The bombing is done visually and five Forts are lost to flak. No contact is made with enemy fighters. On the way out thirty-five Mustangs from the Group land in France due to poor weather at East Wretham. Maj. Niven K. Cranfill, of the 368th FS, washes out his landing gear while attempting to land at East Wretham.

On Jan. 6, 1945, Lt. Robert V. Beaupre crashed and was killed while taking off on a mission to Kempernich, Germany. He held the Air Medal with seven clusters and was only twenty-seven hours short of completing his tour. The severity of the impact is witnessed by the engine which parted company with its bearers (see bottom photo). The pilot of a P-51 was never in danger of the engine being driven back into the cockpit for the bearers were designed to shear the bolts that held them to the firewall which was fabricated from armor grade steel plate. Beaupre's Mustang was coded CV-X and the serial number was 44-14509.

Above, the twisted and broken hulk of a 453rd BG B-24 Liberator named *Sweet Sue*, which crashed near East Wretham on Jan. 8, 1945. It was a miracle no one was killed, considering the Lib's lack of structural integrity. The Luftwaffe considered the B-24 a much easier kill than the rugged B-17. Below, the shredded remains of Capt. Karl K. Shearer's P-51. This crash took place on Jan. 13, 1945 about eight miles north of East Wretham, at Ashill. It was assumed Shearer was the victim of icing. Judging from the depth and length of the trench his Mustang dug it must have been traveling at a good clip when it nosed in. It's rather ironic Shearer was a former B-24 pilot and had survived thirty-three missions in the infamous Liberator.

285   January 14, 1945 (1054-1544)

Lt.Col. Roy W. Evans leads today as the 359th furnishes penetration, target and withdrawal support for B-24s blasting the oil industry at Hemmingstedt, Germany. The Group puts up thirty-six P-51s and four return early. R/V is made west of Heligoland Island, Germany at 1230 and 31,000'. The bombing results are noted to be excellent, with much black smoke rising from the target. No bombers are lost and no contact is made with enemy fighters during escort. Escort is dropped at 1300 and the 359th goes down to look for ground targets. At 1355, Capt. Charles C. Ettlesen, of the 368th FS, strafes a train in the Hannover area, destroying the locomotive and damaging ten flatcars, loaded with about twenty staff cars

and trucks. From 1330-1415, Red and Blue Flights of the 370th FS engage Fw190s in the vicinity of Dummer Lake. At 1330, Capt. Ray S. Wetmore is leading Red Flight when he notices a bandit doing lazy-eights and chandelles, east of Hannover. Red Flight drops their tanks and chase the German fighter all the way to Dummer Lake, where pursuit is dropped. The flight is then vectored to an airfield northwest of the lake but nothing is found. As they turn back to the lake a R/T informs them bandits are in the vicinity of Vorden. Wetmore then spots four Fw190s zooming below him in trail, headed for an airfield and he bounces them. The first 190 to fall is hit from 300 yards out; the pilot tries to crash land the fighter unsuccessfully and dies in the attempt. Wetmore hits the second bandit with a short

Lt. Jack E. McCoskey became a POW during the mission of Jan. 14, 1945. McCoskey, on the left in the photo above, discusses a combat situation with "Pop" Doersch who also played a prominent part in the same mission. Photo was taken during Aug. of 1944. Right, Dr. Chandu a Special Service officer for Indian soldiers living in the Thetford area gave two talks at the Aero Club, one Jan. 14 and another Feb. 11. Subjects were varied and included; how Britain gained control of India, India's opinion of the United States, Indian troops in the British Army, Indian troops and their white girl friends and Indian taboos. Chandu's talks were described as humorous, subtle, provocative and attention holding.

burst from dead astern, at very close range. The enemy pilot tries to break but snaps into the ground and explodes. Victim number three is taken from the rear, at 300 yards. He spins into the ground and explodes. Wetmore then helps his wingman, Lt. Werner J. Rueschenberg, shoot down another 190 by catching it in a cross-fire. The German pilot manages to belly his stricken fighter in on the airfield but Wetmore strafes it, killing the pilot and setting the wreckage on fire. Wetmore spots two more 190s and a P-51 which has a red and white checked nose (339th FG). The Mustang from the 339th nails one of the bandits and the pilot bails out. Firing from 400 yards and 30° deflection, Wetmore scores hits on the remaining 190 and its pilot bails out. Blue Flight of the 370th FS, led by Capt. George A. Doersch, arrives on the scene as Wetmore scores his third kill of the day. Doersch notes a 190 circling 200' above the perimeter of the airfield and within the protective range of 20mm flak guns. Doersch and his wingman, Lt. Jack E. McCoskey, ignore the 20mm fire and go after the 190. Doersch dispatches the enemy fighter then takes on another 190, which is being chased by four P-51s. The bandit turns into Doersch's attack

twice, while making his way to north side of the airfield and its protective flak. "Pop" Doersch makes a pass on the 190, overshoots it, pulls into the vertical and rolls inverted to see what has happened to his quarry. At that moment, McCoskey also overshoots the 190, pulls into a tight turn, goes into a high speed stall (possibly aggravated by having to much fuel left in his fuselage tank, making the Mustang tail heavy), snaps into the ground and explodes. Although "Pop" doesn't see it from his inverted position, McCoskey is thrown clear, survives the crash and is later hospitalized by the Germans. Doersch scores some hits on the 190, the pilot jettisons his canopy and bails out at the top of a hammerhead stall. Enraged at what he thinks is the death of his friend, "Pop" attempts to collapse the German pilot's chute but he cools off and lets the vanquished foe land safely. "Big Ben" contrails are seen in the vicinity of Zwolle, Netherlands.

286   January 15, 1945 (0931-1534)

The 359th flies penetration, target and withdrawal support for B-17s headed for Lechfield, Germany. Maj. James K. Parsons leads *A* group, which starts

Lt. Douglas A. McLean, right, died in the flaming wreckage of his P-51while making a second attempt to take off on Jan. 16, 1945. It would have been his first mission. Note fireman crawling through the foam as he works closer to what remains of the flames.

out with thirty-five Mustangs and has five abort, while Maj. Ralph L. Brown, of the 368th FS, leads *B* group consisting of twenty Mustangs, one of which aborts. The 359th arrives at the R/V point, which is south of Metz, France at 1121 and 18,000'. The assigned bombers are not found; the 359th proceeds to the target, giving general support to the bomber stream. The primary target is obscured by clouds so the Forts bomb their secondary target, which is the marshalling yards at Augsburg, Germany, using radar. The Luftwaffe is absent and no Forts are lost to flak. On the return flight three Mustangs land at Reims, France. The pilots are Capt. Elby J. Beal, of the 368th FS, who returns on the 17th and a Lt. Kelly and Tracey E. Millis of the 369th FS.

287   January 16, 1945 (1005-1400)

Lt.Col. John P. Randolph leads the Group as they provide penetration, target and withdrawal support for B-24s bombing the synthetic oil industry at Ruhland, Germany. Lt. Douglas A. MacLean, a new pilot in the 368th FS, is killed as his fuel laden P-51 crashes during a second attempt to take-off. The P-51 explodes and is almost entirely consumed by fire. Of the fifty-five Mustangs that do take-off only one aborts. On the way in, Lt. Graham Lupton, also of the 368th FS, has oil pressure failure over Amersfoort, Netherlands at 1100. Although Lupton bails out and lands safely, he is later reported killed. R/V is made and the 359th sweeps ahead of the Libs for a period before dropping back to give close support in the vicinity of Verdun, France. Once again no contact is made with the Luftwaffe but flak claims two of the Libs. A R/T is received ordering the 359th to land on the continent because East Wretham is closed due to weather. The Group lands at Creil and Merville, France, takes on fuel and returns to base the next day. F/O Boyd N. Adkins, of the 368th FS, crash-lands at Merville but is not injured.

288　January 20, 1945 (0906-1426)

The 359th flies penetration, target and withdrawal support for B-17s blasting a railway bridge at Mannhiem, Germany. Lt.Col. Roy W. Evans leads *A* group comprised of thirty P-51s, while Maj. James W. Parsons leads *B* group consisting of nine P-51s that are to provide escort for chaff dropping Forts. There are no aborts today. A V-2 is spotted north of Rotterdam, Netherlands at 1000. R/V occurs north of Arlon, Belgium at 1150 and 28,000'. One Fort is seen exploding over the target and it is the only loss of the day. The results of the raid are not observed. No enemy aircraft are encountered and the 359th returns to England without incident. Lts. Richard H. Daniels and Cornelius J. Collins, of the 368th FS, land at the Woodbridge emergency airfield due to the poor weather. Two concrete and masonry pillboxes, at the south end of the runway at East Wrethham, are purposely destroyed by explosives today. The structures were deemed a hazard to aircraft with power failure during takeoff.

* **January 21-27, 1945 (bad weather)**

289　January 28, 1945 (0953-1446)

Col. John P. Randolph leads the Group as they furnish escort for B-17s bombing the marshalling yards at Cologne, Germany. Forty-one P-51s leave East Wretham and seven abort. R/V is made over Turnhout, Belgium at 1115 and 23,000'. The bombing is done by radar and no enemy aircraft are encountered. The flak downs three Forts, one is seen exploding near the target. Another 172 are damaged.

290　January 29, 1945 (0912-1445)

Today the 359th provides escort for B-17s raiding rail targets at Siegen, Germany. Lt.Col. Roy W. Evans leads *A* group, while Maj. James K. Lovett, of the 370th FS, leads *B* group. *A* group takes off with thirty-four P-51s while *B* group starts with fourteen. One Mustang from each group returns early. R/V is made over Hoorn, Netherlands at 1055 and 20,000'. Before reaching the target Lt. Cornelius J. Collins, of the 368th FS, drops a fuel tank and is forced to land at Tours, France returning to base on February 1. The bombing is done by radar and the results are

hidden by cloud cover. No bombers are lost and the 359th makes no contact with the Luftwaffe. The 369th FS breaks escort north of Giessen, Germany at 1200 and drops down to strafe, with these results: 0-20 boxcars, 0-15 oil tank cars, 6-0 Fw190 wings on a flatcar, 1-1 trucks and 1-0 powerhouse. The 368th FS drops escort at 1215 and lets down in the Giessen area to strafe, making the following claims: 3-1 locomotives, 0-20 box-cars, 1-0 oil tank car, 3-0 trucks, 2-0 staff cars, 1-0 powerhouse, 0-2 electric towers and 0-1 barge. Lt. Richard H. Daniels inadvertently strafes an American installation at Ingwiller, France. During Daniels' second pass he is given a warning burst of fire, but persists and on the third pass his Mustang is hit by the American gunners. Daniels is killed when his P-51 crashes about three miles away, at Bauxwiller, France. The 368th also loses Lt. John M. Marr for a couple of weeks, when he bails out over Sanites, France and is hospitalized with a leg injury. On returning to England, Lt. Garland F. Madison, also of the 368th FS, who is low on fuel encounters adverse weather and bails out safely over Exeter.

* **January 30, 31, 1945 (bad weather)**

As February begins only eight of the eighty-six original pilots that constituted the 359th FG are still flying. They are: Niven Cranfill, "Pop" Doersch, Al Homeyer, John Hunter, Dan McKee, Andy Lemmens, Bob Thompson and Ray Wetmore.

It is a strange month that sees the Group scoring not a single victory in the air. Perhaps part of the answer is that the Germans are concentrating much of their remaining airpower in the east in an attempt to stem the Russian advance.

Ground attack action, on the other hand, is ferocious with fourteen of the Group's pilots failing to return during the month's seventeen missions. These losses during strafing are common to all the fighter groups and reach such staggering proportions that at the end of the month a stop order on all opportunity strafing is issued by Wing Command.

291　February 1, 1945 (0921-1450)

Lt.Col. Daniel D. McKee leads A group and Maj. Ralph L. Brown, of the 369th FS, leads B group as the 359th flies penetration, target and withdrawal support for B-17s bombing the marshalling yards at Mannheim, Germany. A and B groups put up eighteen and twenty-nine P-51s respectively, with one fighter returning early from each. R/V occurs over

Lt. Henry L. Thompson vanished without a trace after bailing out off the coast from Filey, England on February 7, 1945. He was on a gunnery training flight when the prop governor in his P-51 failed.

Bastogne, Belgium at 1104 and 24,000'. The bomber formations are noted to be good but not in the proper sequence. The bombing is done by radar, no Forts are lost and no enemy aircraft are encountered. Escort is dropped at Charleroi, Belgium.

Lt. Lawrence A. Zizka, of the 370th FS is making a landing approach at East Wretham, at 1210, when a high wind causes his P-51 to crash and explode in the woods behind the Squadron Operations Building. Zizka, who is returning from a ninety minute test flight, is killed instantly.

***   February 2, 1945 (bad weather)**

292   February 3, 1945 (0835-1431)

Lt.Cols. Roy W. Evans and Daniel D. McKee lead *A* and *B* groups respectively as the 359th flies penetration, target and withdrawal support for B-17s raiding the marshalling yards at Berlin, Germany. *A* group starts out with thirty-three P-51s and has one abort. *B* group sets out with twenty-one Mustangs and has no aborts. R/V is made southwest of Meppel,

Netherlands at 1000 and 25,000'. Today the weather is excellent and the bombing results are outstanding. No enemy fighters are encountered but flak claims fourteen bombers. On the way out Capt. Charles E. Ettlesen's flight, from the 368th FS, strafes and turns in the following claims: 6-0 locomotives, 0-25 railcars and 0-2 switch towers.

***   February 4,5, 1945 (bad weather)**

293   February 6, 1945 (0904-1410)

Lt.Col. John P. Randolph leads *A* group and Maj. Edwin F. Pezda, of the 369th FS, leads *B* group as the 359th provides penetration, target and withdrawal support for B-17s headed for Wenzendorf, Germany. *A* group begins the mission with thirty-seven fighters and five abort. *B* group consisting of eighteen Mustangs has no aborts. R/V is made over Egmond, Netherlands at 16,000'. 9/10 cloud cover obscures the primary target so the Forts hit the secondary, which is the marshalling yards at Chemnitz, Germany. Three Forts are lost to flak and ten more are reduced to flying junk. Enemy fighters are not encountered and escort is maintained until reaching Suhl, Germany. The 359th returns to England without incident.

***   February 7, 1945 (bad weather)**

A gunnery training flight flown by three pilots, of the 368th FS, ends in tragedy. Lts. James J. Ferris III, George W. Long and Henry L. Thompson are over the North Sea when Thompson reports his prop governor has failed. He bails out and is seen to land safely in the water, ten to fifteen miles off the coast, from Filey, England. A search made by ASR aircraft and ships fails to find a trace of the downed pilot.

***   February 8, 1945 (bad weather)**

294   February 9, 1945 (1022-1559)

Lt.Col. Daniel D. McKee leads *A* group and Maj. Ralph L. Brown, of the 368th FS, leads *B* group as they provide penetration, target and withdrawal support for B-17s bombing the synthetic oil industry at Lutzkendorf, Germany. *A* and *B* groups consist of thirty-six and sixteen P-51s respectively. There are five aborts in *A* group and two from *B*. R/V is made north of Brussels, Belgium at 1130 and 23,000'. The bomber formations are noted to be ragged. The target is bombed visually and one Fort is downed by flak. The Luftwaffe is not encountered and as the bombers exit the target, Blue Flight of the 368th, led by Capt. Charles E. Ettlesen, does some strafing. At 1310, near Gotha, Germany Ettlesen damages one of two unidentified aircraft parked on a field. Moving on he quickly destroys two locomotives and is banking sharply for an attack on a third, when the flight enters a rain squall. As Lt. Marvin F. Boussu emerges from the rain he sights a train and makes a pass, exploding the locomotive's boiler. Noticing that Ettlesen has not rejoined the flight, attempts are made to contact him by R/T to no avail and the rest of Blue Flight heads for base. 'Last seen making a head-on attack on a train', a poetic epitaph for a pilot who helped write the book on attacking ground targets, as a member of Bill's Buzz Boys. Blue Flight from the 370th FS, also strafes and the total claims for the day are: 0-1 aircraft, 8-0 locomotives, 2-0 railcars, 0-2 powerhouses and 0-2 power lines.

*   February 10, 1945 (bad weather)

295   February 11, 1945 (0845-1215)

The Group is off on a fighter sweep in the vicinity of Paderborn, Germany with Lt.Col. John P. Randolph leading *A* group and Maj. James W. Parsons leading *B* group. *A* and *B* groups consisting of thirty-two and seventeen Mustangs respectively, have no aborts. The 359th arrives over the target at 0950, on the deck. Total claims for the day include: 24-10 locomotives, 6-111 railcars, 0-2 electric trains, 8-10 vehicles, 2-0 fuel tanks, 1-0 switch house, 0-13 buildings, 0-1 radar station, 0-1 power line, 0-15 barges and 0-3 boats. F/O Harry L. Schector, of the 370th FS, whose P-51 is damaged by flak, lands at St. Trond, Belgium and returns on the 14th.

*   February 12, 13, 1945 (bad weather)

296   February 14, 1945 (0947-1532)

Lt.Cols. Roy W. Evans and Daniel D. McKee lead *A* and *B* groups respectively as the 359th flies penetration, target and withdrawal support for B-17s raiding the marshalling yards at Dresden, Germany. *A* group starts out with thirty-seven P-51s, while *B* group has eighteen; both however have two return early. The

359th encounters no enemy fighters and after breaking escort they drop to strafe. Total claims are: 26-12 locomotives, 4-112 boxcars, 2-17 oil tank cars, 0-14 medium tanks on flatcars, 7-9 vehicles, 1-1 staff cars, 2-0 fuel storage tanks, 0-11 switch houses, 0-6 railway buildings, 0-3 factories, 0-1 radar installation, 1-0 high tension line, 0-19 barges and two soldiers killed. During this action Lt.Col. Evans' P-51 is hit and the engine loses oil pressure. The Merlin then begins to overheat, forcing Evans to bail out near Plauen, Germany where he is taken prisoner. Lt. Roy W. Garrett, of the 368th FS, also becomes a POW, when his P-51 pops its coolant near Meppel, Netherlands and he bails out directly into the hands of German troops. The remainder of the 359th returns without incident.

On this mission the pilots begin carrying small silk Russian flags and identification cards to be used in case of a forced landing in Russian occupied territory.

297   February 15, 1945 (0857-1445)

Lt.Col. John P. Randolph leads *A* group and Maj. Edwin F. Pezda, of the 369th FS, leads *B* group as they furnish penetration, target and withdrawal support for B-17s headed for Bohlen, Germany. Five of *A* group's thirty-four P-51s abort and two from *B* group's sixteen Mustangs. R/V is made over Egmond, Netherlands at 0950 and 18,000'. Due to poor weather the Forts bomb their secondary target, the marshalling yards at Dresden, Germany. No bombers are lost and no enemy fighters are encountered. Near Weisbaden, Germany the P-51 flown by Lt. John W. Lamont, of the 370th FS, is hit by flak but he returns safely. On the way out, Lt. Antony D. Maiorano, of the 368th FS, notices his Merlin begin to smoke over South Beveland Island, Netherlands. He turns toward the mainland and bails out safely. After an overnight stay in Steenbergen, Maiorano is taken to Brussels, Belgium where he catches a transport plane back to England on the 18th.

*   February 16-18, 1945 (bad weather)

298   February 19, 1945 (1210-1617)

Maj. Edwin F. Pezda, of the 369th FS, leads the Group as they fly penetration, target and withdrawal support for B-17s hitting an oil refinery at Dortmund, Germany. The 359th fields forty-three fighters today and only two abort. R/V is made north of Bergen,

Feb. 11, 1945 was a big day for strafers and four of those who scored are shown above. Top left, Lt. David P. Dunmire of the 368th FS, shared in the destruction of four locos and damaging fifteen boxcars. Top right, Lt. Albert E. Wolfe of the 370th FS, shared in the destruction of 8 locos and four boxcars. Bottom left, Lt. Raymond E. Magee of the of the 369th FS shared in damaging seven oil tank cars. Bottom right, Lt. Donald Eugene Cannon of the 369th, shared in the destruction of one loco and the damaging of three locos and fourteen boxcars. Consult the Destruction Diary at the back of this book for a complete list of targets.

Netherlands at 1320 and 25,000'. Prior to the bombing run, eight Mustangs from the 368th FS pull ahead of the B-17s and drop chaff to blind the German radar. No enemy aircraft are encountered and despite heavy flak over the target no bombers are lost. On the way out, near Trier, Germany Lt. Antony D. Maiorano's replacement Mustang pops its coolant and he bails out, briefly being caught on the tail empennage. Maiorano lands safely but becomes a POW. Escort is dropped over the North Sea at 1506.

299   February 20, 1945 (1000-1515)

Lt.Col. Daniel D. McKee leads *A* group and Maj. Niven K. Cranfill, of the 368th FS, leads *B* group as the 359th flies penetration, target and withdrawal

Lts. Vernon T. Judkins and Bert M. Montague were two 369th FS pilots who took part in the strafing on Feb. 11, 1945. Top, a close-up shot of the nose of Jukins' P-51D Babe IV-W serial number 44-15015. Note the photo of his wife applied to the cowling above and to the right of the *e*". Posing with Babe, left to right, Sgt. Charles F. Dunne, armorer and S/Sgt. Archie W. Crawford, crew chief. Bottom left, Judkins and his English wife Margaret. Bottom right, Bert M. Montague. Notice how the black ID band on the wing has been worn away.

support for B-17s blasting the marshalling yards and rail station at Nürnburg, Germany. *A* group takes off eighteen strong and has no aborts, while three of the thirty P-51s forming *B* group return early. R/V occurs over Koblenz, Germany at 1141 and 25,000'.

The bombing is carried out with the use of radar, due to 10/10 cloud cover over the target. The Luftwaffe is absent today but flak downs two B-17s. Escort is dropped northeast of Metz, France at 1350 and the 359th returns safely to England.

Top, a Fw200C Condor maritime reconnaissance-bomber. The Condor was a very successful bomber despite being designed initially as a commercial transport. On Feb. 21, 1945 Lt. Fred S. McGehee damaged a Condor while strafing. McGehee is pictured in his P-51 at the bottom left. Note flight leader stripes on the dorsal strake. Lower right, Capt. John Fraser Buniowski of the 369th FS. Irish, as he was called, strafed and destroyed a loco on Feb. 22, 1945. Note the plexiglass fairing housing the rear-view mirror.

300 February 21, 1945 (0900-1430)

Col. John P. Randolph leads *A* group and Maj. Edwin F. Pezda, of the 369th FS, leads *B* group as the 359th provides penetration, target and withdrawal support for B-17s raiding the marshalling yards at Nürnberg, Germany. *A* and *B* groups consist of twenty-seven and fourteen Mustangs respectively and there is only one abort, that being from *B* group. R/V occurs south of Antwerp, Belgium at 0945 and 18,000'. The target is hit through heavy cloud cover and the results are not observed. No Forts are lost even though the flak is heavy. No enemy fighters are encountered. On a prearranged signal the 369th FS drops escort and splits into two sections to strafe airfields. The 368th and 370th FSs continue to provide escort until they are just east of Selestadt at 1245. Meanwhile Red and Yellow Flights, of the 369th FS, fly south-west from Nürnberg and strafe an airfield near Nordlingen at 1205, with these results: Maj. Fred S. Hodges, one Fw200 bomber damaged, Capt. Robert C. Thomson, one Fw190 and one twin engine aircraft damaged plus one wooden, decoy aircraft destroyed, Lt. Arthur B. Morris, one Ju88 and a gas truck destroyed plus one Me410 damaged and Lt. Fred S. McGehee, one Fw200 and Me410 damaged. At 1220 White and Blue Flights attack an airfield at Schweinfurt, with these claims being made: Maj. Edwin F. Pezda, one multi-engine aircraft destroyed, Lt. Robert M. Francis, one Me410 damaged and Lt. Dale L. Kelly, one hangar damaged. During Francis' attack his oil tank filler cap comes off and oil covers his windscreen. Francis thinks he is hit in an oil line but returns safely. Pezda and Kelly are lucky their claims are witnessed, because their gun cameras are not loaded with film.

301   February 22, 1945 (0945-1505)

This is the first day of *Operation Clarion*, an all-out assault on the German railway and other transportation systems. The 8th AF gambles on this mission by ordering the bombers to be flown at 10,000', less than half the usual altitude.

Maj. Edwin F. Pezda of the 369th FS and Capt. Ray S. Wetmore of the 370th FS lead *A* and *B* groups respectively as the 359th flies another penetration, target and withdrawal support mission for B-17s. Today's targets are in the vicinity of Perleburg, Germany. *A* group starts with thirty-one fighters and has two that return early, while there are no aborts among the thirteen P-51s that make up *B* group. Lt. Russell E. Masters, of the 369th FS, loses oil pressure and bails out off the coast from Ijmuiden, Netherlands at 1038. His chute opens but is not seen on the water. Masters is listed as MIA, on this his first mission. R/V is made northeast of Zwolle, Netherlands at 1053 and 15,000'. A few minutes after R/V, Lt. David P. Dunmire, of the 368th FS, experiences his engine cutting out and with Lt. James W. McCormack as escort, drops down to 10,000', where the Merlin smooths out. The pair rejoins the squadron but a few minutes later drop out of formation to strafe a locomotive. After climbing back into position, for a brief time, the pair then goes down to strafe an airfield.

Dunmire's P-51 is hit in both wings, tail surfaces and the engine, by flak. Unable to climb, Dunmire has McCormack go up for a position fix. At 20,000' he loses sight of Dunmire but gives him a heading for friendly territory, by R/T. The route takes the damaged 51 over Dusseldorf, Germany where at an altitude of 500', it is again hit by flak and begins losing coolant. Radio contact is then lost and Dunmire is listed as MIA. North of Gardelegen, Germany, as the force nears the target area, six Me262s attack the Forts, downing one before quickly outdistancing the escorting P-51s. This is the only B-17 shot down today and the fear of high losses due to the low altitude proves to be unfounded. At 1230, the 370th FS jumps a single Me262, flying at low level, near Pritzwald. Capt. Ray S. Wetmore and Lt. Robert L. McInnes fire on the jet at long range but it vanishes in the haze. About one minute after losing sight of the jet Lt. Donald L. Windmiller spots an airfield, where he damages a Me410 and a decoy aircraft. Windmiller and his wingman also notice a crashed Me262 on the airfield and while they are confident it is the very one fired on by Wetmore and McInnes, unfortunately it cannot be claimed. Moving on "Windy" is separated from his flight and hunts solo, strafing a horse-drawn wagon. Near Parchim he damages a barge but turns for home when two guns jam. On the way out, near Hagenau, Germany, "Windy" damages a locomotive with his two operative guns. In an overlapping action the 369th's Red Flight strafes an airfield near Parchim at, 1240, with these results: Lt. Fred S. McGehee, one Ju88 destroyed and two damaged, Lt. Harold Tenenbaum, one twin engine aircraft and two horse-drawn wagons damaged and for Capt. William F. Collins, two Ju88s destroyed and one damaged. Another flight from the 369th, consisting of Lts. Robert W. Davison, Ralph R. Klaver and Tracey E. Millis share in the destruction of two locomotives and twelve boxcars, loaded with explosives, west of Muritz Lake. Other claims made are listed in the destruction diary.

302   February 23, 1945 (0902-1455)

Lt.Col. Daniel D. McKee, of the 370th FS and Capt. George A. Doersch, of the 368th FS, lead *A* and *B* groups respectively as the 359th flies penetration, target and withdrawal support for B-17s bombing rail and transportation targets across central Germany to Zwickau. This is day two of Operation CLARION. *A* group gets up twenty-six P-51s, with two aborts, while *B* group has three of its sixteen Mustangs re-

Top row: pilots didn't return during Feb. of 1945. On the left, Lt. Roy C. Garrett who became a POW on Feb. 14. Center, Lt. Antony D. Maiorano who bailed out over the Netherlands, after his P-51 popped its coolant, on February 15 and returned to base four days later. On Feb. 19 his second P-51 also popped its coolant but this time he is near Trier, Germany and became a POW. Right, Lt. Lawrence F. Meyer who was listed as MIA on February 23. The bottom row is composed of pilots who completed their tours during March of 1945. Left, Lt. Arnold F. Mettel. Center, Capt. Jimmy C. Shoffit who damaged a Me163 on Aug. 16, 1944. Right, Lt. Edward L. Welch.

turn early. R/V is made east of the Zuider Zee at 1003 and 20,000'. Escort is provided through the target area, no bombers are lost and no enemy fighters are encountered. The 370th FS loses two pilots today, Capt. Washington D. Lyon is listed MIA and Lt. Malcom C. Paulette is listed as KIA; both are last seen near Zwickau at 1215. Escort is dropped at 1230 and the Mustangs head down to strafe. All claims for the 368th FS are made by Capt. George A. Doersch's flight, consisting of himself, Capt. James L. Way Jr., Lts. James W. McCormack and Henry B. Kreuzman. Their claims, scored near Fulda, Germany are: 2-0 locomotives, 0-15 boxcars, 1-0 rail passenger car (streamlined and camouflaged), 0-1 switch house and 1-0 automobile. Doersch's P-51 is damaged by debris from an exploding target, forcing him to land at Heddington Heath, England for repairs. The 369th FS adds these claims to the Group's total: 2-2 locomotives, 0-8 boxcars and 2-0 trucks. Lt. Lawrence F. Meyer, of the 369th, crashes into a hill and his P-51 burns while making a strafing attack. Meyer is listed as MIA. Lt. Garland J. McGregor, of the 370th, who is flying radio relay, is last seen near East Wretham flying into the overcast and not responding to R/Ts. It is later learned he was killed in a crash at Watton. On returning to England the Group finds their base is closed due to weather so they land elsewhere.

303   February 24, 1945 (1050-1505)

Maj. Edwin F. Pezda, of the 369th FS, leads the Group on a penetration, target and withdrawal support mission for B-17s hitting a railway bridge at Wesel, Germany. Only twenty-nine Mustangs fly this mission and there are no aborts. R/V is made over Tilberg, Netherlands at 1220 and 24,000'. No direct hits on the bridge are observed but a large fire is started at the north end of the span. The flak is moderate and no enemy fighters come up to do battle. One Big Ben contrail is spotted today. The 359th crosses out over Egmond, Netherlands at 1340.

304   February 25, 1945 (0825-1452)

8th Air Force B-17s are on their way to bomb the marshalling yards at Munich, Germany and the 359th flies escort. Col. John P. Randolph leads *A* group and Capt. Ralph L. Cox, of the 369th FS, leads *B* group. *A* group starts out with twenty-eight P-51s and has two aborts, while *B* group loses none of its fourteen P-51s to mechanical woes. R/V occurs over Strasbourg, France at 1030 and 23,000'. The bombs are dropped at 1128 and the results are observed to be excellent, with numerous fires being started. One Fort is seen exploding over the target and another is seen on fire, near Sigmaringen, Germany. Nine chutes are counted from the burning Fort. The Mustang flown by Lt. Henry D. Semple, of the 370th FS, is hit by flak and he bails out near Kalterberg. After getting a jeep ride to an airfield, Semple hitches an airplane ride back, returning to base at 1430. The 369th FS does some strafing, with Maj. Edwin F. Pezda, Lts. Robert D. Erwin and Lee Patton sharing in the destruction of a locomotive and damaging six boxcars.

305   February 26, 1945 (0940-1534)

Capt. Ray S. Wetmore, of the 370th FS and Capt. Robert C. Thomson, of the 369th FS, lead *A* and *B* groups respectively as the Group flies escort for B-17s raiding three railway stations in the Berlin area. *A* group begins the mission with fourteen P-51s and has two return early, while *B* group starts with thirty-two and suffers eight aborts. The entire route is covered by 10/10 cloud and the bombing is done in concert with radar equipped, pathfinder aircraft. The flak is once more moderate and no enemy fighters are encountered. All of the 359th's pilots and planes return safely.

306   February 27, 1945 (1112-1649)

Lt.Col. Daniel D. McKee, of the 370th FS, and Maj. Niven K. Cranfill, of the 368th FS, lead *A* and *B* groups respectively as the 359th FG provides penetration, target and withdrawal support for B-17s blasting the railway and communication center at Leipzig, Germany. *A* group leaves East Wretham with thirteen Mustangs and has no aborts. *B* group leaves with thirty-one P-51s and five return early. Radar is employed to drop the bombs as 10/10 cloud cover persists, over Germany. No bombers are lost and no enemy fighters are seen. The 370th FS strafes in the vicinity of Sonnenberg, Germany and makes the claims shown in the Destruction Diary.

307   February 28, 1945 (0730-1231)

Today's mission is a fighter sweep in the area of Munich, Germany. Col. John P. Randolph leads the 359th and of the forty-four Mustangs that leave East Wretham only one returns early. The Group arrives over the target area at 0930 and 14,000'. The 368th FS scores during the following actions: at 0935, near Ingolstadt, Lt. George W. Long destroys one locomotive and damages four others plus five boxcars. From 0945-1030, Lts. John F. Collins Jr. and John D. Cooley Jr. share in the damaging of a locomotive and two boxcars. They also make two passes on a lumberyard, starting two fires. From 1010-1020, between Augsburg and Gunzburg, Lts. Allan G. Martin and George H. Blackburn catch two trucks, each towing a Me109, driving on the Autobahn. Martin destroys one of the fighters and its tow truck plus another truck further down the highway, while Blackburn destroys the other 109 and tow truck. Blackburn also damages a factory and an electric tower. Martin's P-51 is damaged by flak, forcing him to land at Le Culot, Belgium for repairs. His Mustang is then damaged while taxiing out to take off and he returns by transport plane on March 3. Blackburn has a problem with his P-51 and also lands at Le Culot, returning in his Mustang on March 2. Maj. Edwin F. Pezda, of the 369th FS, is strafing a truck convoy, when ground fire severs an oil line, forcing him to bail out. Pezda is captured and becomes a POW. Capt. Harry L. Matthew, also from the 369th, flies through some power lines while attacking a train, and loses his coolant. Matthew is also taken prisoner, after bailing out, but is freed three weeks later by American ground forces. Other claims made today are included in the Destruction Diary.

The location of photos related to a specific mission or event have been kept on the page opposite the corresponding text where possible. This selection is one of the exceptions. The pilots shown above joined the Group after Jan. of 1945 and missed the great hunting days, for the Luftwaffe was only a shadow of its former self; but that doesn't diminish their contribution. Top row starting on the left are three pilots assigned to the 370th FS, Lt. Gwyn W. Bell, Lt. Albert C. Brickner and Lt. Jack W. Brinkmeyer. Bottom row left to right, Lt. Robert H. Elliot (368th) Lt. Marlyn C. Ford (370th) and F/O Joseph M. Hill Jr. (368th).

* March 1, 1945 (bad weather)

During the month of March caliber .50 API ammunition is in short supply and practice firing is forbidden. 50,177 rounds of API will be expended this month.

The gripe of the month is the high number of engine changes required due to the use of 150 octane 'pep-gas.' While formulated to keep spark plugs clean it introduces a set of new problems, burned valve seats and stretched valve stems.

308 March 2, 1945 (0757-1340, A) (0900-1425, B)

The 359th is split into *A* and *B* groups to furnish an overlapping escort for B-17s bombing the synthetic oil plant at Böhlen, Germany. Maj. Niven K. Cranfill, of the 368th FS, and Maj. James K. Lovett, of the 370th FS, lead *A* and *B* groups respectively. *A* group leaves East Wretham with twenty-eight P-51s, while *B* group starts with eighteen. One Mustang aborts from each group. *A* group makes R/V southwest of

Koblenz, Germany at 0910 and 24,000', with *B* group joining the escort at 1050 and 24,000' over Jena, Germany. A low overcast is noted over Böhlen and one box of B-17s bombs the secondary targets at Griz. The 359th encounters no enemy aircraft, although other fighter groups do. Three Forts are lost today and on the way out the 368th FS observes three RAF Lancasters explode over Cologne, Germany as a result of flak. The 359th returns to England without loss.

Lts. Leon J. Levitt and Merle G. Aunspaugh, of the 368th FS, who remain behind today, are scheduled to fly a practice gunnery mission at Polebrook, England. Taking off behind the bombers, at 1307, Levitt and Aunspaugh climb to 2,000' and turn back toward Polebrook from four miles out to make a simulated strafing attack on the base. As he drops down Levitt checks his wingman's position, before reaching the field and pulls up to 1,500' on the far side. Levitt then makes a quarter circuit of the field and makes a second pass, before calling his wingman. Receiving no reply he then notices smoke rising from the woods north of the base. Aunspaugh had struck a tree and died in the resulting crash. This buzz-job led to a trial the result of which was a reprimand and 500 dollar fine, for Levitt.

309   March 3, 1945 (0832-1309)

The 359th flies penetration, target and withdrawal support for B-17s raiding Hannover, Germany. Lt.Col. Daniel D. McKee, of the 370th FS, leads *A* group and Maj. James W. Parsons leads *B* group. *A* and *B* groups begin the mission with thirty-two and fourteen Mustangs respectively and only two P-51s from *A* group abort. Col. John P. Randolph, who is leading *A* group, is the first to turn back, when one of the landing gear on his P-51 fails to retract. R/V is made over Wangeroog Island, Germany at 1010 and the bombing is done at 1040, with the help of radar. No results of the raid are observed due to the weather. After dropping escort the 368th FS drops down to strafe. Lt. Albert A. Cowie damages a training aircraft parked near Hannover, Germany but his P-51 is hit by flak. Cowie's engine quits, he crash-lands near Gandersheim, Germany and is taken prisoner. Other claims are in destruction diary.

310   March 4, 1945 (0806-1324)

Col. John P. Randolph leads the Group as they provide penetration, target and withdrawal support for B-17s bombing munitions dumps and marshalling yards in the area of Ulm, Germany. Forty-two Mustangs leave East Wretham and only one returns early. R/V occurs over Schlettstadt, France at 0940 and 24,000'. The weather is poor today and over 300 of the 1,028 bombers dispatched abort. The Forts escorted by the 359th are noted to be in good formation. The Forts make two runs over the target before dropping their loads and there is no flak. No bombers are lost and no enemy aircraft are encountered.

311   March 5, 1945 (0725-1245)

Lt.Col. Daniel D. McKee, of the 370th FS, leads the 359th on another penetration, target and withdrawal support mission. Today the Forts are being sent to destroy a synthetic oil plant at Ruhland, Germany. The Group leaves East Wretham with forty-two Mustangs and there are nine aborts. The assigned bombers are not in the proper position at the R/V point so, the 359th provides roving support along the entire bomber stream, until reaching the target, where the assigned Forts are found. The primary target is obscured by an overcast and secondary targets at Chemnitz and Plauen, Germany are hit, with the aid of radar. One B-17 is lost and no enemy fighters are encountered. Lts. Earle S. Newcomer and Madison H. Newton, of the 370th FS, land at St. Trond, Belgium on the way out. Newton returns to base after taking on fuel, while Newcomer returns in a B-25 as his Mustang requires an engine change.

*   March 6,7, 1945 (bad weather)

The first P-51D-20 Mustangs arrive at East Wretham on the 6th. On the 7th pilots are briefed on the tail warning radar to be installed in their P-51s this month.

312   March 8, 1945 (1226-1621, A) (1217-1645, B)

Maj. James W. Parsons leads *A* group and Maj. Niven K. Cranfill, of the 368th FS, leads *B* group as the 359th flies area support/patrol for B-17s bombing marshalling yards and an aircraft factory in the Ruhr Valley. Both groups start the mission with twenty-six Mustangs and the only fighter to abort is from *A* group. *B* group makes R/V over Lippstadt, Germany at 1340 and 18,000', while *A* group achieves R/V over Dummer Lake at 1358 and 23,000'. The weather is notably bad today. Although several vectors are received and investigated, no enemy aircraft are encountered. No bombers or fighters are lost on this mission.

Left, Lt. Merle G. Aunspaugh who was killed in a flying accident on March 2, 1945. Right, Lt. Albert A. Cowie. On March 3, 1945, Cowie's P-51 was hit by flak while strafing an aircraft near Hannover, Germany and he crash-landed near Gandersheim, Germany where he was taken prisoner.

313   March 9, 1945 (0804-1240)

Col. John P. Randolph leads *A* group and Capt. Ray S. Wetmore, of the 370th FS, leads *B* group as the 359th flies penetration, target and withdrawal support for B-17s blasting the marshalling yards and munitions industry at Kassel, Germany. *A* and *B* groups are comprised of thirty-three and fourteen P-51s respectively and only one aborts, that being the Mustang flown by Lt. Arthur B. Morris Jr., of the 369th FS, from *A* group. Morris aborts when his Merlin loses oil pressure over Germany and barely makes it back over the English coast, at Clacton on Sea, before catching fire and forcing him to bail out at 1000'. Morris' chute opens at 400' causing him to land heavily, breaking his ankle in three places. R/V occurs over Egmond, Netherlands at 0850 and 20,000'. The bombing is done visually, with excellent results observed. Three Forts are lost and no contact is made with the Luftwaffe.

314   March 10, 1945 (1112-1720)

The 359th flies penetration, target and withdrawal support for B-17s raiding the marshalling yards at Hagen and Schwerte, Germany. Lt.Col. Daniel D. McKee, of the 370th FS, leads *A* group, while Capt. Ralph L. Cox, of the 369th FS, leads *B* group. *A* group is made up of twenty-four P-51s, one of which returns early and *B* group has twenty-five Mustangs. R/V is made over Egmond, Netherlands at 1210 and 24,000'. There is 10/10 cloud cover over the target and the bombs are dropped by radar at 1312. The 370th FS searches for jetties reported over Koblenz but finds nothing. Escort is maintained until reaching a point southeast of Koblenz, where a R/T is received ordering the Group to patrol an area east of the Remagen bridgehead. A second call directs the 359th to the Ludendorff bridge at Remagen, to search for Fw190s and Ar234 jet bombers attacking the span. Unfortunately the American anti-aircraft gun-

Capt. James L. Way Jr. poses with his crew chief in front of P-51D CV-Z Happy 2 44-72281. Way was flying a P-51K on March 3, 1945 when he shared in damaging 2 loco's, 10 boxcars, 1 switch house, 1 factory and a horsedrawn wagon.

ners at the bridge are not told of the approaching Mustangs and the 359th comes under intense friendly fire as well as fire from a German 20mm flak gun located on a hillside. At 1525 two P-51s, from the 368th FS, piloted by Lts. George H. Blackburn and James W. McCormack are hit by the German gunner while flying at 1,000'. McCormack is killed as his P-51 crashes immediately after being hit and his body is buried near the crash site. Blackburn's P-51 crashes into a wooded area near Windhagen, which is 2½ miles away and according to witnesses he died in the crash. Capt. Ray S. Wetmore, of the 370th FS, takes a hit in the right wing of his P-51 starting a fire. The fire dies out, enabling Wetmore to fly his Mustang to St. Trond, Belgium where he bellies in with fuel starvation problems and a jammed canopy. Wetmore's fighter sustains considerable damage but he escapes injury and returns to East Wretham on the 12th.

315   March 11, 1945 (1130-1538)

Col. John P. Randolph is in the lead as the 359th fur-

nishes penetration, target and withdrawal support for B-17s bombing the U-boat yards at Bremen, Germany. A total of fifty-three Mustangs take off on this mission and five return early. R/V is made at 1230 over the North Sea. 10/10 cloud cover makes observation of the results of the bombing, which is done by radar, impossible. No bombers are seen to go down due to the flak, which is heavy. The Deputy Group C.O., Lt. Col. James V. Wilson, pops his coolant north of the Frisian Islands and nurses his P-51 south until reaching Rysum, Germany where he bails out half a mile from a flak battery and is taken prisoner. No enemy aircraft are encountered and no bombers are lost.

316   March 12, 1945 (0940-1525)

Today the 359th flies penetration, target and withdrawal support for B-17s and B-24s bombing the marshalling yards near Swinemünde, Germany. Maj. Niven K. Cranfill, of the 368th FS, leads the Group. Fifty-one Mustangs begin the mission and three abort. R/V occurs over Schleswig, Germany at 21,000'. Once again the bombers are confronted with 10/10 cloud cover and resort to bombing by radar, at 1239. No contact is made with the Luftwaffe. The 359th returns to England without incident.

Left, Sgt. George R. Travis Section Head of the Photo Lab (85th Service Group) explains the mounting of the K-25 camera to Cpl. Albert E. Ziffiro Line Photo Technician from the 368th FS on Feb. 24, 1945. Right photo was taken on March 6, 1945 and shows the completed K-25 Camera installation. Note a cap has been placed on top of the canopy where the radio antenna entered on a small pulley enclosed in a clear plastic blister. The camera mount is obviously hand crafted and attached to the armor plate behind the pilot's head by four bolts. It was a similar installation that kept Ray Wetmore's canopy from jettisoning on March 10, 1945. His P-51 was on fire and he forgot to crank the canopy back until the canopy frame's crossbrace, below the camera mount, was clear before pulling the jettison lever. It took about twenty minutes for rescuers, using crow bars, to pry the jammed canopy off Wetmore's Mustang.

* March 13, 1945 (bad weather)

Capt. Andrew T. Lemmens, of the 370th FS, left East Wretham at 1230 in the piggyback P-51B to inspect an airfield at Cambrai, France. Lt.Col. Grady L. Smith rode in the jump-seat. They return the next day. Indications of a possible move to the continent by the Group will never bear fruit.

317 March 14, 1945 (1242-1725)

Col. John P. Randolph leads *A* group and Maj. James W. Parsons leads *B* group as the 359th provides penetration, target and withdrawal support for B-17s blasting a bridge at Minden, Germany. *A* group consists of thirty-five P-51s and has three aborts, while *B* group starts out with eighteen P-51s and has two aborts. R/V is made at 1400 and 21,000' over St. Vith, Belgium. The bombing is done visually at 1518 and several fires are noted, but the results are hidden by a haze. No enemy aircraft are encountered and one bomber is lost to flak.

318 March 15, 1945 (1211-1746)

Today the 359th is split into *A* and *B* groups, with Maj. Niven K. Cranfill, of the 368th FS, leading *A* group and Lt.Col. Daniel D. McKee, of the 370th FS, leading *B* group. *A* and *B* groups start with thirty-one and eighteen Mustangs respectively and three P-51s from *B* group return early. This mission is one the history books refer to as 'thousand plane raids.' 1,310 bombers and 764 fighters fill the skies over Germany. The B-17s escorted by the 359th are to bomb the marshalling yards at Oranienburg, just north of Berlin and Army Headquarters in Berlin. R/V is made over Zwolle, Netherlands at 1326 and 22,000'. At 1500 Capt. Ray S. Wetmore is leading Red Flight, of the 370th FS, southwest of Berlin at 25,000', when he spots two Me 163s circling at 20,000' twenty miles to the north, in the vicinity of Wittenberge. Wetmore engages one of the rocket fighters which goes into a 70° climb at full power. Suddenly the rocket motor stops and the German pilot heads for the deck, evidently out of fuel. Wetmore is right behind the Komet, his P-51 registering 560 to 600 m.p.h. At 2,000' the Komet levels off and Wetmore opens fire from 200 yards astern. Pieces begin to fly off the 163 and it makes a sharp right turn. A second burst of fire from the P-51 tears off half of the 163's left wing and starts a fire. The pilot bails out and the Komet crashes. Wetmore has expended 222 rounds of API for this his last kill of the war and the only enemy aircraft shot down by the entire 8th AF fighter command today. Wetmore ends the war as the 359th's top ace and top active duty ace of the 8th AF. The bombing is done visually but the results are obscured by smoke and fires. There is no flak over the target but nine bombers are lost.

Top, two 368th FS pilots that were casualties of flak at Remagen, Germany on March 10, 1945. Lts. James W. McCormack, left and George H. Blackburn right, died as their Mustangs crashed after being hit by a German 20mm gun positioned on a hillside. At left, Lt.Col. James V. Wilson of Headquarters. Wilson's P-51 popped its coolant north of the Frisian Islands on March 11, 1945. He nursed his P-51 south to Rysum, Germany before bailing out. Luckily he landed near a flak battery and was quickly taken prisoner. At this stage of the war it was not good to be captured by German civilians who were venting their frustration on downed Allied airmen.

*   **March 16, 1945 (bad weather)**

319   March 17, 1945 (1003-1605)

The 359th flies escort for B-17s blasting the synthetic oil plant at Böhlen, Germany. Col. John P. Randolph leads *A* group while *B* group is led by Capt. Ralph L. Cox, of the 369th FS. *A* group begins the mission with twenty P-51s and two return early, while *B* group has one abort out of the thirty-four Mustangs that take off. R/V is made over Koblenz, Germany at 1118 and 27,000'. Due to 10/10 cloud cover the target is hit by using radar and the results are not observed. One Fort is lost and no contact is made with the Luftwaffe. Escort continues through the target, ending at 1345. Back at East Wretham Lt. Frank Rea Jr., of the 368th FS, bellies his Mustang in but escapes injury.

Two photos of the 368th's two seat P-51B taken on Dec. 18, 1944. Needless to say this was a field conversion. To make room for the passenger the fuselage fuel tank was removed and the radio equipment relocated. Topping off this professional looking job is British Malcolm Hood. Notice the neat fairing added to the trailing edge of the Malcom Hood makes it look almost like the canopy of a late model Navy Corsair. This is the Mustang used by Capt. Andrew T. Lemmens to fly Lt.Col. Grady L. Smith to Cambrai, France on March 13, 1945.

320   March 18, 1945 (0845-1426)

The 359th is divided into *A* and *B* groups today as they provide penetration, target and withdrawal support for B-17s raiding the marshalling yards at Berlin, Germany. *A* group is comprised of eighteen P-51s from the 369th FS and is led by Capt. Ralph L. Cox, of that squadron. *B* group's thirty-four P-51s which come from the 368th and 370th FSs, are led by Capt. Ray S. Wetmore, of the 370th FS. Six P-51s from *B* group abort. The 359th makes R/V over Dummer Lake, Germany at 1010 and 26,000'. *A* group leaves the Forts at Dummer Lake to make a sweep northeast to Berlin. *B* group remains with the Forts and one Me 262 is spotted over Stendal, sixty miles west of Berlin. A pilot from the 368th FS chases

the jettie until his P-51 develops a runaway prop. At 1110 the target is bombed from 21,000' but due to a haze over the area that reaches to 30,000', no results are observed. Meanwhile *A* group has encountered flak as they pass over Tempelhof Airfield at 18,000', causing Yellow Flight to become separated from the rest of the 369th FS. Capt. Cox then leads Red, White and Blue Flights north to Settin and sweeps down the Oder River to Königsberg. While cruising at 10,000', Cox spots two unidentified aircraft headed southeast and leads the P-51s in pursuit. The two bogies are caught over an airfield at Zackerick, north of Kustrin, Germany. They are then identified as Russian Yak-9s but four other fighters are spotted over the airfield. These fighters have radial engines and are assumed to be German Fw190s, attacking

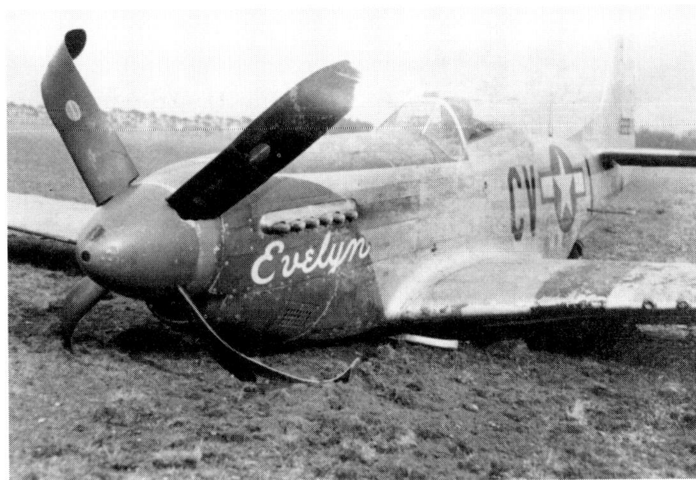

Left, on March 17, 1945 Lt. Frank Rea Jr. bellied in his P-51D Evelyn CV-I 44-11222 at East Wretham. It appears the main gear failed to extend but the tail wheel did. Note hoisting bar inserted through the lower fuselage aft of the insignia. Right, Lt. Robert J. Guggemos (The Wolverine), poses on the wing of a P-51 named *The Cork*. Mr. Webster uses one word in particular to describe a wolverine, ferocious. A fitting description of a true fighter pilot. Guggemos was a brief participant in and occupied a ringside seat during the Russian incident of March 18, 1945.

the field. The 369th FS makes a diving attack, with the following incidents taking place: Lt. Robert J. Guggemos latches onto what he identifies as a Fw190 and fires on it from 500 yards, without scoring any hits. As Guggemos moves in closer both fighters enter a haze and when it clears he is then behind a Yak-9. Guggemos attempts to break off the engagement but the Yak becomes aggressive, gets on his tail and begins firing. At this point Guggemos' wingman, Lt. Robert E. McCormack clobbers the Yak in the wing roots and the Russian fighter disintegrates. Guggemos and McCormack then climb to 12,000' and look down on the area. The sky below them is filled with burning fighters. In the meantime, Cox is leading an attack on the four fighters thought to be Fw190s. Cox singles out the leader of the flight and fires a long burst from ninety down to 40° deflection, scoring heavily and causing the fighter to catch fire and crash. Cox then quickly dispatches two more bogies before being apprized he is in combat with Russians. The leader of Red Flight, Lt. Rene L. Burtner, also scores a kill at this time. Reverting to Yellow Flight, that was separated from *A* group over Tempelhof, we find Lt. Robert S. Gaines Jr. has led his flight to the same general area as the rest of the group. Gaines leads his flight in bouncing what appears to be three Me109s, near Joachimsthal. As they close in on the trio, which are flying at 2,000', the bogies go into a diving left turn. Gaines fires a long burst into the lead aircraft, which is bluish in color, with no visible markings. The stricken fighter plummets straight into Werbellin Lake and explodes. F/O Harley E.

Berndt (Yellow 4) damages the number two fighter in the flight, scoring hits in the wing roots and cockpit, beginning at a range of 600 and closing to 200 yards. The bogie then breaks right and down and Berndt rejoins his flight. Lt. Bryce H. Thomson (Yellow 3) bounces what he thinks is a Me109 but as he closes in for the kill realizes it is not a German aircraft. While engaged with this fighter Thomson looks over his shoulder and finds he in turn is being fired on by another fighter. Breaking hard Thomson gets on the tail of his attacker. In one 360° turn he identifies it as a Yak-9. He then pulls up beside the Yak, waggles his Mustang's wings, points to the star insignia and then waves at the Russian pilot. Ivan hesitates, then waves in return. Thomson retires and joins another flight of P-51s. As this action is taking place, the combat over the airfield continues as Burtner leads Red Flight on a strafing pass across the field and he torches two Yak-9s taxiing out to take off. Simultaneously Lt. Robert W. McIntosh fires on a fighter that is landing and his gun camera film shows a pattern of fire cutting up the ground between the fighter that is landing and one taxiing. One of these two fighters ground loops. Capt. Ray S. Wetmore, who has been monitoring the battle on his radio, heads for the scene with *B* group. Wetmore bounces ten bogies flying on the deck but as he closes in notices red stars on their fuselages. Breaking off violently he narrowly escapes shooting down a La-5. Once more Wetmore's famous 'x-ray eyes' have proven invaluable. As the fight continues over Zackerick, Maj. Niven K. Cranfill of the 368th FS

On March 18, 1945 the 359th FG engaged Soviet Yak-9 aircraft north of Berlin. In this photo we have a flight of Yak-9Ds belonging to an elite Guards unit. Note the tailwheel door hanging down on the Yak in the foreground. Construction was mixed: The wing was wood; the fuselage was a welded steel tube frame covered with metal panels from the nose to just aft of the cockpit, where the top and bottom were then covered with curved plywood the sides were fabric. The use of fabric was not uncommon; even the mighty Corsair's outer wing panels were canvas covered. Also check the lack of insignia on top of the wing. SMITHSONIAN NATIONAL AIR AND SPACE MUSEUM

bags two Yak-9s. By now the Russians on the ground are putting up considerable flak and Cox orders his pilots to break off combat. The 359th retires from the area without a loss and returns safely to base but the real fireworks are about to begin.

Joseph Stalin has all surviving Russian pilots involved in this incident shot, then demands President Franklin D. Roosevelt order the execution of all American pilots involved. The only pilot court-martialed is Lt. Robert W. McIntosh. His gun camera film is the only evidence of the days events, the other films being "lost in the developing tank." The story goes he is fined a dollar, given a carton of cigarettes and told to go home. McIntosh is considered, by some of the other pilots, to be lucky for they remain in England, months after the war, completing their tours and sweating a decision concerning their fate. Lt.Gen. James H. Doolittle, Commander of the 8th AF, wasn't about to hang any of his boys and round filed all complaints concerning the matter. Eventually all of the pilots went home and the incident died a quiet death.

How did this international incident happen? Despite the lapse of half a century many of the facts are still not known and probably never will. First is the matter of aircraft identification. From the rear a Fw190 and a La-5 look very similar, as do the Me109 and Yak-9. Only when you get close in can small details, such as the shape of the horizontal stabilizers and the location of coolant scoops, be noted. These are small differences, not visible from every angle. Nor are they relevant when a Russian pilot is determined to kill you and your main concern is survival. Adding to the identification problem is the fact the Russians *usually* didn't paint the red star insignia on top of their fighters wings, instead positioning them under the wings (great for troops on the ground) and on the sides of the fuselage and vertical stabilizer. Another factor that may have entered the equation is the Russians flew a lot of captured Fw 190s. The Russians were also neglectful and paranoid, about letting the Allies know just how far they had advanced, so it is possible the airfield in question was still listed as German held. Considering all of the data available, two things are apparent; some of the Russians refused to break off their engagements and paid dearly and the much vaunted Yak-9 was definitely no match for the P-51. The score was nine destroyed in the air and two on the ground, most being Yak-9s.

321   March 19, 1945 (1111-1711)

The 359th flies area support for B-17s scheduled to bomb Halle, Germany. *A* group is led by Capt. Ray S. Wetmore, of the 370th FS, while *B* group is led by

March 19, 1945, was Maj. Nevin Kendall Cranfill's day for he scored the Group's only victory. Adding to the sweetness was the fact the victory was scored over a Me262. "Cranny" also damaged another 262 that was attacking a Mustang, saving the life of an unknown pilot. Photo shows the P-51 Cranny flew that day, CV-Q 44-15717.

Maj. Fred S. Hodges. *A* and *B* groups start the mission with sixteen and thirty-five P-51s respectively and two return early from *B* group. R/V is made over Sangerhausen, Germany at 1307 and 15,000'. Due to poor visibility the Forts hit secondary targets at Jena (motor transportation) and Zwickau (optical works), plus other targets of opportunity. The bombs are dropped mostly by radar and four B-17s are lost. Maj. Niven K. Cranfill is leading the 368th FS south of Dessau when, at 1400, three Me262s are seen passing overhead. As most of the squadron drops their tanks to give chase, Cranfill spots fifteen Me262s below him, heading south towards a box of Forts, which they attack. As the jetties break off their attack Cranfill is in position to bounce them. Seeing one of the 262s on the tail of a P-51, he goes for it first, scoring hits on the wings and saving the endangered Mustang. Following the damaged jettie north Cranfill comes across another 262 and starts shooting at it from slightly below and astern, at 600-800 yards. Hits on the bottom of the fuselage cause the 262 to begin a diving turn to the left. A second, longer burst hammers the spiralling fighter and it crashes and explodes. As he watches the jettie crash, Cranfill also notices a second explosion, on the ground, about a quarter of a mile away. It is assumed his wingman, Lt. Clifton Enoch Jr. crashed at this location (near Halle), between 1410 and 1415. The 369th and 370th also report spotting Me262s, at a distance, but they are not overtaken due to their superior speed.

322   March 20, 1945 (1518-1936)

Col. John P. Randolph is in the lead as the Group flies escort for twenty RAF Lancasters, whose target is a railway bridge at Nienburg, Germany. This mission causes a lot of excitement when the pilots are told the British will be dropping their new 22,000 lb. Grand Slam bombs. Forty-eight Mustangs leave East Wretham and two abort. R/V occurs near Egmond, Netherlands at 1557 and 13,000'. The Mustangs sweep ahead of the bombers, then rejoin them over the target. The 359th's pilots are disappointed to see the Lancs drop common 2,000 lb. bombs, instead of the Grand Slams. Many near misses are observed and a fire is started at the eastern approach to the bridge, but the span is left standing. As the Group lands at East Wretham, Lt. Robert W. Hopkins, of the 369th FS, is caught in the prop wash of the preceding Mustang and his fighter flips over. Hopkins emerges uninjured but his P-51 is totaled.

323   March 21, 1945 (0752-1245)

Maj. Niven K. Cranfill, of the 368th FS, leads today as the Group provides escort for B-17s bombing an airfield at Handorf, Germany. The 359th repeats yesterdays performance by getting forty-eight Mustangs aloft and having two abort. R/V is made at 0900, southwest of Meppel, Netherlands. Huge fires and explosions are noted at the target. After escort for the Forts is dropped the 359th provides top cover for P-51s of the 55th and 4th FGs as they strafe airfields at Bohmte and Rheine, Germany. No enemy aircraft are encountered and the Group returns without incident.

324   March 21, 1945 (1636-1940)

The second mission today is led by Maj. James W. Parsons as the 359th flies escort for B-24s raiding an airfield at Mulheim, Germany. Thirty-five P-51s begin this mission and only one aborts. R/V is made at 1721 and 20,000' over Walcheren, Netherlands. The target is hit visually at 1803 and the results of the

On March 22, 1945 Lt. Jack R. Schulte (Hot Shot Charlie) of the 370th FS, was landing his flak damaged P-51 when it suddenly flipped over. Although it took nearly thirty minutes to extract him, he was not seriously injured. Note the paint on the prop blades was rubbed off and the tires show indications that the wheels were locked, dirt being evident only on a small patch of the treads. The seat and armor plate assembly has been removed and is lying in the foreground. This P-51 was probably used for spare parts rather than bother trying to make it air-worthy again; after all they were still rolling off the production lines. Today with the venerable Mustang bringing $500,000 on the market, almost ten times its original cost, there is no doubt a similarly damaged 51 would be rebuilt.

bombing of the airfield and adjacent marshalling yard are noted to be excellent. No bombers are lost and there is no encounter with the Luftwaffe. On the way out Lt. John F. Collins, of the 368th FS, is forced to land on the continent due to engine trouble but he returns later in the day.

325   March 22, 1945 (0945-1347)

Today the 359th flies penetration, target and withdrawal support for B-17s bombing an airfield at Alhorn, Germany. Maj. Niven K. Cranfill, of the 368th FS, leads *A* group and Lt. Robert W. Davison, of the 369th FS, leads *B* group, after Maj. Fred S. Hodges aborts. Hodges is the only pilot to return early as *A* and *B* groups put up fifteen and thirty-three Mustangs respectively. R/V is made west of Egmond, Netherlands at 1033 and 16,000'. The target is bombed visually and the destruction is almost total. It is described as "the best bombing ever witnessed by the 359th". The only B-17 lost today is a damaged one being escorted out by Capt. Albert G. Homeyer, of the 368th FS. The Fort makes a safe belly landing near Meppen, Germany. On returning to base the flak-damaged P-51 flown by Lt. Jack R. Schulte, of the 370th FS,

flips over while landing. Although Schulte's extraction takes almost thirty minutes, he is not seriously injured.

326   March 23, 1945 (1134-1639)

Today sees a change from the usual escort duty to that of a fighter sweep south-east of Kassel, Germany. Capt. Ray S. Wetmore leads twenty-three P-51s on this mission and none abort. The 359th arrives over the target area at 1256. At 1445, in the vicinity of Salzwedel, White Flight of the 368th FS, led by Capt. George A. Doersch, spots two Ar96s at about 8,000'. Doersch and Lt. Kenneth E. Barber score hits on one Arado, which crashes and explodes. The other aircraft circles over an airfield where it is protected by flak guns. As Doersch and Barber exit, Lt. Marvin F. Boussu, of the 368th's Blue Flight, makes a single pass across the field damaging a He 111 bomber that fails to burn. At this stage of the war it is standard Luftwaffe practice to drain the fuel from all parked aircraft. This not only keeps aircraft from burning or exploding if strafed but also saves the now priceless fuel. The 370th FS chases two Me163s during the sweep but fails to overtake them.

Top left, Maj. James W. Parsons wearing a British helmet and Mae West poses with his crew chief Sgt. Floyd Myers. On March 24, 1945 Parsons scored a victory over a Me109 while flying Wild Will, the P-51D in the background. Parsons named his Mustang in honor of his first squadron commander Maj. William Miller of the 42nd FS, 54th FG in the Aleutians. Miller was shot down over Kiska during November of 1942. Top right, Capt. Robert C. Thomson who shot down two Me109s on March 24. Below, the P-51D flown by Lee Patton when he damaged two Me109s in the air on March 24.

327   March 24, 1945 (0556-1135)

Maj. Niven K. Cranfill, of the 368th FS, leads the Group on the first of three missions today. The first assignment is an area patrol in the vicinity of Hamm, Germany. Twenty-five P-51s take off and none abort. Time over the target is 0735 at 15,000'. All of the action on this mission is ground attack and the claims include: 7-4 locomotives, 10-0 boxcars, 6-0 oil tank cars, 13-0 trucks, 5-3 staff cars, 0-1 high tension tower and communications facilities. Against these claims only one Mustang receives noteworthy damage, that being the P-51 flown by Lt. John T. Marron, of the 368th FS. Although flak blows the entire landing flap off the Mustang's right wing, Marron flies it back to base for a safe landing.

328   March 24, 1945 (1010-1525)

Maj. James W. Parsons leads the second mission which is an area patrol northeast of Hamm, Germany. The P-51s sent out on the first mission have not yet returned when twenty-four take off on the second mission. Four of these Mustangs abort. At 1300, after patrolling for more than an hour, the 369th FS spots fifteen Me109s, which are setting up a landing pattern over the airfield at Eiklon. Diving on the bandits, the 369th inflicts the following losses: Capts. Robert C. Thomson and William F. Collins, Lts. Robert T. Lancaster and Fred S. McGehee, two kills each. Maj. James W. Parsons, Lts. Dale E. Kelly, Harold Tenenbaum and Bryce H. Thomson, one kill each. Tenenbaum and Kelly share a kill and Lt. Lee Patton damages two. The total is 13-0-2, with no losses. The only damage sustained by the 369th occurs when a 20mm shell passes through the P-51 flown by Capt. Robert C. Thomson. The projectile narrowly misses oil and coolant lines before exiting through the cockpit, where it also misses the pilot. Thomson brings the Mustang back for an uneventful landing. The 370th FS strafes and the claims are in the destruction diary.

The crosses on some of the German fighters engaged today are reported to be painted in such a way that they appeared to be circular at first glance. Capt. Robert C. Thomson reports holding his fire until aircraft identification was positive.

329   March 24, 1945 (1552-1907)

The third and final mission today is penetration, target and withdrawal support for B-17s bombing Twente Airfield at Enshede, Germany. Capt. John B. Hunter, of the 368th FS, leads and of the twenty-five P-51s that begin the mission three abort. R/V is made west of Egmond, Netherlands at 1650 and 21,000'. The bombing is observed as good, with considerable damage done to all runways. The flak is moderate but accurate. No bombers are lost and no enemy aircraft are encountered.

*   March 25, 1945 (bad weather)

330   March 26, 1945 (1103-1659)

Col. John P. Randolph leads as the 359th flies penetration, target and withdrawal support for B-17s blasting the synthetic oil plant at Zeitz, Germany. Forty-one Mustangs leave East Wretham and five return early. R/V occurs over the target area at 1400 and 24,000'. The bombing takes place at 1410, through breaks in the clouds and it is noted many of the bombs fell wide of their target. Flak over the target is intense. The Group returns safely to base.

The weather today is described by veteran pilots as being, **"very hazardous and constituting a greater risk than was warranted by any results that could be obtained."**

*   March 27-29, 1945 (bad weather)

331   March 30, 1945 (1218-1900)

Capt. Ralph L. Cox, of the 369th FS, leads *A* group and Col. John P. Randolph leads *B* group as the 359th furnishes penetration, target and withdrawal support for B-17s raiding the U-boat yards and a railway bridge at Vegesack, near Bremen, Germany. *A* and *B* groups put up thirty-seven and nineteen fighters respectively and there are three aborts from *A* group. *B* group makes R/V over Hoorn, Netherlands at 1345 and 20,000', with *A* group joining the armada eighteen minutes later, north of Zwolle, Netherlands at 25,000'. Excellent bombing results are noted and the escort is maintained until reaching the Netherlands coast on the way out. No enemy aircraft are encountered. At 1652 a R/T is received asking for help on an ASR search. Four pilots from the 368th FS, Capt. George A. Doersch, Lts. John D. Cooley, James J. Ferris III and Lewis L. Fraser take the job, arriving in position at 1735. Ferris and Fraser search until 1800, when low fuel forces them to return to base. Doersch and Cooley then locate the pilot, in his dinghy, four miles off the northeast tip of Schiermon-

Left, Lt. John D. Cooley Jr. poses with crew chief S/ Sgt. Charles Doersom in front of his P-51D *Janet* (Cooley's girlfriend's name) CV-V 44-11685. Right, the flip side of Cooley's Mustang's nose. No idea who Elva May was. On March 30, 1945 Cooley and Pop Doersch, who were part of an ASR search effort, located a pilot in his dinghy four miles off the northeast tip of Schiermonnikoog Island. DOERSOM

nikoog Island. The pair leaves the area at 1820 and land at Beccles, England for fuel, returning to East Wretham the next morning.

332 March 31, 1945 (0710-1255)

Lt.Col. Daniel D. McKee, of the 370th FS, leads *A* group, while Lt.Col. Niven K. Cranfill, of the 368th FS, leads *B* group as the 359th flies penetration, target and withdrawal support for B-17s hitting Strassfurt, Germany. *A* group consists of thirty-four P-51s and has three aborts. *B* group has no aborts among its nineteen Mustangs. R/V is made north of Gotha, Germany at 0900. The results of the bombing are not observed and there is no contact with the Luftwaffe. The flak is moderate to heavy. Escort is maintained through the target and dropped near Vechta, Germany.

* April 1, 1945 (bad weather)

333 April 2, 1945 (1434-1839)

Lt.Col. Niven K. Cranfill, of the 368th FS, leads the Group today as they provide penetration, target and withdrawal support for B-17s and B-24s scheduled to bomb the Galsted Air Depot in Denmark. Fifty-four Mustangs leave East Wretham on this mission and only one aborts. R/V occurs over the North Sea at 1520 and 11,000'. At a point thirty miles south of Blaavands Huk, Denmark the force turns back due to 10/10 cloud cover over the Danish peninsula. No enemy aircraft are encountered. One B-24 flies to Sweden with engine trouble and crashes there. The 359th returns to East Wretham intact.

The clocks are set forward one hour today, for the British equivalent of daylight savings time.

334 April 3, 1945 (1422-1916)

Lt.Col. Daniel D. McKee, of the 370th FS, leads *A* group and Lt.Col. Niven K. Cranfill, of the 368th FS, leads *B* group as the 359th flies penetration, target and withdrawal support for B-17s hitting the U-boat yards at Kiel, Germany. *A* group consists of eighteen P-51s and they experience two aborts. *B* group begins the mission with thirty-five Mustangs and has only one abort. R/V is made over the North Sea at 1601 and 24,000'. At 1630, near Flensburg, Germany Capt. George A. Doersch leads Red Flight, of the 368th FS, in an attack on five suspected bandits. As they close in the bandits are found to be yellow-nose Mustangs (361st FG). Directly behind the Mustangs are three

Me262s, closing in for the kill. Lt. Olin G. Everhart attacks, getting hits in the fuselage and both wings of a 262. The jettie begins to burn, enters a vertical dive and explodes as it hits the ground. Everhart expends only 88 rounds of API for the kill. Unfortunately the victory is not awarded. The bombs are dropped at 1641 but the results are not observed due to an overcast. Flak over the target is heavy but inaccurate. Lt. Charles E. Stubblefield, of the 369th FS, is the apparent victim of oxygen equipment failure when his P-51 falls out of formation sixty miles off the coast from Lowestoft, England. He is listed MIA.

335   April 4, 1945 (0809-1417)

Today the 359th furnishes penetration, target and withdrawal support for B-17s blasting an airfield and control station at Fassburg, Germany. Col. John P. Randolph leads *A* group, on this his last mission, before being sent home. Lt.Col. Daniel D. McKee, of the 370th FS, leads *B* group. *A* and *B* groups put up eighteen and thirty-six Mustangs respectively, with two returning early from *A* group and three from *B* group. R/V is made near Helgoland Island at 0924 and 16,000'. The bombing results are noted to be good, as is the camouflage on the Me109s on the airfield. Only one bomber is lost and no enemy aircraft are encountered.

*   April 5, 1945 (bad weather)

A complaint that drop tanks were released on Sudbury, England at 1230 on March 31st is received. It is later proved the 359th FG was not responsible.

336   April 6, 1945 (0714-1312)

Capt. George A. Doersch, of the 368th FS, leads the 359th as they fly penetration, target and withdrawal support for B-17s bombing the rail station and marshalling yards at Leipzig, Germany. Forty P-51s leave East Wretham and three abort. R/V occurs over Koblenz, Germany at 0845 and 23,000'. The bombs are dropped at 1006 but the results are not observed due to an overcast. Near Grimma, which is south of the target, three Forts are seen colliding and spinning down. Only one chute is noted. No contact is made with the Luftwaffe.

337   April 7, 1945 (1203-1732)

Today the 359th flies penetration, target and withdrawal support for B-17s raiding an airfield at Reinsehlen, Germany. Lt.Col. Daniel D. McKee, of the 370th FS, leads *A* group and Capt. George A. Doersch, of the 368th FS, leads *B* group. *A* group begins the mission with sixteen P-51s and none abort, while *B* group's thirty- eight Mustangs suffer three aborts. R/V is made over Bocholt, Germany at 1325 and 18,000'. The bombs are dropped at 1515 and the results are noted to be excellent. The Group returns to base without incident, but there is heavy fighting by other groups.

338   April 8, 1945 (0836-1413)

Maj. James W. Parsons leads *A* group and Capt. Ray S. Wetmore, of the 370th FS, leads *B* group as the 359th flies penetration, target and withdrawal support for B-17s bombing Zerbst, Germany. Of the seventeen Mustangs assigned to *A* group one aborts, while there are no aborts form the thirty-five Mustangs in *B* group. R/V occurs over Treysa, Germany at 1038 and 19,000'. The bombs are dropped visually at 1142, with results noted to be excellent. Four B-17s fall to flak and the Luftwaffe fails to show. Escort is dropped at 1222, south of Kassel, Germany.

339   April 9, 1945 (1334-1931)

The 359th flies penetration, target and withdrawal support for B-17s blasting a jet airfield at Obershleischeim, Germany (north of Munich). Lt.Col. Daniel D. McKee leads fifty Mustangs off and two abort. R/V is made east of Heidelburg, Germany at 1535 and 22,000'. Part of the Group maintains close escort over the target, which is bombed visually, with excellent results observed. At 1600, a flight from the 368th FS, led by Capt. George A. Doersch, times a strafing run to occur just after the bombs have hit the targeted airfield. On the first pass Lt. Robert H. Elliot damages two Ju88s. During the second pass no aircraft are visible, due to dust in the air from the bombing, so Elliot strafes a gun emplacement. At 1645, near Augsburg on the return leg of the mission, Capt. Marvin F. Boussu is leading Red Flight, of the 368th FS, when he spots three Me262s beginning a head-on attack on some B-17s that are directly ahead. Red Flight drops their tanks and moves forward to engage. The jetties divert from the Forts toward the Mustangs. The 262s zip past Red Flight, with Red 3 and 4 breaking off in pursuit. F/O Raymond C. Muzzy and Lt. Frank Rea Jr. both score hits on the jetties, with Muzzy claiming one damaged and one damaged/shared with Rea. After the Me262s

Two pilots participating in "The Great Jet Massacre" of April 10, 1945 were Lt. Ralph R. Klaver, at the top and Lt. Harold Tenenbaum below. Klaver's P-51 was named *Born to Lose* IV-R serial number 44-15588 but was not the Mustang he flew on April 10. On the right is a sequence taken from Lt. Robert J. Guggemos' gun camera footage showing the Me262 he destroyed on April 10th. Note in the final frame the landing gear is down and at this point the German pilot was still hopeful of getting down in one piece.

have outdistanced Muzzy and Rea, Boussu sights them at 10,000', while he is flying at 21,000'. As Red 1 and 2 dive on the three bandits they are spotted and the trailing 262 breaks right. Boussu gets one burst into the jettie's fuselage before it speeds off. At 1650, while separated from the 368th's White Flight, Lt. Leon J. Levitt finds approximately 200 Ju88s parked among the trees bordering the Autobahn, south of Munich. Levitt makes two passes, flaming two Ju88s. He also tries to contact his squadron by radio but fails and leaves the area. At 1700, Capt. George A. Doersch and his wingman attack

Germering Airfield, located west of Munich. On his first pass Doersch sets a Fw 190 on fire and it explodes. On the second pass Pop pulls out of his dive, toward the target, so low he can't aim his guns but fires anyway. As Pop pulls up to exit the field his prop slices into a He111 bomber and at that instant a delayed action bomb explodes under the Mustang. Flying debris dents the P-51's spinner, cracks the bullet proof windscreen and knocks the rear-view mirror off the windscreen frame. The coolant temperature rises and Pop opens both radiator shutters to the max. With the temperatures reading in the green he heads home but fifty miles west of Frankfurt the Merlin catches fire and Doersch makes a safe belly landing. Pop then makes his way to the American lines and hitches a ride back to base.

340   April 9, 1945 (1530-1930)

The second mission today is escort for three photo-recon P-38s (F-5s), headed for Dessau, Germany. Capt. Ivan B. Holloman, of the 369th FS, leads the escort flight, consisting of six Mustangs. All nine aircraft arrive over the target at 1735 but low cloud cover prevents the F-5s from accomplishing their mission. No enemy aircraft are encountered and the planes return safely to England.

341   April 10, 1945 (1159-1753)

Capt. Ralph L. Cox, of the 369th FS leads *A* group and Capt. Albert G. Homeyer, of the 368th FS, leads *B* group as the 359th provides penetration, target and withdrawal support for B-17s hitting munitions dumps and Army Headquarters at Oranienburg, Germany. The 359th puts up fifty-nine fighters to-day: Forty in *A* group, which has one P-51 return early and nineteen in *B* group, which also has one abort. R/V is made over Osnabruck, Germany at 1340 and 21,000'. Capt. Robert F. Boussu and Lt. John T. Marron, both from the 368th FS, chase a Me262 briefly, near Wittstock, with Marron scoring hits in the jet's aft fuselage. The jettie then dives, lead-ing the Mustangs into flak and terminating the pur-suit. In the same area, the 370th FS witnesses five Me262s make an attack on the Forts, with two of the bandits falling to gunners on the bombers. The bombing takes place at 1450, with the results noted to be excellent but the fight for the skies continues to be savage. Lt. Harold Tenenbaum of the 369th FS and his wingman, Lt. Albert S. Freeman, are cruis-ing at 14,000' when a B-17 explodes directly in front of them. Tenenbaum then spots six Me262s attack-ing the Forts above him and climbs to engage the bandits. On reaching 16,000', another 262 is spotted below, being chased by Mustangs. Abandoning his climb, Tenenbaum dives after the 262, closing the gap until the jettie initiates a shallow climb and speeds off. Now Tenenbaum notices two jets below him, distantly pursued by more Mustangs. Diving from 8,000' he overhauls one of the bandits and be-gins firing from 500 yards, at 60° deflection. As the German pilot lowers his jet's landing gear, in prepa-ration to land at Gardelegen Airdrome, Tenenbaum

closes to 100', opens fire and sets the 262's right engine on fire. The 262 touches down at mid-field and contin-ues on for 400 yards, before exploding. Tenenbaum catches a second Me262 trying to land and scores some hits before being driven off by flak. As Tenenbaum exits, Lts. Robert J. Guggemos and Horace E. Garth III, both from the 369th FS, arrive and catch a third jet trying to land. Guggemos pulls in behind the 262 and closing to 100' fires a long burst. The jet bursts into flames, goes into a steeper glide and crashes on the field. Lt. Ralph R. Klaver also damages a 262 at this location. Finding the flak has driven off his wingman, Garth, Guggemos joins with Mustangs from the 361st FG heading west and later helps them strafe an airfield at Dannefeld, Germany. After hitting one Me109, parked in a tree line, he makes a second pass for camera confirmation. As Guggemos opens fire a second 109, previously hidden from view, explodes. Eight or nine Me109s are left in ruins as a result of this joint effort.

April 10, 1945 is known as the day of *The Great Jet Massacre*, with the 8th AF claiming twenty Me 262s in the air. Total losses for the Luftwaffe on the 10th were 311 destroyed and 237 damaged, while the Mighty 8th's losses were nineteen bombers and eight Mustangs.

342   April 11, 1945 (1015-1634)

The 359th flies penetration, target and withdrawal support for B-17s bombing a target in the Kreuz-linger Forest, near Munich, Germany. Capt. Ray S. Wetmore, of the 370th FS, leads *A* group and *B* group is lead by Capt. Albert G. Homeyer, of the 368th FS. *A* group begins the mission with thirty-eight Mustangs and has three abort, while two Mus-tangs of the nineteen that form *B* group abort. No strafing is permitted on this mission. R/V is made over Neustadt, Germany at 1202 and 25,000'. *A* group maintains close escort, while *B* group makes a sweep in the area of Munich. The bombing is done visu-ally, from 1247-1252 with excellent results observed. The flak is very heavy over the target but only one Fort is lost. No enemy aircraft are encountered and the 359th returns to base without incident.

*   April 12, 1945

President of The United States of America, Franklin Delano Roosevelt dies.

343   April 13, 1945 (1334-1843)

Lt.Col. Donald A. Baccus leads the 359th for the first

Top left, Lt.Col. Donald A. Baccus, commander of the 359th FG from April 8 to Sept. of 1945. Baccus came from the 356th FG where he was the commander of the 359th FS. He led the 359th FG into combat for the first time on April 13, 1945 and destroyed an enemy aircraft on the ground on April 17, 1945 bringing his total for the war to 5½ in the air and 4 on the ground. Lt. John W. Herb, top right, of the 368th FS didn't return from the mission of April 13, 1945. Herb strafed an airfield and destroyed two Me110s and two Do217s. While making one of several passes on the airfield Herb struck some trees and tore the scoop from his P-51. He tried to belly in on a nearby field but fell short and hit more trees, before crashing on the field and perishing in the flaming wreckage. Right, Baccus' P-51D CV-U 44-72746.

time, as they furnish penetration escort for B-17s raiding the marshalling yards at Neumunster, Germany to be followed by strafing. Forty-two Mustangs leave East Wretham and seven abort. R/V occurs over the North Sea at 1500 and 24,000'. The 370th FS maintains escort until 1530, when the bombs are dropped. No enemy aircraft are encountered and one bomber is lost. Ground claims for today are summarized as follows:

(1518-1530) The 368th FS strafes south of Neumunster, Germany. Blue Flight hits an airfield, with three pilots getting four kills each. Lt. John A. Denman: four Me110s plus a locomotive later on; Lt. Kenneth E. Barber; three Me110s plus an unidentified single engine aircraft; and Lt. John W. Herb, two Me110s and two Do217s. While making a pass on the airfield Herb strikes some trees, tearing the ventral scoop from his Mustang. He tries to belly-in on a nearby field but falls short by thirty yards and hits more trees before crashing on the field and perishing in the flaming wreckage.

(1518) Red Flight from the 368th, led by Capt. George A. Doersch, strafes between Lübeck and Neumunster and claims four locomotives destroyed.

(1530) Yellow Flight from the 368th, led by Capt. John B. Hunter, strikes an air depot at Lüneburg, Germany. Hunter bags a He111 and Lt. Garland E. Madison destroys a Me210 and one unidentified

Top left, Lt.Col. Daniel D. McKee commander of the 370th FS, at the time of the April 13, 1945 mission. He destroyed two Ar196s on the ground that day. Top right, Capt. Eugene Surowiec of the 370th shared in damaging a tugboat and four barges with Lt. Benjamin D. Schwartz Jr. Left, Lt. Kenneth E. Barber of the 368th FS and his crew chief S/Sgt. Stephen Almasy. Barber added three Me110s and a single engine aircraft destroyed on the ground to the Group's total on April 13.

single engine aircraft. Both P-51s sustain flak damage during the attack but return safely to base.

(1540-1630) Thirteen Mustangs of the 370th FS, led by Lt.Col. Daniel D. McKee, strafe in the area of Ratzeburg and Schwerin Lakes. McKee and Lt. Madison H. Newton destroy two Arado 196 aircraft each. Other claims for the 370th are: 11-3 locomotives, 5-5 oil tank cars, 1-1 tugboats and 1-8 barges.

* April 15, 1945

Memorial services for President Roosevelt are held, at 1500, in the Station Theater.

344 April 16, 1945 (1330-1930)

Today Capt. Ralph L. Cox, of the 369th FS, leads *A* group and they fly a strafing mission in the Prague area of Czechoslovakia. Capt. John B. Hunter, of the 368th FS, leads *B* group as they provide target support for B-17s bombing the marshalling yards at Platting and Regensburg, Germany to be followed by strafing. *A* group consists of thirty-four P-51s from the 370th and 369th FSs. *B* group contains twenty P-51s coming from the 368th FS. There are three aborts from *A* group while only one Mustang returns early from *B* group. *A* group arrives over Prague to find large numbers of aircraft drawn into the city, where they are protected by heavy flak. The flak is so intense no attempt is made to strafe. Meanwhile *B* group observes excellent bombing results at Platting before dropping down to strafe. At 1555 the 368th FS, less Blue Flight, strafes an airfield adjacent to the marshalling yards at Platting. The dust from the bombs hitting the airfield and marshalling yards hasn't settled when the 368th makes a single pass on about twenty Me109s, parked wing-tip to wing-tip. Capt. John B. Hunter destroys one and damages one, Lt. John T. Marron destroys two and Lt. James H. McDonald destroys two and damages one.

On April 13, 1945, Lt. Frank Rea Jr., top left, destroyed a loco and shared in the destruction of three others. It's interesting he was still flying a B model P-51. On April 16, 1945, Lt. James H. McDonald, top right, destroyed two Me109s on the ground. Left, the P-51D flown by Lt. John B. Hunter on April 16 when he destroyed a Me109 on the ground. Name on the nose is *Addie II*. BISHER

345   April 17, 1945 (1120-1716)

The 359th is once more split into *A* and *B* groups to perform two missions. First *A* group, led by Lt.Col. Donald A. Baccus, flies a strafing job in the Prague-Linz-Salzburg, Czechoslovakia and Munich-Regensburg, Germany sector. *B* group, led by Maj. James W. Parsons, provides escort for B-17s raiding the marshalling yards at Dresden, Germany. *A* group puts up thirty-six fighters and has eight return early. *B* group only has one abort from its complement of eighteen P-51s. R/V is made over Coburg, Germany

at 1330 and 18,000'. At 1400, thirty miles west of Dresden, Capt. William F. Collins (White 3) and his wingman, Lt. Fred S. McGehee, bounce a Me262 that is shadowing the bomber stream. They give up the chase after five minutes and return to the Forts. At 1456, Collins and McGehee drop down to investigate a bandit reported near an airfield. Collins finds the field and spots a well camouflaged Fw190 parked there. He destroys it on his first pass but decides not to stick around when tracers are seen coming up in his direction. At 1345 the 370th FS, which is part of *A* group, begins hunting at Prague. Three airfields,

Top, 9th AF B-26B-55 Marauders. Although the Martin Marauder was called, among other things, the *Baltimore Whore* (built in Baltimore and having no visible means of support, referring to its small wing) at the end of the war it had the enviable record of the lowest loss rate per sortie of all U.S. bombers. ANDREW TREAT

northeast of the city, are each found littered with the tattered remains of over 100 enemy aircraft. Lt.Cols. Donald A. Baccus and Daniel D. McKee strafe the airfields at Ganacker and Platting, Germany. At Ganacker, McKee destroys a Fw190 and notes about fifty previously strafed aircraft, along with intense light caliber flak. Moving to Platting, Baccus destroys an unidentified twin engine aircraft and damages a Me 109. The 359th returns to England without incident.

346 April 18, 1945 (0840-1444)

For this mission the 359th is divided into *A*, *B* and *C* groups, led by Capt. John B. Hunter, of the 368th FS, Capt. Ralph L. Cox, of the 369th FS and Lt.Col. Daniel D. McKee, of the 370th FS, respectively. *A* group begins the mission with eighteen P-51s and has no aborts. *B* group starts with seventeen fighters and has the only abort, while *C* group is comprised of sixteen P-51s. The assignment is penetration, tar-

A lineup of 368th Mustangs. This photo was probably taken after the end of the war since the IFF tail warning radar antennas are visible on the first three aircraft. CV-J, serial number 44-15711, was flown by Lt. J. F. Collins Jr. who took part in the strafing on February 28 and March 3, 1945. Next in line is CV-I, serial number 44-11222, flown by Lt. Emory C. Cook when he shot down a Me109 on December 23, 1944. The third Mustang is CV-K, serial number 44-63689, and is seen elsewhere in this book. Notice the yellow spiral painted on the spinners.

get and withdrawal support for 9th AF B-26 Marauders. The target is an oil storage facility, in a wooded area, southwest of Neuberg, Germany. R/V is made over Mannheim, Germany at 1010 and 9,000'. The bombing takes place at 1210, with a good concentration of hits made on the target. The B-26s are left at the target and the 359th returns safely to base.

347   April 19, 1945 (0827-1407)

Today the Group flies escort for B-17s bombing the marshalling yards at Falkenburg, Germany. Capt. Ray S. Wetmore, of the 370th FS, leads *A* group and Maj. Fred S. Hodges leads *B* group. There are eighteen Mustangs in *A* group, which has two return early and thirty-four in *B* group, which has only one abort. Just after takeoff, Lt. John J. Murray, of the 370th FS, crash lands at Croxton. Murray is not injured but his P-51 is Category E. R/V occurs over Hamelin, Germany at 1005 and 25,000'. During the escort, a top turret gunner from the 457th BG fires on the Mustangs of the 368th's Blue Flight. Luckily none of the fighters are hit. The bombs are dropped at 1103, with excellent results being observed. No Forts are lost, but twenty-seven are hit by flak. No contact is made with the Luftwaffe and the 359th returns to England without incident.

Lt. Eugene F. Dauchert of the 368th FS crashes the Group's A-20 at base.

348   April 20, 1945 (0826-1411)

Capt. Ralph L. Cox, of the 369th FS, leads *A* group and Lt.Col. Daniel D. McKee, of the 370th FS, leads *B* group as the 359th flies penetration, target and withdrawal support for B-17s blasting the marshalling yards at Seddin, Germany. The 359th fields forty-two P-51s in *A* group, which has two aborts and nineteen in *B* group, that has only one abort. R/V takes place over Hague, Netherlands at 0921 and the escort is routine. The bombs are dropped at 1124 and good results are noted. No enemy aircraft are encountered.

*   April 24, 1945

Lt.Col. Donald A. Baccus leads eighty-three Mustangs on a non-operational flight over East Anglia. It is a record launch for the Group.

349   April 25, 1945 (0732-1345)

This is the last day the 8th AF will fly a heavy bombardment mission in Europe. All succeeding missions will be to drop food, or bring back former

POWs. This assignment catches the Group off guard, as they are not expecting to fly today.

The target of the B-17s is the Pilzen-Skoda armament works at Pilzen, Czechoslovakia. Capt. Ray S. Wetmore, of the 370th FS, now the leading ace in the 8th AF still in combat, leads *A* group and Capt. Robert C. Thomson, also of the 370th FS, leads *B* group. *A* group leaves East Wretham with seventeen Mustangs and two abort. *B* group begins the mission with thirty-six P-51s and four return early. The bombing takes place at 1130 and the results are observed as excellent, with large fires started and gigantic clouds of smoke rising to 10,000'. No enemy fighters are encountered but seven Forts are seen lost to flak, three spinning down over the target. Fifteen chutes are noted, along with the fact the airmen who bailed out were fired on by 20mm flak guns. On returning to England four bombers are declared Category E, while 180 require repairs. As the 359th is returning to base, the P-51 flown by F/O Jack D. Highfield, of the 368th FS, has prop failure. Highfield bellies his Mustang in on a bombed-out airfield, twelve miles south of Dortmund, Germany and returns to base several days later. As the Group lands at East Wretham, Lt. Clarence R. Brown, of the 369th FS, noses his P-51 over, but escapes injury.

At 0940 hours on May 7, 1945, the 359th FG received the following Teletype from 8th AF Headquarters:

1. "A representative of German High Command signed the unconditional surrender of all German land sea and air forces in Europe to the Allied Expeditionary Forces and simultaneously to the Soviet High Command at 1041 hours Central Europe Time, 7 May, under which all forces will cease active operations at 0001 B May 9."

2. "Effective immediately all offensive operations by Allied Expeditionary Force will cease and troops will remain in present positions. Moves involved in occupational duties will continue. Due to difficulties of communications there may be some delay in similar orders reaching enemy troops so full defensive precautions will be taken."

A few days later word was passed down that training, for transfer to the Pacific, would soon commence and last for about one month. This never materialized.

POWs Lt. Elmer N. Dunlap and Edward J. Maslow, of the 370th FS, return to East Wretham in May after being liberated. They report German intelligence had photos of the 370th's pilot status board as well as the names of all personnel.

During June and July men were being sent home, while those remaining on duty kept the base and equipment running. Lt. James J. Ferris III, of the 368th FS, was killed when his P-51B crashed during a simulated combat training flight, on June 19, 1945. His body was found near the wreckage and it is assumed his chute failed to open after successfully bailing out. The cause of the crash is unknown.

Late in June a New York newspaper ran the following headline, "Last of the Eighth Air Force returns to the States." That came as a shock to the 359th FG, which was still soundly entrenched at East Wretham. July saw the 359th touring historical sites and the enlisted men attending special schools.

Lt. Eugene F. Dauchert of the 368th FS, who was serving with the 3rd Gunnery and Tow-Target Flight at East Wretham, was landing an A-35B at Martlesham Heath on July 7 when its engine caught fire. Dauchert bellied the aircraft in and extracted his passenger, Lt. Jett of the 356th FG. Jett later died from his injuries and Dauchert received 1st and 2nd degree burns about the face and head. For his heroic action in removing Jett from a burning aircraft in the face of an imminent explosion Dauchert is awarded the Soldiers Medal.

While on a routine training flight, on July 9, the P-51 being flown by Lt. George Turinsky lost oil pressure and crashed six miles west of Great Massingham. Turinsky suffered small cuts and bruises about the face but the Mustang was totaled.

Tragedy struck again on July 23, when F/O John H. Klug Jr., of the 368th FS, died in the wreckage of his P-51, shortly after taking off. When the engine began to lose power Klug turned back toward the base but realizing his fighter wouldn't make the runway he selected an open field to land on. The P-51 suddenly snapped inverted and crashed. The 368th FS had suffered its final loss.

August came to East Wretham and with it the welcome news Japan had surrendered. Paradoxically the 359th FG's morale hit a low point, for there was no longer a reason for their existence. All that remained on most of their minds was going home. By this time only eighteen Mustangs were available for all of the pilots to fly and these were being serviced by one engineering section.

On Nov. 4, 1945, the Group's remaining personnel, that had accumulated enough points to ship home*, boarded the Queen Mary and arrived at New York on the 9th. The Group was then transferred to Camp Kilmer, New Jersey. The cosmic wheel had come full circle and the 359th was inactivated the next day.

*Pilots who were still short on hours transferred to the 9th AF and completed their tours as part of the occupational forces. Some of these men returned home as late as Sept. of 1946.

Top left, Lt. George Turinsky (Turk) of the 370th FS. Turinsky flew B-17s before transferring to the 370th on April 16, 1945. Too late to fly combat he did stay with the 370th until they folded their tent in September, then transferred out. On July 9 the Mustang Turinsky was flying on a training mission lost oil pressure and he crash landed near Great Massingham suffering minor cuts and bruises. The P-51 was totaled. Top right, a line up of 368th FS Mustangs during May 1945. Barely visible are the yellow spirals painted on the spinners. Line up includes: CV-Y, *Kitten*, 44-63776; CV-N, *Lady*, 44-14965; CV-T, *Silky*, 44-11758; CV-Z, *Happy, 2* 44-72281; and CV-Q 44-15717. ALMASY Right, Lt. Vernon T. Judkin's P-51D, *Babe*. This photo was also taken after the war and several things are worth noting. First the ground crews have outlined the black code letters in red (it's easy to tell when the pace slows down); second, the flight color has been applied to the canopy frame; and third, the tail warning radar has been installed.

Four late model Mustangs are shown above. The top two photos are of P-51K CS-<u>M</u>, 44-11574, flown by Capt. William F. Stepp. Name painted on the right side of the nose is *Miss Virginia* with *Marilyn Beth* on the left side. Note the M on the left side is positioned much higher. Middle left, 'Pop' (my boy), in small letters below 'Pop', was flown by Lt. John T. Marron when he destroyed two Me109s on April 16, 1945. *Pop* was a P-51D-20NA, CV-K, 44-63689. WILLIAM HESS Middle right, Lt. John W. Herb leans against the nose of *Mary Lou*, another P-51D-20NA; CV-E, 44-72260. SID WHEELER The two bottom photos are of Lt. Robert W. McIntosh, his groundcrew and *Dilbert*, a P-51D-10NA; IV-E, 44-14127. In the bottom left photo we have crewchief S/Sgt. Floyd Myers on the left, McIntosh in the center and assistant crewchief Sgt. Robert Pollak. The same trio appears in the photo on the right but in reverse order. The right side of Dilbert's nose is sporting the name *Lil' Marge* and the underlined fuselage code letter E is barely visible on the extreme left, under the wing.

Top left, Lt. Warner C. Jennings' P-51K *Michigan Mauler;* IV-I serial number 44-11572. Top right, Lt. Jennings and his crew. Middle left, Capt. Robert W. Hopkins and his P-51D *Saucy Sal;* IV-M serial number 44-72344. Note the Mustang's nose has just been painted; the cowling fasteners have not been turned resulting in a loss of paint on the heads. Middle right, another shot of Hopkins and his 51. This one shows the female figure added by Tony Chardella. Bottom left, Capt. Jimmy C. Shoffit lands his P-51D, *Josephine II;* CS-T, serial number 44-15102. Bottom right, another line of Mustangs at East Wretham, very late in the war is a good guess since the flight color has been applied to the canopy frame, flight leader stripes applied to the vertical strake and the tail warning radar installed on *Gloria Mac;* P-51D IV-J, serial number 44-72425, Lt. Robert E. McCormack's 51.

Top, Standiford Field, Louisville, Ky. in the Spring of 1947. Note the Kentucky Mustangs carry the national insignia on the fuselage unlike the early W. Va. Mustangs. It also happens to be the standard late WW II insignia, which doesn't have the red horizontal stripe in the center of the white bars. Below is the ill-fated trainer that bellied-in during the summer camp of 1953, at Camp Greyling, Michigan. Lt. Bill Gast was piloting the TF-51D when a coolant line under the cockpit floor blew, filling the cockpit with scalding steam. Gast and his passenger were pulled from the wreckage by Airman James Evans.

Postwar Assignments

When the Air National Guard was ordered activated on Jan. 30, 1946 Army Air Force units, previously inactivated, were selected to fill the slots thus created. Since a numbering system of 100 through 200 was being used for Air National Guard units, that meant the World War II unit designations would change.

The 368th FS became the 165th FS, stationed at Louisville, Kentucky. The 369th FS resurfaced as the 167th FS and was based at Charleston, West Virginia. Sadly the 370th FS was not reincarnated, its glorious history ending with the termination of WW II. The third squadron forming the group was the 156th FS from Charlotte, North Carolina. This unit's history is linked to the 360th FS of the 356th FG, 8th AF. The 156th, 165th and 167th FSs were put under the command of the 123rd FG, based at Louisville, Kentucky. The 123rd was a new unit, as WW II fighter groups were not resurrected . Since the Kentucky and West Virginia units are those with direct ties to the 359th FG, this book will not deal with the North Carolina squadron.

165TH FS—KENTUCKY, ANG

The 165th FS was federally recognized on February 16, 1947. The squadron was based at Standiford Field, Louisville, Kentucky and equipped with the P-51D. On January 7, 1948 Capt. Thomas F. Mantell was leading a flight of four Mustangs, being ferried from Marietta, Georgia when the control tower operator at Godman Field, Fort Knox, Kentucky asked him to investigate an unidentified flying object reported in the area. One of the Mustang pilots reported he was low on fuel and was given permission to continue to base. Mantell and the two remaining pilots, Lts. A. W. Clements and B. A. Hammond, then turned to find the UFO, with the help of the men in the control tower, who could now see the object. Mantell pulled ahead of the others so far they could barely see him. The tower then received a R/T from Mantell at 1445, stating he had the object in sight, that it appeared to be metallic and was tremendous in size. At this time the others in the flight were at 15,000' and broke off, because none of the fighters were carrying oxygen. Mantell's last words were, "It's above me and I'm gaining on it. I'm going to 20,000 feet." He continued the chase and a few minutes later, near Franklin, Kentucky, his P-51 crashed. This event triggered the UFO craze that is still very much alive. Mantell's death has been attributed to everything from a head-on collision, with the object in question, to a mysterious death ray, but the true cause is in all probability anoxia. Mantell evidently lost consciousness and his P-51 went into an uncontrolled dive, during which the left wing snapped off. The big question is what was so enticing that a seasoned combat pilot would risk passing out from a lack of oxygen to see? Officials would have us believe it was a Navy Skyhook balloon. The remains of Mantell's P-51 were taken to Stadiford Field where they remained for a couple of years.

During the summer camp of 1949, which was held at New Castle, Delaware the 123 FG distinguished themselves by successfully repelling an attack, made by an aggressor force of bombers. It was an event that must have seemed a paradox for Lt.Col. Phil Ardery commander of the 123rd FG and Lt.Col. James K. McLaughlin, commander of the 167th FS, former bomber pilots. Ardery was the pilot of the last B-24 Liberator to cross the burning oil fields of Ploesti, Romania on August 1, 1943. To have survived that gauntlet was a miracle. McLaughlin had likewise survived the brutal battle of the first Schweinfurt mission.

A group photo of 165th pilots taken during 1954. Colonel Ardery is standing in front of the 7 on the Mustang's nose.

The 123rd FG was called to arms for the Korean War on October 10, 1950 and was redesignated the 123rd Fighter Bomber Group. On October 26 the 123rd was redesignated a Wing, the first of five ANG Wings employed during the war. All three squadrons, the 156th, 165th and 167th, gathered at Godman Field, where operations involved three main thrusts. These operations were; refresher training in the P-51 for immediate combat duty in Korea, transitioning to the F-84E Thunderjet for deployment to England and using a cadre of experienced Mustang pilots to train new pilots in the employment of the P-51 in the ground attack role.

The initial command structure was as follows:
Wing Commander—Col. Phillip Ardery
Executive Officer—Lt. Col. James K. McLaughlin
123rd FBG Commander—Lt. Col. William J. Payne
165th FBS Commander—Maj. Lee J. Merkel
156th FBS Commander—Maj. Albert W. Clements
167th FBS Commander—Maj. Joseph T. Crane

Kentucky lost five ANG men in action, one being Capt. John Shewmaker, for whom the 123rd's base in Louisville was later named. Shewmaker's F-84 was lost in Korea and he is thought to be one of thirty-seven Air Force POWs sent to Russia.

During this period the Air Force issued a directive requiring magna-fluxing the landing gears of all P-51s with 600 or more hours flying time and 74 of the unit's 82 Mustangs were inspected. 34 were found to have cracked pivot bearings and were grounded for repairs.

Pilots adapting to the F-84 went to RAF Base Manston, England, in November of 1951. Their role was to bolster NATO forces against an escalation of Russian forces, which was a direct result of our intervention in Korea. During April of 1952 the 123rd went through an Operational Readiness Inspection, and received an excellent rating. All was not roses, though, as the Group lost over twenty F-84s, mostly to engine problems. Several pilots were forced to eject over the North Sea, after engine failure. Capt. Ken Walker was among those rescued.

With the units returning to state control in July of 1952, the Charleston and Charlotte squadrons, or what was left of them, returned home. Lt.Col. Lee Merkel, along with a few key officers, returned to Kentucky from England and began to rebuild the 123rd. Col. Ardery returned home during the Fall of 1952 and reassumed command.

At the summer camp of 1953, held at Camp Greyling, Michigan, the 165th lost its dual-control TF-51. Capt. Lyle Carter had just given William Marland, the Governor of West Virginia, a demonstration ride in the Mustang trainer. Then Lt. Bill Gast, of the 165th, took someone up for a ride. The TF-51 blew a coolant line, located under and to the side of the cockpit floor, filling the cockpit with scalding steam. Gast crash landed the Mustang and Airman James Evans pulled the two injured fliers

A Kentucky P-51D serves as a target tug during a 1956 gunnery meet. This fighter has its lightning bolt, entire nose, tail and wing tips painted yellow and edged in black. Note the release cable for the target sleeve running from the flare pistol port to the ground wire bracket under the aft fuselage. Note the serial number on the vertical tail surfaces is applied at an angle.

out of the ill-fated trainer. Evans was rewarded by having his request for pilot training approved.

In September of 1953 four members of the Kentucky ANG tried to rescue survivors trapped in the wreckage of a C-46 that crashed at Standiford Field. In recognition of their efforts Walter Carter, Howard Curtis, Charles Simmons and Jesse Brown received the Soldiers Medal and the first issues of the Kentucky Medal for Valor.

Lt.Col. Lee Merkel didn't live to see the transition to jets take place, as he died in the crash of his Mustang near Bedford, Indiana, on January 31, 1956. During the Spring the 165th began training in the T-28 and T-33 in preparation for the arrival of the F-86. The Mustang was nearing the end of its service life and two were lost, although the pilots escaped injury, during the 1956 Summer Camp held at Travis Field, Savannah, Georgia. The 165th continued to fly the P-51 until the fall, when conversion to the F-86A Sabre took place.

January of 1958 was the beginning of a new era for the 165th, when its mission changed to photo recon and they re-equipped with the Martin RB-57B Canberra. Likewise the 123rd was reorganized, with the 123rd Tactical Reconnaissance Wing at the top, followed by the 123rd Tactical Recon. Group and the 165th Tactical Recon. Squadron.

During 1959 the RB-57Bs were used to penetrate the borders of the United States, testing the Air Defence Command's radar and interceptors. These missions were a part of Operation Eye Opener.

Operation Willow Freeze was a 1961 exercise conducted in Alaska. Two RB-57Bs and a C-47 were sent north in January and the photo ships mapped 210 square miles that would later be used as a drop zone during the exercise. In February seven more of the RB-57Bs were sent to participate. Other operations during the year included exercises flown from Puerto Rico and the participation of three Canberras, flying out of Christmas Island, in the Pacific, in nuclear weapons tests. The next mission of note was the aerial mapping of 78,000 acres of land at Oak Ridge, Tennessee for the Atomic Energy Commission.

In January of 1965 the Air Force notified the Kentucky ANG they were reclaiming the RB-57s for use in Vietnam. In recognition of the 123rd TRWs outstanding performance with the trusty Canberra the unit was awarded the Spaatz Trophy, the highest honor bestowed on Air National Guard units.

July of 1965 saw the first RF-101 Voodoo arrive and by the end of the year Kentucky would receive twenty-four Voodoos. These were F-101A and C model fighters from the 81st Tactical Fighter Wing stationed at Bentwaters, England and as such would require modification to perform photographic missions.

Near the middle of 1966 the unit had mastered flying and servicing their supersonic aircraft and sent

Top, Kentucky F-86As at the summer camp of 1957. Although these fighters ushered the 165th into the jet age they didn't last long for the unit was given a photo-reconnaissance mission and re-equipped with RB-57Bs in January of 1958. Bottom, a B-57B Canberra lands at Martinsburg, W. Va. Although the official name the U.S. Air Force gave this bomber was the Intruder the British name stuck and the Navy's A-6 would fly to everlasting glory with the Intruder moniker. Martin Aircraft Company was given the contract to build the B-57, which was a British design, and in the process made several changes that vastly improved the aircraft. Time proved the B-57 to be a versatile aircraft and it has soldiered on for lo these many years in many guises.

fourteen RF-101s, three T-33s, two C-47s and 635 men to summer camp at Travis Field, Savannah, Georgia. The deployment was interrupted by Hurricane Alma and in the interest of safety the Voodoos returned to Kentucky until the storm passed. Before the year ended another of their aircraft was reclaimed by the Air Force. C-47 number 43-48101 was modified to an AC-47 gunship for use in Vietnam. In its place they received a C-54, which served for several years.

Early in 1967 Kentucky lost its first 101 in a take-off accident. Lt. William Irion's Voodoo lost power during a takeoff from Shewmaker ANG Base and although making a successful trap on the cable at the end of the runway, the Voodoo drug the cable, along with its two 50,000 lb. ship anchor chains off the end. The 101 then caught fire, with Irion escaping safely before the jet was destroyed.

Operation Guard Strike, a month long exercise staged during the summer of 1967, gave the Kentucky ANG a chance to show their proficiency, not only with their flying but with their newly acquired film and print processors. The 165th exposed nearly 5,000' of film and printed over 1,000 photo enlargements, proving its abilities were on a par with active duty Air Force units.

The entire 123rd Tactical Recon Wing was called to active duty on January 26, 1968 during the *Pueblo* Crisis. The Navy intelligence gathering ship USS *Pueblo* had been captured by North Korean gunboats, after venturing into enemy waters. In response President Lyndon B. Johnson activated the reserves to counter the North Korean action, as the active military forces were stretched thin by the war in Vietnam. The first notable objective of the 123rd was to rotate one of the Group's squadrons, for a temporary assignment, to Itazuke Air Base, Japan. The 154th from Arkansas was the first to rotate during the call-up, leaving on July 23. They were replaced, in turn, by the 192nd from Nevada and then the 165th from Kentucky. Kentucky's tour in Japan started during January of 1969. During their stay the 165th flew 750 recon missions, and during March accumulated 735 flying hours, a wing record.

The 165th's temporary duty in Japan ended during April of 1969, which happened to correspond to the wing's deactivation. The 165th received a commendation from the commander of the 5th AF and the entire wing was judged the best during the call-up, which earned them the Air Force Outstanding Unit Award. The unit's departure from Itazuke was covered by the Japanese press and their cameras recorded a spectacular but non-fatal takeoff crash. Capt. Bill Seiber retracted his gear when he felt it unload and seconds later the 101 settled back onto the runway. Seiber rode his blazing fighter until the arresting barrier sheared off the external fuel tanks, it slid to a halt; he then walked away. While there was no loss of life abroad, the 165th did lose Capt. Francis (Buzz) Sawyer in a flying accident in Missouri.

In 1971 tragedy struck again, when the 165th lost Capt. Roger M. Sanders and his Voodoo in a takeoff accident at Shewmaker ANG Base. Sander's fighter struck another aircraft just after lift-off and at an altitude too low to eject. This was the last accident involving the modified RF-101G and H models, for during the fol-lowing year the Kentucky ANG would be re-equipped with twenty, standard production, RF-101Cs.

Tornados ravaged Louisville and other parts of Kentucky during April of 1974 and the ANG not only helped cleanup but the photographs taken by their Voodoos were instrumental in speeding up the release of federal disaster relief funds.

A change in equipment came in the spring of 1976, with the arrival of RF-4C Phantom IIs. These aircraft, like the first Voodoos flown by the 165th, were previously stationed in England and came from the 10th TRW at Alconbury. The Phantom, unlike the Voodoo, required a second crewman, the Photographic Systems Officer (PSO), the equivalent of a Weapons Systems Officer in a fighter. This meant bringing in men to fill the back seats of the nineteen F4s eventually assigned to the 165th.

Beginning in late February and lasting into March of 1978, seventeen Kentucky Phantoms deployed to Norway, to take part in a NATO training exercise named *Coronet Snipe*. The objective of this exercise was to test the ability of the Air National Guard to deploy to Europe and operate efficiently while flying from unfamiliar turf. *Coronet Snipe* was a great success and in the coming years the Kentucky ANG would become a familiar sight in Europe.

1982 was a big year for Kentucky, with another deployment to Europe to train with NATO forces and again garnering the Spaatz Trophy. A near tragedy also took place that year, when Capt. Mike Sams and Lt. Mike Bell were forced to exit their Phantom due to a fire that disabled their F4 over the Cherokee National Forest some forty miles southeast of Knoxville, Tennessee. This was the only RF-4C the 165th would lose.

The next change in missions was a truly big one and for many a real heart-breaker. The 165th became a Tactical Airlift Squadron in 1989 and was re-equipped with the venerable C-130B Hercules. This must have come as quite a shock to the 165th since it had recently won the title of the best photo-recon unit in the entire Air Force. The cosmic wheel had turned again, with the three old Mustang squadrons, the 156th,165th and 167th, again flying the same aircraft.

On February 6, 1992 Kentucky lost one of its C-130Bs, which was a former 167th Herk, when it crashed into the side of a four-story hotel and adjacent restaurant in Evansville, Indiana. The six man

Top photo is an excellent view of a RF-101C Voodoo. Notice the last three digits of the serial number are 101, very chic. This Voodoo is from the second lot the 165th was equipped with and they were standard production aircraft, unlike the modified F and G models of the first lot. The C models gave the 165th much better service and there were no fatal mishaps involving these birds during their four years in service. The Voodoo was a huge fighter being 69'-3" long but with a wing-span of only 39'-8". By comparison the RF-101C was 2'-5" longer than the WW II B-24H heavy bomber. The wing of the Voodoo was 1'-1" shorter than the wing of a P-47D Thunderbolt and the visual effect of those small appendages mated too such a large fuselage is awe inspiring. Below, RF-4C Phantom full serial number 64-1075 photographed in 1981. Notice Shewmaker ANG Base being painted out on the hangar as the base becomes Standiford Field once more.. Many books have been written about the legendary Phantom and it is sufficient to say here that it was truly a great aircraft. C. ARRINGTON PHOTOS

crew and eleven people on the ground died in this tragic accident. The C-130 had been making touch-and-go landings at a nearby airport. Killed were: pilot Maj. Richard A. Strang; co-pilots Capt. Warren J. Klingaman and Lt. Vincent D. Yancar; flight engineer Master Sgt. William G. Hawkins and loadmaster Master Sgt. John M. Medley.

On May 16, 1992 the Kentucky ANG held an Arrival Ceremony for the first of twelve factory fresh C-130Hs they were receiving. Their first C-130H was 91-1231, which happens to be the 2,000th Hercules built. It was also the first C-130 with a built-in defensive capability. They carry a missile detection system plus a chaff and flare dispensing system to thwart missiles.

167TH FS—WEST VIRGINIA, ANG

Federal recognition for the 167th came on March 7, 1947. The unit's first commander was Lt.Col.

Both photos on this page were taken by Ross Taylor. Ross was a crew chief for P-51s in the 325th FG and their unofficial photographer. After the war Ross ran an aerial mapping and photography business out of Kanawha Airport, placing him in the perfect position to take pictures of the 167th's activities. At the top is a lineup of 167th P-47D Thunderbolts. Below, a P-51D in its "Blue Nosed Bastards of Bodney" paint job prepares for takeoff. Note that the national insignia was not applied to the fuselage; only to the top left and bottom right positions on the wing. Also note the tread patterns on the tires don't match; a point of interest for scale modelers.

James K. McLaughlin, a native West Virginian with 350 combat hours in B-17s with the 8th AF. General Mac, as he would later be known, flew the lead plane, for Col. Bud Peaslee on the famous "Black Thursday" mission against the ball bearing factories at Schweinfurt, Germany. Under McLaughlin's expert guidance the 167th was molded into what was arguably the finest fighter squadron in the ANG.

Until the runways at Kanawha Airport (now Yeager Airport) were finished the Squadron operated ten T-6 Texans from Clark Field, a grass strip just out-side of St. Albans, West Virginia. On November 3, 1947 Kanawha Airport was formally dedicated. It was rainy and cold and the facility was a sea of mud despite eleven acres of perforated steel planking. Among those present was World War I ace Capt. Eddie Rickenbacker.

The first Air Force Advisor assigned to the 167th was Maj. Edwin L. Heller. An ace from the 352nd FG, Heller had accumulated 146 combat missions and destroyed twenty-two German aircraft, five and a half in the air and three of those in a single dogfight. Among his decorations were the Distinguished Flying Cross with four oak-leaf clusters, the Air Medal with fifteen clusters and the Croix de Guerre.

During November and December of 1947 the 167th was equipped with P-47Ds. Also acquired were three A-26 Invaders, two C-45 "Bug Smashers" and two of the ever-present C-47 Gooney Birds. During the few months the 167th flew the Jug there was one crash. Lt. Leonard Bostic was making a landing approach at Kanawha Airport when the engine in his P-47 lost power and the fighter dropped into a wooded area, plowing a 200 yard path. Bostic suffered, among other injuries, a fractured skull and broken pelvis. A fire started and Bostic was saved from certain death when three Negro men pulled him from the wreckage. The rescuers were awarded Bronze Medals from the Carnegie Hero Commission and Bostic was back flying within a year.

In the spring of 1948 the Nebraska ANG, which was flying Mustangs, was re-equipped with the P-80 and West Virginia received fifteen of their P-51s. By August of 1948 the Thunderbolts were gone and the 167th attended their first summer camp, flying P-51D Mustangs. The noses of the P-51s were painted strato-blue, which is close to a royal blue, in the manner of the 352nd FG, Heller's old unit.

The ANG no longer has summer camps like those held in the Mustang era. Those gatherings of eagles gave the fighter pilots a chance to fire their guns at ground targets, as well as drop practice bombs and fire rockets. Pilots were required to accumulate thirty hours of flight time during camp, which went toward their yearly minimum of 110 hours. Lt. Kenneth C. Hoylman was Top Gun in the 167th. Hoylman once scored 190 hits out of a possible 200 on a standard five foot square bulls-eye.

The following is a list of summer camps attended by the 167th during the years they flew fighters:

1. 1948, Columbus, Indiana: Atterbury AFB
2. 1949, Newcastle, Delaware: Newcastle County Airport
3. 1950, Columbus, Ohio: Lockbourne AFB (now Rickenbacker)
4. 1953, Grayling, Michigan: Camp Grayling
5. 1954, Grayling, Michigan: Camp Grayling
6. 1955, Savannah, Georgia: Travis Field
7. 1956, Savannah, Georgia: Travis Field (last round-up of Mustangs)
8. 1957, Savannah, Georgia: Travis Field
9. 1958, Savannah, Georgia: Travis Field
10. 1959, Camp Douglas, Wisconsin: Volk Field
11. 1960, Alpena, Michigan: Phelps-Collins ANG Base

At summer camp of 1949 Sgt. James Keeler and several others from the armaments section were sent to Fort Dix, New Jersey to set up and man the firing range for the 123 FG's Mustangs. It was a cloudy day so the 123rd decided to stand down. The Ohio ANG was up and contacted the gunnery range, by R/T, obtaining permission to use the range. While ground control was giving the Ohio pilots instructions for approaching the targets, the rest of the team was enjoying a hearty lunch prepared by the Army NG. However, unknown to the pilots, the R/T was broken and the last thing they heard was, "Do you see the building with the red cross on the roof ?" Thinking that was the target the Mustang pilots began their attack, using 100 lb. practice bombs. These bombs had a five pound charge of powder with the remainder of the casing filled with sand. Practice bombs could be destructive if they scored a direct hit but the powder charge is mainly to create smoke to spot hits.

When Keeler and his buddies saw the first P-51 release its bombs directly at them and the storage building, they pitched their meals in the dirt and took cover. The bombs destroyed the wooden building and the rest of the Mustangs began their runs. The range officer grabbed a flare pistol to ward them off and without checking the pistol he fired a green flare, which meant continue. Keeler who was taking cover under a six-by truck, ran for the box of flares, found a double star red and tossed it to the frantic officer. The officer fired the flare stopping the debacle before there were any casualties.

Chuck Yeager flew to Charleston frequently, to visit his parents in nearby Hamlin and chat with his cousins Randall and Raymond Yeager, who were ground crewmen in the 167th. Chuck would often take a Mustang up and take on anyone who felt lucky, in a mock dogfight. He never lost.

The good times were not to last long, for the clouds of war were gathering again. On June 25, 1950 North Korea invaded South Korea and once more the venerable P-51 was in the forefront of the battle. Twenty prop-driven Russian aircraft would fall to their guns during the first year of the fighting and although never given credit for downing any MiG-15s, at least four in all likelihood went down as a result of being hosed by Mustangs.

The 167th was activated for the Korean War on October, 10, 1950 and moved to Godman Field, Fort Knox, Kentucky. As previously explained in the 165th's history, training centered on either flying the P-51 or transitioning to the F-84.

Lee F. Barrows Jr., Jack Darby and Kenneth C.

Top, no history of the 167th is complete without mentioning Kanawha Airport, now named Yeager Airport. Construction of this engineering marvel required moving 9,000,000 cubic yards of earth from three mountain tops of Coonskin Ridge. This required 2,500 gallons of diesel fuel each day to keep the earth moving machinery running and a grand total of 2,000,000 pounds of explosives. Below, a photo of some of the 167th's personnel during its formative period. Seated left to right on the Mustang's wing; Lts. Harry K. Blackhurst and J. B. Dooley. Standing on the left is Maj. Edwin L. Heller, their first Air Force Advisor; in the center is the head honcho, Lt.Col. James K. McLaughlin and on his left are T/Sgt. Gordon E. Renstrom and S/Sgt. Fred K. Dotson. Kneeling is S/Sgt. John B. Shelton. Photo contributed by the 167th's first First Sergeant Paul M. Taylor.

Hoylman were sent to England to fly F-84s. While on a maximum range training flight, from Manston to Munich, Germany the float-valve in the main tank of Hoylman's F-84, stuck in the open position, allowing fuel being transferred from the other tanks to constantly flow into the main fuel tank, which then vented out the overflow tube. When his fuel supply became critical Hoylman decided to eject. Alas, the seat wouldn't fire so Hoylman reverted to his WW II training, rolling the fighter on its back and dropping out of the seat. Fate hadn't achieved it's full measure of fun this day as Ken found himself dangling from a tree, fifty feet off the ground. After hanging helplessly for what seemed an eternity he managed to attract the attention of a local farmer who summoned help. Meanwhile the F-84 plunged into a fish hatchery killing 8,000 trout, which the U.S. government paid for.

Jack Darby and Lee Barrows elected to remain in Europe when the West Virginia ANG was inactivated. Barrows was later killed when the F-86 he was flying crashed on December 2, 1953.

The following 167th pilots are known to have gone to Korea and what is known of their service there is as follows:

Lyle E. Carter—111th Fighter Bomber Squadron; 100 missions, 205 combat hours in F-84Es.

U. G. Copenhaver—12th FBS; 25 missions in P-51s plus numerous hours in C-47 and C-54 transports.

George Coyle—18th Fighter Bomber Group; 84 missions in P-51s before being shot down by anti-aircraft fire. After bailing out of his burning Mustang, at 900', Coyle was surrounded by about twenty enemy troops, shooting one before being taken prisoner. During his imprisonment Coyle was a constant source of annoyance to his hosts and never signed the confession they wanted.

J. T. Crane—CO of the 12th FBS of the 18th FBG; 74 missions in P-51s.

R. C. Fogelsong—45th Tactical Recon. Squadron; shot down by anti-aircraft fire after completing 12 missions in P-51s. Still listed as missing in action. Fogelsong was the first pilot from the 167th to die in combat.

Lee A. Harper—39th FBS of the 18th FBG; the second member of the 167th to die in Korea. Harper's P-51 took a fatal hit while attacking a ground target and he bailed out too low for his parachute to open.

George H. Looney—12th FBS, 49 ground support missions. Looney's P-51 was shot up eight times but always brought him back. Targets were mainly trains and truck convoys.

Fred Thomas—67th FBS of the 18th FBG, 100 missions, 161 hours in P-51s.

Ed Heller, the 167th's first Air Force Advisor, was promoted to Lt.Col. during the Korean War and completed fifty-eight missions in F-86 Sabres. Heller was credited with the destruction of 3.5 MiG-15s before being shot down in January of 1953. He was taken prisoner and released in May of 1955.

Even though the air war in Korea was taking a heavy toll in men and machines the worst loss of the period came stateside, when a double tragedy struck the 167th. On April 5, 1951, Maj. Woodford (Jock) Sutherland had just completed a training flight in Florida and his P-51 was rolling along a taxi strip when another Mustang hit him head-on. The impact threw Sutherland forward, causing his head to strike the windscreen fame killing him instantly. A witness stated that the noise made by the prop slicing into Jock's plane "sounded like gears being stripped in the transmission of a large truck". The body was returned to Charleston for burial.

The worst was yet to come, when two C-47s loaded with167th personnel left Godman to attend the funeral. It was Sunday morning, April 8, 1951, when a C-47 with Capt. Edwin K. Whittington at the controls slammed into a ridge four miles short of Kanawha Airport. Nineteen men died in the flaming wreckage and two more would succumb to burns and massive injuries in the next three days. The reason for the crash was never determined. There was a heavy fog, which caused the second C-47, piloted by Lt.Col. McLaughlin, to turn back but aside from that both engines were determined to have been running perfectly at the time of impact. Those who perished and were identified include: Capt. Edwin K. Whittington, pilot; 1st Lt. Harry B. Kesler, co-pilot; Tech. Sgt. William H. Shelton, crew chief; Staff Sgt. David Rollyson, Sgt. Winson A. Schoonover, Sgt. James E. Creasy, Cpl. Columbus Hall, Capt. Charles E. Cobb, Cpl. Dennis I. Meeks, Cpl. John R. Price and Pfc. Jimmy Dolan. Unidentified were 1st Lts. Drexel Crites, Lyle F. Finley, Herman F. Winter, Charles R. Michaelson, William J. Frank, Staff Sgt. Kenneth C. Amick, Sgt. Richard F. Hazeltine and Pfc. James R. Lewis. Capt. Harry K. Blackhurst of the 167th and Maj. Issac Bonifas of another unit, died in the hospital.

Operation Southern Pine, conducted during August 13-17, !951, was a prime example of the caliber of pilots to be found in the 167th. During this exercise the 167th was to defend its base, near Fort Bragg,

Chuck Yeager (in the flight jacket) and his father are standing on the wing of the P-80B-5-LO he flew under the Dickinson Street Bridge in downtown Charleston, W. Va. Not many people had seen a jet and Chuck's buzz job caused a real sensation. One of those witnessing that event was a young boy named Jimmy O. Bail. Years later J.O. retired from the 167th and was the last pilot on duty to be trained for combat in the P-51. ROSS TAYLOR COLLECTION

North Carolina, from attack by an aggressor squadron of F-80 Shooting Stars. Gun camera footage of the first day's encounter showed that all of the F-80s were destroyed, except for one that ran. This would-be escapee was singled out for special humiliation by John Darby. Darby went to full military power and pulled alongside the jet and its astonished pilot at 475 m.p.h. The F-80 pilots improved after their initial thrashing but still lost to the 167th's Mustangs.

Not all of the pilots were "top drawer," as the unit was involved in training new comers. Sgt. James Keeler, who was an armorer, recalled watching a greenhorn apply too much power to his P-51 just as it touched down. The Mustang spun 180° and began rolling down the runway backwards. Gathering his wits the pilot kept his fighter tracking down the runway and by a smooth application of power braked to a halt.

When the 167th was deactivated on July 9, 1952, the remaining personnel in Kentucky packed and started back to Charleston, but they had to leave their P-51s. Back in Charleston the squadron began to reorganize and fill its depleted ranks. On January 29, 1953, Capt. Leonard Hash was returning to Charleston from Dobbins AFB, Georgia, where he had picked up gaskets for a C-47 engine. Hash was making excellent time, running full bore, when the Merlin engine in his P-51H, serial number 44-64542, swallowed a dozen valves. Hash tried in vain to restart the engine and in the process dropped too low to bail out.

He bellied the '51 in on a farm near Liberty, South Carolina. The canopy was jammed shut and the aircraft started to burn. Hash, a man of considerable strength and certainly motivated, used his helmet and shoulders as a battering ram, to free the canopy. A local doctor teated his feet and legs for burns and he was then taken to Donaldson AFB Hospital, where he was treated and released. Hash's legs would eventually require some skin grafts.

When it was time for the summer camp of 1953 the 167th was still equipped with two P-51H Mustangs, not counting trainers or utility types, and was forced to borrow ten P-51Hs from the 164th FS, of the Ohio ANG. From late 1953 through 1954 the 167th received a mixed bag of P-51D and H models, which brought it back to full strength. H models were not popular with the mechanics and were quickly passed on to other units operating that type. During this period the 167th also got its first jet, a well worn F-84E Thunderjet, which was dubbed the *Earthworm*. Its airworthiness was dubious, so it was grounded and used only to practice jet-starts and run-ups. Eventually it was sold for scrap, loaded on a flatbed and hauled away.

Summer camp 1955 saw the 167th at Travis Field, Savannah, Georgia; memorable for its smell if nothing else (those who have experienced the aroma of a paper pulp mill know whereof I write). Camp broke up early when a tropical storm moved towards

Early in 1950 the blue noses were dispensed with and the national insignia added to the fuselage sides. 44-72800 in the top left photo is in the process of acquiring the insignia and the unicorn is still displayed on the nose. Paul Taylor. Top right, a smiling Armament Chief, T/Sgt. James H. Guthrie, watches as Sgt. Jack B. Van Devender on the left and Flight Chief Sgt. James Keeler look busy for a photo. One of Guthrie's many assignments during WW II was to help train the armorers of the 99th FS of the 332 FG (all Negro unit) in removing the Bendix hydraulic gun-chargers from their P-40s (before leaving the U.S.) and instructing them how to bore sight the P-40's guns. The hydraulic chargers were removed because they were a potential fire hazard and the guns were manually charged prior to takeoff. Middle left, Capt. John B. Darby (Jack) poses with his P-51 which sprung a massive oil leak while taking off from Godman AFB, Ky. The pilot's manual, states that a pilot should not turn back and attempt a landing but Darby did successfully, thus saving a valuable aircraft. Middle right, a F-84G flown by the 167th pilots based at Manston, England. The nose and wingtip tanks are dark blue. Bottom left, a view showing some of the F-84Es at Godman. Note the coontail on the helmet lying near the open door. Bottom center, a P-51 from the 45th Tactical Recon. Sqd. in Korea, Roma C. Fogelsong's unit. Note the camera pods under the wings. Don Harless of Dunbar, West Virginia, a pilot in the 45th, furnished this photo. He also stated the camera pods didn't work well. Color scheme was dark blue spinner and wingtips with white polka dots. Bottom right, Capt. Lee Franklin Barrows Jr. on the left poses with Jack Darby. Barrows would perish in the crash of a F-86 in Dec. of 1953. HOYLMAN

the area. On the way home a pilot from the 167th skirted the South Carolina coast in search of adventure. Spotting a freighter he gave it a good buzzing. After landing he was informed the ship was Russian and the buzz-job had almost caused an international incident.

On September 8, 1955, the 167th lost P-51D serial number 45-11383 in a landing accident, at Kanawha Airport. Capt. Jessie Birchett landed long and flipped over at the end of the runway. The Mustang slid tail first down the grassy embankment, stopping short of going into Elk River. Birchett, who was

In the top left corner is Lee Harper in the cockpit of a 111th TRS P-51 he flew during WW II. Harper flew 85 missions in the Mediterranean Theater of Operations and completed 80 in Korea before perishing when he bailed out of his mortally stricken P-51 to low for his parachute to open. Right, the remains of the C-47 that crashed on April 8, 1951, killing twenty men of the 167th FS. Bottom left photo is of Roma Fogelsong the first 167th pilot to die in combat in Korea. Fogelsong, who had been openly critical of the way the air war was being conducted, died on his thirteenth mission when his P-51 was hit by ground fire and exploded at an altitude of about 500', officially the Air Force lists him as MIA. In the center is Jock Sutherland who was killed in a ground collision at the end of a P-51 training mission in Florida. He was a co-pilot on the naval version of the B-24 during WW II and received a DFC and a Gold Star for heroism. His unit, Bombing Squadron 104, received a Presidential Unit Citation for its action against Japanese shipping. The last photo is of George Coyle who bailed out of his burning P-51 after being hit by ground fire while on an attack mission in Korea. Coyle shot one North Korean soldier before being taken prisoner. George is one of those individuals who made his captors regret having kept him for almost two years. Notice that the helmets of both Coyle and Sutherland have coontails, the badge of the Coonskin Boys.

trapped in the wreckage and hanging inverted in his safety harness, was dug out by hand since the use of shovels might ignite the gasoline which was leaking profusely from a ruptured fuel tank. Birchett received a scratched arm but 383 was fit only to serve as a source of parts for the remaining Mustangs.

Big changes were in the wind and the 167th was sure to be affected. The Jet Age was at hand and Kanawha Airport's runways were deemed too short to safely handle jet fighters on an operational level. Political pressure was being applied to move the squadron to the new Raleigh County Airport at Beckley, West Virginia. T-6 trainers were posted there and minor construction was carried out by members of the 167th, but in the end Martinsburg, West Virginia was chosen as the unit's new home.

The 167th moved in December of 1955. It was similar to summer camp, but cold. Facilities were still under construction and supplies were stored in tents, which also served as work quarters for the mechanics, a rather Spartan condition that would exist in varying degrees for the next three years.

It was a difficult time in many ways. The P-51 which had held its own against the early jets was now clearly outpaced by a new generation of jet fighters. The old war horse was suffering structural failures and rebuilt engines were a "luck of the draw" affair, the Mustang was suffering from a malady racers call "tired iron." The supply of high octane gasoline required by the 167th ran short at times, requiring trips to Navy bases to obtain fuel. Having to borrow from the Navy was an embarrassment and a logistical burden. Despite these many handicaps the ground crews did an outstanding job of maintaining an accident-free record during this period.

Col. Joseph T. Crane was the Base Commander and Maj. Joseph W. Hass joined the 167th during 1956 to become the Squadron Commander. Hass was a much decorated WW II fighter pilot, having flown eighty-five missions with the 87th FS of the 79th FG, based on Corsica. Most of his missions were ground support for the British 8th Army in Italy. He also participated in the invasion of southern France, providing support for American forces there. For these actions he was awarded the Distinguished Flying Cross and the Air Medal with three Oak Leaf Clusters. He also wore the prestigious British Desert Air Force patch for his service with the 79th FG. Hass was replaced as Squadron Commander on Nov. 10, 1958 when Capt. Martin J. Bambrick took the helm.

Another WW II veteran joining the 167th, at Martinsburg, was James L. Miller. Miller joined the Royal Canadian AF in 1940 because the U.S. Army Air Corps required a minimum of two years of college for pilots, while Canada only required a high school diploma. So at age nineteen, Miller and eleven other young American men went north to fly military aircraft. In May of 1942, after becoming a pilot, Miller returned to the U.S. and joined the Army Air Force, eventually being assigned to a transport squadron and sent to the China-Burma-India theatre of operations.

During WW II Miller flew 167 missions in transports and became frustrated at flying unarmed aircraft, while being shot at. Between supply missions Miller met some of his old comrades from Canada who were now flying fighters for the Royal Air Force in Calcutta, India. Circumventing official channels Miller managed to fly as a substitute with his friends, accumulating over twenty-five ground support missions in a variety of British fighters, including the Spitfire, Hurricane and Typhoon.

Staying on with the Air Force after WW II, Miller ended up in the 41st FS of the 35th Fighter Interceptor Group, flying patrol along the 38th parallel in Korea, just before the beginning of hostilities there. While these flights were officially unarmed the pilots made sure they had hot guns and on one occasion a North Korean transport plane that brazenly crossed the line received a warning burst of fire from Miller's Mustang, giving notice to the "reconnaissance" plane's pilots they were not welcome. They took the hint and turned back north. Miller left the 35th FIG, for a Stateside assignment with the 20th Fighter Bomber Group that flew F-84G Thunderjets with a nuclear weapon delivery mission.

At Langley AFB in Virginia, Miller supervised the loading of the first nuclear bomb to an operational F-84G. The 20th FBG was then sent to England and after three years there Miller returned to the U.S.

Miller joined the Air Force Reserve and took a civilian job with Fairchild Aviation while he furthered his education. When the 167th appeared in Martinsburg with their Mustangs he quit Fairchild and signed up.

The last roundup for the Mustang was the summer camp of 1956, with the Ky. and W. Va. ANGs still operating the P-51, while N. Carolina was flying F-86A Sabres. West Virginia was also flying T-28As, which were equipped with tricycle landing gear, to acclimate pilots to landing with a nose wheel, in preparation for the arrival of their Sabres. During the winter of 1956–57 the 167th began delivering their Mustangs to Sacramento, California for salvage.

The Air Force arranged a decommissioning ceremony for the Mustang at Wright-Patterson AFB, Dayton, Ohio, for Jan. 27, 1957. Only two P-51s were found still on inventory and both were assigned to the 167th. Serial number 44-74936 was en route to Sacramento, for salvage and was the first choice because it had a combat record.

936 developed engine trouble and landed at Cheyenne, Wyoming for repairs. The 130th Troop Carrier Squadron from Charleston, W. Va., furnished a SA-16 Albatross to take crew chief John Boone Harris, to preflight 936; and Lt.Col. Joseph T. Crane base commander of the 167th; who would fly 936, his personal mount, back to Dayton. They arrived in time to be grounded by a blizzard.

When it became doubtful that 936 would make the ceremony on time, the focus switched to 44-72948, which was still at Martinsburg. Maj. James L. Miller

A P-51H being warmed-up for a training flight. While the H was the ultimate model of the Mustang and the pilots enjoyed its performance, it was considered to be a pain in the ass by the mechanics. LT.COL. R. C. SUTHERLAND

flew 948, which had a recently installed engine, to Charleston. As luck would have it, Sgt. Sheldon Miller (no relation to the pilot), once the crew chief on 948 and whose name was still on the Mustang, was on duty. When word came that 936 was definitely not going to make it on time, Sheldon prepared his old charge for its final flight from Charleston and Maj. Miller flew 948 and himself into everlasting glory.

The scene at Dayton was staged with the Mustang and a F-100 Super Sabre scheduled to make three 270 m.p.h. fly-bys for the motion picture cameras and press. On the third pass the F-100 was supposed to pull away from the P-51 in a show of superior speed. When the pair of North American fighters reached a predetermined point Major Milton E. Nelson lit the F-100's afterburner but before the jet could spool up Miller firewalled his Merlin for a wail of defiance at the Jet Age. The Mustang leaped ahead of the F-100 then made a sharp climbing turn to the left that would have torn the wings off the F-100. A fourth anticlimactic pass produced the same results with the P-51 breaking left before being passed.by the F-100. Old 948 was flown back to Charleston by Lt. Col. James K. McLaughlin where it was scheduled for display. Miller left Dayton the next day for Wyoming and flew 936 back to Dayton a few days later where it is on permanent display along with a spare Merlin engine from the 167th.

Two pilots were killed on March 10, 1957, when their T-28A rolled over and crashed while approaching Shepherd Field. The official cause was attributed to carbon monoxide entering the cockpit. From that point on all pilots flying the T-28 were required to wear oxygen masks at all times. Killed in the accident were Capts. Max F. Swartz and Earl P. Farmer. Swartz was an Air Force veteran of WW II and Korea. Farmer was a Navy pilot during WW II.

The 167th was supposed to receive F-86As like its sister units but on June 28, 1957, they got twenty-four F-86Es, which were passed on three months later, when F-86H-1s were received. This made the 167th the first ANG unit to be equipped with the H model. This also broke the 167th's long association with the 123rd FG, and they became part of the 113th Tactical Fighter Wing. Be that as it may, when summer camp of 1957 rolled around the 167th was still flying T-28A trainers, a real come-down from the Mustang; some wondered if the P-51's retirement was a bit premature. The first two pilots from the 167th to be checked out in the Sabre did so during camp and later in the year several others flew to Kentucky in T-28s where they were checked out in the 165th's Sabres.

A Capital Airlines DC-3 crashed near Shepherd Field during June of 1958. Lt. Edwin Strickland and Staff Sgt. Kenneth Evans were awarded the Soldiers Medal, the highest peace time award for bravery, for risking their lives to rescue three men from the burning wreckage. Governor of West Virginia Cecil Underwood made the presentation.

In Oct. of 1958 the 167th held an Open House for the general public to visit their newly completed base. On hand for the event were Bob Hoover, famed dem-

Left, photo taken at the 53 camp shows, left to right, Harloe Sheets, Ashford (Spad) Kelly and John A. Wilson III. Sheets was a former B-17 pilot with eight combat missions over Europe. Sheets would join the 130th Troop Carrier Squadron and remain in Charleston, while the 167th moved to Martinsburg. He died on December 12, 1960 when the SA-16 he was flying crashed after hitting telephone lines and burned near Richmond, Va. Kelly was called Spad by the younger pilots who jokingly claimed he was so old he learned to fly when the WW I Spad was a front-line fighter. Wilson's military career began in WW II as a B-24 pilot in the Pacific. Wilson flew mostly anti-shipping missions and sank two cargo ships. One patrol mission he flew lasted an amazing 22 hours and five minutes. He attained the rank of Maj.Gen. and retired as the Adjutant General of West Virginia in 1988. Right: group shot of the Coonskin Boys taken during Governors Day at Camp Greyling, Michigan, 1953. Governor William C. Marland of W. Va is on the far left.

onstration pilot for North American Aviation; Maj. James Jabara, an ace and a veteran of both WW II and Korea; and the" Minutemen," a F-86E precision flying team from the Colorado ANG's 120th TFS.

Now that the 167th had become a jet unit, they had to become proficient at flying and maintaining their Sabres. Their first O.R.I. (operational readiness inspection) placed them in 36th spot. Bambrick wrote a letter requesting the O.R.I. team return to Martinsburg and show them where improvements could be made. It was an extraordinary request that pleased the team and they did return. One year later the 167th was rated 4th in the nation and they have never looked back.

Tragedy reared its ugly head again on Jan. 10, 1960. Paul Ash, an ROTC officer getting in his required monthly flight time, had a flame-out not far from Shepherd Field. Ash tried to stretch his glide to reach the runway and failed. The mistake that ultimately cost him his life was failure to jettison his drop tanks immediately. Instead he waited until within sight of the runway before dropping the tanks; by then his airspeed was so low the tanks would not fall free, but rolled along the bottom of the wings, the right tank eventually flipping over the leading edge, destroying the pitot tube and rendering the air speed indicator useless. Without this vital instrument landing was pure guesswork. The Sabre stalled, impacted on its belly and slid into a tree. When the rescue vehicles arrived Ash was still in his seat, lying on top of the wrecked fuselage.

Fortunately the aircraft was not completely de-stroyed by fire and an investigation of the wreckage determined the flame-out had been caused by the failure of an oil supply line that lubed the shaft in the engine's compressor stage. All of the Sabres were grounded until their engines were inspected. This would be the last fatality suffered by the 167th for thirty-three years.

The 167th participated in a special training exercise during 1960 when they flew six of their fighters to Alaska for joint maneuvers with the Army. Ground support personnel followed their charges in a C-119. Sgt. William O. Starks, maintenance chief during the deployment, described the month-long mission as "the slickest job we ever performed, not one hitch during the entire stay. Everything functioned perfectly; not even an engine change was required."

The pilots were at their peak as well. It was just like the good old Mustang days but a lot faster. The usual pranks expected of fighter pilots abounded but the two most notable took place during mock combat exercises. First to fall victim was an Army general being chauffeured over the battlefield as a referee, in a helicopter. He thought he was flying pretty low until a Sabre zoomed under his helicopter, giving all concerned a rush. The general ordered his copter to land and refused to go back up as long as those "crazy Sabre pilots" were still there. The next victims were the crew of a tank that was a target for a mock strafing demonstration. The Sabre pilot bore in on the tank straight and level forcing it off the road. The angry tank commander radioed the pilot that, if he repeated that stunt again, he would hit him with a shovel!

The 167th flew the P-51 longer than any other U. S. unit and was one of the few with extensive nose art. Like the 368th FS they used cartoon characters which often had an association with the pilot or crew chief. Starting in the top left corner, crewchief Max Richardson with *Little Max* (from the Joe Palooka strip), P-51D 45-11381; c/c John Bailey and *Beetle Bailey*, 44-72718; c/c Ed Morton and *The Phantom*, 44-74694; c/c Fuzzy Johnson and *Shook* (Daffy Duck), 45-11633; c/c Critt Guthrie and artist John Boone Harris with *One Hop* (frog), 44-74936; left to right are Jim Brown, William Starks and c/c Kemp Copenhaver with *Stump Jumper* (Woody Woodpecker), 44-63810; and c/c Gordon Palmer on the wing of *Dennis the Menace*, 45-11700. Other toons included *Wimpey* on 45-11383; *Casper* (the ghost) on 44-74949; *Daisy* (Dagwood's dog) chasing a cat on 44-74962; *Sad Sack* on a P-51D named *Tilt*, 44-73081, Bugs Bunny on a P-51D named *Wham-Bam*, 44-72948 and *Wile E. Coyote* on 44-73574. *Nancy* and *Sluggo* were also used but no record remains to indicate which P-51s they were on.

Top left, P-51D, serial number 45-11383, came to an sad end on Sept. 8, 1955 at Kanawha Airport. Captain Jessie Birchett ran out of runway, nosed over at the end and slid to a stop just short of going into Elk River. Right, a scene from summer camp 1956. This P-51, alias *Shook*, is being leveled on stands in preparation for having its guns bore-sighted. Bottom left, one of the first T-28A trainers received by the 167th. The Mustangs are still visible in the background. George Archer, one of the crew chiefs, commented that the T-28 seemed flimsy in comparison to the P-51 and it was not one of his favorite aircraft. The T-28A was powered by an anemic 800 h.p. Wright radial engine that pulled it along at a less than breathtaking speed of 283 m.p.h. Right, the first F-86E delivered to Martinsburg, serial number 51-2780, still in the markings of its previous owners the 141st FIS of New Jersey. The twenty-four F-86Es the 167th received were "high time" fighters and were not flown extensively. The E models were passed on to the 156th FIS of N. Carolina in October of 1957.

The F-86s stay of four years was short in comparison with the P-51s nine. When the Sabres passed from the scene on April 1, 1961 the fighter era also passed from the 167th. Fifteen hard core fighter pilots left and found positions in other squadrons.

1st Lt. Don Slack was one of those who departed. Slack transferred to the 141st TFS of the New Jersey ANG. The 141st was called to active duty during the Berlin Crisis in Oct. of 1961 and moved to Chaumont Air Base, France. Slack died during a routine training flight when his F-84F struck a cloud covered mountain in the French Alps. Richard Bach's book, *Stranger to the Ground*, is dedicated to his former squadron mate, Don Slack.

The 167th was now an Aeromedical Transport Squadron. Their new mission was the evacuation and care of sick and wounded personnel. This would later be extended to include hauling military cargo.

The Flying Boxcars received by the 167th were described by Maj. Martin J. Bambrick as "the sorriest lot of C-119s I had ever seen." These seven aircraft required the hiring of twenty-two additional mechanics. Transition to the C-119 took three months and an Air Force mobile training detachment assisted during this period.

Maj. Bambrick stepped down as air commander of the 167th on December 1, 1961, and Lt.Col. Robert H. Veller took his place. Veller's Air Force career started during WW II and continued through the Korean War, when he flew C47s for fourteen months of combat air evacuation with the 21st Troop Carrier Squadron known as the "Kyushu Gypsies."

On July 2, 1963, the *Centennial Queen*, the first of eight C-121G Super Constellations landed at Martinsburg; it was a welcome change in aircraft. The 167th now operated as a part of the Military Air Transport Service (MATS) but their mission was still primarily Aeromedical.

P-51D serial number 44-72948 holds a unique spot in Air Force history being the Mustang that took part in the official retirement ceremony of the type on Jan. 27, 1957. 948 served briefly overseas during WW II, had nine engine changes, served in at least seven squadrons, and accumulated 1,555 flying hours. In this picture Maj. Jim Miller's press interview is in progress (note B-29 with tip tanks in background). Later that day Miller would be interviewed, via telephone by Walter Cronkite.

In Nov. of 1963 the 167th flew its first over-water mission, to Puerto Rico. In April Of 1964 the unit made its first flight to Europe with stops in England, Germany and Spain.

Beginning in Aug. of 1964 the 167th assisted in the emergency transportation of cargo during the Vietnam War. Christmas that year in Vietnam was made merrier when the 167th delivered several tons of gifts from home to the servicemen there. By February of 1966 the unit was flying three missions a month to Southeast Asia, which stretched their support to the limit. In November of 1966 an aircrew from Martinsburg earned the *Tiger Award* for the fastest turnaround time on a flight to DaNang Air Base, Vietnam. It was the first of five such awards the unit would earn during the war.

Col. Robert H. Veller retired during Aug. of 1965 and his position was filled by Col. William J. Denton Jr. in November. Denton had served in WW II and in Korea for two years as a pilot.

On January 1, 1966, the command of the 167th changed to Military Airlift Command (MAC) formerly MATS. Things began to look very gloomy when Defence Secretary Robert McNamara started to make budget cuts. There was no projected program for the unit after July 1, 1967. During February of 1967 the *Air Force Times* publication announced that the 167th would be phased out along with units in California, Pennsylvania and New York.

Senator Robert C. Byrd of W. Va. came to the defence of the 167th. This move was unexpected, as Byrd had earlier fought the relocation of the unit to Martinsburg. But as a member of the Senate Armed Services Committee, Byrd exerted pressure to either retain the 167th in its present role or give it a new mission and he pushed a bill through Congress that retained all of the imperiled Air Guard units.

During this period of political infighting the 167th received several awards, the most coveted of which was the 21st AF Reserve Forces Award of Operational Excellence. What better time to receive such an honor. On April 9, 1967, the 167th got the results of an ORI. They had passed with flying colors, but their future was still questionable.

During this time the C-121G models were replaced by C-121C models, a better aircraft with more load carrying ability, despite the C designation which made it appear, on paper, the older of the two models.

December of 1968 brought a change of missions for the unit. Their intercontinental flights were changed to off-shore feeder routes transferring patients from hospitals in Alaska, Newfoundland, Labrador, Bermuda, Puerto Rico, the Canal Zone and Guantanamo Bay, Cuba. The situation had stabilized but the need for extra crew members and personnel required for intercontinental flights was gone and the unit lost a few men.

On June 1, 1970, all Air Guard near off-shore aeromedical flights were discontinued and the job was taken over by the regular Air Force, using jet aircraft. The 167th was now relegated to training missions.

1971 found the 167th once again involved in intercontinental missions as part of *Operation Creek Guard Lift*, in support of the United States Air Force Europe (USAFE) Command Centralized Courier System. Trips started to Spain and soon expanded to include Germany, Italy, Greece and Turkey. These missions continued until March 31, 1972.

During this period the unit performed outstanding assistance to Shepardstown, W. Va., by trucking two million gallons of water there from Martinsburg when Shepardstown's water purification plant could not meet demand. Also, the 167th's fire fighters gave prime as-

Top, a fine study of a typical F-86H-1. This particular Sabre serial number 52-2044 was flown by 1st Lt. A. R. Ogden and was one of the few Sabres to carry nose art which in this case was "Howdy Doody." 52-2044 and 52-2040 now reside in dismantled condition in a junk yard at Front Royal, Va. Below the pilots of the 167th gather for a farewell party for Air Force Advisor Maj. Nolan I. Jones. First row starting on the left: WO1 Gaines M. Timberlake, Capt. James H. Hamilton, 1st Lt. G. W. Guessford, Maj. Joseph W. Haas, 1st Lt. G. C. McKinney, 1st Lt. Robert L. Kearse, 2nd Lt. J. W. Hearne and Capt. Edwin C. Strickland. Second row: 1st Lt. B. J. Morrison, Capt. Kenneth E. Steryous, 1st Lt. C. D. Porter, Capt, Herman Floyd, Maj. Nolan I. Jones, 1st Lt. J. O. Bail, 1st Lt. Donald B. Atkins and Capt. J. N. Mellor. Third row: 1st Lt. A. R. Ogden, 1st Lt. Donald E. Slack, Capt. Elwood Sterling, Capt. G. W. Heindel, Capt. Martin J. Bambrick, 1st Lt. D. W. Arnett, Col. Joseph T. Crane Jr. and Capt. Kenneth Parker. BOTH PHOTOS BY DOUG WILBURN

Left, crew chief Kenny Evans and Maj. Martin Bambrick standing next to his F-86H-1 serial number 52-2043. Although Bambrick was tops in gunnery school, he was assigned as a wingman for aces and as a result only scored one kill while covering the tail of his leaders. Marty was also part of a team that volunteered to steal a Mig-15. Right, Lt. Don Slack stands on the wing of a T-28A trainer. Slack would leave the 167th to continue flying jet fighters and eventually lost his life when the F-84 Thunderstreak he was flying slammed into a mountain in the French Alps.

sistance fighting a gasoline-fueled holocaust at Pikeside, W. Va.'s Community Oil Company bulk plant.

As 1971 came to an end ominous rumors began to circulate. MAC had no C-121 aircraft in its plans after June 30th, 1972. Brig. Gen. James K. McLaughlin, assistant adjutant general for air, wrote West Virginia's congressmen in hope their influence would result in a prestigious aircraft that would re-equip the 167th. When 1972 began with no announcement of a new mission for the unit, Senator Robert C. Byrd went to bat for them again. As a result, during the first quarter of 1972 there was an announcement that the 167th would become part of the Tactical Air Command (TAC) and would receive newer, modern aircraft.

On April 21, 1972, the first C-130A, appropriately named *The City of Martinsburg*, landed on the rainswept runway at Shepherd Field. As a part of their new mission the 167th would be making cargo drops by parachute. Conversion to the C-130 was not as difficult as envisioned and on Dec. 1, 1972, they made their first drop, at their on-base drop zone.

During May of 1972 Col. William J. Denton Jr., the base commander, retired and Col. Joseph T. Crane assumed the dual role of base and air commander.

A massive military budget and record funding was announced for the fiscal year 1973. Then on Dec. 21, 1973 an unforeseen complication threatened. The National Guard Bureau announced that all flying by the unit was banned for an indefinite period due to the energy crisis. What a dilemma! Newly acquired aircraft, freshly trained crews and no fuel.

During the second week of Jan. 1974 the flying ban was lifted and training flights resumed. On March 9 and 10 the unit underwent its first ORI with the C-130 and got a Combat Ready C-2 rating. The highlight of 1974 was the units sweep of its three sister units, of the 118th Tactical Airlift Wing, in a Tactical Airlift competition conducted at Nashville, Tennessee July 15-17. In competition with the 167th were the 145th Tactical Airlift Group (TAG) of Charlotte N. Carolina, 166th TAG of Newcastle Del. and the 118th TAG of Nashville, Tennessee. The 167th amassed 1,651 points of a possible 2,700 with their closest competitor the 118th scoring 1,600 points. Quite an accomplishment for the unit since it was their first competition flying the C-130.

On Dec. 8, 1974, Capt. Samuel B. Cusimano was awarded the Bronze Star with *V* device for his previous service in Vietnam. Cusimano was a B-52 copilot whose bomber was shot down by a SAM over North Vietnam. Cusimano was taken prisoner and listed as MIA. The Bronze Star was awarded for his exemplary actions while a POW.

As a part of the Air Guard's primary function in assisting in domestic disasters the 167th flew to St. Croix and Thomas in the Virgin Islands performing emergency airlifts where torrential rains had caused millions of dollars in damage and many deaths.

In 1977 Col. Kenneth Gornall assumed the position of base commander from Col. Crane and the unit was assigned to Operation Volant Oak, which is still in effect as of this writing. The base of opera-

Top photo shows the remains of F-86H-1 serial number 52-2022. This is the aircraft Paul Ash perished in when he attempted to land after a flame-out. Below, the infamous "Dollar Nineteens" arrive at Martinsburg. To quote Martin Bambrick, "they were the sorriest lot of C-119s I had ever seen." Six of the 167th's C-119Cs were sent to the 130th in Charleston during the first ten days of Oct. 1963. A thorough inspection revealed the cost of re-wiring these birds alone made them beyond economical repair. Indeed two C-119s went directly from Martinsburg to Davis Monthan for salvage. One of those two birds, 48-0344, was nicknamed the *Ramp Rooster*, indicating it spent an inordinate amount of time on the ground being repaired, and it had a large rooster painted on its nose similar to Foghorn Leghorn. This view of the C-119 shows the landing gear struts to good advantage. These were subject to constant attention since the slightest play in this unit would cause a severe vibration in the airframe, leading to structural failure. The props were prone to shedding their tips which in turn caused the engine to part company with the airframe, not exactly endearing qualities. DOUG WILBURN

tions for *Volant Oak* is Howard Air Base in Panama, the hub of military traffic to all parts of South and Central America. Several ANG units rotate duty there, flying in supplies and providing transportation for personnel stationed there. Howard AB is the focal point for defence of the Canal Zone.

As a guest of the 167th TAG during the last VIP tour to Panama, in Aug. of 1987 (before Operation Just Cause), and as an observer on a support mission across Nicaragua to Palmerola, Honduras, I was impressed by the extent of our involvement in those countries, but it was much later I learned Palmerola was the base created by Ollie North for supplying arms to the Contras. The United States must maintain a presence in Panama to insure no subversive foreign power gains control of the Canal. Those malevolent forces were there and one had only to drive by the American Embassy and see the splotches of red paint on its white walls to verify that fact.

Russia had a keen interest, and probably still has, in what's happening in Central America. While over the coastal waters approaching Howard AB for a landing I saw a Russian nuclear submarine submerging. I was informed this type of activity was not unusual, and the Russians monitor our radio traffic.

Col. Jack Koch replaced Col. Gornall as base commander in March of 1980. Koch joined the 130th Troop Carrier Squadron on July 14, 1956, and attended summer camp that year as an airman. On returning from camp he went directly to flight training at Lackland AFB, Texas. After initial single engine training he opted to go into multi-engine training and Travis Hoover, a former Doolittle Raider and pilot of the second B-25 to leave the *Hornet*'s flight deck, gave Koch his first multi-engine instruction in a TB-25.

After graduation Koch returned to Charleston and flew the SA-16, C-119 and C-130 mission aircraft while also becoming proficient in the U-6A Beaver, VC-47 Gooney Bird and VC-54D Skymaster.

In July of 1979 Koch was appointed active duty liaison with the 130th in Panama. It was a non-flying

Top photo shows one of the first lot of C-121G Connies flown by the 167th. These were previously operated by the U.S. Navy under the designation R7V-1. They were flown to Martinsburg from Moffet Naval Air Station, California. The main visible difference between this version and the later C models were the square windows that replaced the port holes. The Connie was considered to be one of the best transports in civilian and military use, easy to fly and maintain. On one of the many supply missions flown to Vietnam J.O. Bail's Connie took a 20mm hit in the tailplane during the landing approach. Luckily the damage was only superficial. Below, a photo taken by Ray Boarman, of a 167th C-121C being unloaded at Tan Son Nhut Air Base, South Vietnam. For this particular mission the unit was awarded one of the five *Tiger Awards*, for the fastest turn-around time, they would earn during the Vietnam War.

position but Cookie managed to sneak in enough hours flying the C-130 to retain his proficiency. When Col. Koch retired as base commander of the 167th he had logged more than 12,500 flying hours, with over 3,000 of those in the Hercules.

Col. V. Wayne Lloyd assumed the position of group commander in March of 1989 and a change in aircraft soon followed. On Sept. 27, 1989, the 167th flew its last C-130B to Standiford Field, Louisville, Ky, where it was turned over to the 165th TAG. The 167th was re-equipped with twelve C-130Es. While these were newer models they had not received the meticulous care the 167th is noted for and all underwent thorough inspection and maintenance, before entering service.

Both of West Virginia's ANG units, the 167th and 130th TAGs were commited to Operation Desert Shield. The 167th was the first unit to be asked for

volunteers and thirty members of their aeromedical evacuation team were flown to Saudi Arabia. Following close behind were another 121 volunteers including support personnel to help load and unload cargo. Some of the later group remained stateside to beef-up other units involved with logistical movements connected to *Desert Shield*.

Then came the orders activating both units. The 167th was in command of *Operation Volant Pine*, flying out of Mildenhall, England. The following units contributed aircraft and personnel to that operation.

1. 167th TAG—Martinsburg, W. Va. (Command)
2. 133rd TAW—Minneapolis, Minn.
3. 135th TAG—Baltimore, Maryland
4. 143rd TAG—Providence, R. I.
5. 146th TAW—Van Nuys, Calif.

The majority of the aircraft involved in *Volant Pine* were older C-130Es and not sent to the desert

Six fliers with long and distinguished careers grace this page. Top left, Lt. Kenneth C. Hoylman in the cockpit of his P-40N of the 51st FG, 14th AF. Ken completed 111 ground support missions. HOYLMAN Top right, David W. Arnett who flew 85 ground support missions in P-47s of the 58th FG, 5th AF. Dave is seen here in a P-38. Middle left, left to right, crew chief Antalio, Capt. Joseph Haas and armorer McIntosh. Haas flew P-47s in ground support while assigned to the 79th FG operating out of Corsica. Middle right, Lyle Carter who flew 62 missions in P-51s of the 339th FG, 8th AF. He destroyed one Me109 in the air and three on the ground, damaged three Me109s and a Me262. In Korea he flew 100 missions in F-84Es of the 111th FBS. Bottom left, Lt. Col. J. O. Bail, the last combat trained P-51 pilot on active duty when he retired in August of 1988. J.O. loves to tell of flying through the apple orchards near the Martinsburg area with their P-51's vertical stabilizers looking like shark fins moving through the trees. M. R. KILMER Bottom left, M/Sgt. Don Horine the last WW II aerial gunner to leave active flying status when he retired with 42 years of continuous service in 1984. He flew 33 missions in B-24s of the 449th BG(H), 15th AF. WOLFINGER

Left, in competition with all other U. S. Air Force units and several from foreign countries at *Volant Rodeo* 1985, the 167th was judged to have the best Hercules in the world. No small feat when you consider 58-0753 was an early B model. The same aircraft almost won Volant Rodeo 1986 but was disqualified by a judge who argued that one circuit breaker was incorrect. It wasn't, but that's a long story. If you visit the 167th's base you will find a sign on the front of their main hangar stating "*World's Best Maintenance Volant Rodeo 1985,*" and they aren't kidding for during the many years they have competed they have never been rated less than fifth in the world! Right, the Air Force's high time combat crew. Standing, left to right: Col. Jack Koch now a retired Brig. Gen. (pilot) 10,366.2 hrs., Lt.Col. Ed B. Kuempel (co-pilot) 9,094.4 hrs., Col. Del R. Wightman (navigator) 11,955.2 hrs., Kneeling, left to right: CM/Sgt. Gary D. Albright (loadmaster) 9,952.6 hrs., CM/Sgt. David N. Fraizer (engineer) 22, 453.9 hrs. and SM/Sgt. Ray T. Boarman (loadmaster) 10,697.0 hrs. Total flying time for this crew when the photo was taken in March of 1989 was 74,519.3 hours.

because of the accelerated wear their aging airframes would have been subjected to. The bulk of their missions were of a logistical nature and ranged as far as Incirlik, Turkey.

After the stunning defeat of Iraq's military forces, the 167th was back to the usual grind when an event that is still spreading ripples across the face of the world occurred in Russia, the collapse of communist rule. In a short time the tiny states that had been overrun and assimilated into the U.S.S.R. were raising their flags of independence. The Baltic states, a constant source of turmoil throughout history, erupted into violence causing the senseless death of untold numbers of civilians. A war that was not only fueled by political differences but religious intolerance as well, a "worst case" scenario.

The 167th began flying relief missions into Sarajevo, Bosnia-Hercegovina during July of 1992. Rhein-Mein Air Base at Frankfurt, Germany is the base used for Operation Provide Promise, the airlifting of food and medical supplies into the airport at Sarajevo.

The perils involved in these flights are considerable. The airport at Sarajevo is a tactical nightmare, surrounded on three sides by mountains and possessing only one runway. Landings are a rush when the airport is being shelled and the engines are left run-

ning for a speedy exit. If a C-130 took a hit that prevented it from taking off, it would simply be pushed off the runway, becoming mortar bait and the crew would have to wait for a ride out of the war zone. One of the 167th's Herks was hit in a hydraulic line during a flight into Sarajevo and the crew managed to improvise a shunt that saved them from having to shut down their engines and probably lose their aircraft.

While still flying missions in Bosnia the unit suffered its first loss since 1960, in a tragic stateside

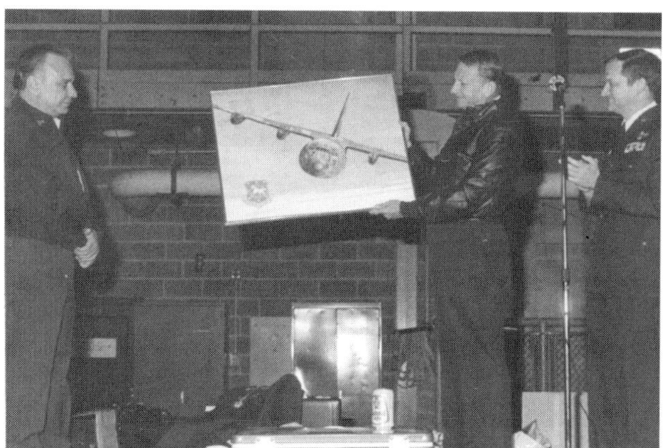

Left, Col. Jack Koch accepts an oil painting of a C-130B from the artist T/Sgt. Frank Sierra. Behind Cookie is the 167th's incoming commander Lt.Col. V. Wayne Lloyd. Photo taken during March of 1989 by Floyd Ferrell.

F-86H-1NA, serial number 52-2058, a former 167th bird was reclaimed from Grissom Air Force Base after its closing. The Sabre was dismantled by a team of retirees from the unit and brought home aboard two C-130s. This Sabre was flown by Lt. Bob Kearse and the crew chief was Lawrence Long.

The only concession to authentic markings was the replacement of the yellow flight tail band with a red tail band which was the 369th FS's rudder color and the tail-band on 167th Herks.

PHOTOS BY BILL WOLFINGER

accident. On Oct. 7, 1992, a C-130E flying a low level practice mission, near Berkeley Springs, W Va., struck unmarked power lines that resulted in the loss of the aircraft and all aboard. Witnesses to the crash said the pilot nosed the burning Hercules into the ground, to avoid hitting a house in its path.

The local media indulged in a bit of yellow journalism by suggesting part of the crew was intoxicated, after obtaining a copy of the coroner's report which stated traces of alcohol were found in samples of body tissue belonging to two of the crewmen. The media neatly omitted the fact that when a body is burned the sugar in it turns to alcohol. It was also suggested the aircraft was being flown in a restricted area which was pure rubbish. Five years previous to this accident a DC-3 spraying gypsy moths struck the same lines and the pilot was decapitated.

The names of the crew were: Pilot Lt.Col. Alfred J. Steinberger; copilot Capt. Dallas O. Adams; flight engineer M/Sgt. George F. Griffith; flight engineer S/Sgt. James T. Hinchman; and loadmasters S/Sgt. Frederic E. Jones and T/Sgt. John R. Funkhouser.

The 167th received the first of twelve new C-130Hs on Dec. 21, 1994. It was an unique experience as they had never been equipped with new aircraft. This was long overdue for a unit that is always in the eye of the storm, making history as did their illustrious predecessors, the 369th FS, in the skies over *Fortress Europe*.

Top, Lt. T. P. Smith poses with *Caroline* his P-51D CS-E 44-13893. Note kill marks on the canopy frame representing two Fw190s destroyed on November 21, 1944. T. P. also got credit for damaging two 190s that day. A look through the destruction diary will show this was a very busy Mustang flown by several other pilots. From appearances this photo was taken while the Group was still flying combat. The paint on the nose is the Group's standard forest green. Below is a post war lineup of Mustangs at East Wretham. In the foreground is Smith's *Caroline* with an olive drab nose. Note also the dark blue canopy frame and the red outline added to the black I.D. bands on the wing and the horizontal stabilizer visible in another view not published. Second in the line is Capt. Ray Wetmore's former ride, CS-L 44-14733 devoid of the scrolled name *Daddy's Girl*, but now with red outlines on the fuselage code letters. Compare the green on the other three 51s in this picture with the olive drab on *Caroline*. T. P. SMITH COLLECTION

In the top photo we see *Caroline* has sprung a bad oil leak around the prop governor. Engine oil under high pressure controled blade pitch and if a seal blew this was the mess the wrench turners had to endure. Note the engine bearers are dark chromate (interior) green instead of the more common chromate yellow. Today it's common knowledge that when dirty engine oil laden with heavy metals is absorbed into the skin it can lead to terminal cancer but little thought was given to this kind of thing fifty years ago and mechanics labored long hours on oily engine parts to keep the birds of war flying. The bottom photo is one of the finest examples of a well kept hack ever seen. A lot of the Group still held a warm spot in their hearts for the P-47D and the care taken to maintain this Jug is evident. Note the gun ports in the wing of *Blondie II*, CS-X, 42-74676 are faired over and the entire aircraft is spotless; that's no easy task for a plane powered by an air-cooled radial engine. T. P. SMITH COLLECTION

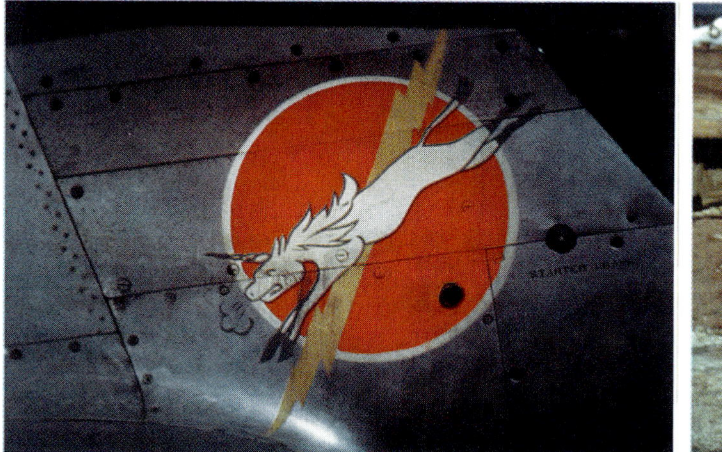

W. Va. ANG P-51D painted in the style of the 352nd FG but not yet adorned with the 369th FS unicorn. 44-73570 was in Red Flight and Jack Darby's mount. The muddy conditions that accompany a pierced steel plank runway and parking area are evident and reminiscent of the horrible conditions the 359th FG endured at East Wretham. Bottom left, close-up of the 369th FS badge as applied to 167th FS Mustangs from 1948 through early 1950. On the right a Packard built Rolls Royce Merlin being readied for installation somewhere in Florida during the Korean War. Modelers take note this engine is semi-gloss black and not the mysterious *engine grey* referred to in many kits. Mechanic facing the camera is Sgt. W. O. Starks. KEN HOYLMAN PHOTOS

The F-84 Thunderjet shown at the top was stationed at RAF Manston, England and flown by Ken Hoylman. Note the nose and tip tanks are 167th blue. KEN HOYLMAN PHOTO. A stunning shot of 522056, a F-86H-1 Sabre belonging to Green Flight. This was the aircraft flown *backwards* by North American Aviation's famed demonstration pilot Bob Hoover at the 167th's open house in 1958. Model builders will note the service stenciling was painted on a metallic grey tape which in turn was applied to the aircraft, so much for clear coats and fretting about silvering under your decals. F. C. HARTMAN VIA JEAN-PIERRE HOEHN

On this page are two of the world's all-time great aircraft. At the top is a Kentucky RF-4C Phantom. From the Vietnam War and up to and including the time of this writing the Phantom still carries on. The 165th was re-equipped with F4s early in 1976 and operated the type until mid 1989 when their mission became that of Tactical Airlift and they received C-130B Hercules aircraft. Below, a milestone C-130H is delivered to the 165th on May 16, 1992. This particular Hercules happened to be the 2,000th unit built. Being the Mecca of the horse racing fraternity no doubt inspired the Kentucky Air National Guard to name eleven of its Herks after Kentucky Derby winners with the odd ball being named Man 'O' War, which was a great horse that didn't win that race. For those interested here are the names with the serial number: 91-1231, *Man 'O' War*; 91-1232, *Secretariat*, 91-1233, *Exterminator*; 91-1234, *Bold Venture*; 91-1235, *His Eminence*; 91-1236, *Citation*; 91-1237, *Flying Ebony*; 91-1238, *Fools Pleasure*; 91-1239, *Assault*; 91-1651, *Brokers Tip*; 91-1652, *Strike the Gold*; and 91-1653, *Chateaugay*. C. ARRINGTON COLLECTION

Appendix

359TH COMMANDERS

Col. Avelin P. Tacon Jr.—Jan. 15, 1943 to Nov. 11, 1944.
  West Point.
Col. John P. Randolph—Nov. 12, 1944 to April 7, 1945.
Lt.Col. Donald A. Baccus—April 8, 1945 to Sept. of 1945.
Lt.Col. Daniel D. McKee—Sept. 16, 1945 to Oct. of 1945.
Maj. Andrew T. Lemmens—Oct. 29, 1945 to Nov. 10, 1945

359TH HEADQUARTERS PILOTS

Lt.Col. Niven K. Cranfill—July 1944 to Aug. of 1944.
Lt.Col. Roy W. Evans—Nov. 1944 to Feb. 14, 1945.
Maj. Rockford V. Gray—Oct. 1943 to Feb. of 1944.
Maj. Fred S. Hodges—March 1944 to Sept. of 1945.
Maj. Chauncey S. Irvine—Feb. 1944 to April of 1944.
Capt. Karl H. Kirk—July 1944 to Sept. of 1944, transferred out.
Maj. Andrew T. Lemmens—April 1945 to Oct. of 1945.
Lt.Col. Daniel D. McKee—Fall 1943 to Feb. of 1944 then
  from April 1945 to Sept. of 1945.
Capt. Leslie D. Minchew—May 1945 to Nov. of 1945.
Lt.Col. James W. Parsons—Nov. 1944 to April of 1945.
Capt. Samuel R. Smith—April 1944 to Aug. of 1944, trans. out.
Lt.Col. William H. Swanson—April 1944 to October of 1944.
Lt.Col. James V. Wilson—Feb. 1945 to Mar. 11, 1945, POW.
  West Point.

SQUADRON COMMANDERS

368th FS
Lt.Col. Albert R. Tyrrell
Maj. Clifton Shaw
Maj. Niven K. Cranfill
Maj. William C. Forehand
Capt. Charles E. Ettlesen
Maj. Benjamin H. King
Capt. Charles E. Ettlesen
Lt.Col. Niven K. Cranfill
Lt.Col. James W. Parsons
Capt. Marvin F. Boussu
Capt. Cosgrove
Maj. Donald J. Walter

369th FS
Maj. Rockford V. Grey
Lt.Col. William H. Swanson
Maj. Chauncey S. Irvine
Capt. Lester G. Taylor
Maj. Chauncey S. Irvine
Maj. James A. Howard
Maj. Edwin F. Pezda
Maj. Fred S. Hodges
Maj. Edwin F. Pezda.
Maj. Fred S. Hodges
Maj. Ralph A. Cox
Capt. Rene L. Burtner
Capt. Joseph A. Webster

370th FS
Lt. Allen C. Bears
Lt.Col. John B. Murphy
Capt. James K. Lovett
Lt.Col. Daniel D. McKee
Maj. Ray S. Wetmore

PILOTS—368TH FS

Lt. Robert H. Addleman—completed tour (CT)
Lt. Boyd N. Adkins Jr.—CT
Lt. Robert S. Alexander—April 1945 to Sept. of 1945.
Lt. John C. Allen—KIA
Lt. Carl M. Anderson—POW
Lt. David B. Archibald—POW
Lt. Joseph M. Ashenmacher—CT
Lt. Merle G. Aunspaugh—killed in flying accident.
Capt. Glen C. Bach Jr.—CT
Capt. George F. Baker Jr.—CT
Lt. Arlen R. Baldridge—KIA
Lt. Kenneth E. Barber—Jan. 1945 to Sept. of 1945.
Lt. Louis E. Barnett—MIA
Lt. Merle B. Barth—MIA
Lt. Clifford L. Bartlett—KIA
Capt. Elby J. Beal—CT
Lt. Robert V. Beaupre—KIA
Capt. Robert E. Benefiel—CT

368th FS pilots beginning in the top left with Maj. Clifton Shaw the Squadron's commanding officer from June 22, 1944 to Aug. 12, 1944. Top right, Lt. David B. Archibald in the cockpit of a P-51B (note badly weathered paint and the freshly painted I.D. band). Second row left, Capt. Billy D. Kasper and his crew chief, S/Sgt. Charles Doersom. Kasper's P-51B-15NA is CV-V, 42-106949. On the right Lt. Merle B. Barth in the cockpit of his P-51D-5NT *California Cowboy*, 44-11158. Bottom left, Lt. Louis E. Barnett. Barnett bailed out of his stricken Mustang on Sept. 12, 1944 but his parachute failed to open fully and he died on impact with the ground. German civilians burried him in a cemetary at Wutike. Bottom right, Capt. Joseph Powers Kelsey (Cho).

Lt. George H. Blackburn—KIA
Capt. Wayne N. Bolefahr—KIA, West Point.
Lt. Raymond L. Botsford—killed in flying accident.
Capt. Marvin F. Boussu—Sept. 1944 to Sept. of 1945.
Lt. Ray A. Boyd Jr.—POW
Lt. Eugene F. Britton—CT
Lt. Cecil R. Brown—KIA
Maj. Ralph L. Brown—CT

Maj. Wayne R. Brown—killed in flying accident.
Lt. Robert E. Burton—April 1943 to April of 1944, then to 370th FS.
Lt. George J. Byron—March 1945 to Sept. of 1945.
Lt. Leonard D. Carter—CT
Lt. Emer H. Cater—KIA.
Lt. Cornelius J. Cavanaugh—CT
Lt. Donald W. Chatfield—CT

Eight pilots from the 368th FS. Starting in the top left and moving to the right; Lt. Robert H. Addleman, Lt. Donald W. Chatfield, Lt. Eugene F. Dauchert, Capt. Clarence M. Lambright, Capt. Thomas S. Lane, Capt. Wilbur H. Lewis, Lt. James J. Lubien and Lt. John M. Marr.

Space doesn't allow the placement of pictures of all the pilots within the War Diary but this doesn't diminish their importance. Above are eight pilots from the 369th FS. Starting in the top left corner and moving right; Lt. Robert William Campbell (Bogey), Lt. George M. Givan, Capt. Charles H. Kruger, Lt. Paul Eugene McClusky, note D-Day stripes on wing of his P-51B, Lt. Stanley Emerson Sackett (Sad Sack), Lt. Robert Brunner Sander, name on the nose of his P-47 is *Jean's Warrior*, Lt. Alma Ronald Smith and Lt. Charles W. Staley with crossed arms.

More pilots from the 369th FS beginning in the top left, Lt. Clifford Eugene Carter one of the "Buzz Boys." Top right, Capt. Lester George Taylor a West Point man. Second row on the left, Lt. Ferris C. Suttle, his ground crew and his Mustang *Darling Earline*. Left to right are; Sgt. William Wall assistant crew chief, Suttle, Sgt. James F. Foley, armorer and S/Sgt. Floyd Myers, crew chief. Second row right, Lt. Robert S. Gaines. Bottom, Lt. Douglas G. Lindsey and his P-51D-20NA *Gravel Gertie* 44-72???

Lt. Willis J. Cherry—POW

Lt. William L. Cimino—Mar. 1945 to Sept. of 1945.

Lt. Buell R. Clark—Mar. 1945 to Sept. of 1945.

Lt. Edward L. Clark—Mar. 1945 to Sept. of 1945.

Lt. Cornelius J. Collins—Oct. 1944 to July of 1945, trans. out.

Capt. John F. Collins Jr.—Oct. 1944 to July of 1945, trans. out.

Lt. Emory C. Cook—CT

Lt. John D. Cooley Jr.—January 1945 to Sept. of 1945.

Capt. Cosgrove—Sept. 1945 to Oct. of 1945. Trans. from the 9th AF.

Lt. Albert A. Cowie—POW

Capt. Lewis G. Crane—CT

Lt.Col. Niven K. Cranfill—CT

Lt. Richard H. Daniels—KIA.

Lt. Eugene F. Dauchert—Aug. 1944 to April of 1945, trans. out.

Capt. John A. Denman—Oct. 1944 to Sept. of 1945.

Maj. George A. Doersch—CT

Lt. Olin P. Drake—Jan. 1944 to June 10, 1944, shot down, evaded and returned.

Lt. David P. Dunmire—MIA

Lt. Robert H. Elliot—Feb. 1945 to Sept. of 1945.

Lt. Clifton Enoch Jr.—MIA

Capt. Charles E. Ettlesen—KIA, West Point.

Lt. Olin C. Everhart—Feb. 1945 to July of 1945, trans. out.

Lt. James J. Ferris III—killed in flying accident.

Lt. Jack O. Flack—CT

Capt. Oscar R. Faldmark—CT

Capt. Howard L. Fogg Jr.— May 1943 to May 1944, then to the 370th FS. Back with the 368th FS July 1944 to Sept. of 1944, completed tour.

Maj. William C. Forehand—CT

Some of the 370th's pilots beginning top left and moving right; Lt. Kenneth M. Braymen, Lt. Harold D. Hollis and Capt. Milton S. Berry. Second row; Maj. George A. Doersch and his crew chief S/Sgt. Fred Schuster, Doersch who flew his first tour with the 370th, was now with the 368th and his P-51D-20NA was named *Ole Goat* CV-R 44-72067. Second row, right, Lt. Donald Page and his P-51D named *Oh Nurse!* Bottom: Capt. Thomas C. Sutton. Those boyish looks belie the fact he had flown combat in the African and Italian campaigns before coming to the 370th FS.

Lt. William B. Foster Jr.—Feb. 1945 to July of 1945, trans. out.

Lt. Lewis L. Fraser—Feb. 1945 to July of 1945, trans. out.

Lt. Roy C. Garrett—POW

Capt. Chester R. Gilmore—CT

Lt. John T. Gordon—July 1944 to Feb. of 1945, April 1945 to July of 1945, CT.

Lt. Robert J. Guggemos—April 1945 to Sept. of 1945.

Lt. James H. Haas—POW

Lt. Benjamin M. Hagen III—POW

Lt. Frank Hanzalik—CT

Capt. Robert B. Hatter—CT

Capt. Robert W. Hawkinson— April 1943 to Aug. 2, 1944, shot down, evaded and returned.

Lt. William J. Heim—April 1945 to Sept. of 1945.

Lt. John W. Herb—KIA

F/O Jack D. Highfield—Mar. 1945 to July of 1945, trans. out.

F/O Joseph M. Hill Jr.—Mar. 1945 to Sept. of 1945.

Capt. Albert G. Homeyer Jr.—CT

Lt. Lester W. Hovden—KIA

Lt. Clyde M. Hudelson Jr.—KIA

Capt. John B. Hunter—CT

Lt. Edward J. Hyland—KIA

Capt. Raymond B. Janney III—CT

Lt. Edward G. Kaloski—June 1944 to Sept. 1, 1944, trans. out.

Capt. Billy D. Kasper—CT

Capt. John S. Keesey—CT

Capt. Joseph P. Kelsey—CT

Lt. Ralph E. Kibler—April 1943 to Jan. of 1944, then to the 370th FS.

Maj. Benjamin H. King—Aug. 1944 to Dec. of 1944, completed tour. Had previously flown with the 347th FG in the Pacific.

F/O Richard E. Klock—Mar. 1945 to Sept. of 1945.

F/O John H. Klug Jr.—killed in flying accident.

Lt. George J. Kosc—CT

Lt. Henry B. Kruezman—Jan. 1945 to Sept. of 1945.

Lt. Arvy F. Kysely—CT

Capt. Clarence M. Lambright—CT

Capt. Thomas S. Lane—CT

F/O John T. Lanier—Mar. 1945 to Sept. of 1945.

Lt. John F. Lauesen—Aug. 1944 to Sept. 25, 1944, KIA. Previous service in Eagle Squadron, 150 hrs. in Spitfires.

Maj. Andrew T. Lemmens—June 1943 to May of 1944, then to the 370th FS.

Lt. Leon J. Levitt—Jan. 1945 to July of 1945, trans. out.

Capt. Wilbur H. Lewis—CT

Lt. Emil L. Loehr—Feb. 1945 to Sept. of 1945.

Lt. George W. Long—Dec. 1944 to Sept. of 1945.

Lt. James J. Lubien—June 1944 to Dec. of 1944, trans. out.

Lt. Graham Lupton—KIA

Lt. Douglas A. MacLean—KIA

Lt. Garland F. Madison—Dec. 1944 to Sept. of 1945.

Lt. Antony D. Maiorano—POW

Lt. John S. Marcinkiewicz—POW

Lt. Clifford H. Marcus—Oct. 1944 to Sept. of 1945.

Lt. John M. Marr—Dec. 1944 to Sept. of 1945, trans. out.

Lt. William J. Marshall—Jan. 1945 to Sept. of 1945.

Lt. Alfred D. Marson—Dec. 1944 to July of 1945, trans. out.

Lt. Allen G. Martin—Dec. 1944 to Sept. of 1945.

Lt. James C. Martin—May 1945 to Sept. of 1945.

F/O Robert G. Mason—Mar. 1945 to Sept. of 1945.

Lt. James W. McCormack—KIA

Lt. James H. McDonald—Jan. 1945 to Sept. of 1945.

Capt. Thomas J. McGeever—KIA

Capt. Charles E. Mosse—POW

Lt. Donald L. Murphy—MIA

F/O Raymond G. Muzzy—Jan. 1945 to Sept. of 1945.

Lt. Paul E. Olson—POW

Lt.Col. James W. Parsons—April 1945 to Sept. of 1945.

Capt. Earl P. Perkins—CT

Lt. James R. Pino—POW.

Lt. Gaston M. Randolph—CT

Lt. Frank Rea Jr.—Jan. 1945 to Sept. of 1945.

Capt. Wilbur W. Seller Jr.—May 1945 to Sept. of 1945.

Maj. Clifton Shaw—CT

Lt. William R. Simmons—KIA

Lt. James B. Smith—POW

Lt. Henry L. Thompson—Jan.1945 to Feb. 7, 1945, missing after bailing out over the Eng. Channel on a training flight.

Lt.Col. Albert R. Tyrrell—POW

Maj. Donald J. Walter—Sept. 1945 to Oct. of 1945, came from 9th AF.

Capt. James L. Way Jr.—Jan. 1945 to Sept. of 1945.

Lt. Samuel A. White—CT

PILOTS—369TH FS

Capt. Benjamin H. Albertson—April 1943 to Oct. of 1943, then to the 370th FS.

Capt. Glen C. Bach—Jan. 1943 to Jan. of 1944, then to the 368th FS.

Lt. Lawrence A. Bearden—killed in flying accident.

F/O Harley E. Berndt—Jan. 1945 to Aug. of 1945, trans. out.

Lt. Robert J. Booth—POW

Lt. Robert M. Borg—April 1943 to Jan. of 1944, then to the 370th FS.

Lt. Lawrence W. Bouchard—completed tour and trans. out.

Lt. Richard H. Broach—POW. West Point.

Capt. Carey H. Brown—April 1943 to Oct. of 1943, then to the 370th FS. West Point.

Lt. Clarence R. Brown—Mar. 1945 to Sept. of 1945.

Lt. Grover W. Brown—Mar. 1945 to Sept. of 1945.

Lt. Charles R. Bruening—MIA

Lt. Lowell W. Brundage—KIA

Capt. John F. Buniowski—CT

Lt. Thomas G. Bur—July 1944 to May of 1945, trans. out.

Lt. Harold R. Burt—KIA

Capt. Rene L. Burtner—Aug. 1944 to Aug. 18, 1944, shot down, evaded and returned. Sept. 1944 to Sept. of 1945.

Capt. Herbert C. Burton—April 1944 to Aug. of 1944, trans. out.

Lt. Robert W. Campbell—CT

Lt. Walter J. Carroll—Mar. 1945 to Sept. of 1945.

Lt. Donnald E. Cannon—CT

Lt. Clifford E. Carter—MIA assumed KIA

Lt. Richard G. Carter—Mar. 1945 to Sept. of 1945.

Lt. Vernon E. Chaffee—Mar. 1945 to Sept. of 1945, trans. out.

Capt. William F. Collins—Aug. 1944 to Sept.of 1945.

Maj. Ralph L. Cox—Feb. 1945 to Sept. of 1945.

Lt.Col. Niven K. Cranfill—Oct. 1943 to Aug. of 1944, then to the 368th FS.

Lt. Cecil W. Crawford—MIA

Capt. Claude J. Crenshaw—CT

Lt. Harry F. Cuzner Jr.—CT

Capt. Robert W. Davison—CT

Lt. Grover C. Deen—POW

Capt. Charles E. Ettlesen—Dec. 1943 to May 25, 1944, shot down, evaded and returned. Moved to the 368th FS.

Lt. Robert D. Erwin—Sept. 1944 to Sept. of 1945.

Lt. Frank S. Fong—Feb. 1944 to Feb. of 1945, trans. out.

Capt. Robert M. Francis—Sept. 1944 to Nov. of 1945.

Lt. Albert S. Freeman—Feb. 1945 to Sept. of 1945.

Capt. Robert S. Gaines Jr.—CT

Lt. Horace E. Garth III—Feb. 1945 to July of 1945, trans. out.

Lt. Harold R. Gates—Feb. 1945 to July of 1945, trans. out.

Lt. George M. Givan—killed in flying accident.

Maj. Rockford V. Grey—March 1943 to Oct. of 1943, then to Headquarters.

Lt. Robert J. Guggemos—Oct. 1944 to April of 1945, then to the 368th FS.

Lt. Maurice N. Haines—POW

Lt. LeRoy D. Hess Jr.—POW

Lt. Kenneth L. Hobson—POW

Maj. Fred S. Hodges—Sept. 1944 to Mar. of 1945, then to Headquarters. Previous service with the AVG/Flying Tigers.

Lt. Frank W. Holliday—MIA assumed KIA

Capt. Ivan B. Hollomon—May 1944 to Sept. 11, 1944, shot down, evaded and returned. Dec. 1944 to July of 1945.

Capt. Albert G. Homeyer— April 1943 to Jan. of 1944, then to the 368th FS.

Capt. Robert W. Hopkins—Oct. 1944 to Sept. of 1945.

Maj. James A. Howard—KIA

F/O Conrad Z. Hruby—Mar. 1945 to Sept. of 1945.

Lt. John E. Hughes—MIA assumed KIA

Lt. James F. Hutton—MIA

Maj. Chauncey S. Irvine—CT

Lt. Russell H. Jenner—KIA

Lt. Warner C. Jennings—Sept. 1944 to Sept. of 1945.

Lt. Vernon T. Judkins—Aug. 1944 to Sept. of 1945.

Lt. Dale E. Kelly—Oct. 1944 to Sept. of 1945.

Lt. John J. Kelly III—Aug. 1944 to Sept. of 1945.

Capt. Joseph P. Kelsey—June 1943 to Nov. of 1943, then to the 368th FS.

Lt. John E. Keur—CT

Capt. Karl H. Kirk—Feb. 1944 to July of 1944, then to Headquarters.

Lt. Ralph R. Klaver—Sept. 1944 to Sept. of 1945.

Lt. Thomas J. Klem—Aug. 1944 to July of 1945, trans. out.

Capt. Charles H. Kruger—CT

Lt. D. H. Laing—POW

Lt. Robert T. Lancaster—Sept. 1944 to Sept. of 1945.

Lt. Howard A. Linderer—POW

Lt. Douglas G. Lindsey—Jan. 1945 to Sept. of 1945.

Capt. Washington D. Lyon—Oct. 1944 to Nov. of 1944, then to the 370th FS.

Capt. Raymond E. Magee—CT

Lt. Russell E. Masters—MIA

Capt. Harry L. Matthew—POW

Lt. Paul E. McCluskey—KIA

Lt. Robert E. McCormack—Dec. 1944 to Sept. of 1945.

Lt. Fred S. McGehee—Dec. 1944 to Sept. of 1945.

Lt. Robert W. McIntosh—Jan. 1945 to Sept. of 1945.

Capt. Joseph W. Mejaski—CT

Lt. Donald S. Melrose—MIA

Lt. Arnold F. Mettel—CT

Lt. Lawrence F. Meyer—MIA.

Lt. Tracey E. Millis—Dec. 1944 to Sept. of 1945.

Lt. Bert M. Montague—Dec. 1944 to Sept. of 1945.

Lt. Myron C. Morrill Jr.—MIA

Lt. Arthur B. Morris Jr.—Oct. 1944 to June of 1945, trans. out.

Capt. Charles E. Mosse—April 1943 to Oct. of 1943, then to the 368th FS. POW

Capt. John H. Oliphint—April 1943 to June 8, 1944, shot down, captured and escaped. Later returned to England.

Capt. Eugene R. Orwig Jr.- CT

Capt. Jefferson C. Painter—June 1943 to May of 1944, trans. out.

Lt. James R. Parsons Jr.—killed in flying accident.

Lt.Col. James W. Parsons—Aug. 1944 to Nov. of 1944, then to Headquarters. Previous service with the 54th FG in the Aleutians.

Lt. Lee Patton—Jan. 1945 to Sept. of 1945.

Capt. Grant M. Perrin—CT

Maj. Edwin F. Pezda—Oct. 1943 to May of 1944, then to Headquarters. Back with the 369th FS from Nov. 1944 to Feb. 28, POW. West Point.

Capt. Robert L. Pherson—KIA

Lt. Roger W. Porter—CT

Lt. Luster H. Prewitt—CT

Capt. Gilbert R. Ralston Jr.- CT

Lt. Homer L. Rodeheaver—KIA

Lt. Stanley E. Sackett—KIA

Lt. Robert B. Sander—KIA

Lt. Virgal E. Sansing—Mar. 1944 to June 20, 1944, shot down, evaded and returned.

Capt. Karl K. Shearer—KIA

Lt. Edwin L. Sjoblad—MIA

Lt. Alma R. Smith—CT

Lt. Byron N. Sonderman—Jan. 1945 to Sept. of 1945.

Lt. Charles W. Staley—April 1943 to Aug. of 1944, completed tour and trans. out.

Capt. Jack D. Stevens—CT

Lt. Charles E. Stubblefield—MIA

Lt. Ferris C. Suttle—KIA

Lt.Col. William H. Swanson—April 1943 to April of 1944, then to Hdqrtrs.

Capt. Lester G. Taylor—CT, West Point.

Lt. Harold Tenenbaum—Oct. 1944 to Sept. of 1945.

Capt. Robert L. Thacker—CT

Lt. Wendel G. Thomas—April 1945 to June of 1945, trans. out.

Lt. Bryce H. Thomson—Sept. 1944 to July of 1945, trans. out.

Maj. Robert C. Thomson—CT

Lt. Edward J. Thorne—POW.

Capt. Joseph A. Webster—Sept. 1945 to Nov. of 1945.

PILOTS—370TH FS

Capt. Benjamin H. Albertson—POW

Capt. Vincent W. Ambrose—CT

Lt. Wilson K. Baker Jr.—interned in Sweden.

Lt. Jack H. Bateman—April 1943 to May of 1944, trans. out.

Lt. Paul H. Bateman—CT

Lt. Claire A. Becker—(Jungle Jolly) Mar. 1945 to Sept. of 1945.

Lt. Gwyn W. Bell—Mar. 1945 to Sept. of 1945.

Lt. John E. Bell— Mar. 1945 to Sept. of 1945.

Lt. Emidio L. Bellante—(Dago) Mar. 1945 to July of 1945 trans. out.

Lt. Albert F. Benneyworth—Mar. 1945 to Sept. of 1945.

Lt. Robert M. Borg—CT

Lt. Kenneth M. Braymen—Mar. 1945 to Sept. of 1945.

Lt. Albert C. Brickner—(Brick) Mar. 1945 to Sept. of 1945.

Lt. Jack W. Brinkmeyer—April 1945 to Sept. of 1945.

Capt. Carey H. Brown—killed in flying accident.

Lt. William E. Buchanan—CT

Capt. James E. Buckley—KIA, West Point.

Capt. Will D. Burgsteiner—CT

Lt. Robert E. Burton—CT

Left photo, ground officers of the 369th FS. Kneeling left to right; Lt. Arnold Winford Coleman (Sparks)—Communications / radio, Capt. Paul D. Bruns—Flight Surgeon, Lt. John Elbert Regan Jr. (Spy-'Y')—Assistant Intelligence Officer, Lt. Marshall Caldwell Carpenter (Carp)—Armaments. It's interesting that Doc Bruns felt he wasn't contributing enough to the war and joined the 82nd Airborne Div. Standing, Lt. Clifton Philip Englund (Cliff) Communications/radar, Capt. Frank George Hahn (Spy-'X')—Intelligence, Lt. Solomon Chernus—Supply, Capt. Roger Van Gorder—Adjutant, Lt. Francis W. Hankey—Ordnance and Maj. Jefferson K. Fraley—Exec. Right photo, the 370th's top dogs. Kneeling; Maj. Daniel D. McKee—Commander (and the only flier in this group), Lt. John L. McDowell, Capt. Allen C. Bears—Exec. and Lt. Karl S. Elebash—Assistant Intel. Officer. Standing; Capt. John M. Benton—Intel., Capt. George W. Crouse—Flt. Surgeon, Lt. Don E. Caskey—Armament, Capt. Willis A. Dutton—Engineering and Lt. Herbert S. Rothman—Communications.

Lt. James W. Cadenhead—Did not leave for Eng. with the Group.

Lt. Vernon L. Caid—CT

Capt. Robert M. Callahan—CT

Lt. Dick D. Connelly—KIA

Lt. Alexander M. Cosmos—killed in flying accident.

Maj. Ralph L. Cox—Sept. 1944 to Feb. of 1945, then to the 369th FS.

Lt.Col. Niven K. Cranfill—April 1943 to Oct. of 1943, then to the 369th FS.

Capt. Charles V. Cunningham—CT

Maj. George A. Doersch—April 1943 to Feb. of 1945, then to the 368th FS.

Lt. John L. Downing—CT

Lt. Elmer N. Dunlap—POW.

Capt. Howard L. Fogg Jr.—May 1944 to July of 1944, then to the 368th FS.

Lt. Marlyn C. Ford—(Buck) Mar. 1945 to Sept. of 1945.

Lt. Arthur J. Giese Jr.—(Goose) Feb. 1945 to July of 1945, trans. out.

Lt. Howard E. Grimes—KIA

Lt. Lynn W. Hair—KIA.

Lt. Robert E. Hall—April 1943 to Oct. of 1943.

Lt. William H. Hastings Jr.—CT

Capt. Charles W. Hipsher—CT

Capt. William R. Hodges—April 1943 to May 11, 1944, shot down, evaded and returned. Sept. 1944 to Dec. of 1944, CT

Lt. Harold D. Hollis—KIA

Capt. Samuel J. Huskins Jr.—CT

Maj. Chauncey S. Irvine—Oct. 1943 to Feb. of 1944, then to Hdqrtrs.

Lt. Emory G. Johnson—CT

Lt. Cyril W. Jones Jr.—KIA

Lt. John E. Kerns—MIA

Lt. Ralph E. Kibler Jr.—KIA

Lt. Herman E. King—April 1943 to April 16, 1944, transferred to 56th FG.

F/O Harold E. Koenig—Mar. 1945 to Sept. of 1945.

Lt. John W. Lamont—CT

Capt. Raymond B. Lancaster Jr.—interned in Sweden.

F/O Eric H. Leathley—(The Bug) Jan. 1945 to Sept. of 1945, trans. out.

Maj. Andrew T. Lemmens—May 1944 to April of 1945, then to Hdqrtrs.

Maj. James K. Lovett—CT

Capt. Frank O. Lux—CT

Capt. Washington D. Lyon—MIA

Lt. Ross O. Major—April 1943 to Oct. of 1944, trans. out.

Capt. Frank R. Marshall Jr.—CT

Lt. James C. Martin—(Pete) Jan. 1945 to May of 1945, then to 368th FS.

Lt. Edward J. Maslow—POW

Lt. John F. McAlevey—(The Bum) CT

Lt. John W. McAllister Jr.—Aug. 1944 to Mar. of 1945, trans. out.

Lt. Jack E. McCoskey—POW

Lt. Garland J. McGregor—KIA

Capt. Robert L. McInnes—CT

Lt.Col. Daniel D. McKee—April 1943 to Oct. of 1943, then to Hdqrtrs. Back with the 370th from Feb. 1944 to April of 1945 then to Hdqrtrs again.

Capt. John W. McNeill Jr.—CT

Capt. Milton S. Merry—CT

Lt. George D. Miller—Feb. 1945 to Sept. of 1945.

Lt. Thomas W. Morris—(Baldy) Dec. 1944 to Sept. of 1945.

Lt.Col. John B. Murphy—completed tour, had previously flown with 343rd FG, Alaska.

Lt. John J. Murray—Dec.1944 to Sept. of 1945.

Lt. Wallace C. Murray—MIA

Left, 369th FS Armament and Ordnance Sections (sorry, no list of names). If these men failed to service their charges correctly the entire mission would be for naught. A fighter with jammed guns or unjettisonable bombs is almost worthless. Right, 370th FS 'A' Flight armorers. Sitting on ground left to right; Wagner, Delbert Jaques and Kenneth Coleman. Second row; Hyman Bernfield, George Thiehaud (with mascot) and Howard Martin. In truck; Dave Kingery.

Lt. Warren R. Newberg—CT

Lt. Earle S. Newcomer—(Chippie) Dec. 1944 to July of 1945, trans. out.

Lt. Madison H. Newton—(Dusty) Dec. 1944 to Sept. of 1945.

Lt. Albert T. Niccolai—MIA assumed KIA

Lt. Robert G. Oakley—CT

Lt. James H. O'Shea—CT

F/O James J. O'Shea—MIA.

Lt. Donald G. Page—Oct. 1944 to Sept. of 1945.

Lt. Malcom C. Paulette—KIA

Maj. Edwin F. Pezda—April 1943 to Oct. of 1943, then to the 369th FS.

Lt. Alan C. Porter—KIA

Lt. Richard O. Rabb—interned in Sweden.

Capt. Galen E. Ramser—CT

F/O Luther C. Reese—MIA

Lt. Werner J. Rueschenberg—CT

Lt. James J. Ruggles—Dec. 1944 to Sept. of 1945.

Lt. Harry L. Schecter—(The Count) Dec. 1944 to July of 1945, trans. out.

Lt. Jack R. Schulte—Dec. 1944 to July of 1945, trans. out.

Lt. Benjamin D. Schwartz Jr.—Dec. 1944 to Sept. of 1945.

Lt. Harry D. Semple—(Dean) Jan. 1945 to July of 1945, trans. out.

Capt. Jimmy C. Shoffit—CT

Lt. Gordon M. Shortness—MIA

Lt. Russell E. Shouse—(Junior) Dec. 1944 to Sept. of 1945.

Lt. Joseph E. Shupe—MIA

Lt. Robert W. Siltamaki—POW

Capt. Samuel R. Smith—Oct. 1943 to April of 1944, then to Hdqrtrs.

Lt. Seymour Smith—(Smith Bar) Dec. 1944 to Sept. of 1945, trans. out.

Lt. Thomas P. Smith—Feb. 1944 to April 11, 1944, ran out of fuel over the Netherlands. POW, escaped and returned. Sept. 16, 1944 to April of 1945.

Lt. Connie L Stanley—April 1945 to July of 1945, trans. out.

Capt. Homer A. Staup—Aug. 1944 to May of 1945, trans. out.

Lt. Stanley F. Stegnerski—MIA

Capt. William F. Stepp—Sept. 1944 to Sept. of 1945.

Lt. Howard E. Steussey—POW

Lt. Richard P. Straub—(Blue Blazes) Jan. 1945 to Sept. of 1945.

Lt. Paul E. Sundheim—POW

Capt. Eugene L. Surowiec—Oct. 1944 to Sept. of 1945.

Capt. Thomas C. Sutton—April 1945 to Sept. of 1945.

Lt. Earl W. Thomas Jr.—KIA

Lt. Elbert W. Tilton—CT

Lt. Daniel R. Tuchscherer—CT

Lt. William N. Tucker Jr.—KIA

Lt. George Turinsky—April 1945 to Sept. of 1945, trans. out.

Lt. Benjamin J. Vos Jr.—MIA

Lt. Edward L. Welch—CT

Lt. Frank E. Westall Jr.—KIA

Maj. Ray S. Wetmore—CT

Lt. Bennie F. White—MIA

F/O Walter W. Wiley—POW

Lt. John W. Wilson—CT

Lt. Harvey C. Williams—July 1944 to Sept. of 1945, trans. out.

Lt. Theophalus A. Williams—KIA

Capt. Donald L. Windmiller—June 1944 to Sept. of 1945.

Capt. Albert E. Wolfe—CT

Capt. Robert M. York—CT

Lt. Lawrence A. Ziska—killed in flying accident.

ACES

Pilots that scored all of their victories while flying with the 359th FG. Air victories only.

	ACES
1. Maj. Ray S. Wetmore—370th FS	21.25
2. Maj. George A. Doersch— 370th & 368th	10.5
3. Lt. Robert J. Booth—369th	8
4. Capt. Claude J. Crenshaw—369th	7
5. Lt.Col. John B. Murphy—370th	6.25
6. Lt. Cyril W. Jones Jr.—370th	6
7. Lt. David B. Archibald—368th	5
8. Maj. Ralph L. Cox—370th & 369th	5
9. Lt.Col. Niven K. Cranfill—368th, 369th, 370th & Hdqrtrs.	5
10. Capt. William R. Hodges—370th	5
11. Lt. Paul E. Olson—368th	5
12. Capt. Robert M. York—370th	5

Top, photo of 370th FS pilots taken before Sept. 11, 1944. Front row left to right; F/O Jack McCoskey, Capt. John McNeill Jr., Lt. Ross Major, Capt. Ray Wetmore and Lt. Lawrence Zizka. Second row; Lt. Edward Welch, F/O James J. O'Shea, Lt. Dick Connelly, Capt. Samuel Huskins Jr., Lt.Col. Daniel McKee, Maj. James Lovett, Lt. Emory Johnson, Lt. Robert Oakley and Lt. Warren Newberg. Third row; Capt. Will Burgsteiner, Capt. George Doersch, Capt. Ralph Cox, Lt. Robert York, Lt. Robert McInnes, Lt. Homer Staup, Lt. John McAllister, Lt. Milton Merry, Lt. Harvey Williams and Lt. Galen Ramser. Fourth row; Capt. William Hodges, Lt. Thomas Smith, Lt. Stanley Stegnerski, Lt. Frank Marshall, Lt. Albert Wolfe, Lt. John Lamont, Lt. Werner Rueschenberg, Lt. James Shoffit and Lt. Elbert Tilton. Note the diversity of uniforms. Below, Flying Control personnel (sorry no names).

Gun camera action. Starting in the top left corner and moving to the right; C. J. Cavenaugh scores good hits on a Fw190 on Aug. 8, 1944; D. D. Connelly destroys a truck on Aug. 8, 1944; Rene Burtner in a low level attack on trains (no date); D. D. Connelly pounces a flak tower on Aug. 8, 1944; Cyril Jones pumps API into a Me109 on Aug. 9, 1944; a Me109 trails smoke after an attack by J. W. Wilson on Aug. 9, 1944; the boiler starts to explode on this loco strafed by Claude Crenshaw on Aug. 10, 1944, massive boiler failure on another train during the mission of Aug. 10 COURTESY J. D. STEVENS; BV 138 seaplane gets a working over on Oct. 7, 1944 (see Destruction Diary); Yak 9 about to bite the dust on Mar. 18, 1945; a Me109G being lined up by D. E. Kelly on Mar. 24, 1945.

Destruction Diary

Abbreviations and terms used in Destruction Diary

Adm. Bldg.=Administration Building
Armed Trawler (boat)
Ctl. Tw'r=Control Tower
Elec. Loco=Electric powered RR Locomotive
(g)=ground target
HQ Bldg.=Headquarters Building
Marsh. Yd.=Marshalling Yard (RR complex)
Med. Tank=Medium Tank (Panther category armored
    fighting vehicle)
Motor Vehicles (automobiles, trucks and motorcycles)
M/E/AC=Multi-Engined Aircraft (claims read thus
    when gun-camera film wasn't clear enough to make a
    positive identification)
Observ. Tw'r=Observation Tower

Oil Tank=RR Oil Tanker Car
Pass. Cars=RR Passenger Cars (coaches)
Power Launch (boat)
Round House (RR facility for turning locomotives
    around)
(sh)=shared claim
Signal Tower (most often associated with the RR)
S/E/AC=Single Engine Aircraft
Switch House (RR building)
T/E/AC=Twin Engine Aircraft
T/E/Trnsp't=Twin Engine Transport Aircraft
U/AC=Unidentified Aircraft
U/S/E/AC=Unidentified Single Engine Aircraft
U/Grd./Tgt.=Unidentified Ground Target

SIGNIFICANT MISSIONS

1. First aerial kill on mission # 17, January 29,1944.

2. Group receives a letter of commendation from Gen. Spaatz for action during mission #26, February 10, 1944.

3. First mission for Bill's Buzz Boys, March 26, 1944.

4. Lt. Frank Fong, the only Chinese-American pilot in the E.T.O. scores a kill during mission #57, March 27, 1944.

5. First bombing assignment, mission #61, March 30, 1944.

6. First all Mustang outing, mission #88, May 6, 1944.

7. First trip to Berlin, mission #96, May 19, 1944.

8. First Chattanooga Choo-Choo mission, mission #98, May 21, 1944.

9. First use of P-51Bs as dive bombers, mission #102, May 23, 1944.

10. D-Day June 6,1944, the Group flies six missions.

11. Operation Zebra, mission #148, June 25, 1944.

12. Col. Tacon makes the first official spotting of the Me163 rocket powered fighter during mission #176, July 28, 1944.

13. Operation Buick, mission #179, August 1, 1944.

14. Three pilots land in Sweden, mission #182, August 4, 1944.

15. 370th FS destroys two Me163s (the first) in aerial combat during mission #196, August 16, 1944.

16. Lt. Lawrence Zizka makes the only kill of the entire VIII Fighter Command on mission #204, August 27, 1944.

17. Combat with Swiss aircraft, mission #214, September 10, 1944.

18. Distinguished Unit Citation for mission #215, September 11, 1944.

19. Jack-in-the-box barrage balloons encountered on mission #241, October 24, 1944.

20. With all fifteen fighter groups of the 8th AF up, the 359th accounts for one third of the locomotives destroyed during mission #248, November 5, 1944.

21. Lts. Archibald and Olson become aces in a single day on mission #269, December 18, 1944.

22. A rare He280 jet fighter is spotted in flight during mission #270, December 24, 1944.

23. First day of Operation Clarion, mission #301, February 22, 1945.

24. Remagen bridgehead incident on mission #314, March 10, 1945.

25. Capt. Wetmore scores the only kill made by the entire VIII Fighter Command, which also happens to be the third Me163 destroyed by the 359th FG, on mission #318, March 15, 1945.

26. Combat with Russian aircraft during mission # 320, March 18, 1945.

27. Provided escort for RAF Lancasters on mission #322, March 20, 1945.

28. Worst weather ever encountered, mission #330, March 26, 1945.

29. The Great Jet Massacre, mission #341, April 10, 1945.

DATE	SQ	PILOT	NO.	DEST.	NO.	PROB.	NO.	DAM.	A/C	SER. NO.	CODE
Jan. 29 1944	368	Shaw, C.					1	Me110	P-47		CV-
	369	Prewitt, L.H.					1	Me110	P-47		IV-
		Gray, R.V.	.5	Me110					P-47		IV-
		Oliphint, J.H.	.5						P-47		IV-
Jan. 30 1944	369	Prewitt, L.H.					1	Ju88	P-47		IV-
		Thacker, R.L.	1	Ju88					P-47		IV-
		Pherson, R.L.					1	Ju88	P-47		IV-
		Gray, R.V.	1	Me109					P-47		IV-
		Booth, R.J.	1	Me109					P-47	42-8695	IV-F
		Cranfill, N.K.					1	Me109	P-47		IV-
Feb. 3 1944	369	Thomson, R.C.	1	Fw190					P-47	42-75270	IV-R
Feb. 10 1944	369	Ettlesen, C.C.	1	Me109E					P-47		IV-
		Carter, C.E.					1	Me109G	P-47		IV-
	370	Brown, C.H.	1	Me109					P-47	42-75136	CR-N
		Kibler, R.E. Jr.	1	Me109					P-47	42-74632	CR-D
		Major, R.O.	1	Me109					P-47	42-8578	CR-V
		Hodges, W.R.	2	Me109					P-47	42-74719	CR-O
		Wetmore, R.S.	1	Me109					P-47	42-8663	CR-G
Feb. 22 1944	368	Cater, E.H.	1	Me109					P-47	42-75141	CV-1
		LemMens, A.T.	1	Me109					P-47	42-8617	CV-M
	370	Doersch, G.A.	1	Fw190D					P-47		CR-
		Murphy, J.B.			1	Me109			P-47		CR-
		Niccolai, A.T.					1	Me109	P-47		CR-
Feb. 24 1944	368	McGeever, T.J.	1	Fw190					P-47	42-74633	CV-W
		Tyrrell, A.R.	2	Fw190s					P-47	42-75111	CV-A
	370	Murphy, J.B.	1	Me109					P-47	42-8613	CR-A
Mar. 2 1944	370	McKee, D.D.					1	Fw190	P-47	42-75118	CR-Z
Mar. 4 1944	369	Broach, R.H.			1	Me109F			P-47	42-75210	IV-I
	370	Bateman, P.H.	.5	Fw190D					P-47	42-74737	CR-P
		Murphy, J.B.	.5	Fw190D					P-47	42-8613	CR-A
		Bateman, P.H.	.25	Me109					P-47	42-74737	CR-P
		Murphy, J.B.	.25						P-47	42-8613	CR-A
		Porter, A.C.	.25						P-47	42-8578	CR-V
		Wetmore, R.S.	.25						P-47	42-8663	CR-G
		Murphy, J.B.					1	Me109	P-47	42-8613	CR-A
		Wetmore, R.S.					1	Me109	P-47	42-8663	CR-G
		Mosse, C.E.					1	Me109	P-47	42-8611	CR-N
		Hodges, W.R.			1	Me109			P-47	42-74719	CR-O
		Hollis, H.D.					1	Me109	P-47	42-75409	CR-X
Mar. 6 1944	368	Bolefahr, W.N.	1	Me109G					P-47	42-22786	CV-B
		Janney, R.B. III					1	Me109G	P-47	42-75141	CV-I
		Cater, E.H.					1	Fw190	P-47	42-74721	CV-K
	369	Pherson, R.L.	1	Me109F					P-47	42-75210	IV-I
		Booth, R.J.	1	Fw190					P-47	52-75048	IV-Z
		Carter, C.E.					1	Steamship	P-47	42-75054	IV-V
Mar. 8 1944	368	Janney, R.B. III					1	Me109G	P-47	42-75141	CV-I
	369	Staley, C.W.					1	Fw190	P-47	42-75054	IV-V
Mar. 15 1944	368	McGeever, T.J.			1	Me109	2	Me109	P-47	42-75111	CV-A
	369	Kruger, C.H.	1	Me109F	1	Me109F			P-47	42-74642	IV-K
					1	Loco					
		Thacker, R.L.			1	Loco			P-47	42-8698	IV-X
Mar. 16 1944	369	Linderer, H.A.	1	Me109					P-47	42-74666	IV-O
	370	Wetmore, R.S.	2	Fw190					P-47	42-75068	CR-P
Mar. 26 1944	369	Oliphint, J.H.	1	T/E/AC(g)	1			HE 177(g)	P-47		IV-
			1	Hangar			2	Hangars			
							1	Building			
							1	Water Tower			
Mar. 27 1944	369	Pherson, R.L.	1	Me109E					P-47		IV-
		Fong, F.S.	1	Fw190					P-47		IV-
	370	McKee, D.D.			1	Fw190	1	Me109	P-47	42-75118	CS-Z
Mar. 29 1944	369	Carter, C.E.	2	Me410s(g)				P-47		IV-
			1	Boxcar	1	Hangar	5	Locos			
		Ettlesen, C.C.					1	S/E/AC(g)	P-47		IV-
							1	Loco			
		Thacker, R.L.					4	Locos	P-47		IV-
		Ettlesen, C.C.					1	Hangar	P-47		IV-
		Oliphint, J.H.					1	Building	P-47		IV-
		Oliphint, J.H.	5	Soldiers			2	Flak Towers			
		Carter, C.E.	2	Coal Trains					P-47		IV-
		Oliphint, J.H.							P-47		IV-
		Carter, C.E.	1	Train			20	RR Cars	P-47		IV-
		Thacker, R.L.							P-47		IV-
		Oliphint, J.H.							P-47		IV-
		Ettlesen, C.C.							P-47		IV-

DATE	SQ	PILOT	NO.	DEST.	NO.	PROB.	NO.	DAM.	A/C	SER. NO.	CODE
Apr. 1 1944	369	Carter, C.E.					1	Me109	P-47		IV-
							3	Locos			
							1	Tugboat			
		Thacker, R.L.					8	Locos	P-47		IV-
		Ettlesen, C.C.									
		Carter, C.E.	1	Tugboat			1	Tugboat	P-47		IV-
		Ettlesen, C.C.							P-47		IV-
Apr. 8 1944	369	Oliphint, J.H.	3	Locos			1	Tugboat	P-47		IV-
		Ettlesen, C.C.	5	Tugboats			1	Power	P-47		IV-
		Thacker, R.L.						Launch	P-47		IV-
							1	Barge			
							3	Coal Barges			
							1	Canal Bridge			
								Control Station			
Apr. 11, 1944	370	Doersch, G.A.	1	Fw190					P-47	42-8558	CS-J
		Kibler, R.E. Jr.					1	Me109	P-47	42-75413	CS-U
		Smith, S.R.	2	Fw190s(g)	1.00	Fw190			P-47	42-8613	CS-A
		Dunlap, E.N.	1	Fw190			1	Fw190	P-47	42-75079	CS-B
		Burgstiener, W.D.	4	Fw190s(g)			1	Fw190(g)	P-47	42-7894	CS-I
		Wetmore, R.S.	1	Ju88(g)			2	Ju88s(g)	P-47	42-75068	CS-P
		Callahan, R.M.					5	Fw190(g)	P-47	42-8042	CS-H
		Shupe, J.E.	1	Ju88(g)			1	Ju88(g)	P-47	42-8498	CS-T
		McKee, D.D.	1	Ju88(g)			2	Ju88(g)	P-47	42-75118	CS-Z
		Hollis, H.D.	1	Ju88(g)					P-47	42-75409	CS-X
		Ambrose, V.W.	1	Ju88(g)					P-47	42-78611	CS-N
		Borg, R.M.					10	U/AC(g)	P-47	42-8566	CS-N
							1	T/E			
								Trns'p(g)			
		Porter, A.C.					1	Ju88(g)	P-47	42-8578	CS-V
							1	Ctl. Tower			
							1	Barracks			
Apr. 12 1944	369	Oliphint, J.H.	1	Train					P-47		IV-
			2	Boxcars							
Apr. 15 1944	368	Huddleston, C.M.					1	Powerline	P-47	42-75111	CV-A
		Beaupre, R.V.					1	Coast Watchers Radar Unit	P-47	42-8592	CV-L
		Bolefahr, W.N.					1	Barracks Area	P-47	42-8485	CV-B
		Hawkinson, R.W.					1	Loco	P-47	42-22468	CV-S
		Hunter, J.B.					12	RR Cars	P-47	42-74721	CV-K
		Baldridge, A.R.							P-47	42-8645	CV-M
		Fogg, H.L.							P-47	42-75088	CV-G
		Fogg, H.L.					1	Radar Tower	P-47	42-75088	CV-G
		Baldridge, A.R.	1	Loco			2	Flak Towers	P-47	42-8645	CV-M
		Hunter, J.B.					1	Loco			
							1	Radar Tower			
							1	Barracks Area			
	370	Doersch, G.A.					1	Ju88	P-47	42-8558	CS-J
		Hollis, H.D.			1	Ju88(g)			P-47	42-75068	CS-P
		McKee, D.D.					1	U/AC(g)	P-47	42-75118	CS-Z
							1	U/SE/AC(g)			
							1	Gun Position			
		Callahan, R.M.	1	Ju88(g)					P-47	42-75894	CS-L
		Bateman, J.H.					1	Barracks Area	P-47	42-74745	CS-D
Apr. 19 1944	369	Ettlesen, C.C.	1	Switch Tower	1	Loco	4	Locos	P-47		IV-
		Thacker, R.L.	1	Loco					P-47		IV-
		Sansing, V.E.							P-47		IV-
Apr. 22 1944	369	Booth, R.J.	1	Fw190					P-47		IV-
		Matthew, H.L.	1	Fw190			1	Loco	P-47		IV-
			1	Loco							
		Pezda, E.F.			1	Loco			P-47		IV-
		Oliphint, J.H.	2	Locos			1	Factory	P-47	42-74666	IV-O
			1	Searchlight			4	Wagons			
	370	Hollis, H.D.	1	Fw190D					P-47	42-75409	CS-X
		Kibler, R.E. Jr.	2	Fw190s					P-47	42-75515	CS-B
		Lancaster, R.B.	1	Fw190			1	Fw190	P-47	42-75253	CS-S
		Wetmore, R.S.	1	Fw190					P-47	42-76282	CS-O
		Brown, C.H.	1	Train			1	Train	P-47		CS-
							1	Barge			
							1	Tanker			
		Tuchscherer, D.					2	Trains	P-47		CS-
		Major, R.O.	1	Train			1	Switch House	P-47		CS-
					1	Switchman	1	RR Station			

DATE	SQ	PILOT	NO.	DEST.	NO.	PROB.	NO.	DAM.	A/C	SER. NO.	CODE
Apr. 24, 1944	368	Burton, R.E.	2	Hangars			1	Adm. Bldg.	P-47	42-74721	CV-K
		Janney, R.B.					1	Barracks	P-47	42-75128	CV-R
		Lemmons, A.T.					1	Power Line	P-47	42-8645	CV-M
		Mosse, C.E.							P-47	42-8485	CV-B
	370	Wetmore, R.S.	1	Me109(g)			1	Me109	P-47	42-75068	CS-P
		Smith, S.R.	1	U/S/E/AC(g)					P-47	42-76308	CS-Y
		Porter, A.C.	1	Me109(g)					P-47	42-75118	CS-Z
		Bateman, P.H.	1	Me109(g)					P-47	42-76282	CS-O
		Bateman, P.H.	.33	U/T/E/AC(g)					P-47	42-76282	CS-O
		Smith, S.R.	.33						P-47	42-76308	CS-Y
		Wetmore, R.S.	.33						P-47	42-75068	CS-P
Apr. 25 1944	369	Booth, R.J.	1	Me109					P-47	42-8695	IV-F
			1	Radar Station							
	370	Callahan, R.M.	1	Fw190(g)					P-47	42-2480	CS-K
		Grimes, H.E.					1	Barracks Area	P-47	42-76308	CS-Y
Apr. 29 1944	370	Cunningham, C.V.			1	Fw190			P-47	42-76416	CS-H
		Hodges, W.R.	2	Locos			3	Locos	P-47	42-8643	CS-Q
		Maslow, E.J.	4	Locos			3	Locos	P-47	42-75894	CS-L
		Hipsher, C.W.	7	Locos					P-47	42-75413	CS-U
		Porter, A.C.	1	Loco					P-47	42-75118	CS-Z
		Bateman, P.H.					1	Loco	P-47	42-76282	CS-O
Apr. 30 1944	368	Mosse, C.E.	1	Me210(g)					P-47	42-8485	CV-B
		Janney, R.B.	1	Me210/410(g)	1			Me210/410(g)	P-47	42-8402	CV-M
		Mosse, C.E.	1	Ammo Dump			?	Hangars	P-47	42-8485	CV-B
		Janney, R.B.							P-47	42-8402	CV-M
		White, S.A.							P-47	42-74721	CV-K
		Burton, R.E.							P-47	42-76598	CV-V
May 4 1944	368	Hawkinson, R.W.					5 or 6	Barracks	P-47	42-75128	CV-R
							1	Hangar			
May 8 1944	368	Bolefahr, W.N.	1	Me109			1	Me109	P-51B	43-24764	CV-B
		Homeyer, A.B.					1	Me109	P-51B	42-106949	CV-V
		Hogan, B.M. III			.5	Me109			P-51B	42-106898	CV-D
	369	Burton, H.C.	1	Me109					P-51B	42-106818	IV-U
		Ettlesen, C.C.	1	Me109					P-51B	42-106853	IV-V
		Booth, R.J.	2	Me109					P-51B	43-7199	IV-F
			1	Fw190							
			1	Loco							
		Cranfill, N.K.			.5	Me109			P-51B	42-106848	IV-N
	370	Doersch, G.A.	1	Fw190			1	Fw190	P-51C	42-103345	CS-D
			1	Me109							
		Shupe, J.E.	2	Fw190					P-51B	42-106851	CS-X
			1	Loco							
May 11 1944	370	Hollis, H.D.	1	Me410(g)					P-51B	42-106851	CS-X
		Wetmore, R.S.					2	Flak Towers	P-51B	42-106894	CS-P
							2	Gun Positions			
		McKee, D.D.					?	Hangars	P-51	42-106878	CS-A
May 12 1944	369	Laing, D.H.	1	T/E/AC(g)					P-51B	42-106599	IV-W
		Ettlesen, C.C.	.5	T/E/AC(g)			1	T/E/AC(g)	P-51B	42-106853	IV-V
		Thacker, R.L.	.5	T/E/AC(g)					P-51B	42-106607	IV-X
May 19 1944	369	Mosse, C.E.	1	Me109					P-51B	43-6962	CV-Y
		Janney, R.B.	1	Me109					P-51B	42-106619	CV-J
		Cater, E.H.	2	Locos	4	RR Cars	1	Power Line	P-51B	43-6491	CV-E
		Drake, O.P.	1	Ammo Car			1	Oil Derrick	P-51B	42-106667	CV-L
							1	Hq. Bldg.			
							1	Control Tower			
							3	Gun Positions			
	369	Thomson, R.C.	1	Me109					P-51B	42-106841	IV-Q
		Burton, H.C.	2	Me109					P-51B	42-106670	IV-C
		Kruger, C.H.	1	Me109					P-51B	42-106629	IV-K
		Oliphint, J.H.	1	Me109					P-51B	43-6620	IV-R
			1	Oil Tank			1	Oil Tank			
							1	Flak Tower			
		Ettlesen, C.C.	.5	Me109					P-51B	42-106853	IV-V
		Rodeheaver, H.					1	Barge	P-51B	42-106818	IV-U
		Rodeheaver, H.	1	Barge			1	Barge	P-51B	42-106818	IV-U
		Oliphint, J.H.							P-51B	43-6620	IV-R
		Thomson, R.C.							P-51B	42-106841	IV-Q
		Morrill, M.C. Jr.							P-51C	42-103354	IV-B
	370	Wetmore, R.S.	2	Me109s					P-51B	42-106894	CS-P
		Hipsher, C.W.					1	Me109	P-51B	42-106935	CS-U
		Bateman, P.H.	1	Fw190D					P-51B	42-106926	CS-O

DATE	SQ	PILOT	NO.	DEST.	NO.	PROB.	NO.	DAM.	A/C	SER. NO.	CODE
May 21 1944	368	McGeever, T.J.	1	Ju52 or Ju86					P-51B	42-106809	CV-H
			1	U/AC(g)							
			.5	Ju52 (g)							
		Drake, O.P.					1	HE 111(g)	P-51B	42-106995	CV-Q
							1	GO 242(g)			
		Hatter, R.B.	6	U/AC(g)			3	U/AC(g)	P-51C	42-103197	CV-H
		Homeyer, A.G.	1	Fw190(g)			1	Fw190(g)	P-51B	42-106949	CV-V
			1	Seaplane (g)							
		Bach, G.C.	2	Fw190(g)			4	U/AC(g)	P-51B	42-106867	CV-1
		Lane, T.S.	2	Fw190s(g)			3	U/AC(g)	P-51B	42-106618	CV-W
		Randolph, G.M	.5	Ju52(g)			3	U/AC(g)	P-51B	42-106577	CV-X
		Hagan, B.M. III	1	Trainer(g)			2	Trainers(g)	P-51B	42-106898	CV-D
							2	Locos			
							1	Radio Tower			
		Addleman, R.H.					1	Loco	P-51B	42-106667	CV-L
		Huddleson, C. Jr.					1	Warehouse	P-51B	42-106620	CV-G
							1	Power Line			
		McGeever, T.J.	1	Loco			1	Loco	P-51B	42-106809	CV-H
		Randolph, G.M.							P-51B	42-106577	CV-X
		Bach, G.C.	1	Loco					P-51B	42-106867	CV-I
		Homeyer, A.G.							P-51B	42-106949	CV-V
		Baldridge, A.R.					?	RR Bldgs.	P-51B	43-6962	CV-Y
							1	Radar Tower			
							1	Telegraph Line			
		Hunter, J.B.					1	RR Bldg.	P-51B	42-106702	CV-X
							4	Box Cars			
							1	Radar Tower			
							1	Power Line			
							1	Flak Position			
		Drake, O.P.	1	Loco			2	Locos	P-51B	42-106995	CV-Q
		Baldridge, A.R.							P-51B	43-6962	CV-Y
		Hunter, J.B.							P-51B	42-106702	CV-X
	369	Broach, R.H.	.5	U/LW/AC					P-51B	42-106771	IV-I
		Sander, R.B.	.5						P-51		IV-
		Orwig, E.R.	1	T/E/AC(g)			1	T/E/AC(g)	P-51B	42-106916	IV-D
							1	Loco			
		Rodeheaver, H.	1	Barge(s)			1	Barge(s)	P-51B	42-106818	IV-U
							1	Barge			
		Oliphint, J.H.	1	Loco			3	Locos	P-51B	42-106620	IV-R
			1	Switch Eng.			2	Bld'gs			
							1	Radar Tower			
		Thacker, R.L.	4	Locos					P-51B	42-106607	IV-X
		Orwig, E.R.							P-51B	42-106916	IV-D
		Campbell, R.W.							P-51	42-106757	IV-Z
		Kruger, C.H.							P-51B	42-106629	IV-K
		Rodeheaver, H.R.							P-51B	42-106818	IV-U
		Oliphint, J.H.							P-51B	42-106620	IV-R
		Kruger, C.H.	4	Locos					P-51B	42-106629	IV-K
		Thacker, R.L.							P-51B	42-106607	IV-X
		Matthew, H.L.							P-51B	43-24798	IV-T
		Oliphint, J.H.							P-51B	42-106620	IV-R
		Fong, F.S.							P-51		IV-M
		Matthew, H.L.	3	Locos					P-51B	43-24798	IV-T
		Oliphint, J.H.							P-51B	42-106620	IV-R
		Fong, F.S.							P-51		IV-
		Campbell, R.W.							P-51		IV-
		Matthew, H.L.	1	Loco					P-51B	43-24798	IV-T
		Campbell, R.W.							P-51		IV-
		Kruger, C.H.							P-51B	42-106629	IV-K
		Thacker, R.L.							P-51		IV-
		Thacker, R.L.					10	Tank Cars	P-51		
		Campbell, R.W.							P-51		
		Kruger, C.H.							P-51B	42-106629	IV-K
		Oliphint, J.H.							P-51B		
		Matthew, H.L.							P-51B	43-24798	IV-T
		Fong, F.S.							P-51		
		Broach, R.H.	1	Loco			1	Radar Tower	P-51B	42-106771	IV-I
		Sander, R.B.					3	RR Cars	P-51		IV-
		Thacker, R.L.					1	Signal Tower	P-51		IV-
		Kruger, C.H.					2	Signal Towers	P-51B	42-106629	IV-K
	370	Callahan, R.M.	1	Ju88(g)			1	Ju88(g)	P-51B	42-106851	CS-X
							1	Loco			
							1	Radar Station			

DATE	SQ	PILOT	NO.	DEST.	NO.	PROB.	NO.	DAM.	A/C	SER. NO.	CODE
		Newberg, W.R.					2	Ju88(g)	P-51B	43-24791	CS-D
							1	Loco			
							2	Radar Stations			
		Shupe, J.E.	4	Ju88s(g)			3	Ju88s(g)	P-51		CS-
		McKee, D.D.	2	Locos	1	Boxcar	1	Radar Tower	P-51B	42-106941	CS-B
		Lancaster, R.B.					1	RR Station	P-51B	42-106805	CS-F
		Cunningham, C.V.					1	Water Tank	P-51B	42-106799	CS-Y
		Doersch, G.A.					1	Switch House	P-51B	43-24810	CS-J
		Wetmore, R.S.					1	Round House	P-51B	42-106894	CS-P
		Lemmens, A.T.							P-51C	42-103294	CS-O
		Hipsher, C.W.							P-51B	42-106935	CS-U
		Doersch, G.A.	2	Locos(s)			1	Loco	P-51B	43-24810	CS-J
			1	Power Station			?	Boxcars			
							1	Round House			
							1	T/E/AC			
		Borg, R.M.					1	Radar Station	P-51B	42-106879	CS-T
							1	Switch House			
							1	Small Factory			
May 24 1944	368	Hunter, J.B.	.5	Me109					P-51B	43-7155	CV-C
		McGeever, T.J.					1	Loco	P-51B	42-106727	CV-F
							1	Power Line			
	369	Sansing, V.E.	.5	Me109			1	Radar Tower			
							1	Tugboat			
		Campbell, R.W.	1	Loco					P-51B	43-6757	IV-Z
		Thacker, R.L.	1	Loco					P-51B	42-106607	IV-X
			1	Oil Car							
		Oliphint, J.H.	2	Oil Cars			1	Medium Tank	P-51B	42-106620	IV-R
		Brundage, L.W.	1	Oil Car					P-51B	42-106691	IV-H
		Orwig, E.R.					1	Tugboat	P-51B	42-106670	IV-C
		Ettlesen, C.C.	1	Gas Tank			1	Tugboat	P-51C	42-103354	IV-B
							3	Barges			
							1	Cargo Ship			
							1	High Tension Tower			
		Orwig, E.R.	1	Loco					P-51B	42-106670	IV-C
		Campbell, R.W.							P-51B	43-6757	IV-Z
		Broach, E.R.	2	Locos					P-51B	42-106771	IV-H
		Fong, F.S.							P-51B	43-7199	IV-F
		Sander, R.B.							P-51B	42-106906	IV-L
		Ettlesen, C.C.	1	Loco					P-51C	42-103354	IV-B
		Brundage, L.W.							P-51B	41-106691	IV-H
		Ettlesen, C.C.	2	Locos					P-51C	42-103354	IV-B
		Brundage, L.W.							P-51B	42-106691	IV-H
		Thacker, R.L.							P-51B	42-106607	IV-X
		Orwig, E.R.							P-51B	42-106670	IV-C
		Oliphint, J.H.							P-51B	42-106620	IV-R
		Cambell, R.W.							P-51B	43-6757	IV-Z
		Sansing, V.E.							P-51B	43-24756	IV-V
		Orwig, E.R.	2	Oil Cars					P-51B	42-106670	IV-C
		Campbell, R.W.							P-51B	43-6757	IV-Z
		Sansing, V.E.							P-51B	43-24756	IV-V
May 29 1944	368	Hatter, R.B.	1	Me109					P-51C	42-103197	CV-Y
		Hagan, B.M.	1	Me109					P-51B	42-106898	CV-D
	369	Thacker, R.L.	1	Me109					P-51		IV-
		Booth, R.J.	1	Fw190					P-51B	43-7199	IV-F
	370	Grimes, H.E.	2	Fw190s					P-51B	42-106791	CS-Y
		Lancaster, R.B.	1	Me109	1	Me109			P-51B	42-106805	CS-F
		Murphy, J.B.	1	Fw190					P-51B	42-106878	CS-A
		Murphy, J.B.	.5	Fw190					P-51B	42-106878	CS-A
		Doersch, G.A.	.5						P-51B	43-24810	CS-J
		Siltamaki, R.W.	.5	Fw190					P-51B	42-106975	CS-N
		Doersch, G.A.	.5						P-51B	43-24810	CS-J
		Wetmore, R.S.	2	Fw190s					P-51B	42-106894	CS-P
May 30 1944	368	Forehand, W.C.	1	Me109					P-51B	42-106577	CV-X
		Hawkinson, R.W.	.5	Me109					P-51B	42-106611	CV-K
		Hunter, J.B.	.5						P-51B	42-106702	CV-X
	HQ	Tacon, A.P.					1	Fw190(g)	P-51C	42-103329	CV-Z
	369	Booth, R.J.					1	Ju88(g)	P-51B	42-106916	IV-D
							1	Loco			
							1	Oil Car			
							1	Oil Derrick			
		Pherson, R.L.					1	Staff Car	P-51		IV-
		Broach, R.H.	1	Barge					P-51		IV-
	370	Grimes, H.E.	.5	Me109					P-51B	42-106799	CS-Y
		Hipsher, C.W.	.5						P-51B	43-22810	CS-J
		Hipsher, C.W.	.5	Me109					P-51B	43-24810	CS-J
		Siltamaki, R.W.	.5						P-51B	42-106926	CS-O

DATE	SQ	PILOT	NO.	DEST.	NO.	PROB.	NO.	DAM.	A/C	SER. NO.	CODE
June 6 1944	368	Tyrell, A.R.	1	Loco					P-51		CV-
		McGeever, T.J.							P-51		CV-
	369	Oliphint, J.H.	1	Truck					P-51B	42-106679	IV-O
		Oliphint, J.H.	1	Loco					P-51B	42-106679	IV-O
		Pherson, R.L.							P-51B	42-106803	IV-A
		Oliphint, J.H.	30/40	Ammo Cars			10	Boxcars	P-51B	42-106679	IV-O
		Pherson, R.L.					2	Tank Cars	P-51B	42-106803	IV-A
		Cuzner, H.F.							P-51B	42-106469	IV-G
		Oliphint, J.H.	1	Transformer Station					P-51B	42-106679	IV-O
		Cuzner, H.F.							P-51B	42-106469	IV-G
		Burton, H.C.	2	Locos			1	Radio Tower	P-51B	42-106670	IV-C
		Booth, R.J.	8-10	RR Cars			1	Truck	P-51B	43-7199	IV-F
		Ralston, G. Jr.							P-51B	43-24756	IV-V
	370	Fogg, H.L.					1	Loco	P-51B	43-6879	CS-T
		Hastings, W.H.					1	Tank Car	P-51B	43-24810	CS-J
		Connelly, D.D.							P-51B	42-106925	CS-V
June 7 1944	368	Marcinkiewicz					1	Truck	P-51		CV-
							3	Trailers			
	370	Borg, R.M.	1	Ammo Train & Loco			10	Boxcars	P-51B	42-106749	CS-M
		Murphy, J.B.	5	Light Tanks			12	Light Tanks	P-51B	42-106878	CS-A
		Grimes, H.E.	6	Trucks			15	Trucks	P-51B	42-106799	CS-Y
		Hipsher, C.W.	2	Signal Trucks					P-51B	42-106935	CS-U
		Downing, J.L.							P-51B	42-106580	CS-I
		Reese, L.C.							P-51B	42-106474	CS-M
		Tuchscherer, D.							P-51B	43-24778	CS-H
		Lancaster, R.B.							P-51B	42-106805	CS-F
		Rabb, R.O.							P-51B	42-106975	CS-N
		Hollis, H.D.							P-51B	42-106941	CS-B
		Ambrose, V.W.							P-51C	42-103319	CS-R
		Wetmore, R.S.							P-51B	43-6879	CS-T
		McNeill, J.W. Jr.							P-51B	42-106692	CS-T
June 8 1944	370	Cunningham, C.V.	1	Loco			2	Boxcars	P-51B	42-106704	CS-H
			2	RR Cars							
		McKee, D.D.	10	Boxcars	2	Trucks	1	Loco	P-51B	42-106878	CS-A
		Lancaster, R.	3	Trucks			4	Boxcars	P-51B	42-106805	CS-F
		Callahan, R.M.					3	Motor Vehicles	P-51B	42-106894	CS-P
		Cunningham, C.V.							P-51B	42-106704	CS-H
		Baker, W.J. Jr.							P-51B	42-106925	CS-N
		Hastings, W.H.					2	Trucks	P-51B	42-106799	CS-Y
		Bateman, P.H.					4	Flatcars	P-51B	42-10926	CS-O
		Doersch, G.A.							P-51	43-24810	CS-J
June 10 1944	368	Drake, O.P.	2.00	Me 109s					P-51C	42-103329	CV-Z
	369	Cranfill, N.K.	1	RR Tunnel					P-51		IV-
	370	Doersch, G.A.	1.00	Me 109					P-51B	42-106580	CS-I
		Ambrose, V.W.					1.00	Me 109	P-51B	43-7013	CS-E
		McKee, D.D.	4	Boxcars			1	RR Track	P-51B	42-106799	CS-Y
		Lancaster, R.							P-51B	43-24791	CS-D
		Ambrose, V.W.							P-51B	43-7013	CS-E
		Bateman, P.H.							P-51B	42-106894	CS-P
		Hastings, W.H.							P-51B	43-6826	CS-W
		Doersch, G.A.							P-51B	42-106580	CS-I
		Callahan, R.M.					1	Elec. Loco	P-51B	42-106716	CS-L
		Fogg, H.L.					5	Boxcars	P-51B	43-6879	CS-T
		Newburg, W.R.							P-51B	42-106474	CS-M
		Rabb, R.O.					1	Med. Tank	P-51B	42-106805	CS-F
		Lemmens, A.T.					1	Med. Tank	P-51B	42-106704	CS-H
		Borg, R.M.	2	Trucks					P-51B	42-106749	CS-M
		Hipsher, C.W.	1	Truck					P-51B	42-106935	CS-U
June 11 1944	370	Hipsher, C.W.	1	RR Station					P-51B	42-106935	CS-U
		Cunningham, C.	2	Oil Cars					P-51B	42-106805	CS-F
		Lancaster, R.	1	Truck			1	Horsedrawn Caisson	P-51		CS-
		Hollis, H.D.							P-51B	42-106749	CS-M
		Ambrose, V.W.							P-51B	43-7013	CS-E
		Downing, J.L.							P-51B	42-106580	CS-I
		Fogg, H.L.	1	RR Track					P-51B	43-6879	CS-T
		Hastings, W.H.							P-51B	42-106799	CS-Y
		Callahan, R.M.					3	Boxcars	P-51B	42-106716	CS-L
		Newburg, W.R.							P-51B	43-24791	CS-D
		Callahan, R.M.	1	Truck			2	Trucks	P-51B	42-106716	CS-L
		Newburg, W.R.	2	Trucks			1	Truck	P-51B	43-24791	CS-D
		Doersch, G.A.	1	Truck	6	Occupants of Staff Car	1	Staff Car	P-51B	43-24810	CS-J
		McNeill, J. Jr.	1	Boxcar			1	Truck	P-51B	42-106692	CS-T
			1	Flatcar			1	RR Track			
			1	Truck							

DATE	SQ	PILOT	NO.	DEST.	NO.	PROB.	NO.	DAM.	A/C	SER. NO.	CODE
		Lemmons, A.T.	1	Gun Carrier			2	Trucks	P-51B	42-106941	CS-B
							1	Jeep			
							1	Civilian Car			
		Bateman, P.H.					1	Truck	P-51B	42-106894	CS-P
							1	Staff Car			
June 12 1944	369	Hess, L.D.	2	Fw190s					P-51		IV-
		Irvine, C.S.					1	Me109(g)	P-51B	42-106803	IV-A
							1	Hangar			
							1	Light Tower			
June 20 1944	369	Burton, H.C.	.5	Me410					P-51B	42-106670	IV-C
		Perrin, G.M.	.5						P-51	?-6730	IV-R
	370	Murphy, J.B.					1	Train+Loco	P-51D	44-13513	CS-A
		Ambrose, V.W.	1	Truck					P-51C	42-103319	CS-R
		McNeill, J. Jr.					1	Marsh. Yard	P-51B	42-106692	CS-T
		Baker, W.K. Jr.					1	Loco	P-51B	42-106941	CS-B
							1	Flak Tower			
		Grimes, H.E.	2	Tank Cars			1	Loco	P-51B	42-106799	CS-X
			1	Truck			3	Tank Cars			
		Callahan, R.	1	Tank Car			2	Locos	P-51B	42-106716	CS-L
							5	Tank Cars			
							1	Truck			
		Borg, R.M.					1	Train+Loco	P-51B	42-106749	CS-M
							1	Marsh. Yard			
		Downing, J.L.					1	Marsh. Yard	P-51B	42-106580	CS-I
		Doersch, G.A.	1	Truck			1	Loco	P-51B	42-106935	CS-U
							1	Staff Car			
		Newburg, W.R.					1	Train+Loco	P-51B	43-4791	CS-P
							1	Marsh. Yard			
June 21 1944	368	Lubien, J.J.					2	T/E/AC(g)	P-51B	42-106929	CV-B
		Tyrrell, A.R.	1	Me410(g)					P-51		CV-
			1	Fw189(g)							
			1	Me110(g)							
July 11 1944	370	O'Shea, J.H.	1	Loco					P-51B	42-106799	CS-Y
		Baker, W.K. Jr.					3	Locos	P-51B	43-6461	CS-Q
July 17 1944	370	Siltamaki, R.					1	Loco	P-51B	43-12147	CS-W
							20	Boxcars			
							2	Trucks			
		Buchanan, W.	1	Truck			1	Loco	P-51B	42-106894	CS-P
							2	Boxcars			
							2	Trucks			
							?	Sheep			
		Reese, L.C.					2	Locos	P-51B	42-106479	CS-M
		Hipsher, C.W.	6	Oil Tank Cars			2*	Locos	P-51D	44-13529	CS-D
			1	Truck							
		Shortness, G.					5*	Locos	P-51B	42-106902	CS-C
							2	Tank Cars			
		Windmiller, D.	15	Tank Cars			1*	Loco	P-51B	43-6961	CS-L
							2	Trucks			

*5 Locos strafed by three pilots in overlapping claims

DATE	SQ	PILOT	NO.	DEST.	NO.	PROB.	NO.	DAM.	A/C	SER. NO.	CODE
		Cunningham, C.	1	Truck			2	Trucks	P-51B	42-106704	CS-H
		Tilton, E.W.	2	Trucks			2	Locos	P-51B	42-106805	CS-F
		Caid, V.L.	1	Truck			3	Trucks	P-51D	44-13513	CS-A
July 20 1944	370	Baker, W.K. Jr.	1	Me109			1	Fw190	P-51B	43-6461	CS-Q
		Reese, L.C.					1	Me109	P-51B	43-7013	CS-E
July 21 1944	368	McGeever, T.J.	2	Locos			?	Boxcars	P-51C	42-103386	CV-N
		Gilmore, C.R.							P-51B	42-106995	CV-Q
		Cherry, W.J.							P-51B	42-106436	CV-T
	HQ	Tacon, A.P. Jr.					1	T/E/AC(g)	P-51D	44-13404	CS-Z
	370	Murphy, J.B.	1	Me109					P-51D	44-13513	CS-A
		Siltamaki, R.W.	1	Ju52(g)			3	He111s(g)	P-51B	43-12147	CS-W
			1	Ju88(g)			4	T/E/AC(g)			
		Wiley, W.W.	1	Ju88(g)			10	Ju88s(g)	P-51D	44-13604	CS-U
							1	Loco			
							2	Oil Storage Tanks			
		Reese, L.C.	1	Ju88(g)					P-51B	43-7013	CS-E
July 24 1944	368	Kelsey, J.P.					1	T/E/AC(g)	P-51D	44-13762	CV-D
		Chatfield, D.W.					2	T/E/AC(g)	P-51C	42-103318	CV-U
	HQ	Tacon, A.P. Jr.					1	T/E/AC(g)	P-51D	44-13404	CV-Z
	370	Callahan, R.M.	1	S/E/Biplane					P-51C	42-103394	CS-B
		Newburg, W.R.	1	S/E/Biplane			1	Hangar	P-51B	42-106805	CS-F
							?	Boxcars			
		Tilton, E.W.	1	S/E/Biplane			1	Hangar	P-51D	44-13513	CS-A

DATE	SQ	PILOT	NO.	DEST.	NO.	PROB.	NO.	DAM.	A/C	SER. NO.	CODE
July 26 1944	370	Borg, R.M.	4	Locos					P-51B	42-106878	CS-O
		Lancaster, R.	1	Boxcar					P-51D	44-13529	CS-D
		Williams, T.A.	2	Vehicles					P-51B	43-6461	CS-Q
		Hastings, W.H.							P-51B	42-106851	CS-X
		McNeil, J.W. Jr.							P-51D	44-13893	CS-E
		Ramser, G.E.							P-51B	43-24778	CS-H
July 28 1944	370	Hipsher, C.W.	1	Loco					P-51D	44-13604	CS-U
		Shofitt, J.C.	1	Loco					P-51B	42-106894	CS-H
		Tuchscherer, D.	1	Loco					P-51D	44-13996	CS-M
Aug 4 1944	368	Swanson, W.H.					1	Armed Trawler	P-51		CV-
		Chatfield, D.W.						(Schooner)	P-51		CV-
		Cherry, W.J.							P-51		CV-
		Keesey, J.S.							P-51		CV-
	370	Baker, W.K. Jr.	1.00	Me110					P-51B	43-6461	CS-Q
	369	Burt, H.R.	1.00	Me110					P-51C	42-103799	IV-F
		Holliday, F.W.					1	Me109	P-51C	42-103785	IV-K
		Pezda, E.F.	1.00	Me109					P-51D	44-13301	IV-B
		Sjoblad, E.L.	1.00	Me109					P-51B	42-12434	IV-P
		Taylor, L. Jr.	1.00	Fw190					P-51D	44-13689	IV-H
			1	Loco							
Aug 5 1944		Pezda, E.F.	1	Loco					P-51D	44-13301	IV-B
		Crenshaw, C.J.							P-51D	44-13606	IV-I
		Mejaski, J.W.							P-51B	42-103793	IV-G
		Hutton, J.F.							P-51B	42-106916	IV-D
Aug 6 1944	369	Thacker, R.L.	1	Loco			55	RR Cars	P-51		IV-
		Kruger, C.L.							P-51		IV-
		McCluskey, P.E.							P-51		IV-
		Bur, T.G.							P-51		IV-
	370	Ramser, G.E.	1	Loco			4	Boxcars	P-51D	44-13966	CS-K
		Murphy, J.B.					2	Coal Cars	P-51B	42-106799	CS-Y
		Caid, V.L.							P-51B	43-24799	CS-H
Aug 7 1944	368	Forehand, W.C.					1	Tank	P-51		CV-
		Beal, E.J.							P-51		CV-
		Cook, E.C.							P-51		CV-
Aug 8 1944	368	Keesey, J.S.	1	Fw190			3	Fw190s	P-51B	42-106581	CV-V
		Cavanaugh, C.J.					1	Fw190	P-51C	42-103197	CV-Y
		Britton, E.F.					2	Trucks	P-51		CV-
		Hatter, R.B.							P-51		CV-
		Barth, M.B.							P-51		CV-
		Boyd, R.A. Jr.							P-51		CV-
	370	Shoffit, J.C.	1	Truck			6	Boxcars	P-51B	42-106692	CS-T
		Connelly, D.D.							P-51D	44-14096	CS-V
		Connelly, D.D.	1	Staff Car			2	Flak Towers	P-51D	44-14096	CS-V
		O'Shea, J.H.	5	Trucks					P-51D	44-13633	CS-R
		Ramser, G.E.							P-51B	43-24778	CS-H
		Buchanan, W.E.							P-51B	42-106894	CS-P
		Wilson, J.W.							P-51D	44-13604	CS-U
		Cunningham, C.	1	Truck					P-51B	42-106704	CS-H
		Vos, B.J. Jr.							P-51D	44-13645	CS-M
		Lux, F.O.							P-51D	44-14948	CS-J
		Newburg, W.R.					20	Boxcars	P-51D	44-14038	CS-G
		Tilton, E.W.					1	Truck	P-51B	42-106902	CS-C
		York, R.M.							P-51D	44-13893	CS-E
		Merry, M.S.							P-51D	44-13529	CS-D
Aug 9 1944	368	Cook, E.C.					1	Me109	P-51B	43-12478	CV-P
		Keesey, J.S.			1	Fw190			P-51B	42-106581	CV-V
	370	Tilton, E.W.	1	Me109			1	Me109	P-51D		CS-
		Jones, C.W. Jr.	1	Me109			1	Me109	P-51D	44-13529	CS-D
		Lux, F.O.	1	Me109					P-51D	44-13893	CS-E
		Murphy, J.B.	1	Fw190					P-51D	44-13604	CS-U
		York, R.M.	1	Me109					P-51B	42-106862	CS-U
		Wilson, J.W.			1	Me109			P-51B	42-24778	CS-H
Aug 10 1944	369	Keur, J.E.	2	Locos					P-51B	43-12439	IV-Q
		Keur, J.E.	2	Locos			2	Locos	P-51B	43-12439	IV-Q
		Pezda, E.F.							P-51		IV-
		Buniowski, J.F.							P-51		IV-
		Crenshaw, C.J.							P-51		IV-
		Stevens, J.D.					3	Locos	P-51		IV-
		Mejaski, J.W.							P-51		IV-
		Perrin, G.M.							P-51		IV-
		Taylor, L.G.					3	Locos	P-51		IV-
		Suttle, F.C.							P-51		IV-
		Thorne, E.J.							P-51		IV-
		Melrose, D.S.							P-51		IV-
		Cuzner, H.F.							P-51		IV-

		Cuzner, H.F.	3	RR Cars					P-51		IV-
		Deen, G.C.							P-51		IV-
	370	Callahan, R.M.	2	RR Sheds			1	Loco	P-51D	44-13966	CS-K
		Jones, C.W. Jr.	1	Road Bridge			4	Boxcars	P-51D	44-13529	CS-D
		York, R.M.							P-51B	42-106894	CS-P
		O'Shea, J.H.							P-51B	42-106704	CS-H
		Newberg, W.R.							P-51D	44-13604	CS-U
		Wilson, J.W.							P-51B		CS-
		Vos, B.J. Jr.							P-51D	44-14948	CS-J
		Oakley, R.G.							P-51B	42-106799	CS-Y
		O'Shea, J.H.	1	Loco			1	Loco	P-51D	44-13893	CS-E
		Williams, T.A.	1	RR Tracks			2	Boxcars	P-51B	42-106580	CS-I
		Lux, F.O.	1	Switch Tower					P-51B	43-24778	CS-H
		McInnes, R.L.	1	RR Shed					P-51B	42-106862	CS-U
Aug 12 1944	369	Porter, R.W.	3	Boxcars			10	Boxcars	P-51		IV-
		Cuzner, H.F.							P-51		IV-
		Burt, H.R.							P-51		IV-
		Deen, G.C.							P-51		IV-
		Kruger, C.H.	16	Soldiers					P-51		IV-
		Kruger, C.H.	2	Trucks			25	Boxcars	P-51		IV-
		Mettel, A.F.							P-51		IV-
		Crenshaw, C.J.							P-51		IV-
		Melrose, D.S.							P-51		IV-
		Cusner, H.F.	3	Locos					P-51		IV-
		Deen, G.C.							P-51		IV-
	370	Newberg, W.R.					1	Loco	P-51D	44-13604	CS-U
		Rueschenberg, W.J.					1	Truck	P-51B	42-106692	CS-T
		Westall, F.E.							P-51B	42-106851	CS-X
		Lux, F.O.							P-51D	44-13633	CS-R
		O'Shea, J.H.							P-51D	44-13394	CS-B
		Buchanan, W.E.							P-51B	42-106704	CS-H
		Ramser, G.E.							P-51B	43-24778	CS-H
		O'Shea, J.H.					1	Truck	P-51D	44-13394	CS-B
		Lux, F.O.							P-51D	44-13633	CS-R
		Buchanan, W.E.							P-51B	42-106704	CS-H
		Westall, F.E.							P-51B	42-106851	CS-X
Aug 13 1944	370	McInnes, R.L.					10	Boxcars	P-51B	42-106580	CS-I
		Lux, F.O.					3	Trucks	P-51D	44-13966	CS-K
		Ramser, G.E.					1	Tank	P-51		CS-
		Westall, F.E.							P-51		CS-
		Hastings, W.H.							P-51B	42-106851	CS-X
		Wilson, J.W.							P-51B	42-106902	CS-C
		Zizka, L.A.							P-51D	44-13645	CS-M
		Lux, F.O.	1	Truck			2	Trucks	P-51D	44-13966	CS-K
		Cunningham, C.					1	Tank	P-51B	42-106580	CS-H
		Vos, B.J. Jr.					1	RR Track	P-51D	44-13633	CS-R
		O'Shea, J.H.					2	RR Tracks	P-51D	44-14948	CS-J
		McInnes, R.L.					1	Water Tower	P-51B	42-106580	CS-I
							1	Tank			
		Johnson, E.G.					2	RR Tracks	P-51B	42-106692	CS-T
		McNeil, J.W. Jr.					1	Flak Tower	P-51D	44-13893	CS-E
		Oakley, R.G.					1	Truck	P-51B	42-106799	CS-Y
		Merry, M.S.							P-51D	44-14096	CS-V
		Hastings, W.H.	2	Trucks			1	RR Intersection	P-51B	42-106851	CS-X
		Wilson, J.W.					1	Tank	P-51B	42-106902	CS-C
		Zizka, L.A.							P-51D	44-13645	CS-M
		York, R.M.					1	Highway Bridge	P-51D	44-13604	CS-U
		McInnes, R.L.							P-51B	43-24778	CS-H
		Buchanan, W.E.							P-51B	42-106894	CS-P
		Oakley, R.G.							P-51B	42-106799	CS-Y
Aug 14 1944	369	Pezda, E.F.	1	Loco					P-51		IV-
		Hughes, J.E.							P-51		IV-
		Buniowski, J.F.							P-51		IV-
	370	Merry, M.S.					24	Boxcars	P-51B	42-106805	CS-F
Aug 16 1944	HQ	Cranfill, N.K.	1	Me109					P-51D	44-13301	IV-B
	370	Lux, F.O.	1	Me109					P-51D	44-14948	CS-J
		Murphy, J.B.	1	Me163					P-51D	44-13966	CS-K
		Jones, C.W. Jr.	1	Me163					P-51D	44-13529	CS-D
		Shoffit, J.C.					1	Me163	P-51B	42-106692	CS-T
Aug 17 1944	369	Perrin, G.M.	6	Locos					P-51		IV-
			2	Ammo Trucks							
		Hutton, J.F.					1	Loco	P-51		IV-
							10	Boxcars			

DATE	SQ	PILOT	NO.	DEST.	NO.	PROB.	NO.	DAM.	A/C	SER. NO.	CODE
		Campbell, R.W.	1	Loco					P-51		IV-
			1	Truck							
			1	Trailer							
			1	Flak Tower							
	370	Hipsher, C.W.	3	Trucks					P-51D	44-13604	CS-U
			1	Armored Car							
		Burgsteiner, W.D.	3	Boxcars			1	Loco	P-51D	44-14062	CS-Q
		Zizka, L.A.							P-51D	44-13645	CS-M
		Hastings, W.H.							P-51B	42-106851	CS-X
		Merry, M.S.							P-51B	42-106805	CS-F
		Vos, B.J. Jr.	5-7	Ammo Cars			4	Locos	P-51B	42-106704	CS-H
		York, R.M.	10	Vehicles			30	Oil Tank Cars	P-51D	44-13966	CS-K
		McAllister, J.	1	RR Track			1	Truck	P-51D	44-14038	CS-G
		Williams, T.A.							P-51B	42-10692	CS-C
		Shoffit, J.C.					3	Trucks	P-51B	42-106692	CS-T
		McInnes, R.L.	1	Highway Bridge					P-51B	42-106862	CS-U
		York, R.M.	1	Truck					P-51D	44-13966	CS-K
Aug 18 1944	369	Burtner, R.L.	3	Me109s(g)			1	Ju88(g)	P-51B	43-2186	IV-R
							1	Ju52(g)			
							4-5	Gun Emplacements			
		Crenshaw, C.J.	1	Ju88(g)			1	Ju88(g)	P-51D	44-13606	IV-I
			1	Ju52(g)							
		Pezda, E.F.					2	Ju88s(g)	P-51D	44-13301	IV-B
Aug 24 1944	368	Britton, E.F.	1	Loco					P-51B	42-106611	CV-K
		Barth, M.B.							P-51C	42-103898	CV-A
		Barth, M.B.					1	Armed Trawler	P-51C	42-103898	CV-A
Aug 25 1944	368	Archibald, D.	1	S/E/AC(g)			1	Destroyer	P-51D	44-13404	CV-Z
			1	Loco							
Aug 27 1944	368	Cavanaugh, C.J.	1	Loco			5	Passenger Cars	P-51C	42-103197	CV-Y
							1	Tugboat			
		Archibald, D.B.	1	Loco					P-51B	43-12145	CV-W
		Archibald, D.B.	2	Locos					P-51B	43-12145	CV-W
		King, B.H.							P-51C	42-103898	CV-A
		Kosc, G.J.							P-51B	42-106693	CV-M
	369	Pezda, E.F.	1	Loco			1	Barge	P-51D	44-13301	IV-B
		Hutton, J.F.	1	Loco					P-51D	44-13520	IV-U
		Pezda, E.F.	2	Locos			3	Tugboats	P-51D	44-13301	IV-B
		Crenshaw, C.J.	1	Tugboat					P-51D	44-13606	IV-I
		Hutton, J.F.							P-51D	44-13520	IV-U
		Porter, R.W.							P-51B	42-106853	IV-V
		Crenshaw, C.J.					5	Passenger Cars	P-51D	44-13606	IV-I
		Campbell, R.W.	2	Locos					P-51D	44-13336	IV-Y
		Hobson, K.L.							P-51C	42-103789	IV-F
		Burt, H.R.							P-51C	42-103793	IV-M
	370	Zizka, L.A.	1	T/E/AC					P-51D	44-13394	CS-B
		Vos, B.J. Jr.					1	Loco	P-51D	44-13966	CS-K
		Welch, E.L.					14	RR Cars	P-51B	42-106894	CS-P
		York, R.M.					1	Tugboat	P-51D	44-13893	CS-E
		Sundheim, P.E.					1	Switch House	P-51B	42-106580	CS-I
		Jones, C.R. Jr.	1	Loco			4	Boxcars	P-51D	44-13529	CS-D
		O'Shea, J.H.	5	Locos			39	Boxcars	P-51D	44-14122	CS-W
		McInnes, R.L.							P-51D	42-106862	CS-U
		Jones, C.W. Jr.							P-51D	44-13529	CS-D
		Rueschenburg, W.J.							P-51D	44-15067	CS-L
		Hastings, W.H.	2	Locos			15	Boxcars	P-51B	42-106851	CS-X
		McAllister, J.	2	Trucks					P-51D	44-14038	CS-G
		Ramser, G.E.							P-51D	44-14778	CS-H
		Zizka, L.A.							P-51D	44-13394	CS-B
Aug 28 1944	368	Fladmark, O.R.	1	Ju52(g)			6	RR Cars	P-51B	42-106879	CV-R
			1	Loco							
		Kelsey, J.P.	3	Locos			15	Boxcars	P-51C	43-103943	CV-Q
		Gilmore, C.R.	1	Truck			5	Pass. Cars	P-51B	42-106727	CV-F
		Gordon, J.T.	2	Soldiers			3	Trucks	P-51B	43-12433	CV-C
		Kasper, B.D.					1	Armored Car	P-51B	42-106809	CV-H
		King, B.H.	1	Loco					P-51C	42-103898	CV-A
		Haas, J.H.	1	Loco					P-51B	42-106581	CV-V
		King, B.H.	3	Locos			25-30	Boxcars	P-51C	42-103898	CV-A
		Haas, J.H.					26	Pass. Cars	P-51B	42-106581	CV-V
		Olson, P.E.					4	Oil Tanker Cars	P-51B	42-106917	CV-J
		Archibald, D.B.	1	Loco					P-51C	42-103669	CV-I
			1	Truck							
		Cook, E.C.					2	Locos	P-51B	43-12478	CV-P
							6	Pass. Cars			
							2	Boxcars			

	369	Crenshaw, C.J.	3	Locos			2	Locos	P-51D	44-13606	IV-I
		Magee, R.E.	2	Boxcars			35	Boxcars	P-51B	42-106680	IV-J
		Majeski, J.W.	1	Truck					P-51D	44-13390	IV-N
		Holliday, F.W.	1	Trailer					P-51B	43-24798	IV-T
		Campbell, R.W.	4	Locos			10	Boxcars	P-51D	44-13336	IV-Y
		Suttle, F.C.	5	Boxcars			7	Trucks	P-51B	43-24756	IV-V
		Parsons, J.R.	1	Staff Car					P-51B	42-106803	IV-A
		Bur, T.G.	8	Trucks					P-51B	43-12434	IV-P
		Bur, T.G.	1	Flak Gun					P-51B	43-12434	IV-P
		Taylor, L.G.	1	Loco			1	Loco	P-51D	44-13689	IV-H
		Deen, G.C.	2	Boxcars			12	Boxcars	P-51C	42-103799	IV-F
		Gaines, R.S. Jr.					2	Troop Cars	P-51C	42-103793	IV-G
		Holliday, F.W.							P-51B	43-24798	IV-T
		Deen, G.C.	1	Loco			1	Loco	P-51C	42-103799	IV-F
		Gaines, R.S. Jr.	2	Boxcars			5	Boxcars	P-51C	42-103793	IV-G
		Holliday, F.W.							P-51B	43-24798	IV-T
		Ralston, G. Jr.	1	Train+Loco					P-51D	44-13520	IV-U
		Perrin, G.M.							P-51B	43-12444	IV-X
		Hughes, J.E.							P-51B	42-106853	IV-V
		Cannon, D.E.							P-51D	44-13301	IV-B
		Ralston, G. Jr.					7	Boxcars	P-51D	44-13520	IV-U
		Hughes, J.E.					3	Barges	P-51D	42-106853	IV-V
	370	McNeil, J.W. Jr.	7	Locos			12	Boxcars	P-51D	44-13893	CS-E
		Johnson, E.G.	1	Oil Storage Tank			1	Round House	P-51D	44-15067	CS-L
		Jones, C.W. Jr.							P-51D	44-14948	CS-S
		Shoffit, J.C.							P-51D	44-14096	CS-V
		York, R.M.	10	Boxcars			2	Locos	P-51D	44-13966	CS-K
		Lux, F.O.					30	Boxcars	P-51D	44-14122	CS-W
		Oakley, R.G.					1	Truck	P-51D	44-13394	CS-B
		Staup, H.A.					1	Trailer	P-51B	42-106894	CS-P
							1	Switch House			
		Vos, B.A. Jr.	3	Locos			33	RR Cars	P-51D	44-13645	CS-M
		Zizka, L.A.					5	Vehicles	P-51B	42-106851	CS-X
		Ramser, G.E.							P-51B	43-24778	CS-H
		Lamont, J.W.							P-51D	44-13604	CS-U
Sep 8 1944	368	Ashenmacher, J.	1.00	Ju 52(g)			1.00	Ju 52(g)	P-51B	43-12433	CV-C
		Gilmore, C.R.	1.00	Ju 52(g)					P-51B	42-106727	CV-F
		Baker, C.F. Jr.	0.50	Ju 52(g)					P-51B	44-14081	CV-E
		Benefiel, R.E.	0.50						P-51B	42-106611	CV-K
		Gilmore, C.R.	3	Locos			1	Loco	P-51B	42-106727	CV-F
		Baker, G.F. Jr.	1	Half-Track			1	River Transport	P-51D	44-14081	CV-E
		Benefiel, R.E.	1	Field Piece					P-51B	42-106611	CV-K
		Bartlett, C.L.							P-51C	42-103669	CV-I
	369	Crenshaw, C.J.	5	Locos					P-51D	44-13606	IV-I
		Magee, R.E.	2	Trucks					P-51B	42-106680	IV-J
		Mejaski, J.W.							P-51D	44--14117	IV-M
		Jenner, R.H.							P-51D	44-14218	IV-X
		Buniowski, J.F.	1	Loco			5	Boxcars	P-51		IV-
		Keur, J.E.							P-51		IV-
		Prewitt, L.H.							P-51		IV-
		Bruening, J.F.	1	Loco			3	Trucks	P-51		IV-
		Mettel, A.F.					1	Radar Station	P-51		IV-
	370	Hastings, W.H.	3	Locos			2	Locos	P-51		CS-
							2	Trucks			
							1	Trailer			
		Rueschenburg W.					1	Loco	P-51		CS-
		Vos, B.J. Jr.	1	Loco			1	Loco	P-51		CS-
		Staup, H.A.	8	Trucks			1	RR Car	P-51		CS-
		Oakley, R.G.					3	Trucks	P-51		CS-
		Newburg, W.							P-51		CS-
		York, R.M.	2	Locos					P-51		CS-
		Welch, E.L.	1	Truck					P-51		CS-
			1	German Soldier							
		Pezda, E. F. (369)	1	Loco			2	Locos	P-51		IV-
		Murray, J.W.							P-51		IV-
		Johnson, E.G.							P-51		IV-
		Rueschenburg, W.							P-51		IV-
		Jones, C.W. Jr.	5	Locos			1	Locos	P-51		CS-
		Williams, T.A.	2	RR Cars			20	RR Cars	P-51		CS-
		Ramser, G.A.	1	Motorcycle			1	Motorcycle	P-51		CS-
		Wilson, J.W.	2	Motorcycle Drivers							
			5	Trucks							
Sep 9 1944	369	Burt, H.R.	1	Loco					P-51		IV-
Sep 10 1944	369	Hobson, K.L.	1	S/E/AC*			1	S/E/AC	P-51B	42-106680	IV-J

Identified by the author as a F+W C-3603, Read Mission Text.

DATE	SQ	PILOT	NO.	DEST.	NO.	PROB.	NO.	DAM.	A/C	SER. NO.	CODE
	370	Murray, W.C.	1	Auto			1	Truck	P-51		CS-
		McAllister, J.W.	1	Truck			1	Trailer	P-51		CS-
		Hastings, W.H.					?	Bldgs.	P-51		CS-
Sep 11 1944	368	Benefiel, R.E.					2	Me109s	P-51B	42-106917	CV-J
		Flack, J.O.	.5	Me109					P-51D	44-13786	CV-B
		Lambright, C.	.5	Me109					P-51D	44-14131	CV-T
			2	Locos							
		Flack, J.O.	1	Oil Tank Car					P-51D	44-13786	CV-B
		Lambright, C.	1	Loco					P-51D	44-14131	CV-T
		Lewis, W.H.					1	Me109	P-51B	43-24764	CV-B
		Kysely, A.F.	3	Locos			1	Fw190	P-51B	42-106809	CV-H
		Barnett, L.E.	2	Fw190s	1	Fw190			P-51D	44-13404	CV-Z
		Gilmore, C.R.	1	Fw190					P-51B	42-106727	CV-F
		King, B.H.	2	Fw190s					P-51D	44-14329	CV-X
			1	Me109							
		Baker, G.F. Jr.	2	Fw190s					P-51D	44-14081	CV-E
	369	Klem, T.J.					1	Me109	P-51D	44-13301	IV-B
		Holliday, F.W.	1	Me109					P-51D	44-14307	IV-P
		Keur, J.E.	1	Me109					P-51D	44-14432	IV-Q
		Perrin, G.M.	2	Fw190s	1	Me109			P-51D	44-14218	IV-X
		Crenshaw, C.J.	2	Me109s					P-51D	44-13606	IV-I
			1	S/E/AC(g)							
		Parsons, J.W.	1	Me109					P-51D	44-14127	IV-E
		Ralston, G.W.	1	Fw190					P-51D	44-13520	IV-R
			1	Me109							
		Gaines, R.L. Jr.			1	Me109			P-51C	42-103793	IV-G
		Mejaski, J.W.	2	Ju88s(g)			3	Ju88s(g)	P-51D	44-14117	IV-M
		Parsons, J.R.	1	Ju88(g)			3	Ju88s(g)	P-51D	44-14216	IV-Z
			1	Ju188(g)			3	Ju188s(g)			
		Holloman, I.B.	1	Loco			1	Loco	P-51D	44-13689	IV-H
							4	Boxcars			
	370	O'Shea, J.H.	1	Fw190					P-51D	44-13071	CS-W
		Wilson, J.W.	1	Me109			1	Fw190	P-51D	44-15067	CS-L
		Buchanan, W.E.	1	Me109			1	Ju88(g)	P-51B	42-106894	CS-P
		Jones, C.W. Jr.	4	Me109s			2	Me110s(g)	P-51D	44-13633	CS-R
			1	Ju88(g)			2	Ju88s(g)			
		Murray, W.C.	1	Me109					P-51D	44-14096	CS-X
			1	Ju88s(g)							
		Jones, C.W. Jr.					.5	He177(g)	P-51D	44-13633	CS-R
		Murray, W.C.					.5	He177(g)	P-51D	44-14096	CS-X

For its actions on 11 Sep 1944 the 359th Fighter Group was awarded the Distinguished Unit Citation.

DATE	SQ	PILOT	NO.	DEST.	NO.	PROB.	NO.	DAM.	A/C	SER. NO.	CODE
Sep 12 1944	368	Carter, L.D.	1	Fw190			1	Fw190	P-51B	42-106581	CV-V
		Haas, J.H.	1	Fw190					P-51		CV-
		Hatter, R.B.	2	Fw190s			1	Me109	P-51D	44-14325	CV-N
		Barth, M.B.	1	Me109					P-51D	44-13786	CV-B
		Beal, E.J.	1	Me109					P-51D	44-13539	CV-O
		King, B.H.	1	Me109					P-51C	42-103898	CV-A
	369	Deen, G.C.	1	Fw190					P-51C	42-103799	IV-F
		Burt, H.R.	1	Fw190					P-51C	42-103785	IV-K
		Hughes, J.E.	1	Loco					P-51		IV-
	370	Connelly, D.D.	1	Me109					P-51D	44-14096	CS-V
			1	Fw190							
		McInnes, R.L.	2	S/E/AC(g)					P-51D	44-14192	CS-A
			1	Ju52(g)							
		Lamont, J.W.	2	S/E/AC(g)					P-51B	42-106894	CS-P
		Jones, C.W. Jr.	3	S/E/AC(g)					P-51D	44-14071	CS-W
Sep 18 1944	369	Parsons, J.R.	1	Fw190					P-51C	42-103793	IV-G
		Bur, T.G.	.5	Me109G					P-51D	44-13390	IV-N
		Keur, J.E.	.5						P-51D	44-14432	IV-Q
		Deen, G.C.	1	Fw190					P-51		IV-
		Crenshaw, C.J.	1	Me109					P-51D	44-13606	IV-I
Sep 28 1944	368	Cook, E.C.	2	Locos					P-51B	43-12478	CV-P
		Benefiel, R.E.	3	Locos					P-51D	44-14329	CV-X
			1	Truck							
			1	Trailer							
		Cook, E.C.	2	Locos					P-51B	43-12478	CV-P
		Benefiel, R.E.								P-51D	44-14329	CV-X
Oct 2 1944	370	Buchanan, W.E.	2	Locos					P-51B	42-106894	CS-P
		Welch, E.L.								P-51D	44-13645	CS-M
		Connely, D.D.	3	Locos					P-51D	44-14521	CS-A
		Zizka, L.A.	50	RR Cars					P-51D	44-14265	CS-Q
		Ramser, G.E.								P-51D	44-14429	CS-D
		Lamont, J.W.								P-51D	44-14179	CS-N
		Connely, D.D.	7	Locos					P-51D	44-14521	CS-A
		Zizka, L.A.								P-51D	44-14265	CS-Q

DATE	SQ	PILOT	NO.	DEST.	NO.	PROB.	NO.	DAM.	A/C	SER. NO.	CODE
Oct 6 1944	370	Doersch, G.A.	2	Fw190s			1	Fw190	P-51D	44-14159	CS-Y
		McCoskey, J.E.	1	Fw190					P-51B	42-106851	CS-X
		McInnes, R.L.	1	Fw190			1	Fw190	P-51D	44-14192	CS-S
Oct 7 1944	370	York, R.M.					.5	Bv 138(g)	P-51D	44-14159	CS-Y
		Johnson, E.G.					.5		P-51B	42-106851	CS-X
		Doersch, G.A.	.5	Bv 138(g)					P-51D	44-13914	IV-Y
		McCoskey, J.E.	.5						P-51D	44-14096	CS-V
		Welch, E.L.	2	Locos					P-51		CS-
Oct 24 1944	368	Adkins, B.N. Jr.	1	Fw190			1	Loco	P-51B	42-106693	CV-M
							1	Barge			
							1	Truck			
		Barth, M.B.	1	Fw190					P-51D	44-14131	CV-T
		Beaupre, R.V.	1	Loco			1	Loco	P-51D	44-14509	CV-X
							1	Barge			
							4	Tanks			
		Archibald, D.	6	Locos			10-15	RR Cars	P-51D	44-14652	CV-L
			2	RR Cars							
			1	Flak Gun							
			5	Soldiers							
		Gordon, J.T.	5	Locos			3	Boxcars	P-51D	44-14854	CV-Q
							10-15	RR Cars			
		Brown, R.L.	1	Loco			1	Switch House	P-51D	44-14854	CV-Q
			1	Flatcar							
			1	Boxcar							
			1	Truck							
			3	Tanks							
		Beal, E.J.	3	Locos			1	Truck	P-51C	42-103898	CV-A
		Boyd, R.A. Jr.	2	Locos			5	Boxcars	P-51D	44-14329	CV-X
			1	Flatcar							
			1	Truck							
		Flack, J.O.	2	Locos			1	Switch House	P-51D	44-13786	CV-B
			2	Trucks							
		Brown, R.L.	4	Locos					P-51D	44-14854	CV-Q
		Beal, E.J.	10	RR Cars					P-51C	42-103898	CV-A
		Flack, J.O.							P-51D	44-13786	CV-B
		Boyd, R.A. Jr.							P-51D	44-14329	CV-X
		Gilmore, C.R.	7	Locos			15	Flatcars w/Tanks	P-51D	44-14325	CV-N
		Carter, L.D.	1	Flatcar w/Tank			12	Boxcars	P-51D	44-14062	CV-C
		Fladmark, O.R.	1	Oil Tank Car					P-51D	44-14879	CV-R
		Kasper, B.D.	7	Trucks					P-51D	44-14566	CV-C
		Olson, P.E.	1	Truck			1	Truck	P-51D	44-14444	CV-J
	369	Matthew, H.L.	4	Locos					P-51B	43-24798	IV-T
		Hodges, F.S.							P-51D	44-14315	IV-L
		Erwin, R.D.							P-51B	42-106803	IV-A
		Parsons, J.R.							P-51C	42-103793	IV-G
		Collins, W.F.							P-51D	44-13610	IV-V
		Parsons, J.R.	2	Locos			10	RR Cars	P-51C	42-103793	IV-G
							1	Observation Tower			
		Hodges, F.S.	1	Loco					P-51D	44-14313	IV-L
		Erwin, R.D.							P-51B	42-106803	IV-A
		Parsons, J.R.							P-51C	42-103793	IV-G
		Collins, W.F.							P-51D	44-13610	IV-V
		Collins, W.F.	1	Loco *(shared with unknown pilots)*					P-51D	44-13610	IV-V
		Collins, W.F.	1	Loco					P-51D	44-13610	IV-V
		Tenebaum, H.							P-51B	42-106599	IV-W
		Gaines, R.S. Jr.	1	Loco					P-51		IV-
		Gaines, R.S. Jr.	1	Loco					P-51		IV-
		Klaver, R.R.							P-51		IV-
		Cannon, D.E.	1	Loco					P-51		IV-
		Matthew, H.L.	2	Locos					P-51B	43-24798	IV-T
		Ralston, G. Jr.							P-51		IV-
		Klem, T.J.							P-51		IV-
		Davison, R.W.	3	Locos			1	High Tension Line Support	P-51D	44-13606	IV-I
		Ralston, G. Jr.						5	Boxcars	P-51		IV-
		Klem, T.J.						5	Tanks			IV-
		Thomson, R.C.	2	Locos					P-51		IV-
		Jennings, W.C.							P-51		IV-
		Matthew, H.L.	4	Locos			25	Boxcars	P-51B	43-24798	IV-T
		Davison, R.W.	3	Trucks					P-51D	44-13606	IV-I
		Matthew, H.L.	2	Locos			10	Trucks			
			2	Trucks			20	Passenger Cars			
	370	Hodges, W.R.	1	Loco					P-51D	44-14427	CS-D
		Hastings, W.H.	1	Loco					P-51B	42-106851	CS-X

DATE	SQ	PILOT	NO.	DEST.	NO.	PROB.	NO.	DAM.	A/C	SER. NO.	CODE
		Hodges, W.R.	1	Loco					P-51D	44-14427	CS-D
		Hastings, W.H.	1	Truck					P-51B	42-106851	CS-X
		Connely, D.D.	6	Locos					P-51D	44-14168	CS-I
		Caid, V.L.					1	Loco	P-51		CS-
							1	Truck			
		Wolfe, A.E.	1	Loco			2	RR Wagons	P-51		CS-
		Johnson, E.G.					1	RR Car	P-51		CS-
		Ramser, G.E.	1	Freight Car			1	RR Station	P-51		CS-
		Lovette, J.K.					1	Unidentified Moving Target	P-51		CS-
Nov 2 1944	368	Baker, G.F. Jr.	.5	Me109					P-51D	44-14500	CV-E
		Fladmark, O.R.	.5						P-51D	44-11236	CV-B
		Baker, G.F. Jr.					1	Me109	P-51D	44-14500	CV-E
	369	Klaver, R.R.					1	Me109	P-51D	44-14534	IV-B
	370	Connely, D.D.	1	Me109					P-51D	44-14096	CS-V
		Cox, R.L.	1	Me109					P-51D	44-14983	CS-F
		Huskins, S.J.	.5	Me109 *(shared with pilot from 353rd FG)*					P-51D	44-14427	CS-D
		Wetmore, R.S.	2	Me109s					P-51D	44-14733	CS-L
Nov 4 1944	370	O'Shea, J.H.	1	Loco			2	Boxcars	P-51D	44-4185	CS-Q
			1	Horse							
		McKee, D.D.	1	Loco					P-51D	44-14521	CS-A
		Staup, H.A.							P-51D	44-14168	CS-I
		Zizka, L.A.							P-51D	44-14983	CS-F
Nov 8 1944	369	Burtner, R.L.	1	Loco					P-51		IV-
		Tenenbaum, H.					15	RR Cars	P-51		IV-
Nov 21 1944	368	Keesey, J.S.					1	Fw190	P-51D	44-11236	CV-B
		McGeever, T.J.	1	Fw190(g)					P-51D	44-14870	CV-W
	369	Crenshaw, C.J.	4	Fw190s	1	Fw190			P-51D	44-15016	IV-I
		Tenenbaum, H.	1	Fw190					P-51D	44-15007	IV-Z
	370	Cox, R.L.	3	Fw190s					P-51D	44-14979	CS-H
		Hodges, W.R.	2	Fw190s	1	Fw190	1	Fw190	P-51D	44-14427	CS-D
		Lamont, J.W.					1	Fw190	P-51D	44-14368	CS-Z
		Burgsteiner, W.			1	Fw190			P-51D	44-14192	CS-S
		Smith, T.P.	2	Fw190s			2	Fw190s	P-51D	44-13893	CS-E
		Caid, V.L.	2	Fw190s			1	Fw190	P-51D	44-14773	CS-G
		McKee, D.D.	1	Fw190					P-51D	44-14521	CS-A
		Staup, H.A.	2	Fw190s					P-51D	44-14168	CS-I
Nov 26 1944	HQ	Evans, R.W.	1	Me109			1	Me109	P-51D	44-14988	IV-E
Nov 27 1944	368	Cranfill, N.K.	2	Me109s					P-51D	44-15100	CV-Q
			1	Fw190							
		Daniels, R.H.			1	Fw190			P-51D	44-11236	CV-B
	369	Lancaster, R.T.			1	Me109			P-51D	44-14997	IV-U
	370	Windmiller, D.	2	Me109s					P-51D	44-14987	CS-C
		Wetmore, R.S.	3	Me109s					P-51D	44-14979	CS-H
		Marshall, F.R.	1	Me109					P-51D	44-14368	CS-Z
		York, R.M.	3	Me109s	1	Me109			P-51D	44-14630	CS-R
Dec 18 1944	368	Olson, P.E.	5	Fw190s					P-51D	44-14131	CV-T
		Archibald, D.	5	Fw190s			1	Fw190	P-51D	44-15555	CV-L
Dec 23 1944	368	Benefiel, R.E.	1	Me109					P-51D	44-14769	CV-A
		Cook, E.C.	1	Me109					P-51D	44-11222	CV-I
Dec 24 1944	368	Beal, E.J.	2	Fw190s	1	Fw190			P-51D	44-15618	CV-R
		Boyd, R.A.					1	Fw190	P-51D	44-14329	CV-X
	369	Kelly, J.J. III	1	Me109					P-51B	42-106476	IV-H
		Keur, J.E.					1	Me109	P-51K	44-11572	IV-I
		Thomson, B.H.	1	Me109					P-51D	44-15016	IV-I
	370	Hodges, W.R.	1	Fw190					P-51D	44-15543	CS-X
		Johnson, E.G.	2	Fw190s			2	Fw190s	P-51D	44-14773	CS-G
		Lemmens, A.T.	1	Fw190					P-51D	44-15521	CS-V
		Oakley, R.G.	1	Fw190					P-51D	44-14983	CS-F
		Wilson, J.W.	1	Fw190					P-51D	44-14179	CS-N
Dec 31 1944	368	Baker, G.F. Jr.	2	Fw190s					P-51D	44-14500	CV-E
	369	Collins, W.F.	1	Fw190					P-51D	44-11350	IV-Y
		Collins, W.F.	.5	Fw190					P-51D	44-11350	IV-Y
		Morris, A. Jr.	.5	Fw190					P-51	44-15394	IV-D
		Collins, W.F.	.5	Fw190					P-51D	44-11350	IV-Y
		Morris, A. Jr.	.5	Fw190					P-51D	44-15394	IV-D
		Morris, A. Jr.	1	Fw190					P-51D	44-15394	IV-D
	370	Johnson, E.G.	.5	Me109 *(shared with 4th FG pilot)*					P-51D	44-14773	CS-G
		Lemmens, A.T.	1	Me109					P-51D	44-15521	CS-V
		Lux, F.O.	1	Me109					P-51D	44-14987	CS-C
		Lux, F.O.	.5	Me109					P-51D	44-14987	CS-C
		Zizka, L.A.	.5	Me109					P-51D	44-14129	CS-S
		Ramser, G.E.					1	Me109	P-51D	44-13604	CS-U
		Wetmore, R.S.	1	Me109					P-51D	44-14733	CS-L
		Wetmore, R.S.	.5	Me109					P-51D	44-14733	CS-L
		Rueschenberg, W.	.5	Me109					P-51D	44-11350	CS-D

DATE	SQ	PILOT	NO.	DEST.	NO.	PROB.	NO.	DAM.	A/C	SER. NO.	CODE
		McCoskey, J.E.					1	Me109	P-51D	44-14521	CS-A
Jan 1 1945	368	Adkins, B.N. Jr.	1	Fw190					P-51C	42-103898	CV-A
		Carter, L.D.					1	Fw190	P-51D	44-15067	CV-C
		Kasper, B.D.	1	Me109					P-51K	44-11647	CV-F
	370	Wetmore, R.S.	1	Me109					P-51D	44-14773	CS-L
		York, R.M.	1	Fw190					P-51D	44-14159	CS-Y
Jan 14 1945	368	Ettlesen, C.E.					1	Loco	P-51K	44-11651	CV-V
							10	RR Cars			
							20	Vehicles			
	370	Wetmore, R.S.	4	Fw190s					P-51D	44-14733	CS-L
		Wetmore, R.S.	.5	Fw190					P-51D	44-14733	
		Rueschenberg, W.	.5	Fw190					P-51D	44-13604	CS-V
		Doersch, G.A.	2	Fw190s					P-51K	44-11760	CS-O
Jan 29 1945	368	Ferris, J.J. III	1	Vehicle			5	RR Cars	P-51K	44-11651	CV-V
							1	Staff Car			
		Bossu, M.F.					2	Trucks	P-51D	44-15096	CV-D
		Marron, J.T.					1	Vehicle	P-51K	44-11696	CV-G
		Baker, G.F. Jr.	1	Oil Tank Car			1	Loco	P-51D	44-14500	CV-E
		Brown, R.L.					10	Boxcars	P-51D	44-15371	CV-Z
		McCormack, J.W.					1	Oil Tank Car	P-51D	44-15618	CV-H
							1	Truck			
							1	Barge			
							1	Power Plant			
							1	High Tension Tower			
		Denman, J.A.	3	Locos			10	RR Cars	P-51K	44-11758	CV-T
		Long, G.W.	1	Vehicle					P-51D	44-14650	CV-X
	369	Magee, R.E.					20	Boxcars	P-51D	44-15741	IV-Y
							10	Oil Tank Cars			
							1	Yellow Coupe			
							4-6	Fw190 Wings on Flatcar			
		Gaines, R.S. Jr.	2	Trucks			1	Truck	P-51D	44-11664	IV-G
		Kelly, J.J. III							P-51B	42-106476	IV-H
		Klem, T.J.							P-51D	44-15007	IV-Z
		Thomson, B.H.							P-51K	44-11658	IV-I
		Guggemos, R.J.					12	Boxcars	P-51D	44-15894	IV-D
		Holloman, I.B.					5	Oil Tank Cars	P-51D	44-14315	IV-L
		Guggemos, R.J.	1	Power House					P-51D	44-15894	IV-D
		Holloman, I.B.							P-51D	44-14315	IV-L
Feb 3 1945	368	Ettlesen, C.E.					6	Locos	P-51		CV-
		Carter, L.D.					25	RR Cars	P-51		CV-
		Martin, A.G.					2	Switch Towers	P-51		CV-
		Adkins, B.N.							P-51		CV-
Feb 9 1945	368	Ettlesen, C.E.	2	Locos			1	U/AC(g)	P-51K	44-11651	CV-V
		Boussu, M.F.	1	Loco			2	Power Houses	P-51D	44-15096	CV-D
							2	Power Lines			
		Doersch, G.A.	1	Loco					P-51D	44-13966	CS-K
		Newton, M.H.							P-51B	42-106826	CS-W
		Merry, M.S.					2	Boxcars	P-51D	44-15527	CS-Q
		Newcomer, E.S.					2	Boxcars	P-51D	44-13394	CS-B
Feb 11 1945	368	Brown, R.L.					3	Barges	P-51D	44-15371	CV-Z
		Benefiel, R.E.					3	Boats	P-51K	44-11657	CV-F
		Martin, A.G.					1	Castle	P-51D	44-14500	CV-E
		Ferris, J.J. III					1	Factory	P-51D	44-13721	CV-W
							2	RR Stations			
							1	Radar Tower			
		Denman, J.A.	2	Locos					P-51K	44-11758	CV-T
			1	Truck							
		Hunter, J.B.	1	Staff Car			1	Electric Loco	P-51D	44-14566	CV-C
		Madison, G.F.	1	Truck				& Train	P-51D	44-14650	CV-X
		Gordon, J.T.	1	Truck Driver			3	Trucks	P-51D	44-13762	CV-D
		Hanzalik, F.					12	Barges	P-51K	44-11696	CV-G
							1	Switch House			
		Cranfill, N.K.	4	Locos			4	Locos	P-51D	44-15717	CV-Q
		Dunmire, D.P.					15	Boxcars	P-51D	44-15618	CV-R
		McCormack, J.W.					1	Switch House	P-51D	44-13740	CV-A
		Marron, J.T.					2	RR Stations	P-51D	44-63689	CV-K
							1	Factory			
	369	Judkins, V.T.					2	Locos	P-51		IV-
							1	Marsh. Yard			
							1	Truck			
		Matthew, H.L.	1	Loco			1	Boxcar	P-51		IV-
		Montague, B.M.					1	Switch Tower	P-51		IV-
							1	RR Station			
		Davison, R.W.	2	Locos			1	HQ Car	P-51		IV-
			1	Truck			1	High Tension Line			

DATE	SQ	PILOT	NO.	DEST.	NO.	PROB.	NO.	DAM.	A/C	SER. NO.	CODE
		Collins, W.F.	1	Loco			3	Locos	P-51		IV-
		Cannon, D.E.	1	Soldier			14	Boxcars	P-51		IV-
		Morris, A.B. Jr.					3	Switch Towers	P-51		IV-
		Magee, R.E.					7	Oil Tank Cars	P-51		IV-
		McGehee, F.S.					3	Wagons	P-51		IV-
	370	Doersch, G.A.	3	Locos			1	Loco	P-51D	44-13966	CS-K
			2	Fuel Storage Tanks							
		Newton, M.H.					1	Loco	P-51D	44-14159	CS-Y
		Doersch, G.A.	2	Locos					P-51D	44-13966	CS-K
		Newton, M.H.							P-51D	44-14159	CS-Y
		Merry, M.S.					1	Loco	P-51D	44-15102	CS-T
		Newcomer, E.S.					25	Boxcars	P-51K	44-11574	CS-M
		Lyon, W.D.	8	Locos			4	Boxcars	P-51D	44-14987	CS-C
		Johnson, E.G.	4	Boxcars			5	Trucks	P-51D	44-14773	CS-G
		Morris, T.W.	4	Trucks			3	Trailers	P-51B	42-106826	CS-W
		Wolfe, A.E.					5	Switch Houses	P-51D	44-14979	CS-H
		Lemmens, A.T.	1	Loco			2	Locos	P-51D	44-15521	CS-V
		Shouse, R.E.	2	Tank Cars			8	Boxcars	P-51D	44-14129	CS-S
		Wilson, J.W.							P-51D	44-14179	CS-N
		Schector, H.L.							P-51D	44-14948	CS-J
		Johnson, E.G.	3	Locos			4	Boxcars	P-51D	44-14773	CS-G
			4	Boxcars							
Feb 14 1945	368	Homeyer, A.G.	2	Locos			20	Boxcars	P-51K	44-11797	CV-M
		Denman, J.A.							P-51K	44-11758	CV-T
		Long, G.W.							P-51D	44-13776	CV-Y
		Madison, G.F.							P-51K	44-11696	CV-G
		Benefiel, R.E.	2	Locos					P-51		CV-
			1	Vehicle							
Feb 21 1945	369	Morris, A.B.	1.00	Ju88(g)			1.00	Me410(g)	P-51K	44-11572	IV-I
			1	Gas Truck							
		Francis, R.M.					1.00	Me410(g)	P-51D	44-15242	IV-Q
		Thomson, R.C.	1	Wood A/C(g)			1.00	Fw190(g)	P-51D	44-14625	IV-F
							1.00	T/E/AC(g)			
		Pezda, E.F.	1.00	M/E/AC(g)					P-51K	44-11635	IV-B
		Hodges, F.S.					1.00	Fw200(g)	P-51D	44-14988	IV-E
		McGehee, F.S.					1.00	Fw200(g)	P-51D	44-15588	IV-R
							1.00	Me410(g)			
		Kelly, D.E.					1	Hangar	P-51D	44-15739	IV-J
Feb 22 1945	368	Doersch, G.A.	1	Loco			1	Boxcar	P-51D	44-15067	CV-C
		Way, J.L. Jr.	1	Truck					P-51D	44-15371	CV-Z
		Martin, A.G.	2	Trailers					P-51D	44-11236	CV-B
		Denman, J.A.	2	Locos			1	Boxcars	P-51K	44-11758	CV-T
			1	Ammo Car			1	Boat			
	369	Collins, W.F.	2.00	Ju88s(g)			1.00	Ju88(g)	P-51D	44-15242	IV-Q
		McGehee, F.S.	1.00	Ju88(g)			2.00	Ju88s(g)	P-51D	44-15215	IV-S
		Tenenbaum, H.					1	T/E/AC(g)	P-51D	44-14218	IV-X
							1	Horse & Cart			
							1	Tractor			
							2	Carts			
		Davison, R.W.	1	Loco					P-51D	44-15204	IV-C
		Davison, R.W.	1	Loco			2	Armored Cars	P-51D	44-15204	IV-C
		Klaver, R.R.	12	Boxcars					P-51D	44-15588	IV-R
		Millis, T.E.							P-51K	44-11636	IV-A
		Buniowski, J.	1	Loco					P-51		IV-
		Collins, W.F.					1	Ammo Dump	P-51D	44-15242	IV-Q
		McGehee, F.S.							P-51D	44-15215	IV-S
		Holliman, I.B.	2	Trucks					P-51		IV-
		Jennings, W.C.							P-51		IV-
		Cannon, D.E.							P-51		IV-
	370	Windmiller, D.					1.00	Me410(g)	P-51D	44-14179	CS-R
							1	Loco			
							1	Barge			
							2	Horses & Cart			
Feb 23 1945	368	Doersch, G.A.	2	Locos			15	Boxcars	P-51D	44-15067	CV-C
		Way, J.L. Jr.	1	Streamlined Car					P-51D	44-15371	CV-Z
		McCormack, J.	1	Passenger Car					P-51D	44-13740	CV-A
		Kruezman, H.B.							P-51D	44-15717	CV-Q
	369	Meyer, L.F.	1	Loco					P-51D	44-15394	IV-D
		Matthew, H.L.	1	Loco					P-51D	44-15081	IV-T
		Matthew, H.L.	2	Locos			8	Boxcars	P-51D	44-15081	IV-T
		Meyer, L.F.							P-51D	44-15100	IV-Q
		Francis, R.M.							P-51D	44-15242	IV-Q
		Hopkins, R.W.							P-51K	44-11572	IV-A
		Holliman, I.B.	2	Trucks					P-51D	44-15725	IV-V
		Cannon, D.E.							P-51D	44-15588	IV-R
		Jennings, W.C.							P-51K	44-11572	IV-I

DATE	SQ	PILOT	NO.	DEST.	NO.	PROB.	NO.	DAM.	A/C	SER. NO.	CODE
		Cannon, D.E.	1	Truck Driver					P-51D	44-15588	IV-R
Feb 25 1945	369	Pezda, E.F.	1	Loco			6	RR Cars	P-51K	44-11635	IV-B
		Patton, L.							P-51K	44-11658	IV-I
		Erwin, R.D.							P-51D	44-14117	IV-M
Feb 27 1945	370	McKee, D.D.	1	Loco			1	Switch Tower	P-51		CS-
		Shouse, R.E.							P-51		CS-
		Lemmens, A.T.							P-51		CS-
		Stepp, W.F.	1	Loco					P-51		CS-
			4-5	Military Personnel							
		Surowiec, E.L.						5	Boxcars	P-51		CS-
		Lovett, J.K.								P-51		CS-
		Lamont, J.W.								P-51		CS-
		Morris, T.W.								P-51		CS-
Feb 28 1945	368	Blackburn, G.	1	Me109(g)			1	Power Pylon	P-51K	44-12143	CV-H
			1	Truck			1	Factory			
		Martin, A.G.	1	Me109(g)			1	Truck	P-51D	44-14500	CV-E
		Collins, J.F.						1	Loco	P-51D	44-15711	CV-J
		Cooley, J.D. Jr.						2	Boxcars	P-51D	44-11236	CV-B
								1	Lumber Yard			
		Long, G.W.	1	Loco			4	Locos	P-51D	44-13776	CV-Y
								5	Boxcars			
	369	Cannon, D.E.	1	Vehicle			1	Radar Station	P-51D	44-15588	IV-R
		Lancaster, R.	1	Barn			1	Switch House	P-51D	44-14543	IV-P
								1	Military Camp			
		Francis, R.M.	2	Locos					P-51D	44-15242	IV-Q
			2	Vehicles							
		Guggemos, R.	1	Loco					P-51D	44-15514	IV-O
			6	Vehicles							
			?	Occupants of Staff Car							
		Francis, R.M.	4	Locos			5	Boxcars	P-51D	44-15242	IV-Q
		Guggemos, R.	1	Grain Elevator					P-51D	44-15514	IV-O
		Matthew, H.L.	1	Loco					P-51D	44-15081	IV-T
		Lindsay, D.G.						4	RR Cars	P-51D	44-15204	IV-C
		Pezda, E.F.	2	Vehicles			2	Vehicles	P-51D	44-14625	IV-F
		Stubblefield, C.								P-51D	44-15725	IV-V
		Magee, R.E.						30	RR Cars	P-51		IV-
								1	Vehicle			
		Gaines, R.S. Jr.						1	Truck	P-51		IV-
		Berndt, H.E.								P-51		IV-
		Thomson, B.H.	1	Loco					P-51		IV-
		Kelly, J.J. III	4	Horses			5	Passenger Cars	P-51		IV-
		Thomson, B.H.	2	Wagons			4	Boxcars	P-51		IV-
								1	Tugboat			
		Burtner, R.L.	1	Loco					P-51		IV-
		Sonderman, B.								P-51		IV-
	370	McKee, D.D.	1	Loco			10	Boxcars	P-51		CS-
		Shouse, R.E.	2	Boxcars			2	Switch Towers	P-51		CS-
		Lemmens, A.T.						1	House	P-51		CS-
		Schecter, H.L.						1	Factory	P-51		CS-
		Lux, F.O.	1	Loco			12	RR Cars	P-51		CS-
		Martin, A.G.								P-51		CS-
		Wolfe, A.E.	3	Boxcars			16	Boxcars	P-51		CS-
		Lamont, J.W.	2	Trucks			2	Trucks	P-51		CS-
			1	Civilian Car							
			2	Gestapo Men							
March 3 1945	368	Cowie, A.A.					1	S/E/AC(g)	P-51K	44-11696	CV-G
		Denman, J.A.	2	Locos			3	Passenger Cars	P-51D	44-72067	CV-R
		Cooley, J.D. Jr.						4	Boxcars	P-51D	44-15067	CV-C
		Long, G.W.								P-51D	44-13776	CV-Y
		Barber, K.E.								P-51D	44-14566	CV-C
		Collins, J.F. Jr.						2	Locos	P-51D	44-15711	CV-J
		Muzzy, R.G.						10	Boxcars	P-51K	44-11662	CV-A
		Way, J.L. Jr.						1	Switch House	P-51K	44-11797	CV-M
		McCormack, J.W.						1	Factory	P-51D	44-13740	CV-A
								1	Horsedrawn Wagon			
		Marron, J.T.						1	Factory	P-51		CV-
March 15 1945	370	Wetmore, R.S.	1	Me163					P-51D	44-15521	CS-V
March 18 1945*	369	Berndt, H.E.					1	Me109	P-51D	44-15007	IV-Z
		Cox, R.L.	1	Fw190					P-51D	44-72154	IV-N
		Gaines, R.S. Jr.	1	Me109					P-51K	44-11664	IV-G

As shown in official records for this day. Actual kills follow next

DATE	SQ	PILOT	NO.	DEST.	NO.	PROB.	NO.	DAM.	A/C	SER. NO.	CODE
March 18 1945		*On this date the 359th Fighter Group engaged a large group of Russian aircraft. The following pilots scored the victories listed below. This was the largest engagement with the Russians by the USAAF during World War II.*									
	368	Cranfill, N.K.	2	Yak-9s					P-51D		CV-
	369	Cox, R.L.	3	La-5s					P-51D	44-72154	IV-N
		Burtner, R.L.	1	Yak					P-51D	44-14718	IV-D
			2	Yaks(g)							
		McCormack, R.	1	Yak					P-51D		IV-
		Gaines, R.S. Jr.	1	Yak					P-51K	44-11664	IV-G
		McIntosh, R.W.	1	Yak					P-51D		IV-
		Berndt, H.E.			1			Yak-9		P-51D	44-15007	IV-Z
March 19 1945	368	Cranfill, N.K.	1	Me262			1	Me262	P-51D	44-15717	CV-Q
March 23 1945	368	Barber, K.E.	.5	Ar196					P-51D	44-72260	CV-E
		Doersch, G.A.	.5						P-51D	44-72406	CV-G
		Boussu, M.F.			1			He111(g)	P-51D	44-72143	CV-H
March 24 1945	369	Collins, W.F.	2	Me109s					P-51D	44-11350	IV-Y
		Kelly, D.E.	1	Me109					P-51D	44-72503	IV-F
		Kelly, D.E.	.5	Me109					P-51D	44-72503	IV-F
		Tenenbaum, H.	.5	Me109					P-51D	44-72154	IV-N
		Lancaster, R.	2	Me109s					P-51D	44-15215	IV-S
		Patton, L.			2			Me109s	P-51K	44-11635	IV-B
		Parsons, J.W.	1	Me109					P-51D	44-14127	IV-E
		Tenenbaum, H.	1	Me109					P-51D	44-72154	IV-N
		Thomson, B.H.	1	Me109					P-51K	44-116558	IV-I
		Thomson, R.C.	2	Me109s					P-51D	44-72780	IV-K
		McGehee, F.S.	2	Me109s					P-51D	44-72366	IV-D
	370	Wetmore, R.S.	2	Trucks	4			Locos	P-51		CS-
		Newcomer, E.S.			3			Staff Cars	P-51		CS-
		Leathley, E.H.							P-51		CS-
		Murray, J.J.							P-51		CS-

Capt. Robert W. Hopkins poses with Rene Burtner's P-51D Hubert, flown by Burtner on March 18, 1945, when he destroyed three Yak-9s. Before returning to East Wretham Burtner landed at St. Trond, Belgium, where his ammo was replenished and fresh film loaded in his gun camera. Only Nevin K. Cranfill still refuses to admit his part in the Russian incident and made sure no proof existed by having his gun-camera film burned. After finding the Russians flew against us in Korea such feelings of remorse are a bit misplaced. The Communists held no warm spot in their hearts for Americans.

DATE	SQ	PILOT	NO.	DEST.	NO.	PROB.	NO.	DAM.	A/C	SER. NO.	CODE
		Lux, F.O.					7	Trucks	P-51		CS-
		Ruggles, J.J.							P-51		CS-
		Semple, H.D.							P-51		CS-
		Staup, H.A.							P-51		CS-
		Lemmens, A.T.	1	Truck					P-51		CS-
		Giese, A. J. Jr.	1	Civilian Car					P-51		CS-
		Newton, M.H.	1	Vehicle					P-51		CS-
		Smith, T.P.							P-51		CS-
		Martin, J.C.	2	Trucks			4	Trucks	P-51		CS-
April 9 1945	368	Boussu, M.F.					1	Me262	P-51D	44-72413	CS-H
		Muzzy, R.C.					1	Me262	P-51D	44-13762	CV-D
		Muzzy, R.C.					.5	Me262	P-51D	44-13762	CV-D
		Rea, F. Jr.					.5		P-51B	42-106876	CV-F
		Levitt, L.J.	2	Ju88s(g)					P-51D	44-14652	CV-A
		Elliott, R.H.					2	Ju88s(g)	P-51K	44-11797	CV-M
		Doersch, G.A.	1	Fw190(g)			1	He 111(g)	P-51D	44-72067	CV-R
April 10 1945	368	Marron, J.T.					1	Me262	P-51D	44-13776	CV-Y
	369	Tenenbaum, H.	1	Me262					P-51D	44-72366	IV-D
		Guggemos, R.J.	1	Me262					P-51D	44-15514	IV-O
			2	Me109s(g)							
		Klaver, R.R.					1	Me262	P-51K	44-11664	IV-G
April 13 1945	368	Denman, J.A.	4	Me110s(g)					P-51D	44-72143	CV-H
			1	Loco							
		Barber, K.E.	30	Me110s(g0					P-51D	44-13762	CV-D
			1	S/E/AC(g)							
		Herb, J.W.	2	Me110s(g)					P-51D	44-72260	CV-E
			2	Do 217s(g)							
		Hunter, J.B.	1	He 111(g)					P-51D	44-72331	CV-C
		Madison, G.E.	1	Me210(g)					P-51D	44-11236	CV-B
			1	MeS/E/AC(g)							
		Ferris, J.J. III	1	Loco					P-51K	44-11662	CV-A
		Marshall, W.J.								P-51D	44-14566	CV-C
		Doersch, G.A.	3	Locos					P-51D	44-72281	CV-Z
		Long, G.W.								P-51D	44-13776	CV-Y
		Martin, A.G.								P-51D	44-11223	CV-O
		Rea, F. Jr.								P-51B	42-106876	CV-F
		Rea, F. Jr.	1	Loco					P-51B	42-106876	CV-F
	370	McKee, D.D.	2	Ar 196s(g)					P-51D	44-72823	CS-A
		Newton, M.H.	2	Ar 196s(g)					P-51D	44-14168	CS-O
			1	Loco							
		Merry, M.S.	8	Locos			3	Locos	P-51D	44-14983	CS-F
		Newcomer, E.	5	Oil Tank Cars			5	Oil Tank Cars	P-51D	44-13645	CS-M
		McAlevey, J.F.								P-51K	44-11574	CS-M
		Bellante, E.L.								P-51D	44-72208	CS-C
		Page, D.C.	2	Locos					P-51D	44-11348	CS-R
		Shouse, R.B.	1	Tugboat			4	Barges	P-51D	44-13893	CS-E
		Leathley, E.H.	1	Barge					P-51K	44-11760	CS-J
		Surowiec, E.L.					1	Tugboat	P-51D	44-14733	CS-L
		Schwartz, B.D.					4	Barges	P-51D	44-14521	CS-A
April 16 1945	368	Hunter, J.B.	1	Me109(g)			2	Me109s(g)	P-51D	44-72331	CV-C
		Marron, J.T.	2	Me109s(g)					P-51D	44-63689	CV-K
		McDonald, J.H.	2	Me109s(g)			1	Me109(g)	P-51D	44-13539	CV-O
April 17 1945	HQ	Baccus, D.A.	1	T/E/AC(g)			1	Me109(g)	P-51K	44-11685	CV-U
	369	Collins, W.F.	1	Fw190(g)					P-51D	44-72330	IV-N
	370	McKee, D.D.	1	Fw190(g)					P-51D	44-72823	CS-A
April 25 1945		*No claims made on the last combat mission flown by the 359th Fighter Group.*									

OPERATIONAL TOTALS IN THE EUROPEAN THEATER OF OPERATIONS

LENGTH OF OPERATIONS—17 months · TOTAL SORTIES FLOWN—13,455
LOSSES, INCLUDING ESCAPEES AND EVADERS—125 · BATTLE DAMAGED AIRCRAFT—228
AMMO EXPENDED—924,807 Rounds of Cal. 50 · BOMBS DROPPED—487 (500-lb.), 325 (250-lb.), 80 (100-lb.)
ENEMY AIRCRAFT DESTROYED IN THE AIR—255.5 · ENEMY AIRCRAFT DESTROYED ON THE GROUND—121.33
LOCOMOTIVES DESTROYED—335 · LOCOMOTIVES DAMAGED—147 (pilots named)
RR CARS DESTROYED—237 · RR CARS DESTROYED—1,119 (pilots named)
MOTOR VEHICLES DESTROYED—144

Note: Claims that are screened as a group are shared by the listed pilots.

359th F.C. Aircraft Serial Numbers

Production codes RA=Republic plant at Farmingdale, New York. RE=Republic plant at Evansville, Indiana. NA=North American at Inglewood, California. NT=North American at Dallas, Texas. Fuselage codes and A/C names given where known. Names separated by a comma denote a change while two different names connected by a+indicate names on opposite sides of the nose. Aircraft lost during operations are noted with a *. Three Mustangs interned in Sweden noted *Sweden.

P-47D-2-RA
42-22464*
42-22468 CV-S (Geronimo)
42-22480 CS-K
P-47D-2-RE
42-7894 CS-I
42-8042 CS-H
42-8402 CV-M (Lucky Pearl)
P-47D-4-RA
42-22766 CV-S
42-22776 CV-D (Boots)
42-22786 CV-B
42-22791*
P-47D-5-RE
42-8485 CV-B
42-8498 CS-T
42-8542*
42-8545 IV-L (Mary)
42-8551 IV-W (Green Eyes)
42-8552 CS-J
42-8558 CS-J
42-8578 CR-V, CS-V
42-8592 CV-L
42-8611 CR-N, CS-N
42-8613 CR-A
42-8617 CV-M
42-8636 CR-F*
42-8637 CV-Z
42-8643 CS-Q
42-8645 CV-M
42-8663 CR-G
42-8693 CS-E (Miss Margaret)
42-8695 IV-F (Oily Boid)
42-8698 IV-X
P-47D-6-RE
42-74632 CR-D
42-74633 CV-W
42-74642 IV-K (Nancy June)
42-74645 IV-E, IV-N
42-74666 IV-O (The Mad Rebel)
42-74676 CS-X (Blondie II)
42-74695 CV-E
42-74698 CS-?
42-74719 CR-O
42-74721 CV-K
42-74737 CR-P*
42-74745 CS-D
P-47D-10-RE
42-75048 IV-Z
42-75054 IV-V
42-75068 CR-P, CS-P
42-75079 CS-B*
42-75082 CV-G
42-75085 IV-Q
42-75095 CV-N (Pappy Yokum)
42-75104 CV-?*
42-75108*
42-75111 CV-A
42-75113 CV-O (Daisy Mae)
42-75118 CR-Z, CS-Z
42-75128 CV-R
42-75136 CR-N*
42-75141 CV-I
42-75158 IV-B
42-75210 IV-I (Dotty)
P-47D-11-RE
42-75253 CS-S
42-75263 CS-?*
42-75270 IV-R (Sally)

42-75409 CR-X, CS-X
42-75413 CS-U
42-75515 CS-B
P-47D-15-RE
42-76282 CS-O
42-76308 CS-Y
P-47D-16-RE
42-75894 CS-L
P-47D-20-RE
42-76416 CS-H
42-76598 CV-V
P-51B-1NA
43-12145 CV-W
43-12147 CS-W*
43-12186 IV-R*
43-12208 IV-L (Rose of San Antone)
43-12294 CS-C (Shrimp)
43-12433 CV-C
43-12434 IV-P, IV-R (Dunquerque)
43-12435 IV-Z
43-12439 IV-Q
43-12444 IV-X
43-12463 CS-F* Sweden (Some Joke)
43-12478 CV-P
P-51C-1NT
42-102996 CS-S (Lovin' Lulu)
42-103197 CV-H, CV-Y (Sweet Jean Marie)
42-103294 CS-O
41-103318 CV-U*
42-103319 CS-R
P-51B-5NA
43-6461 CS-Q* Sweden (Hot Pants)
43-6491 CV-E* (Wanna Honey)
43-6757 IV-Z
43-6826 CS-W
43-6879 CS-T
43-6961 CS-L*
43-6962 CV-Y*
43-7013 CS-E
P-51C-5NT
42-103329 CV-Z*
42-103332 CV-?
42-103339 IV-F
42-103343*
42-103345 CS-D
42-103354 IV-B*
42-103386 CV-N (Miss Janet)
42-103394 CS-B
42-103669 CV-I
42-103743 IV-M*
P-51B-10NA
43-7119*
43-7155 CV-C
43-7179* (Oily Boid II)
43-7199 IV-F
42-106436 CV-T
42-106443 IV-Y (Poison)
42-106469*
42-106474 CS-M*
42-106476 IV-H
42-106577 CV-X*
42-106580 CS-I, CS-M*
42-106581 CV-V (Tootser)
42-106599 IV-W
42-106607 IV-X
42-106611 CV-K
42-106618 CV-W
42-106619 CV-J (Die Fledermaus)

42-106620 CV-G, IV-R*
42-106629 IV-K (Nancy June 2nd), (Tojo Peach)
42-106667 CV-L* (Sweet Sue)
42-106670 IV-C*
42-106673 CV-B
42-106679 IV-O* (The Mad Rebel)
42-106680 IV-J
42-106689 IV-S (Briney Marlin)
42-106691 IV-H*
42-106692 CS-T (Josephine)
42-106693 CV-M*
42-106702 CV-X*
42-106704 CS-H
42-106716 CS-L
42-106727 CV-F
P-51C-10NT
42-25067 CS-? (Sandra Lynn)
42-103762 CV-D
42-103785 IV-K* (Nancy June 3rd)
42-103793 IV-G (San'Tone Sweetheart)
42-103797 IV-E (Darling Earline)
42-103799 IV-F*
42-103893 CS-E
42-103898 CV-A (Matilda IV)
42-103943 CV-Q
P-51B-15NA
43-24756 IV-V
43-24764 CV-B (The Beachcomber)
43-24771 IV-I
43-24778 CS-H (Zombie)
43-24786*
43-24791 CS-D, CS-P*
43-24798 IV-T (Pistol Pack'n Mama II)
43-24799 CS-H
43-24810 CS-J*
43-24833 CS-Q
42-106749 CS-M
42-106757 IV-Z
42-106771 IV-I* (Dotty)
42-106775 CV-?
42-106791 CS-Y
42-106799 CS-Y*
42-106803 IV-A
42-106804*
42-106805 CS-F (Galveston Gal)
42-106808 CS-?*
42-106809 CV-H* (Little Liquidator)
42-106818 IV-U*
42-106841 IV-Q*
42-106848 IV-N* (Deviless 2nd)
42-106851 CS-X
42-106853 IV-V (Traveler)
42-106862 CS-U
42-106865 CS-M*
42-106867 CV-I* (Pegelin)
42-106876 CV-F
42-106878 CS-A, CS-O*
42-106879 CV-R
42-106890 CV-B*
42-106893 IV-?*
42-106894 CS-H, CS-P
42-106898 CV-D* (Boots)
42-106902 CS-C
42-106904*
42-106906 IV-L* (Mary)
42-106913 IV-?*
42-106916 IV-D* (Loretta)
42-106917 CV-J (Mari-Helen)

42-106919 IV-?
42-106921 CS-G*
42-106926 CS-O
42-106929 CV-B (Lola Lee)
42-106935 CS-U
42-106941 CS-B
42-106949 CV-V
42-106961 IV-?
42-106975 CS-N
42-106995 CV-Q
P-51D-5NA
44-13301 IV-B
44-13336 IV-Y* (Yankee Clipper)
44-13386*
44-13387 CV-A*
44-13390 IV-N (Deviless 3rd), (Big Noise from Winnetka)
44-13394 CS-B (Betty Jane II)
44-13404 CV-Z*
44-13513 CS-A
44-13520 IV-R, IV-U
44-13529 CS-D* (Pandemonium)
44-13539 CV-O
44-13549 CV-Q
44-13592 IV-C
44-13604 CS-U
44-13606 IV-I (Louisiana Heatwave)
44-13610 IV-V*
44-13633 CS-R* (Satan's Lady)
44-13645 CS-M
44-13669 CV-I* (Pegelin)
44-13688 IV-?
44-13689 IV-H*
44-13721 CV-W
44-13740 CV-A (Little Audrey)
44-13762 CV-D (Moose Nose), (Cookie)
44-13776 CV-Y (Kitten)
44-13786 CV-B
44-13893 CS-E (Caroline)
44-13914 IV-I, IV-Y
44-13939 CS-?* Sweden
44-13966 CS-K
44-13996 CS-M
44-14038 CS-G
P-51D-5NT
44-11222 CV-I (Evelyn)
44-11223 CV-O
44-11236 CV-B
44-11283 IV-X
44-11348 CS-R
44-11350 IV-Y
P-51K-5NT
44-11572 IV-A, IV-I (Michigan Mauler)
44-11574 CS-M (Marilyn Beth) +(Miss Virginia)
44-11635 IV-B (Pauline)
44-11636 IV-A
44-11647 CV-F*
44-11649 CV-F
41-11651 CV-V*
44-11657 CV-F
44-11658 IV-I
44-11662 CV-A
44-11664 IV-G
44-11671 CV-?
44-11675 IV-C
44-11685 CV-U, CV-V (Janet)+(Elva May)
44-11686 1V-?

44-11696 CV-G*
44-11697 CV-C (Little Ann)
44-11758 CV-T (Silky)
44-11760 CS-J, CS-O
44-11797 CV-M
P-51D-10NA
44-14062 CV-C, CV-Q*
44-14071 CS-W* (Dora Dee)
44-14076 CS-V (De De II)
44-14081 CV-E* (Tootsie)
44-14096 CS-X*, CS-V (Dee Dee III)
44-14100 CV-?*
44-14108 IV-?*
44-14117 IV-M (Stinky)
44-14122 CS-W
44-14127 IV-E (Wild Will), IV-E
   (Dilbert)+(Lil Marge)
44-14129 CS-S
44-14131 CV-T*
44-14159 CS-Y (Rudy)
44-14168 CS-I, CS-O
44-14179 CS-R
44-14185*
44-14188 IV-?*
44-14192 CS-A, CS-S (Blondie II)
44-14216 IV-Z*
44-14218 IV-X (X-Terminator)
44-14240*
44-14265 CS-Q
44-14286 IV-?*
44-14307 IV-P*
44-14313 IV-L (Jeepers)
44-14325 CV-N (Mass Kid)
44-14329 CV-X*
44-14368 CS-Z

44-14399 IV-?*
44-14427 CS-D (Blue Blazes)
44-14429 CS-D
44-14432 IV-Q
44-14444 CV-J* (Supermouse)
44-14476 CV-?
44-14500 CV-E
44-14509 CV-X
44-14518 CS-O
44-14521 CS-V, CS-A (Rayner Shine)
44-14534 IV-B
44-14543 IV-P (Precious Pat)
44-14545 IV-?*
44-14566 CV-C
44-14620 CV-F
45-14625 IV-F* (Pauline)
44-14626*
44-14630 CS-R
44-14650 CV-X*
44-14652 CV-A
44-14670*
44-14718 IV-D (Hubert)
44-14733 CS-L (Daddy's Girl)
44-14769 CV-A
44-14773 CS-G*
44-14778 CS-H
44-14793 CV-?
P-51K-10NT
44-12113 CV-H
P-51D-15NA
44-14854 CV-Q
44-14857*
44-14870 CV-W (Peter E. Jr.)
44-14894*

44-14948 CS-J, CS-S
44-14964*
44-14965 CV-N (Lady)+(Nancy)
44-14978 CS-H*
44-14979 CS-H (Little D——)
44-14983 CS-F
44-14987 CS-C*
44-14988 IV-E
44-14997 IV-U
43-15007 IV-Z
44-15015 IV-W (Babe)
44-15016 IV-I (Heatwave)
44-15067 CS-L, CV-C*
44-15081 IV-T* (Pistol Packin'
   Mama III)
44-15096 CV-D*
44-15100 CV-Q
44-15102 CS-T (Josephine II),
   (Skecter's Skooter)
44-15204 IV-C
44-15215 IV-S (Torchy)
44-15242 IV-Q
44-15277 CS-Q (CisCo)
44-15371 CV-Z* (Happy)
44-15394 IV-D*
44-15489 CV-P (Annie)
44-15514 IV-O
44-15521 CS-V (Screamin' Demon)
44-15543 CS-X (Lydia May)
44-15555 CV-L*
44-15588 IV-R (Born to Lose)
44-15618 CV-H, CV-R (Diane)
44-15711 CV-J
44-15717 CV-Q

44-15725 IV-V
44-15739 IV-J
44-15741 IV-Y
44-15857 IV-?
44-15894 IV-D
857 & 894 not in factory allotted numbers
P-51D-20NA
44-63689 CV-K (Pop my boy)
44-63740*
44-637776 CV-Y
44-472067 CV-R (Ole Goat)
44-72143 CV-H
44-72154 IV-N
44-72207 IV-?*
44-72208 CS-C (Delectable)
44-72223 CV-Q
44-72260 CV-E* (Mary Lou)
44-72281 CV-Z (Happy II)
44-72330 IV-N
44-72331 CV-C (Addie II)
44-72344 IV-M (Saucy Sal)
44-72353 CS-P
44-72366 IV-D (Hubert)
44-72406 CV-G
44-72425 IV-J (Gloria Mac)
44-72503 IV-F*
44-72530 IV-M
44-72603 IV-?
P-51D-25NA
44-72746 CV-U
44-72780 IV-K
44-72832 CS-A (Rayner Shine)
44-73102 CS-V (Screamin' Demon II)

Air National Guard Serial Numbers

Nose art and name of aircraft given where known. WWII and Korean service noted. Civ=civilian registry. A * denotes a loss.

West Virginia—167th F.S.

P-51K-5NT
44-11610
P-51D-20NA
44-63636 WWII
44-63703 WWII and Korea
44-63788 Donald Duck WWII, Civ.
44-63810 Woody Woodpecker
   (Stump Jumper) WWII, Civ.
44-63812 WWII
44-72197
44-72278 Korea
P-51D-25NA
44-72718 Beetle Bailey WWII, Civ.
44-72767 WWII, Civ.
44-72933 WWII, to Phillipine AF, Civ.
44-72937
44-72948 Bugs Bunny (Wham Bam)
   WWII, on display ANG
   Charleston, W. Va.
44-72956 WWII
44-73055 WWII, Korea*
44-73075 WWII
44-73081 Sad Sack (Tilt) WWII, Civ.
44-73154 WWII, Korea
44-73175 WWII
44-73235 WWII
44-73249 WWII. Civ.
44-73423
44-73533 Korea*
44-73570 Korea*
44-73574 WWII, Civ.*

44-73579
44-73581 WWII, Korea
44-73626
44-73627 WWII, Korea*
44-73684 WWII, Korea*
44-73818 Korea
44-73832 Civ.*
44-74226 Korea
P-51D-25NT
44-84745 Civ.
44-84933 Civ.
45-11357 to Phillipine AF, Civ.
45-11367 Civ.
45-11381 Little Max Civ.
45-11383* Wimpey
45-11411 Korea
45-11471 to Israeli AF, back to USA
   Civ.
P-51D-30NA
44-74426 to RCAF
44-74428 Korea*
44-74475 Civ.
44-74502 to RCAF. Civ.
44-74522
44-74546
44-74598
44-74694 The Phantom (The
   Phantom) Civ.*
44-74811
44-74827 to Indonesian AF, RNZAF
   Museum
44-47900
44-74936 frog (One Hop) to USAF
   Museum

44-74949 ghost (Casper)
44-74960 to El Salvador
44-74962 Dagwood's dog (Daisy) to
   Indonesia. Returned to USA Civ.
P-51D-30NT
45-11558 Civ.
45-11582 Civ. air museum Chino, Calif.
45-11586 Civ.*
45-11610
45-11620 Civ.*
45-11633 Daffy Duck (Shook) Civ.
45-11688
45-11700 Dennis the Menace Civ.,
   Cuban AF
TF-51
44-84655 two metal nuts (Toulouse
   Nuts) to Bolivia, hulk returned
   to USA.
P-51H-5NA
44-64389
P-51H-10NA
44-64542*
F-86E
50-591
50-674
51-2780
F-86H-1NA
52-1989
52-1992
52-1993 display EAA Museum,
   Oshkosh
52-1996 to Lockheed as chase plane
52-2004 to Anderson Park, Ind. for
   display

52-2005 to Surry, Va. for display
52-2013 map of W.Va. (Rebuilt in
   W. Va. out of Beer Cans) to
   Lockheed as chase plane
52-2015 map of W. Va. (Jodie's
   Place)
52-2022*
52-2023 to Chrisfield, Maryland, for
   display
52-2027
52-2036
52-2040 junk yard Front Royal, Va.
52-2043 to Freeport, Pa. for display
52-2044 Howdy Doody (Howdy
   Doody) junk yard Front Royal,
   Va.
52-2048 to Ellicott City, Maryland,
   for display
52-2054 to Palmdale Plant 42, Calif.
   for display
52-2056
52-2058 ANG display Martinsburg,
   W. Va.
52-2059 ANG display Toledo, Ohio
52-2065 to Avon, Pa. Civil Air
   Patrol
52-2066 to Princess Anne,
   Maryland, for display
52-2071
52-2074 last seen derelict at
   Riverside, Calif.
52-2080
52-2087
52-2089

Kentucky—165th F.S.

P-51D-5NA
44-13626
P-51D-20NA
44-63350 Civ.
44-63473
44-63803
44-63858
44-63869* T. Mantell
P-51D-25NA
44-73006*
44-73043 WWII, Civ.
44-73079
44-73091*
44-73129 to W. Va. ANG
44-73155
44-73260 Civ.
45-73264 to El Salvador. Civ.
44-73265
44-73287 Civ.

44-73320 Civ.
44-73323 Civ.*
44-73344 WWII, Civ.
44-73420 Civ.
44-73423 Civ.
44-73483 Civ.
44-73487
44-73502
44-73510*
44-74202 Civ.
P-51D-25NT
44-84663
44-84753 Civ.
44-84881 to Phillipine AF
44-84983
45-11388 to Phillipine AF, Civ.
45-11392*
45-11401
45-11540 Civ.*
P-51D-30NA
44-74477
44-74797

44-74850 Civ.
P-51D-30NT
45-11628
P-51H-5NA
44-64225*
44-64264
44-64280
44-64282
44-64357
P-51H-10NA
44-64551
44-64554
44-64555
44-64563
F-86A-5NA
48-0289
49-1065 scrapped
49-1071 scrapped
49-1072 scrapped
49-1081 scrapped
49-1084 scrapped
49-1094 scrapped

49-1096
49-1101 scrapped
49-1138
49-1154 scrapped
49-1179*
49-1181 from Bentwaters, Eng.,
      scrapped
49-1185 from Bentwaters, Eng.*
49-1194 from Bentwaters, Eng.,
      scrapped
49-1209 scrapped
49-1228 from Bentwaters, donated
      civ. display
49-1249 scrapped
49-1261 from Bentwaters, Eng.,
      scrapped
49-1279 scrapped
49-1299 scrapped
49-1309 scrapped
49-1312 from Bentwaters, Eng.,
      scrapped

Bibliography

Andrews, Paul M., Adams, William H. and Woolnough, John, H. *Bits & Pieces of the Mighty Eighth*

Army Air Force, *Down to Earth—Fighter Attack on Ground Targets, To The Limit of Their Endurance, 359th Fighter Group 1943–1945*

Birdsall, Steve, *Log of the Liberators and Saga of the Superfortress*

Bowyer, Chaz, *Coastal Command at War*

Boyne, Walter J., *Messerschmitt 262*

Caidin, Martin, *Black Thursday*

Carson, Leonard K., *Pursue and Destroy*

Carter, Kit C. and Robert Mueller, The Army Air Forces in WW II Combat Chronology 1941–1945

Cloe, John H., *The Aleutian Warrriors*

Edwards, Frank, *Flying Saucers—Serious Business*

Ethell, Jeffery L., *Komet the Messerschmitt 163*

Francillon, Rene, *The Air Guard*

Freeman, Roger A., *The Mighty Eighth, The Mighty Eighth War Diary, The Mighty Eighth War Manual, Combat Profile—Mustang*

Green, William, *Warplanes of the Third Reich, Famous Fighters of the Second World War Vols. 1&2*

Hastings, Max, *Bomber Command*

Hess, William N., *Fighting Mustang Chronicle of the P-51*

Miller, Kent, *Jigger, Tinplate & Redcross*

Morris, Danny, *Aces and Wingmen II, Volume I*

Nowarra, Heinz J., *The Messerschmitt 109—A Famous German Fighter*

Pistole, Larry M., *The Pictorial History of the Flying Tigers*

Ruppelt, Edward J., *Unidentified Flying Objects*

Rust, Kenn C. and William N. Hess, *The Slybird Group—The 353rd Fighter Group on Escort and Ground Attack Operations*

Scutts, Jerry, *Lion in the Sky*

Spate, Wolfgang, *Top Secret Bird—The Luftwaffe's Me-163 Comet*

Spenser, Jay P., *Focke-Wulf Fw-190 the Workhorse of the Luftwaffe*

Stafford, Gene B. and Willaim N. Hess, *Aces of the Eighth*

Wagner, Ray, *Mustang Designer*

ABOUT THE AUTHOR

JACK H. SMITH was born January 10, 1941, in Charleston, West Virginia. His father Jessie (Jeff) was from Savannah, Georgia and his mother the former Anna Hagy hails from Abingdon, Virginia. His brother Tom and uncle Jack Hagy served as waist gunners on 8th AF B-17s during WW II and their love of flying and model building had a strong influence on his life. As a young boy he vividly recalls the 167th's Mustangs roaring over Charleston and in particular the day they flew en masse to Kentucky as part of the call-up for the Korean War.

After graduating from Charleston High School in 1958 he became a full time employee for Fireproof Products, now Ferro Products, as a structural steel and architectural draftsman and as of this writing still holds that position. He married in 1960 and from that union came three children—Eric, Linda and Cindy. During these years Jack built a lot of flying scale models that won numerous awards.

From 1968 to 1975 he worked evenings as a part time Yamaha mechanic culminating with the job of boring and finishing cylinders. During this period he also built a 1965 Corvair with a personally modified engine producing nearly 300 horsepower.

Jack married Dianna Clinton on May 20, 1977, and entered a new era of endeavors. Having lost a place to fly models he now began building museum quality plastic display aircraft. This led to the first of several magazine articles for FineScale Modeler. While gathering data for that project, which was a P-51D Mustang, Dick Phillips of the publication Mustang World suggested he gather data on the 167th FS for an article. Mustang World closed shop leaving Jack with a lot of information and no one to print it. Enter Richard Andre who graduated from CHS with Jack and happens to write a lot of local history. Andre suggested gathering more data and photos, write a book and have it published. As a result Jack wrote The Coonskin Boys, Mountaineer Sabres and West Virginia Airpower.

Jack is a 33rd Degree Scottish Rite Mason and a member of the York Rite. He is a member of the United Methodist Church and occasionally teaches an adult class at the First United Methodist Church of South Charleston.